Atul Prakash   Indranil Sen Gupta (Eds.)

Information Systems Security

5th International Conference, ICISS 2009
Kolkata, India, December 14-18, 2009
Proceedings

 Springer

Volume Editors

Atul Prakash
University of Michigan
Electrical Engineering and Computer Science Department
Ann Arbor, MI, USA
E-mail: aprakash@eecs.umich.edu

Indranil Sen Gupta
Indian Institute of Technology Kharagpur
Department of Computer Science and Engineering
Kharagpur, India
E-mail: isg@iitkgp.ac.in

Library of Congress Control Number: 2009939539

CR Subject Classification (1998): C.2, E.3, D.4.6, K.6.5, K.4.4, H.2

LNCS Sublibrary: SL 4 – Security and Cryptology

ISSN   0302-9743
ISBN-10   3-642-10771-0 Springer Berlin Heidelberg New York
ISBN-13   978-3-642-10771-9 Springer Berlin Heidelberg New York

springer.com

© Springer-Verlag Berlin Heidelberg 2009
Printed in Germany

Typesetting: Camera-ready by author, data conversion by Scientific Publishing Services, Chennai, India
Printed on acid-free paper   SPIN: 12803835   06/3180   5 4 3 2 1 0

Message from the General Chairs

The International Conference on Information Systems Security (ICISS), which was first held in 2005 at Jadavpur University, Kolkata, India, has been successfully organized every year in different parts of the country. The fifth conference in this series, ICISS 2009, held during December 14-18, 2009, returned to its city of birth in Kolkata. Even within a short span of its life, the conference has left its mark in the field of information systems security and attracted a large number of submissions (85) from across the globe. With painstaking effort, the Program Committee selected 17 full papers and 4 short papers for presentation.

The program of the conference spanned over five days and included, in addition to a high-quality technical program, tutorials in the first two days delivered by eminent researchers and practitioners in the field, giving young researchers and students an excellent opportunity to learn about the latest trends in information security.

The Program Chairs, Atul Prakash and Indranil Sengupta, along with the Program Committee members did an excellent job in completing a rigorous review process. We take this opportunity to record our appreciation to the Program Committee members. We would also like to thank Marc Dacier, Venu Govindaraju, Angelos Keromytis, and Nataraj Nagaratnam for accepting our invitation to deliver keynote talks at the conference. The effort made by Indrakshi Ray and Indranil Sengupta in selecting tutorial sessions on topics of contemporary interest in this field deserves special mention. We would also like to thank the Tutorial Speakers who kindly agreed to deliver their lectures.

The Organizing Committee, headed by Samiran Chattopadhyay, should be commended for taking the necessary steps to ensure that the conference could be successfully conducted at the Eastern Zonal Cultural Centre, Salt Lake, Kolkata. We are indebted to the sponsors of this conference who contributed significantly even in a period of economic slowdown. We would also like to thank Sudip Misra, the Finance Chair of the conference, for a commendable job.

December 2009   Sushil Jajodia
                                                   Arun Kumar Majumdar

Message from the Technical Program Chairs

Welcome to the proceedings of the 5th International Conference on Information Systems Security, ICISS 2009. This annual event started off in year 2005 as an initiative to promote information security-related research in the country, and has gradually matured into a reputed international conference.

This year we received 85 papers from 19 countries all over the world. After a rigorous review process, the Program Committee selected 21 papers for presentation, with 17 regular papers and 4 short papers. The Program Committee members carefully scrutinized the papers along with the reviews during a two-week on-line discussion phase. We would like to thank the authors of all the papers for submitting their quality research work to the conference. Special thanks go to the Program Committee members and the external reviewers for sparing their time in carrying out the review process meticulously. We would also like to thank Springer for kindly permitting us to publish the proceedings of the conference as an LNCS volume.

We were fortunate to have several eminent experts as keynote speakers. We are thankful to them for participating in the conference. The main conference program was preceded by two days of tutorial presentations and we would like to thank the tutorial speakers. We would like to thank the Tutorial Chair, Indrakshi Ray, for putting a lot of effort in building up a well-balanced tutorial program.

Finally, we would like to thank the General Chairs, Sushil Jajodia and Arun Kumar Majumdar, members of the Steering Committee and the previous Program Committee Chairs, R. Sekar and Patrick McDaniel, on whom we frequently relied upon for advice throughout the year.

We hope that you find the ICISS 2009 proceedings rewarding.

December 2009

Atul Prakash
Indranil Sen Gupta

Message from the Technical Program Chairs

Conference Organization

Steering Committee

Aditya Bagchi	Indian Statistical Institute, Kolkata, India
Sushil Jajodia	George Mason University, USA
Somesh Jha	University of Wisconsin, USA
Arun Kumar Majumdar	Indian Institute of Technology, Kharagpur, India
Chandan Mazumdar	Jadavpur University, Kolkata, India
Gulshan Rai	MCIT, Government of India
R. Sekar	Stony Brook University, USA

General Chairs

Sushil Jajodia	George Mason University, USA
Arun Kumar Majumdar	Indian Institute of Technology, Kharagpur, India

Program Chairs

Atul Prakash	University of Michigan, USA
Indranil Sengupta	Indian Institute of Technology, Kharagpur, India

Tutorial Chairs

Indrakshi Ray	Colorado State University, USA
A. K. Pujari	LNM Institute of Technology, India

Organizing Chair

Samiran Chattopadhyay	Jadavpur University, Kolkata, India

Government Liaison

A. K. Kaushik	MCIT, Government of India

Publicity Chairs

Indrajit Ray	Colorado State University, USA
Aditya Bagchi	Indian Statistical Institute, Kolkata, India

Poster Chair

Raja Datta   Indian Institute of Technology, Kharagpur,
                                    India

Program Committee

Vijay Atluri   Rutgers University, USA
Aditya Bagchi   Indian Statistical Institute, Kolkata, India
Bharat Bhargava   Purdue University, USA
Kevin Borders   Web Tap Security, USA
Bezawada Bruhadeshwar   IIIT Hyderabad, India
David Brumley   Carnegie Mellon University, USA
Sanjay Burman   CAIR, Bangalore, India
Kevin Butler   Penn State University, USA
Scott Coull   Johns Hopkins University, USA
Vinod Ganapathy   Rutgers University, USA
Sujata Garera   Johns Hopkins University, USA
Soumya K. Ghosh   Indian Institute of Technology, Kharagpur,
                                    India
Trent Jaeger   Penn State University, USA
Sushil Jajodia   George Mason University, USA
Somesh Jha   University of Wisconsin, USA
Sam King   University of Illinois, USA
Kristen LeFevre   University of Michigan, USA
Zhenkai Liang   National University of Singapore, Singapore
Alex Liu   Michigan State University, USA
Donggang Liu   University of Texas, USA
Arun Kumar Majumdar   Indian Institute of Technology, Kharagpur,
                                    India
Anish Mathuria   DA-IICT Gandhinagar, India
Chandan Mazumdar   Jadavpur University, Kolkata, India
Patrick McDaniel   Penn State University, USA
Sharad Mehrotra   UC Irvine, USA
Sudip Misra   Indian Institute of Technology, Kharagpur,
                                    India
Shimon Modi   Purdue University, USA
Rajat Moona   Indian Institute of Technology, Kanpur, India
Debdeep Mukhopadhyay   Indian Institute of Technology, Kharagpur,
                                    India
Prasad Naldurg   Microsoft Research Labs, Bangalore, India
Sukumar Nandi   Indian Institute of Technology, Guwahati, India
Lukasz Opyrchal   University of Miami, USA
J.R. Rao   IBM T.J. Watson Research Center, USA
Pramod K. Saxena   SAG, DRDO, India
R. Sekar   Stony Brook University, USA

Jaideep Srivastava   University of Minnesota, USA
Patrick Traynor   Georgia Institute of Technology, USA
Mahesh V. Tripunitara   University of Waterloo, Canada
Xin Zhao   Google, USA

External Reviewers

Chaitrali Amrutkar   Louis Kruger
Mridul Sankar Barik   Daniel Luchaup
Rana Barua   Subhamoy Maitra
S.S. Bedi   Stephen McLaughlin
Ranjita Bhagwan   Thomas Moyer
Yuanzhu Chen   Divya Muthukumaran
John Criswell   Beng Heng Ng
Italo Dacosta   Machigar Ongtang
Raja Datta   Frank Park
Abhijit Das   N. Rajesh Pillai
Manik Lal Das   Matthew Pirretti
Mamadou Diallo   Devin Pohly
Davidson Drew   Venkatesh Prasad Ranganath
Daniel Fabbri   Bimal Roy
Tony Fang   Sandra Rueda
Matt Fredrickson   Nitesh Saxena
Indivar Gupta   Anirban Sengupta
William Harris   Ahren Studer
Bijit Hore   Manachai Toahchoodee
R. Raghavendra   Jeff Zarnett
Saibal K. Pal   Dazhi Zhang
Meena Kumari

Table of Contents

Keynote Talks

Authentication

Verification

Systems Security

Behavior Analysis

Database Security

Cryptography

Short Papers

A Survey of Voice over IP Security Research

Angelos D. Keromytis

Symantec Research Labs Europe, France

Abstract. We present a survey of Voice over IP security research. Our goal is
to provide a roadmap for researchers seeking to understand existing capabilities
and, and to identify gaps in addressing the numerous threats and vulnerabilities
present in VoIP systems. We also briefly discuss the implications of our findings
with respect to actual vulnerabilities reported in a variety VoIP products.

1 Introduction

Voice over IP technologies are being increasingly adopted by consumers, enterprises,
and telecoms operators due to their potential for higher flexibility, richer feature set,
and reduced costs relative to their Public Switched Telephony Network (PSTN) counterparts. At their core, VoIP technologies enable the transmission of voice in any IP
network, including the Internet. Because of the need to seamlessly interoperate with
the existing telephony infrastructure, the new features, and the speed of development
and deployment, VoIP protocols and products have been repeatedly found to contain
numerous vulnerabilities [16] that have been exploited [19]. As a result, a fair amount
of research has been directed towards addressing some of these issues. However, the
effort is unbalanced, with little effort is spent on some highly deserving problem areas.

We have conducted a comprehensive survey of VoIP security research, complement-
ing our previous work that analyzed known vulnerabilities [16]. Our long-term goal is
four-fold. First, to create a roadmap of existing work in securing VoIP, towards reducing
the start-up effort required by other researchers to initiate research in this space. Second, to identify gaps in existing research, and to help inform the security community of
challenges and opportunities for further work. Third, to provide an overall sanity check
on the overall VoIP security research ecosystem, using known vulnerabilities as a form
of ground truth. Finally, in the context of the VAMPIRE project[1] (which supported this
work), to provide guidance as to what further work in needed to better understand and
analyze the activities of VoIP-system attackers. Naturally, such ambitious goals require
significantly more space than is available in a single conference paper.

In this paper, we provide a representative sample of the research works we surveyed.
We classify these works according to the class of threat they seek to address, using the
VoIP Security Alliance (VoIPSA) [54] threat taxonomy. Although we were forced to
omit a large number of related works (which we hope to present in a comprehensive
form in due time), this survey should be a good starting point for anyone interested in
conducting research on VoIP security. We also briefly discuss the implications of our
findings with respect to actual vulnerabilities reported in a variety VoIP products.

---

[1] http://vampire.gforge.inria.fr/

A. Prakash and I. Sen Gupta (Eds.): ICISS 2009, LNCS 5905, pp. 1–17, 2009.

In the remainder of this paper, Section 2 gives a brief overview of SIP, one of the most popular VoIP technologies. Section 3 summarizes the threat model defined by the VoIP Security Alliance. We then present our survey of the research literature on VoIP security in Section 4, and discuss some of the implications in Section 5.

2 SIP Overview

SIP [42] is an application-layer protocol standardized by the Internet Engineering Task Force (IETF), and is designed to support the setup of bidirectional communication sessions including, but not limited to, VoIP calls. It is somewhat similar to HTTP, in that it is text-based, has a request-response structure, and uses a user authentication mechanism based on the HTTP Digest Authentication. However, it is an inherently stateful protocol that supports interaction with multiple network components (*e.g.,* PSTN bridges), and can operate over UDP, TCP, and SCTP.

The main SIP entities are endpoints (softphones or physical devices), a proxy server, a registrar, a redirect server, and a location server. The registrar, proxy and redirect servers may be combined, or they may be independent entities. Endpoints communicate with a registrar to indicate their presence. This information is stored in the location server. A user may be registered via multiple endpoints simultaneously. During call setup, the endpoint communicates with the proxy, which uses the location server to determine where the call should be routed to. This may be another endpoint in the same network (*e.g.,* in the same enterprise), or another proxy server in another network. Alternatively, endpoints may use a redirect server to directly determine where a call should be directed to; redirect servers consult the location server in the same way that proxy servers operate during call setup. Once an end-to-end channel has been established (through one or more proxies) between the two endpoints, SIP negotiates the session parameters (codecs, RTP ports, *etc.*) using the Session Description Protocol (SDP).

In a two-party call setup between Alice and Bob, Alice sends an INVITE message to her proxy server, optionally containing session parameter information encoded within SDP. The proxy forwards this message directly to Bob, if Alice and Bob are users of the same domain. If Bob is registered in a different domain, the message will be relayed to Bob's proxy, and thence to Bob. The message may be forwarded to several endpoints, if Bob is registered from multiple locations. While the call is being set up, Alice is sent RINGING messages. Once the call has been accepted, an OK message is sent to Alice, containing Bob's preferred parameters encoded within SDP. Alice responds with an ACK message. Alice's session parameter preferences may be encoded in the INVITE or the ACK message. Following this exchange, the two endpoints can begin transmitting voice, video or other content using the agreed-upon media transport protocol, typically RTP. While the signaling traffic may be relayed through a number of SIP proxies, the media traffic is exchanged directly between the two endpoints. When bridging different networks, *e.g.,* PSTN and SIP, media gateways may disrupt the end-to-end nature of the media transfer to translate content between the formats supported by these networks.

There are many other protocol interactions supported by SIP, that cover a number of common (and uncommon) scenarios including call forwarding (manual or automatic), conference calling, voicemail, *etc.* Typically, this is done by semantically overloading SIP messages such that they can play various roles in different parts of the call.

SIP can use S/MIME to carry complex authentication payloads, including public key certificates. When TCP is used as the transport protocol, TLS can be used to protect the SIP messages. TLS is required for communication among proxies, registrars and redirect servers, but only recommended between endpoints and proxies or registrars. IPsec may also be used to protect all communications, regardless of transport protocol.

3 VoIP Threats

As a starting point, we use the taxonomy provided by the Voice over IP Security Alliance (VoIPSA) [54]. VoIPSA is a vendor-neutral, not for profit organization composed of VoIP and security vendors, organizations and individuals with an interest in securing VoIP protocols, products and installations. In addition, we place the surveyed vulnerabilities within the traditional threat space of confidentiality, integrity, availability (CIA). Finally, we consider whether the vulnerabilities exploit bugs in the protocol, implementation or system configuration. In future work, we hope to expand the number of views to the surveyed vulnerabilities and to provide more in-depth analysis.

The VoIPSA security threat taxonomy defines the security threats against VoIP deployments, services, and end users. The key elements of this taxonomy are:

1. **Social threats** are aimed directly against humans. For example, misconfigurations, bugs or bad protocol interactions in VoIP systems may enable or facilitate attacks that misrepresent the identity of malicious parties to users. Such attacks may then act as stepping stones to further attacks such as phishing, theft of service, or unwanted contact (spam).
2. **Eavesdropping, interception, and modification threats** cover situations where an adversary can unlawfully and without authorization from the parties concerned listen in on the signaling (call setup) or the content of a VoIP session, and possibly modify aspects of that session while avoiding detection. Examples of such attacks include call re-routing and interception of unencrypted RTP sessions.
3. **Denial of service threats** have the potential to deny users access to VoIP services. This may be particularly problematic in the case of emergencies, or when a DoS attack affects all of a user's or organization's communication capabilities (*i.e.,* when all VoIP and data communications are multiplexed over the same network which can be targeted through a DoS attack). Such attacks may be VoIP-specific (exploiting flaws in the call setup or the implementation of services), or VoIP-agnostic (*e.g.,* generic traffic flooding attacks). They may also involve attacks with physical components (*e.g.,* physically disconnecting or severing a cable) or through computing or other infrastructures (*e.g.,* disabling the DNS server, or shutting down power).
4. **Service abuse threats** covers the improper use of VoIP services, especially (but not exclusively) in situations where such services are offered in a commercial setting. Examples of such threats include toll fraud and billing avoidance [51, 52].
5. **Physical access threats** refer to inappropriate/unauthorized physical access to VoIP equipment, or to the physical layer of the network.
6. **Interruption of services threats** refer to non-intentional problems that may nonetheless cause VoIP services to become unusable or inaccessible. Examples of such threats include loss of power due to inclement weather, resource exhaustion due to over-subscription, and performance issues that degrade call quality.

4   Survey of VoIP Security Research

In the this section, we classify various research papers across the first four elements of the VoIPSA taxonomy (the last two relate to physical and non-security issues). We also include a *cross-cutting* category, which includes work that covers multiple areas (*e.g.*, proposing a security architecture), and an *overviews* category that includes works that survey vulnerabilities, threats, and security mechanisms. We give an indication as to how many total pieces of related work (including those described in the text) could be classified in that category but were omitted due to space limitations. The works that are discussed offer a representative view of the type of research activity in these problem areas.

Overviews (36 items): Persky gives a very detailed description of several VoIP vulnerabilities [32]. A long discussion of threats and security solutions is given by Thermos and Takanen [53]. Cao and Malik [8] examine the vulnerabilities that arise from introducing VoIP technologies into the communications systems in critical infrastructure applications. They examine the usual threats and vulnerabilities, and discuss mitigation techniques. They conclude by providing some recommendations and best practices to operators of such systems.

Butcher *et al.* [7] overview security issues and mechanisms for VoIP systems, focusing on security-oriented operational practices by VoIP providers and operators. Such practices include the separation of VoIP and data traffic by using VLANs and similar techniques, the use of integrity and authentication for configuration bootstrapping of VoIP devices, authentication of signaling via TLS or IPsec, and the use of media encryption. They briefly describe how two specific commercial systems implement such practices, and propose some directions for future research.

Adelsbach *et al.* [2] provide a comprehensive description of SIP and H.323, a list of threats across all networking layers, and various protection mechanisms. A similar analysis was published by the US National Institute of Standards and Technology (NIST) [20]. Anwar *et al.* [3] identify some areas where the NIST report remains incomplete: counter-intuitive results with respect to the relative performance of encryption and hash algorithms, the non-use of the standardized Mean Opinion Score to evaluate call quality, and the lack of anticipation of RTP-based denial of service. They then propose the use of design patterns to address the problems of secure traversal of firewalls and NAT boxes, detecting and mitigating DoS attacks in VoIP, and securing VoIP against eavesdropping.

Seedorf [45] overviews the security challenges in peer-to-peer (P2P) SIP. Threats specific to P2P-SIP include subversion of the identity-mapping scheme (which is specific to the overlay network used as a substrate), attacks on the overlay network routing scheme, bootstrapping communications in the presence of malicious first-contact nodes, identity enforcement (Sybil attacks), traffic analysis and privacy violation by intermediate nodes, and free riding by nodes that refuse to route calls or otherwise participate in the protocol other than to obtain service for themselves (selfish behavior).

Addressing social threats (49 items): Niccolini [29] discusses the difficulties in protecting against IP telephony spam (SPIT) and overviews the various approaches for blocking such calls, identifying the technical and operational problems with each.

Possible building blocks for SPIT prevention include black/whitelists combined with strong identity verification to provide a reliable CallerID system, referral-based systems among trusted SIP domains, pattern or anomaly detection techniques to discriminate SPIT based on training data, multi-level grey-listing of calls based on caller behavior (similar to throttling), computational puzzles and CAPTCHAs, explicit callee consent (a form of capability, required to actually place a call), content filtering on voicemail spam, callee feedback to indicate whether a call was SPIT or legitimate (typically combined with white/blacklisting, and requiring strong identity), changing one's SIP address as soon as SPIT messages arrive, requiring a monetary fee for the first contact, and legal action. Niccolini argues that none of these methods by itself is likely to succeed, promotes a modular and extensible approach to SPIT prevention, and presents a high-level architecture that was designed for use in a commercial SIP router. Mathieu *et al.* [27] describe SDRS, an anti-SPIT system that combines several of these detection schemes and takes into consideration user and operator preferences.

The SPIDER project (SPam over Internet telephony Detection sERvice) released a public project report [38] providing an overview of SPIT threats and the relevant European legal framework (both on an EU and national basis). The second public project report [25] focuses on SPIT detection and prevention, summarizing some of the work done in this space and defining criteria for evaluating the efficiency of anti-SPIT mechanisms. They then classify prior work according to fulfillment of these criteria, expanding on the relative strengths and weaknesses of each approach. The third public project report [37] builds on the previous two reports, describing an anti-SPIT architectural framework. Elements of this architecture include improved authentication, white/blacklisting, behavior analysis, the use of computational puzzles for challenge/response, reputation management, and audio content analysis.

Pörschmann and Knospe [34] propose a SPIT detection mechanism based on applying spectral analysis to the audio data of VoIP calls to create acoustic fingerprints. SPIT is identified by detecting several fingerprints across a large number of different calls.

Schlegel *et al.* [44] describe a framework for preventing SPIT. They argue for a modular approach to identifying SPIT, using hints from both signaling and media transfer. The first stage of their system looks at information that is available prior to accepting the call, while the second stage interacts with a caller (possibly prior to passing on the call to the callee). The various components integrated in their system include white/blacklists, call statistics, IP/domain correlation, and Turing tests. Their system also allows for feedback from the callee to be integrated into the scoring mechanism, for use in screening future calls. The evaluation focuses on scalability, by measuring the response time to calls as call volumes increase.

Quittek *et al.* [35] propose the use of *hidden* Turing tests to identify SPIT callers. As a concrete approach, they leverage the interaction model in human conversation minimizes the amount of simultaneous ("double") talk by the participants, and the fact that there is a short pause at the beginning of an answered call, followed by a statement by the callee that initiates the conversation. By looking for signs of violation of such norms, it is possible to identify naïve automated SPIT callers. The authors implement their scheme and integrated it with a VoIP firewall.

Dantu and Kolan [17] describe the Voice Spam Detector (VSD), a multi-stage SPIT filter based on trust, reputation, and feedback among the various filter stages. The primary filter stages are call pattern and volume analysis, black and white lists of callers, per-caller behavior profile based on Bayesian classification and prior history, and reputation information from the callee's contacts and social network. They provide a formal model for trust and reputation in a voice network, based on intuitive human behavior. They evaluate their system in a laboratory experiment using a small number of real users and injected SPIT calls.

Kolan et al. [18] use traces of voice calls in a university environment to validate a mathematical model for computing the nuisance level of an incoming call, using feedback from the receivers. The model is intended to be used in predicting SPIT calls in VoIP environments, and is based on the history of prior communications between the two parties involved, which includes explicit feedback from the receiver indicating that a call is unwanted (at a particular point in time).

Balasubramaniyan et al. [4] propose to use call duration and social network graphs to establish a measure of reputation for callers. Their intuition is that users whose call graph has a relatively small fan-out and whose call durations are relatively long are less likely to be spammers. Conversely, users who place a lot of very short calls are likely to be engaging in SPIT. Furthermore, spammers will receive few (if any) calls. Their system works both when the parties in a call have a social network link between them, and when such a link does not exist by assigning global reputation scores. Users that are mistakenly categorized as spammers are redirected to a Turing test, allowing them to complete the call if the answer correctly. In a simulation-based evaluation, the authors determine that their system can achieve a false negative rate of 10% and a false positive rate of 3%, even in the presence of large numbers of spammers.

Srivastava and Schulzrinne [49] describe DAPES, a system for blocking SPIT calls and instant messages based on several factors, including the origin domain of the initiator (caller), the confidence level in the authentication performed (if any), whether the call is coming through a known open proxy, and a reputation system for otherwise unknown callers. They give an overview of other reputation-based systems and compare them with DAPES.

Addressing eavesdropping, interception, and modification threats (34 items): Wang et al. [55] evaluate the resilience of three commercial VoIP services (AT&T, Vonage and Gizmo) against man-in-the-middle adversaries. They show that it is possible for an attacker to divert and redirect calls in the first two services by modifying the RTP endpoint information included in the SDP exchange (which is not protected by the SIP Digest Authentication), and to manipulate a user's call forwarding settings in the latter two systems. These vulnerabilities permit for large-scale voice pharming, where unsuspecting users are directed to fake interactive voice response systems or human representatives. The authors argue for the need for TLS or IPsec protection of the signaling. Zhang et al. [62] show that, by exploiting DNS and VoIP implementation vulnerabilities, it is possible for attackers to perform man-in-the-middle attacks even when they are not on the direct communication path of the parties involved. They demonstrate their attack against Vonage, requiring that the attacker only knows the phone number and the IP address of the target phone. Such attacks can be used to eavesdrop and hijack the victims' VoIP calls. The authors recommend that users and operators use signaling and media protection, conduct fuzzing and testing of VoIP implementations, and develop a lightweight VoIP intrusion detection system to be deployed on the VoIP phone.

Salsano et al. [43] give an overview of the various SIP security mechanisms (as of 2002), focusing particularly on the authentication component. They conduct an evaluation of the processing costs of SIP calls that involve authentication, under different transport, authentication and encryption scenarios. They show that a call using TLS and authentication is 2.56 times more expensive than the simplest possible SIP configuration (UDP, no security). However, a fully-protected a call takes only 54% longer to complete than a configuration that is more representative than the basic one but still offers no security; the same fully-protected call and has the same processing cost if the transport is TCP without any encryption (TLS). Of the overhead, approximately 70% is attributed to message parsing and 30% to cryptographic processing. With the advent of Datagram TLS (DTLS), it is possible that encryption and integrity for SIP can be had for all configurations (UDP or TCP) at no additional cost. A similar conclusion is reached by Bilien et al. [6], who study the overhead in SIP call setup latency when using end-to-end and hop-by-hop security mechanisms. They consider protocols such as MIKEY, S/MIME, SRTP, TLS, and IPsec, concluding that the overall penalty of using full-strength cryptography is low. Barbieri et al. [5] had found earlier that when using VoIP over IPsec, performance can drop by up to 63%; however, it is questionable whether these results still hold, given the use of hardware accelerators and the more efficient AES algorithm in IPsec.

Rebahi et al. [39] analyze the performance of RSA as used in SIP for authentication and identity management (via public-key certificates and digital signatures), and describe the use of Elliptic Curve DSA (ECDSA) within this context to improve performance. Using ECDSA, their prototype can handle from 2 to 8 times as many call setup requests per second, with the gap widening as key sizes increase.

Guo et al. [14] propose a new scheme for protecting voice content that provides strong confidentiality guarantees while allowing for graceful voice degradation in the presence of packet loss. They evaluate their scheme via simulation and micro-benchmarks. However, Li et al. [23] show that the scheme is insecure. Kuntze et al. [21] propose a mechanism for providing non-repudiation of voice content by using digital signatures.

Seedorf [46] proposes the use of cryptographically generated SIP URIs to protect the integrity of content in P2P SIP. Specifically, he uses self-certifying SIP URIs that encode a public key (or, more compactly, the hash of a public key). The owner of the corresponding private key can then post signed location binding information on the peer-to-peer network (e.g., Chord) that is used by call initiators to perform call routing.

Petraschek et al. [33] examine the usability and security of ZRTP, a key agreement protocol based on the Diffie Hellman key exchange, designed for use in VoIP environments that lack pre-established secret keys among users or a public key infrastructure (PKI). ZRTP is intended to be used with SRTP, which performs the actual content encryption and transfer. Because of the lack of a solid basis for authentication, which makes active man-in-the-middle attacks easy to launch, ZRTP uses Short Authentication Strings (SAS) to allow two users to verbally confirm that they have established the same secret key. The verbal communication serves as a weak form of authentication at the human level. The authors identify a relay attack in ZRTP, wherein a man-in-the-middle adversary can influence the SAS read by two legitimate users with who he has established independent calls and ZRTP exchanges. The attacker can use one of the legitimate users as an oracle to pronounce the desired SAS string through a number of means, including social engineering. The authors point out that SAS does not offer any security in some communication scenarios with high security requirements, *e.g.,* a user calling (or being called by) their bank. The authors implement their attack and demonstrate it in a lab environment.

Wright *et al.* [58] apply machine learning techniques to determine the language spoken in a VoIP conversation, when a variable bit rate (VBR) voice codec is used based on the length of the encrypted voice frame. As a countermeasure, they propose the use of block ciphers for encrypting the voice. In follow-on work [57], they use profile Hidden Markov Models to identify specific phrases in the encrypted voice stream with a 50% average accuracy, rising to 90% for certain phrases.

Addressing denial of service threats (19 items): Rafique *et al.* [36] analyze the robustness and reliability of SIP servers under DoS attacks. They launch a number of synthesized attacks against four well-known SIP proxy servers (OpenSER, PartySIP, OpenSBC, and MjServer). Their results demonstrate the ease with which SIP servers can be overloaded with call requests, causing such performance metrics as Call Completion Rate, Call Establishment Latency, Call Rejection Ration and Number of Retransmitted Requests to deteriorate rapidly as attack volume increases, sometimes with as few as 1,000 packets/second. As an extreme case of such attacks large volumes of INVITE messages can even cause certain implementations to crash. While documenting the susceptibility to such attacks, this work proposes no defense strategies or directions.

Reynolds and Ghosal [40] describe a multi-layer protection scheme against flood-based application- and transport-layer denial of service (DoS) attacks in VoIP. They use a combination of sensors located across the enterprise network, continuously estimating the deviation from the long-term average of the number of call setup requests and successfully completed handshakes. Similar techniques have been used in detecting TCP SYN flood attacks, with good results. The authors evaluate their scheme via simulation, considering several different types of DoS attacks and recovery models.

Ormazabal *et al.* [31] describe the design and implementation of a SIP-aware, rule-based application-layer firewall that can handle denial of service (and other) attacks in the signaling and media protocols. They use hardware acceleration for the rule matching component, allowing them to achieving filtering rates on the order of hundreds of transactions per second. The SIP-specific rules, combined with state validation of the endpoints, allow the firewall to open precisely the ports needed for only the local and remote addresses involved in a specific session, by decomposing and analyzing the content and meaning of SIP signaling message headers. They experimentally evaluate and validate the behavior of their prototype with a distributed testbed involving synthetic benign and attack traffic generation.

Larson *et al.* [22] experimentally analyzed the impact of distributed denial of service (DDoS) attacks on VoIP call quality. They also established the effectiveness of low-rate denial of service attacks that target specific vulnerabilities and implementation artifacts to cause equipment crashes and reboots. They discuss some of the possible defenses against such attacks and describe Sprint's approach, which uses regional "cleaning centers" which divert suspected attack traffic to a centralized location with numerous screening and mitigation mechanisms available. They recommend that critical VoIP traffic stay on private networks, the use of general DDoS mechanisms as a front-line defense, VoIP-aware DDoS detection and mitigation mechanisms, traffic policing and rate-limiting mechanisms, the use of TCP for VoIP signaling, extended protocol compliance checking by VoIP network elements, and the use of authentication mechanisms where possible.

Sengar et al. [47] describe vFDS, an anomaly detection system that seeks to identify flooding denial of service attacks in VoIP. The approach taken is to measure abnormal variations in the relationships between related packet streams using the Hellinger distance, a measure of the deviation between two probability measures. Using synthetic attacks, they show that vFDS can detect flooding attacks that use SYN, SIP, or RTP packets within approximately 1 second of the commencement of an attack, with small impact on call setup latency and voice quality.

Conner and Nahrstedt [9] describe a semantic-level attack that causes resource exhaustion on stateful SIP proxies by calling parties that (legitimately or in collusion) do not respond. This attack does not require network flooding or other high traffic volume attacks, making it difficult to detect with simple, network-based heuristics used against other types of denial of service attacks. They propose a simple algorithm, called *Random Early Termination* (RET) for releasing reserved resources based on the current state of the proxy (overloaded or not) and the duration of each call's ringing. They implement and evaluate their proposed scheme on a SIP proxy running in a local testbed, showing that it reduces the number of benign call failures when under attack, without incurring measurable overheads when no attack is underway.

Zhang et al. [61] describe a denial of service attack wherein adversaries flood SIP servers with calls involving URIs with DNS names that do not exist. Servers attempting to resolve them will then have to wait until the request times out (either locally or at their DNS server), before they can continue processing the same or another call. This attack works against servers that perform synchronous DNS resolution and only maintain a limited number of execution threads. They experimentally show that as few as 1,000 messages per second can cause a well provisioned synchronous-resolution server to exhibit very high call drops, while simple, single-threaded servers can be starved with even 1 message per second. As a countermeasure, they propose the use of non-blocking DNS caches, which they prototype and evaluate.

Luo et al. [24] experimentally evaluate the susceptibility of SIP to CPU-based denial of service attacks. They use an open-source SIP server in four attack scenarios: basic request flooding, spoofed-nonce flooding (wherein the target server is forced to validate the authenticator in a received message), adaptive-nonce flooding (where the nonce is refreshed periodically by obtaining a new one from the server), and adaptive-nonce flooding with IP spoofing. Their measurements show that these attacks can have a large impact on the quality of service provided by the servers. They propose several countermeasures to mitigate against such attacks, indicating that authentication by itself cannot solve the problem and that, in some circumstances, it can exacerbate its severity. These mitigation mechanisms include lightweight authentication and whitelisting, proper choice of authentication parameters, and binding nonces to client IP addresses.

Addressing service abuse threats (8 items): Zhang *et al.* [63] present a number of exploitable vulnerabilities in SIP that can manipulate billing records in a number of ways, showing their applicability against real commercial VoIP providers. Their focus is primarily on attacks that create billing inconsistencies, *e.g.,* customers being charged for service they did not receive, or over-charged for service received. Some of these attacks require a man-in-the-middle capability, while others only require some prior interaction with the target (*e.g.,* receiving a call from the victim SIP phone device).

Abdelnur *et al.* [1] use AVISPA to identify a protocol-level vulnerability in the way SIP handles authentication [50]. AVISPA is a model checker for validating security protocols and applications using a high-level protocol specification and security-goals language that gets compiler into an intermediate format that can be consumed by a number of lower-level checkers. The attack is possible with the SIP Digest Authentication, whereby an adversary can reuse another party's credentials to obtain unauthorized access to SIP or PSTN services (such as calling a premium or international phone line). This attack is possible because authentication may be requested in response to an INVITE message at any time during a call, and the responder may issue an INVITE message during a call either automatically (because of timer expirations) or through a user action (*e.g.,* placing the caller on hold in order to do a call transfer). While the solution is simple, it requires changes possibly to all end-device SIP implementations. This work is part of a bigger effort to apply testing and fuzzing toward identifying vulnerabilities in SIP protocols, implementations, and deployed systems. It is worth noting that this work has resulted in a number of vulnerability disclosures in the Common Vulnerabilities and Exposures (CVE) database and elsewhere.

Cross-cutting efforts (51 items): Wieser *et al.* [56] extend the PROTOS testsuite with a SIP-specific analysis fuzzing module. They then test their system against a number of commercial SIP implementations, finding critical vulnerabilities in all of them.

Gupta and Shmatikov [15] formally analyze the security of the VoIP protocol stack, including SIP, SDP, ZRTP, MIKEY, SDES, and SRTP. Their analysis uncovers a number of flaws, most of which derive from subtle inconsistencies in the assumptions made in designing the different protocols. These include a replay attack in SDES that completely break content protection, a man-in-the-middle attack in ZRTP, and a (perhaps theoretical) weakness in the key derivation process used in MIKEY. They also show several minor weaknesses and vulnerabilities in all protocols that enable DoS attacks.

Dantu *et al.* [12] describe a comprehensive VoIP security architecture, composed of components distributed across the media gateway controller, the proxy server(s), the IP PBX, and end-user equipment. These components explicitly exchange information toward better training of filters, and creating and maintaining white/blacklists. Implicit feedback is also provided through statistical analysis of interactions (*e.g.,* call frequency and duration). The architecture also provisions for a recovery mechanism that incorporates explicit feedback and quarantining.

Wu *et al.* [59] design an intrusion detection system, called SCIDIVE, that is specific to VoIP environments. SCIDIVE aims to detect different classes of intrusions, can operate with different viewpoints (on clients, proxies, or servers), and takes into consideration both signaling (*i.e.,* SIP) and media-transfer protocols (*e.g.,* RTP). SCIDIVE's ability to correlate cross-protocol behavior, theoretically allows for detection of more complex attacks. However, the system is rules-based, which limits its effectiveness against new/unknown attacks. In follow-on work, Wu *et al.* [60] develop SPACEDIVE, a VoIP-specific intrusion detection system that allows for correlation of events among distributed rules-based detectors. They demonstrate the ability of SPACEDIVE to detect certain classes of attacks using a simple SIP environment with two domains, and compare it with SCIDIVE.

Niccolini *et al.* [30] design an intrusion detection/intrusion prevention system architecture for use with SIP. Their system uses both knowledge-based and behavior-based detection, arranged as a series in that order. They develop a prototype implementation using the open-source Snort IDS. They evaluate the effectiveness of their system in an attack scenario by measuring the mean end-to-end delay of legitimate SIP traffic in the presence of increasing volumes of malformed SIP INVITE messages.

Nassar *et al.* [28] advocate the use of SIP-specific honeypots to catch attacks targeting the Internet telephony systems, protocols and applications. They design and implement such a honeypot system, and explore the use of a statistical engine for identifying attacks and other misbehavior, based on training on legitimate traces of SIP traffic. The engine is based on their prior work that uses Bayesian-based inference. The resulting SIP honeypot effort is largely exploratory, with performance and effectiveness evaluations left for future work.

Rieck *et al.* [41] apply machine learning techniques to detecting anomalous SIP messages, incorporating a "self-learning" component by allowing for periodic re-training of the anomaly detector using traffic that has been flagged as normal. The features used for clustering are based on n-grams and on tokenization of the SIP protocol. To prevent training attacks, wherein an adversary "trains" the anomaly detector to accept malicious inputs are legitimate, they employ randomization (choosing random samples for the training set), sanitization [10], and verification (by comparing the output of the new and old training models). Their experimental prototype was shown to handle 70 Mbps of SIP traffic, while providing a 99% detection rate with no false positives.

SNOCER, a project funded by the European Union, is "investigating approaches for overcoming temporal network, hardware and software failures and ensuring the high availability of the offered VoIP services based on low cost distributed concepts." The first public project report [48] provides an overview of VoIP infrastructure components and the threats that must be addressed (staying primarily at the protocol and network level, and avoiding implementation issues with the exception of SQL injection), along with possible defense mechanisms. There is also discussion on scalable service provisioning (replication, redundancy, backups *etc.*), toward providing reliability and fault tolerance. The second public project report [11] describes an architecture for protecting against malformed messages and related attacks using specification-based intrusion detection, protocol message verification, and redundancy. They use ontologies to describe SIP vulnerabilities, to allow for easy updating of the monitoring components (IDS) [13].

Marshall *et al.* [26] describe the AT&T VoIP security architecture. They divide VoIP equipment into three classes: trusted, trusted-but-vulnerable, and untrusted. The latter consists of the customer premises equipment, which is outside the control of the carrier. The trusted domain includes all the servers necessary to provide VoIP service. Between the two sit various border and security elements, that are responsible for protecting the trusted devices while permitting legitimate communications to proceed. They describe the interactions among the various components, and the security mechanisms used in protecting these interactions.

5   Discussion

In our previous work [16], we surveyed over 200 vulnerabilities in SIP implementations that had been disclosed in the CVE database from 1999 to 2009. We classified these vulnerabilities along several dimensions, including the VoIPSA threat taxonomy, the traditional {Confidentiality, Integrity, Availability} concerns, and a {Protocol, Implementation, Configuration} axis. We found that the various types of denial of service attacks constitute the majority of disclosed vulnerabilities, over 90% of which were due to implementation problems and 7% due to configuration.

Considering the research work we have surveyed (some of which was discussed in this paper), we can see that out of a total of 197 publications, 18% concern themselves with an overview of the problem space and of solutions — a figure we believe is reasonable, considering the enormity of the problem space and the speed of change in the protocols, standards, and implementations. We also see a considerable amount of effort (roughly 25%) going toward addressing SPIT. While SPIT is not a major issue at this point, our experience with email spam and telemarketing seems to provide sufficient motivation for research in this area. Much of the work is focused on identifying SPIT calls and callers based on behavioral traits, although a number of other approaches are under exploration (*e.g.,* real-time content analysis). One of the problems is the lack of a good corpus of data for experimentation and validation of the proposed techniques.

We were also not surprised to see a sizable portion of research (17%) directed at design, analysis (both security- and performance-oriented), and attacking of cryptographic protocols as used in VoIP. The cryptographic research community appears to be reasonably comfortable in proposing tweaks and minor improvements to the basic authentication mechanisms, and the systems community appears content with analyzing the performance of different protocol configurations (*e.g.,* TLS *vs.* IPsec). With a few notable exceptions, much of the work lacks "ambition."

Most distressing, however, is the fact that comparatively little research (9.6%) is going toward addressing the problem of denial of service. Given the numerical dominance of SIP-specific DoS vulnerabilities (as described earlier) and the ease of launching such attacks, it is clear that significantly more work is needed here. What work is being done seems to primarily focus on the server and infrastructure side, despite our finding that half of DoS-related vulnerabilities are present on endpoints. Furthermore, much of the existing work focuses on network-observable attacks (*e.g.,* "obviously" malformed SIP messages), whereas the majority of VoIP DoS vulnerabilities are the result of implementation failures. More generally, additional work is needed in strengthening implementations, rather than introducing middleboxes and network intrusion detection systems, whose effectiveness has been shown to be limited in other domains; taking a black box approach in securing VoIP systems is, in our opinion, not going to be sufficient.

Also disconcerting is the lack of research (4%) in addressing service abuse threats, considering the high visibility of large fraud incidents [19,51,52]. In general, we found little work that took a "big picture" view of the VoIP security problem. What cross-cutting architectures have been proposed focus primarily on intrusion detection. Work is desperately needed to address cross-implementation and cross-protocol problems, above and beyond the few efforts along those lines in the intrusion detection space.

Finally, we note that none of the surveyed works addressed the problem of configuration management. While such problems represent only 7% of known vulnerabilities, configuration issues are easy to overlook and are likely under-represented in our previous analysis due to the nature of vulnerability reporting.

6 Conclusions

We have presented a survey of VoIP security research. While space restrictions prevent us from discussing all surveyed works, we have discussed a representative subset of these. We presented an initial classification using the VoIPSA threat taxonomy, and juxtaposed this against our previous analysis on VoIP security vulnerabilities. We identified two specific areas (denial of service and service abuse) as being under-represented in terms of research efforts directed at them (relative to their importance in the vulnerability survey), and called for additional effort at securing implementations and configurations, rather than taking a black-box approach of VoIP systems. We intend to expand on this work and offer a more comprehensive analysis in the near future.

Acknowledgment. This work was supported by the French National Research Agency (ANR) under Contract ANR-08-VERS-017.

References

1. Abdelnur, H., Avanesov, T., Rusinowitch, M., State, R.: Abusing SIP Authentication. In: Proceedings of the 4th International Conference on Information Assurance and Security (ISIAS), September 2008, pp. 237–242 (2008)
2. Adelsbach, A., Alkassar, A., Garbe, K.-H., Luzaic, M., Manulis, M., Scherer, E., Schwenk, J., Siemens, E.: Voice over IP: Sichere Umstellung der Sprachkommunikation auf IP-Technologie. Bundesanzeiger Verlag (2005)
3. Anwar, Z., Yurcik, W., Johnson, R.E., Hafiz, M., Campbell, R.H.: Multiple Design Patterns for Voice over IP (VoIP) Security. In: Proceedings of the IEEE Workshop on Information Assurance (WIA), held in conjunction with the 25th IEEE International Performance Computing and Communications Conference (IPCCC) (April 2006)
4. Balasubramaniyan, V., Ahamad, M., Park, H.: CallRank: Combating SPIT Using Call Duration, Social Networks and Global Reputation. In: Proceedings of the 4th Conference on Email and Anti-Spam (CEAS) (August 2007)

5. Barbieri, R., Bruschi, D., Rosti, E.: Voice over IPsec: Analysis and Solutions. In: Proceedings of the 18th Annual Computer Security Applications Conference (ACSAC), December 2002, pp. 261–270 (2002)

6. Bilien, J., Eliasson, E., Orrblad, J., Vatn, J.-O.: Secure VoIP: Call Establishment and Media Protection. In: Proceedings of the 2nd Workshop on Securing Voice over IP (June 2005)

7. Butcher, D., Li, X., Guo, J.: Security Challenge and Defense in VoIP Infrastructures. IEEE Transactions on Systems, Man, and Cybernetics, Part C: Applications and Reviews 37(6), 1152–1162 (2007)

8. Cao, F., Malik, S.: Vulnerability Analysis and Best Practices for Adopting IP Telephony in Critical Infrastructure Sectors. IEEE Communications Magazine 44(4), 138–145 (2006)

9. Conner, W., Nahrstedt, K.: Protecting SIP Proxy Servers from Ringing-based Denial-of-Service Attacks. In: Proceedings of the 10th IEEE International Symposium on Multimedia (ISM), December 2008, pp. 340–347 (2008)

10. Cretu, G.F., Stavrou, A., Locasto, M.E., Stolfo, S.J., Keromytis, A.D.: Casting out Demons: Sanitizing Training Data for Anomaly Sensors. In: Proceedings of the IEEE Security and Privacy Symposium, May 2008, pp. 81–95 (2008)

11. Dagiuklas, T., Geneiatakis, D., Kambourakis, G., Sisalem, D., Ehlert, S., Fiedler, J., Markl, J., Rokis, M., Botron, O., Rodriguez, J., Liu, J.: General Reliability and Security Framework for VoIP Infrastructures. Technical Report Deliverable D2.2, SNOCER COOP-005892 (September 2005)

12. Dantu, R., Fahmy, S., Schulzrinne, H., Cangussu, J.: Issues and Challenges in Securing VoIP. Computers & Security (to appear, 2009)

13. Geneiatakis, D., Lambrinoudakis, C.: An Ontology Description for SIP Security Flaws. Computer Communications 30(6), 1367–1374 (2007)

14. Guo, J.-I., Yen, J.-C., Pai, H.-F.: New Voice over Internet Protocol Technique with Hierarchical Data Security Protection. IEE Proceedings — Vision, Image and Signal Processing 149(4), 237–243 (2002)

15. Gupta, P., Shmatikov, V.: Security Analysis of Voice-over-IP Protocols. In: Proceedings of the 20th IEEE Computer Security Foundations Symposium (CSFW), July 2007, pp. 49–63 (2007)

16. Keromytis, A.D.: Voice over IP: Risks, Threats and Vulnerabilities. In: Proceedings of the Cyber Infrastructure Protection (CIP) Conference (June 2009)

17. Kolan, P., Dantu, R.: Socio-technical Defense Against Voice Spamming. ACM Transactions on Autonomous and Adaptive Systems (TAAS) 2(1) (March 2007)

18. Kolan, P., Dantu, R., Cangussu, J.W.: Nuisance of a Voice Call. ACM Transactions on Multimedia Computing, Communications and Applications (TOMCCAP) 5(1), 6:1–6:22 (2008)

19. Krebs, B.: Security Fix: Default Passwords Led to $55 Million in Bogus Phone Charges (June 2009)

20. Kuhn, D.R., Walsh, T.J., Fries, S.: Security Considerations for Voice Over IP Systems. US National Institute of Standards and Technology (NIST) Special Publication SP 800-58 (January 2005)

21. Kuntze, N., Schmidt, A.U., Hett, C.: Non-Repudiation in Internet Telephony. In: Proceedings of the IFIP International Information Security Conference, May 2007, pp. 361–372 (2007)

22. Larson, J., Dawson, T., Evans, M., Straley, J.C.: Defending VoIP Networks from DDoS Attacks. In: Proceedings of the 2nd Workshop on Securing Voice over IP (June 2005)

23. Li, C., Li, S., Zhang, D., Chen, G.: Cryptanalysis of a Data Security Protection Scheme for VoIP. IEE Proceedings—Vision, Image and Signal Processing 153(1), 1–10 (2006)

24. Luo, M., Peng, T., Leckie, C.: CPU-based DoS Attacks Against SIP Servers. In: Proceedings of the IEEE Network Operations and Management Symposium (NOMS), April 2008, pp. 41–48 (2008)

25. Marias, G.F., Dritsas, S., Theoharidou, M., Mallios, J., Mitrou, L., Gritzalis, D., Dagiuklas, T., Rebahi, Y., Ehlert, S., Pannier, B., Capsada, O., Juell, J.F.: SPIT Detection and Handling Strategies for VoIP Infrastructures. Technical Report Deliverable WP2/D2.2, SPIDER COOP-32720 (March 2007)
26. Marshall, W., Faryar, A.F., Kealy, K., de los Reyes, G., Rosencrantz, I., Rosencrantz, R., Spielman, C.: Carrier VoIP Security Architecture. In: Proceedings of the 12th International Telecommunications Network Strategy and Planning Symposium, November 2006, pp. 1–6 (2006)
27. Mathieu, B., Niccolini, S., Sisalem, D.: SDRS: A Voice-over-IP Spam Detection and Reaction System. IEEE Security & Privacy Magazine 6(6), 52–59 (2008)
28. Nassar, M., State, R., Festor, O.: VoIP Honeypot Architecture. In: Proceedings of the 10th IFIP/IEEE International Symposium on Integrated Network Management, May 2007, pp. 109–118 (2007)
29. Niccolini, S.: SPIT Prevention: State of the Art and Research Challenges. In: Proceedings of the 3rd Workshop on Securing Voice over IP (June 2006)
30. Niccolini, S., Garroppo, R.G., Giordano, S., Risi, G., Ventura, S.: SIP Intrusion Detection and Prevention: Recommendations and Prototype Implementation. In: Proceedings of the 1st IEEE Workshop on VoIP Management and Security (VoIP MaSe), April 2006, pp. 47–52 (2006)
31. Ormazabal, G., Nagpal, S., Yardeni, E., Schulzrinne, H.: Secure SIP: A Scalable Prevention Mechanism for DoS Attacks on SIP Based VoIP Systems. In: Proceedings of the 2nd International Conference on Principles, Systems and Applications of IP Telecommunications (IPTComm), July 2008, pp. 107–132 (2008)
32. Persky, D.: VoIP Security Vulnerabilities. White paper, SANS Institute (2007)
33. Petraschek, M., Hoeher, T., Jung, O., Hlavacs, H., Gansterer, W.N.: Security and Usability Aspects of Man-in-the-Middle Attacks on ZRTP. Journal of Universal Computer Science 14(5), 673–692 (2008)
34. Pörschmann, C., Knospe, H.: Analysis of Spectral Parameters of Audio Signals for the Identification of Spam Over IP Telephony. In: Proceedings of the 5th Conference on Email and Anti-Spam (CEAS) (August 2008)
35. Quittek, J., Niccolini, S., Tartarelli, S., Stiemerling, M., Brunner, M., Ewald, T.: Detecting SPIT Calls by Checking Human Communication Patterns. In: Proceedings of the IEEE International Conference on Communications (ICC), June 2007, pp. 1979–1984 (2007)
36. Rafique, M.Z., Akbar, M.A., Farooq, M.: Evaluating DoS Attacks Against SIP-Based VoIP Systems. In: Proceedings of the IEEE Global Telecommunications Conference (GLOBECOM), November/December (2009)
37. Rebahi, Y., Ehlert, S., Dritsas, S., Marias, G.F., Gritzalis, D., Pannier, B., Capsada, O., Golubenco, T., Juell, J.F., Hoffmann, M.: General Anti-Spam Security Framework for VoIP Infrastructures. Technical Report Deliverable WP2/D2.3, SPIDER COOP-32720 (July 2007)
38. Rebahi, Y., Ehlert, S., Theoharidou, M., Mallios, J., Dritsas, S., Marias, G.F., Mitrou, L., Dagiuklas, T., Avgoustianakis, M., Gritzalis, D., Pannier, B., Capsada, O., Markl, J.: SPIT Threat Analysis. Deliverable wp2/d2.1, SPIDER COOP-32720 (January 2007)
39. Rebahi, Y., Pallares, J.J., Kovacs, G., Minh, N.T., Ehlert, S., Sisalem, D.: Performance Analysis of Identity Management in the Session Initiation Protocol (SIP). In: Proceedings of the IEEE/ACS International Conference on Computer Systems and Applications (AICCSA), March/April 2008, pp. 711–717 (2008)
40. Reynolds, B., Ghosal, D.: Secure IP Telephony using Multi-layered Protection. In: Proceedings of the ISOC Symposium on Network and Distributed Systems Security (NDSS) (February 2003)

41. Rieck, K., Wahl, S., Laskov, P., Domschitz, P., Müller, K.-R.: A Self-learning System for Detection of Anomalous SIP Messages. In: Proceedings of the 2nd Internation Conference on Principles, Systems and Applications of IP Telecommunications. Services and Security for Next Generation Networks: Second International Conference (IPTComm), July 2008, pp. 90–106 (2008)

42. Rosenberg, J., Schulzrinne, H., Camarillo, G., Johnston, A., Peterson, J., Sparks, R., Handley, M., Schooler, E.: SIP: Session Initiation Protocol. RFC 3261 (Proposed Standard) (June 2002); Updated by RFCs 3265, 3853, 4320, 4916, 5393

43. Salsano, S., Veltri, L., Papalilo, D.: SIP Security Issues: The SIP Authentication Procedure and its Processing Load. IEEE Network 16(6), 38–44 (2002)

44. Schlegel, R., Niccolini, S., Tartarelli, S., Brunner, M.: SPam over Internet Telephony (SPIT) Prevention Framework. In: Proceedings of the IEEE Global Telecommunications Conference (GLOBECOM), November/December 2006, pp. 1–6 (2006)

45. Seedorf, J.: Security challenges for peer-to-peer SIP. IEEE Network 20(5), 38–45 (2006)

46. Seedorf, J.: Using Cryptographically Generated SIP-URIs to Protect the Integrity of Content in P2P-SIP. In: Proceedings of the 3rd Workshop on Securing Voice over IP (June 2006)

47. Sengar, H., Wang, H., Wijesekera, D., Jajodia, S.: Detecting VoIP Floods Using the Hellinger Distance. IEEE Transactions on Parallel and Distributed Systems 19(6), 794–805 (2008)

48. Sisalem, D., Ehlert, S., Geneiatakis, D., Kambourakis, G., Dagiuklas, T., Markl, J., Rokos, M., Botron, O., Rodriguez, J., Liu, J.: Towards a Secure and Reliable VoIP Infrastructure. Technical Report Deliverable D2.1, SNOCER COOP-005892 (May 2005)

49. Srivastava, K., Schulzrinne, H.: Preventing Spam For SIP-based Instant Messages and Sessions. Technical Report CUCS-042-04, Columbia University, Department of Computer Science (2004)

50. State, R., Festor, O., Abdelanur, H., Pascual, V., Kuthan, J., Coeffic, R., Janak, J., Floroiu, J.: SIP digest authentication relay attack. draft-state-sip-relay-attack-00 (March 2009)

51. The Register. Two charged with VoIP fraud (June 2006),
    http://www.theregister.co.uk/2006/06/08/
    voip_fraudsters_nabbed/

52. The Register. Fugitive VOIP hacker cuffed in Mexico (February 2009),
    http://www.theregister.co.uk/2009/02/11/
    fugitive_voip_hacker_arrested/

53. Thermos, P., Takanen, A.: Securing VoIP Networks. Pearson Education, London (2008)

54. VoIP Security Alliance. VoIP Security and Privacy Threat Taxonomy, version 1.0 (October 2005), http://www.voipsa.org/Activities/taxonomy.php

55. Wang, X., Zhang, R., Yang, X., Jiang, X., Wijesekera, D.: Voice Pharming Attack and the Trust of VoIP. In: Proceedings of the 4th International Conference on Security and Privacy in Communication Networks (SecureComm), September 2008, pp. 1–11 (2008)

56. Wieser, C., Laakso, M., Schulzrinne, H.: Security Testing of SIP Implementations. Technical Report CUCS-024-03, Columbia University, Department of Computer Science (2003)

57. Wright, C.V., Ballard, L., Coulls, S., Monrose, F.N., Masson, G.M.: Spot Me If You Can: Recovering Spoken Phrases in Encrypted VoIP Conversations. In: Proceedings of IEEE Symposium on Security and Privacy, May 2008, pp. 35–49 (2008)

58. Wright, C.V., Ballard, L., Monrose, F.N., Masson, G.M.: Language Identification of Encrypted VoIP Traffic: Alejandra y Roberto or Alice and Bob? In: Proceedings of 16th USENIX Security Symposium, August 2007, pp. 1–12 (2007)

59. Wu, Y., Bagchi, S., Garg, S., Singh, N.: SCIDIVE: A Stateful and Cross Protocol Intrusion Detection Architecture for Voice-over-IP Environments. In: Proceedings of the Conference on Dependable Systems and Networks (DSN), June/July 2004, pp. 433–442 (2004)

60. Wu, Y.-S., Apte, V., Bagchi, S., Garg, S., Singh, N.: Intrusion Detection in Voice over IP Environments. International Journal of Information Security 8(3), 153–172 (2009)

61. Zhang, G., Ehlert, S., Magedanz, T., Sisalem, D.: Denial of Service Attack and Prevention on SIP VoIP Infrastructures Using DNS Flooding. In: Proceedings of the 1st International Conference on Principles, Systems and Applications of IP Telecommunications (IPTCOMM), July 2007, pp. 57–66 (2007)

62. Zhang, R., Wang, X., Farley, R., Yang, X., Jiang, X.: On the Feasibility of Launching the Man-In-The-Middle Attacks on VoIP from Remote Attackers. In: Proceedings of the 4th International ACM Symposium on Information, Computer, and Communications Security (ASIACCS), March 2009, pp. 61–69 (2009)

63. Zhang, R., Wang, X., Yang, X., Jiang, X.: Billing Attacks on SIP-based VoIP Systems. In: Proceedings of the 1st USENIX workshop on Offensive Technologies, August 2007, pp. 1–8 (2007)

Security for a Smarter Planet

Nataraj Nagaratnam

Distinguished Engineer and CTO
IBM India Software Lab
New Delhi, India

Abstract. Bit by bit, our planet is getting smarter. By this, we mean the systems that run, the way we live and work as a society. Three things have brought this about - the world is becoming instrumented, interconnected and intelligent. Given the planet is becoming instrumented and interconnected, this opens up more risks that need to be managed. Escalating security and privacy concerns along with a renewed focus on organizational oversight are driving governance, risk management and compliance (GRC) to the forefront of the business. Compliance regulations have increasingly played a larger role by attempting to establish processes and controls that mitigate the internal and external risks organizations have today. To effectively meet the requirements of GRC, companies must prove that they have strong and consistent controls over who has access to critical applications and data.

Security has to be applied within a business context and fused into the fabric of business and not as a widget to solve the next security threat. This presentation will discuss challenges planet face, what companies, societies, governments need to be doing to address these challenges, and technical approach around a solution.

A. Prakash and I. Sen Gupta (Eds.): ICISS 2009, LNCS 5905, p. 18, 2009.

The WOMBAT Attack Attribution Method: Some Results

Marc Dacier[1], Van-Hau Pham[2], and Olivier Thonnard[3]

[1] Symantec Research, Sophia Antipolis, France
marc_dacier@symantec.com
[2] Institut Eurecom, 2229 Route des Crètes,
Sophia Antipolis, France
van-hau.pham@eurecom.fr
[3] Royal Military Academy, Polytechnic Faculty,
Brussels, Belgium
olivier.thonnard@rma.ac.be

Abstract. In this paper, we present a new *attack attribution* method that has been developed within the WOMBAT[1] project. We illustrate the method with some real-world results obtained when applying it to almost two years of attack traces collected by low interaction honeypots. This analytical method aims at identifying large scale attack phenomena composed of IP sources that are linked to the same root cause. All malicious sources involved in a same phenomenon constitute what we call a *Misbehaving Cloud* (MC). The paper offers an overview of the various steps the method goes through to identify these clouds, providing pointers to external references for more detailed information. Four instances of misbehaving clouds are then described in some more depth to demonstrate the meaningfulness of the concept.

1 Introduction

There is no real consensus on the definition of "attack attribution" in the cyber domain. Most previous work related to that field tend to use the term "attribution" as a synonym for *traceback*, which consists in "determining the identity or location of an attacker or an attacker's intermediary" [25]. In the context of a cyber-attack, the obtained identity can refer to a person's name, an account, an alias, or similar information associated with a person or an organisation. The location may include physical (geographic) location, or any virtual address such as an IP address or Ethernet address. The rationale for developing such attribution techniques is mainly due to the untrusted nature of the IP protocol, in which the source IP address is not authenticated and can thus be easily spoofed. An extensive survey of attack attribution techniques used in the context of IP traceback can be found in [25].

---

[1] Worldwide Observatory of Malicious Behaviors and Threats
- http://www.wombat-project.eu

A. Prakash and I. Sen Gupta (Eds.): ICISS 2009, LNCS 5905, pp. 19–37, 2009.

In this paper, we refer to "attack attribution" as something quite different from what is described here above. We are primarily concerned with larger scale attacks. In this context, we aim at developing an analytical method to help security analysts in determining their root causes and in deriving their *modus operandi*. These phenomena can be observed through many different means (e.g., honeypots, IDS's, sandboxes, web crawlers, malware collecting systems, etc). In most cases, we believe that attack phenomena manifest themselves through so-called "attack events", which can be observed with distributed sensors that are deployed in the Internet. Typical examples of attack phenomena that we want to identify vary from worm or malware families that propagate through code injection attacks [9], to established botnets controlled by the same people and targeting machines in the IP space. All malicious sources involved in the same root phenomenon constitute what we call a *Misbehaving Cloud* (MC).

The structure of the paper is as follows: Section 2 describes the experimental environment used to validate the method presented. Section 3 offers a high level overview of the attack attribution method defined within the WOMBAT project and Section 4 gives some more information on the multi criteria fusion approach used in the method. Section 5 discusses a couple of illustrative examples obtained by applying the method on honeynet traces, and Section 6 concludes the paper.

2   Description of the Experimental Environment

This paper offers an empirical analysis of some attacks collected during two years by a set of low interaction honeypots deployed all over the world by the Leurré.com Project [10]. We refer the interested reader to [8,19] for an in-depth presentation of the data collection infrastructure. From an analytical viewpoint, our attack attribution method builds upon previous results, namely [18,4,16,24,17]. For the sake of clarity, we start by introducing some important terms that have been defined in these previous publications.

2.1   Terminology

1. **Platform:** A physical machine running three virtual honeypots, which emulate three distinct machines thanks to *honeyd* [20]. A platform is connected directly to the Internet and collects tcpdump traces that are gathered on a daily basis in a centralized database [10].
2. **Source:** An IP address that has sent at least one packet to, at least, one platform. An IP address remains associated to a given Source as long as no more than 25 hours[2] elapse between two packets sent by that IP. After such a delay, the IP will be associated to a new source identifier if we observe it again.

---

[2] By grouping packets by originating sources instead of by IPs, we minimize the risk of mixing together the activities of two distinct physical machines (as a side effect of the dynamic address allocation implemented by ISP's).

3. **Attack:** Refers to all packets exchanged between a malicious source and a platform.
4. **Cluster:** All the sources that execute the same attack against any of the platforms constitute an *(attack) Cluster*. In practice, such a cluster groups all malicious sources that have left highly similar network traces on our platforms. How to identify clusters and how those clusters look like are issues that have been explained in other publications [18,8].

2.2   Honeynet Dataset

Machines used in the Leurré.com project are maintained by partners all over the world, on a voluntary basis. Some of these platforms can thus become unavailable. In the context of this paper, we wanted to apply our analytical method on a dataset that would be, as much as possible, unimpacted by these operational issues. Therefore, we have selected a subset of 40 stable platforms from all platforms at our disposal. A total of 3,477,976 attacks have been observed by those platforms. We represent the total number of attacks per day over the whole analysis period (800 days, from Sep 2006 until November 2008), as a time series denoted by TS. Similarly, we can represent, for each platform, the number of attacks observed on it, on a daily basis. This leads to the definition of 40 distinct attack time series (each made of 800 points), denoted by TS_X where X represents a platform identifier.

We can go even further in splitting our time series in order to represent which type of attack was observed on which platform. To do this, we split each TS_X into as many time series as there are *attack clusters*, as defined before. These newly obtained time series are represented by $\Phi_{[0-800),c_i,p_j}$ $\forall$ cluster c_i and $\forall$ platform p_j. That is, the ith point of the time series $\Phi_{[0-800),X,Y}$ represents the amount of sources attacking, on day i, the platform Y by means of the attack defined by the cluster identifier X. We represent by TS_L2 the set of all these observed cluster time series (in total, 395,712 time series).

In [17], it has been shown that a large fraction of these time series barely vary in amplitude on a daily basis. This continuous, low-intensity activity is also referred to as the Internet *background radiation* [13]. In this paper, we do not consider those flat curves, and we instead focus on time series that show some significant variations over time, indicating the existence of some ephemeral phenomena. To automatically identify these time series of interest, we have applied the method presented in [17], which finally gives a subset of time series denoted by TS_L2'. In our dataset, TS_L2' contains now only 2,127 distinct time series. However, they still comprise a total of 2,538,922 malicious sources. TS_L2' represents the set of time series we have used for this analysis.

3   Overview of WOMBAT Attribution Method

The WOMBAT attack attribution method is made of two distinct steps. In the very first one, we identify periods of time where some of the time series from

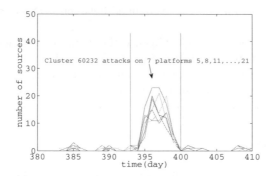

Fig. 1. An example of $\mathcal{M}$-event, composed of seven μ-events (on seven different platforms) that are correlated in the same time interval. Cluster 60332 corresponds to a malicious activity on the VNC port (5900/TCP).

TS_L2' exhibit a pattern that indicate that a specific phenomenon worth of interest is happening. We call a *micro attack event* such period of time for a given time series from TS_L2'. Moreover, we call *macro attack event* a group of micro attack events that are correlated during the same period of time.

The second step of the method consists in characterizing each of these *micro attack events* and in trying to establish connections between them. All micro attack events that share enough features constitute what we call a *Misbehaving Cloud* (MC). We hypothesize that all malicious sources involved in a Misbehaving Cloud have a common root cause. By identifying them and studying their global behavior, we hope to get a better insight into the modus operandi and the strategies of those responsible for them.

We further detail the two steps of the method in the next subsections.

3.1 Step 1: Micro and Macro Attack Events Identification

Definition (μ-event): A *micro attack event* (or μ-event) is defined by a tuple $(\mathcal{T}, \mathcal{C}_i)$ where $\mathcal{T}$ represents a limited period of time (typically a few days) during which a significant attack activity is observed, and $\mathcal{C}_i$ represents the time series corresponding to cluster $\mathcal{C}$ observed on the platform i.

Definition ($\mathcal{M}$-event): A set of micro attack events observed over the same period of time, and during which the corresponding time series are strongly correlated is defined as a *macro attack event* (or $\mathcal{M}$-event).

Figure 1 illustrates this concept by representing a $\mathcal{M}$-event composed of seven μ-events that are correlated in the same time interval.

Identification of μ-events. The micro attack event identification relies mostly on some well-known signal processing techniques. The goal is to segment the time series into periods of interest. Such periods are characterized by some *intense period* of activities isolated by periods of very stable or non existent activities.

Several techniques exist to detect abrupt changes in a signal [1]. In this paper, the method we have used is the one that has been precisely presented in [15].

Identification of $\mathcal{M}$-event. Once we have identified all μ-events of interest in our dataset, we need to identify all those that are strongly correlated over the same period of time, which form thus a $\mathcal{M}$-event. The problem is not as trivial as it may sound, because *i)* μ-events may have overlapping periods, and *ii)* within a given period of time, several distinct phenomena may have taken place. Here too, we have presented and compared various approaches and we refer the interested reader to [17,15] for an in-depth explanation of the algorithms used.

3.2   Step 2: Multi Criteria Fusion of Attack Events Features

The purpose of this second step consists in deciding whether several distinct μ-events are likely due to a same root phenomenon (i.e., the same Misbehaving Cloud), on the basis of different characteristics derived from the network traffic generated by malicious sources involved in such events.

Our approach is based on three components:

1. Attack Feature Selection: we determine which *attack features* we want to include in the fusion process, and we thus characterize each μ-event according to this set of features;
2. Graph-based Clustering: a graph of μ-events is created regarding each feature, based on an appropriate distance for measuring pairwise similarities. Fully connected components can then be identified within each graph;
3. Multi criteria fusion: the different graphs are then combined using an *agregation function* that models some dynamic behavior.

This approach is mostly unsupervised, i.e., it does not rely on a preliminary training phase to attribute μ-events to larger scale phenomena. In the next Section, we describe the three steps of this method.

4   On the Multi Criteria Fusion Approach

4.1   Attack Features Selection

In most clustering tasks, the very first step consists in selecting some key characteristics from the dataset, i.e., salient features that may reveal meaningful *patterns* [6]. In this analysis, we have selected some *features* that we consider useful to analyze the behavior of global phenomena.

One of the key features used in this attribution technique is the spatial distributions of malicious sources involved in μ-events, in terms of originating countries and IP blocks. Looking at these statistical characteristics may reveal attack activities having a specific distribution of originating countries or IP networks, which can help for instance to confirm the existence of "unclean networks" [3]. In practice, for each μ-event, we create a feature vector representing the distribution of countries of sources (as a result of the IP to geolocation mapping), or a vector representing the distribution of IP addresses (grouped by their Class A-prefix, to limit the vector's size).

We have also selected an attack characteristic related to the *targeted plat-forms*. Looking at which specific platform has observed a μ-event is certainly a pertinent feature. At the same time, we combine this information with the $\mathcal{M}$-event identification, since (by definition) $\mathcal{M}$-events are composed of μ-events that are strongly correlated in time (which indicates a certain degree of coordi-nation among them).

Besides the origins and the targets, the *type of activity* performed by the attackers seems also relevant. In fact, worm or bot software is often crafted with a certain number of available exploits targeting a given set of TCP or UDP ports. So, it makes sense to take advantage of similarities between the *sequences of ports* that have been probed or exploited by malicious sources.

Finally, we have decided to compute, for each pair of μ-events, the ratio of common IP addresses. We are aware of the fact that, as time passes, some machines of a given botnet (or misbehaving cloud) might be cured while others may get infected (and thus join the cloud). Additionally, certain ISPs apply a quite dynamic policy of IP allocation for residential users, which means that infected machines can have different IP addresses when we observe them at different moments. Nevertheless, considering the huge size of the IP space, it is still reasonable to expect that two μ-events are probably related to the same root phenomenon when they have a high percentage of IP addresses in common.

To summarize, and to provide a short-hand notation in the rest of this paper, for each μ-event we define a set of features that we denote by:

$$F = \{F_i\}\,,\ i \in \{geo, sub, targ, ps, cip\}$$

where:

$$\begin{cases} geo = \text{geolocation, as a result of mapping IP addresses to countries;} \\ sub = \text{distribution of sources IP addresses (grouped by Class A-subnet);} \\ targ = \text{targeted platforms} + \text{degree of coordination } (\mathcal{M}\text{-event membership);} \\ ps = \text{port sequences probed or targeted by malicious sources;} \\ cip = \text{feature representing the ratio of common IP addresses among sources;} \end{cases}$$

4.2   Graph-Based Clustering

The second component of our attribution method implements an unsupervised clustering technique that aims at discovering groups of strongly connected μ-events, when these are represented within a graph. In [22,23], we have given a detailed description of this graph-based clustering technique. However, to make this paper as self-contained as possible, we briefly describe the high-level prin-ciples of this technique.

As defined by Jain and Dubes in [6], many typical clustering tasks involve the following steps:

i)   feature selection and/or extraction (as described in the previous Subsection);
ii) definition of an appropriate distance for measuring the similarities between pairs of elements with respect to a given feature;
iii) application of a grouping algorithm, such as the classical hierarchical clustering or K-means algorithm;
iv) data abstraction (if needed), to provide a compact representation of each cluster;
v)   optionally, the assessment of the clusters quality and coherence, e.g. by means of validity indices.

Steps (iv) and (v), while important, lie outside the scope of this paper. Instead, we will simply use four anecdotal examples to intuitively demonstrate the quality, i.e., the meaningfulness, of the groups created by the method. Steps (ii) and (iii) are described here after.

Choosing a distance function. How to measure *pairwise similarities* between two feature vectors is obviously an important step, since it will have an impact on the coherence and the quality of the resulting clusters.

When we have to deal with observations that are in the form of probability distributions (or frequencies), like in the case of features F_{geo} and F_{sub}, we need to rely on statistical distances. One commonly used technique is the Kullback-Leibler divergence [7]. Let p_1 and p_2 be for instance two probability distributions over a discrete space X, then the K-L divergence of p_2 from p_1 is defined as:

$$D_{KL}(p_1 \| p_2) = \sum_x p_1(x) \log \frac{p_1(x)}{p_2(x)} \tag{1}$$

which is also called the information divergence (or *relative entropy*). Because D_{KL} is not considered as a true metric, it is usually better to use instead the Jensen-Shannon divergence (JSD) [11], defined as:

$$JS(p_1, p_2) = \frac{D_{KL}(p_1 \| \bar{p}) + D_{KL}(p_2 \| \bar{p})}{2} \tag{2}$$

where $\bar{p} = (p_1 + p_2)/2$. In other words, the Jensen-Shannon divergence is the *average* of the KL-divergences to the *average distribution*.

Finally, to transform pairwise distances d_{ij} to similarity weights sim_{ij}, we still have to define a mapping function. Previous studies found that the similarity between stimuli decay exponentially with some power of the perceptual measure distance [21]. As customary, we can thus use the following functional form to do this transformation:

$$sim(i, j) = exp(\frac{-d_{ij}^2}{\sigma^2}) \tag{3}$$

where σ is a positive real number that affects the decreasing rate of w.

Measuring pairwise similarities for the other considered features (F_{targ}, F_{ps}, F_{cip}) is more straightforward. In those cases, we can use simpler distance functions, such as the *Jaccard similarity coefficient*. Let s_1 and s_2 be two sample sets (for instance with F_{ps}, s_1 and s_2 are sets of ports that have been probed by sources of two μ-events), then the Jaccard coefficent is defined as the size of the intersection divided by the size of the union of the sample sets, i.e.:

$$sim(i, j) = \frac{|s_1 \bigcap s_2|}{|s_1 \bigcup s_2|}$$

The Jaccard similarity coefficient can also be used to compute the ratio of common IP addresses between attack events (F_{cip}). Regarding F_{targ}, a simple weighted means is used to combine two scores: $i)$ one score in $[0, 1]$ as given by the simple comparison of the two targeted platforms, and $ii)$ another score (also in $[0, 1]$) indicating whether two μ-events belong to the same $\mathcal{M}$-event (indicating a time coordination).

Grouping algorithm. In this step, we formulate the problem of clustering μ-events using a graph-based approach. The vertices (or nodes) of the graph represent the patterns (or feature vectors) of the μ-events, and the edges (or links) express the similarities between μ-events, as calculated with the distance metrics described before. Then, we can extract so-called *maximal cliques* from the graph, where a maximal clique is defined as an induced subgraph in which the vertices are fully connected and it is not contained within any other clique. To do this, we use the *dominant sets* approach of Pavan et al. [14], which proved to be an effective method for finding maximal *weighted* cliques. This means that the weight of every edge (i.e., the relative similarity value) is also considered by the algorithm, as it seeks to discover maximal cliques whose total weight is maximized.

By repeating this process, we can thus create an undirected edge-weighted graph G_i for each attack feature F_i, in which the edges are similarity weights $\in [0, 1]$ that can be seen as *relatedness degrees* between μ-events (where a zero value indicates totally unrelated events). Then, the clique algorithm extracts one set of cliques per feature, which reveals the cohesions among μ-events regarding each F_i.

4.3   Multi-Criteria Aggregation

Definition (Aggregation function). An aggregation function is formally defined as a function of n arguments ($n > 1$) that maps the (n-dimensional) unit cube onto the unit interval: $f : [0, 1]^n \longrightarrow [0, 1]$, with the following properties [2]:

(i) $f(\underbrace{0, 0, \ldots, 0}_{n\text{-}times}) = 0$ and $f(\underbrace{1, 1, \ldots, 1}_{n\text{-}times}) = 1$

(ii) $x_i \leq y_i$ for all $i \in \{1, \ldots, n\}$ implies $f(x_1, \ldots, x_n) \leq f(y_1, \ldots, y_n)$

Aggregation functions are used in many prototypical situations where we have several criteria of concern, with respect to which we assess different options. The objective consists in calculating a combined score for each option, and this combined output forms then a basis from which decisions can be made. For example, aggregation functions are largely used in problems of *multi criteria decision analysis* (MCDA), in which an alternative has to be chosen based on several, sometimes conflicting criteria. Usually, the alternatives are evaluated from different attributes (or features) that are expressed with numerical values representing a degree of preference, or a degree of membership.

In our application, we have n different attack features given by the F_i's, and thus a vector of criteria $\mathbf{x} \in [0,1]^n$ can be constructed from the similarity weights, i.e., $x_i = A_i(j,k)$, with A_i being the similarity matrix of graph G_i corresponding to attack feature F_i. Our approach consists in combining the n values of each criteria vector $\mathbf{x}$ (which reflect the set of all relationships between a pair of μ-events), in order to build an aggregated graph $G' = \sum G_i$ from which we can then extract the connected components. A straightforward but rather simplistic approach would consist in combining the criteria using a simple arithmetic mean, or by assigning different weights to each criteria (weighted mean). However, this does not allow us to model more complex behaviors, such as "most of", or "at least two" criteria to be satisfied in the overall decision function. Yager has introduced in [26] a type of operator called *Ordered Weighted Averaging* (OWA), which allows to include certain relationships between multiple criteria in the aggregation process. An OWA aggregation operator differs from a classical weighted means in that the weights are not associated with particular inputs, but rather with their *magnitude*. As a result, OWA can emphasize the largest, smallest or mid-range values. It has become very popular in the research community working on fuzzy sets.

Definition (OWA). For a given weighting vector $\mathbf{w}$, $w_i \geq 0$, $\sum w_i = 1$, the OWA aggregation function is defined by:

$$OWA_w(\mathbf{x}) = \sum_{i=1}^{n} w_i x_{\searrow(i)} = <\mathbf{w}, \mathbf{x}_\searrow> \tag{4}$$

where we use the notation $\mathbf{x}_\searrow$ to represent the vector obtained from $\mathbf{x}$ by arranging its components in decreasing order: $x_{(1)} \geq x_{(2)} \geq \ldots \geq x_{(n)}$.

It is easy to see that for any weighting vector w, the result of OWA lies between the classical **and** (=min) and **or** (=max) operators, which are in fact the two extreme cases when $\mathbf{w} = (0,0,\ldots,1)$ (then $OWA_w(\mathbf{x}) = min(\mathbf{x})$) or when $\mathbf{w} = (1,0,\ldots,0)$ (then $OWA_w(\mathbf{x}) = max(\mathbf{x})$). Another special case is when all weights $w_i = \frac{1}{n}$, which results in obtaining the classical arithmetic mean.

To define the weights w_i to be used in OWA, Yager suggests two possible approaches: either to use some learning mechanism with sample data and a regression model (i.e., fitting weights by using training data and minimizing the least-square residual error), or to give some semantics to the w_i's by asking an expert to provide directly those values, based on domain knowledge. We selected the latter approach by defining the weighting vector as $\mathbf{w} = (0.1, 0.35, 0.35, 0.1, 0.1)$, which translates our intuition about the dynamic behavior of large-scale attack phenomena. It can be interpreted as: *at least three criteria must be satisfied, but the first criteria is of less importance compared to the 2nd and 3rd ones* (because only one correlated feature between two μ-events might be due to chance only).

These weights must be carefully chosen in order to avoid an unfortunate linkage between μ-events when, for example, two events involve IP sources originating from popular countries and targeting common (Windows) ports in the same interval of time (but in reality, those events are not due to the same phenomenon). By considering different worst-case scenarios, we verified that the values of the weighting vector **w** work as expected, i.e., that it minimizes the final output value in such undesirable cases. Moreover, these considerations enable us to fix our decision threshold to an empirical value of about 0.25, which has been also validated by a sensibility analysis. In other words, all combined values that are under this threshold will be set to zero, leading to the removal of corresponding edges in the aggregated graph G'.

Finally, we can easily identify misbehaving clouds by extracting the connected components (or subgraphs) from G'. As a result, for any subset of events of a given MC, we will find a sufficient number of evidences that explain why those events have been linked together by the multi criteria aggregation process.

5   Experimental Results

5.1   Overview

When applying the technique described in Section 3.1 to the dataset described in Section 2.2, we obtain 690 $\mathcal{M}$-events which consist of 2454 μ-events. We use these μ-events as input for the multi-criteria fusion approach (Section 4), and we consequently identify 83 Misbehaving Clouds (MCs), which correspond to 1607 μ-events, and 506,835 attacking sources. The phenomena involve almost all common services such as NetBios (ports 139/TCP, 445/TCP), Windows DCOM Service (port 135/TCP), Virtual Network Computing (port 5900/TCP), Microsoft SQL Server (port 1433/TCP), Windows Messenger Service (ports 1025-1028/UDP), Symantec Agent (port 2967/TCP), and some others. Figure 2a shows the distribution of μ-events per MC. As we can see, in most cases, the MCs contain few μ-events. However, around 20% of MCs contain more than 15 μ-events, and some even contain up to 300 events. Figure 2b represent the CDF of the MCs lifetime. Such lifetime is defined as the time interval, in days, between the very first and the very last attack event of a given MC. As showed in Figure 2b, 67% of MCs exist during less than 50 days but around 22% of them last for more than 200 days.

Figure 2c represents the CDF of the number of platforms targeted by MC. As showed in the Figure, in 94% of the cases, the MCs are seen on less than 10 platforms.

These various characteristics suggest that the root causes behind the existence of these MCs are fairly stable, localised attack processes. In other words, different places of the world do observe different kind of attackers but their modus

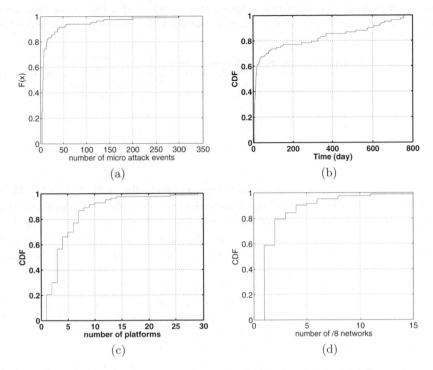

Fig. 2. Some global characteristics of the obtained MCs

operandi remain stable over a long period of time. We are, apparently, not that good at stopping them from misbehaving.

5.2 Case Studies

It is certainly not our intention to detail extensively the behavior and characteristics of every MC that has been found in our 2-year data set. Instead, in this Section, we detail only four MCs, which, although anecdotal, still reflect the kind of findings that our method can provide automatically. Table 1 provides some high-level characteristics of these four MCs phenomena under study. Each MC is analyzed in some detail in the following pages.

MC2: Worm-behaving cloud. MC2 consists of 122 μ-attack events. These μ-events exhibit a shape which is fairly similar to the one left by a typical worm: its trace exists for several days, it has a small amplitude at the beginning but grows quickly, exhibits important drops that can correspond to subnets being cured or blacklisted, and it eventually dies slowly (see [15] for a more formal description of this class of phenomena).

The interesting thing with MC2 is that it is made of a sequence of *worm-like* shaped μ-events. The lifetime of this MC is 741 days! It is composed of μ-events

Table 1. High-level characteristics of four *MCs* under study. The colon *Root cause* refers to the presumed type of phenomenon, based on the results of the attack attribution method.

MC Id	Nr Events	Nr Sources	Duration	Root cause	Targeted ports
2	122	45,261	741	Worm-behaving cloud	1433T (MSSQL), 1025T (RPC), 139T (Netbios), 5900T (VNC), 2967T (Symantec)
3	56	48,007	634	UDP spammers (botnet)	1026U (Windows Messenger)
10	138	26,243	573	P2P	Unusual ephemeral ports (TCP)
20	110	195,018	696	UDP spammers (botnet)	1026U, 1027U, 1028U

that have targeted a number of distinct services, including 1025T, 139T, 1433T, 2967T and 5900T. The results of the multi-criteria fusion algorithm indicate that those μ-events have been grouped together mainly because of the following three features: geographical location, targeted platform, and ports sequence. Moreover, a detailed analysis reveals that an important amount of IP addresses is shared by many μ-events composing this *MC*.

To illustrate the kinds of μ-events found in this *MC*, Figures 3a and 3b represent four μ-events time series. Figure 3a represents two of them, namely e626 and e628, consisting of activities against Microsoft SQL Server (1433/TCP). Whereas Figure 3b represents the other two, namely e250 and e251, consisting of activities against a Symantec Service (2967/TCP). Figure 3c zooms on these last two μ-events from day 100 to day 150. We can observe the slow increase of the two curves that are typical of worm-related attacks [15,27].

The two μ-events on the left (resp. middle) share 528 (resp. 1754) common IP addresses with each other. Given these elements, we are tempted to believe that e626 and e628 (resp. e250 and e251) are generated by the same worm, called *WORM_A* (resp. called *WORM_B*). Both worms, *WORM_A* and *WORM_B*, target the same two platforms: 25 and 64. Furthermore, we found that these four μ-events share an important amount of common compromised machines. This could indicate that both worms, before having contacted our honeypots, had contaminated a relatively similar population of machines. A plausible explanation could be that both had been launched from the same initial set of machines and that they were using the same, or similar, code to choose their targets.

From the attack vector point of view, these two worms have nothing in common since they use very different types of exploits. Furthermore, they have been active in different periods of time. However, the analysis reveals that they exhibit a very similar pattern both in terms of propagation strategy and in terms of success rates. Thus, even if the infection vector differs between the two, the starting point of the infection as well as the code responsible for the propagation are, as explained, quite likely very similar. This reasoning can be generalized to all 122 μ-events, revealing the high probability that all these different attack phenomena have some common root cause(s). This does not, per se, mean that all these attacks are due to the very same person or organisation -even if this is likely- but it indicates that the same core piece of code has probably been reused, from a very similar starting point to launch a number of distinct attacks. This

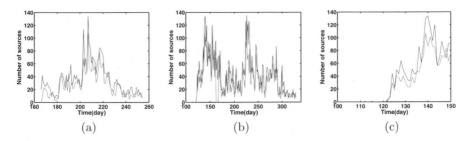

Fig. 3. Attack time series (nr of sources by day) of some μ-events from $MC2$, targeting (a) MS SQL Server (1433/TCP), (b) Symantec agent (2967/TCP). Fig. (c) is a zoom on (b).

reveals some aspect of the modus operandi of those who have launched these attacks and this is an important piece of information for those who are in charge of identifying these misbehaving groups and their tactics.

$MC3$ and $MC20$: Windows Messenger Spammer. In this other case study, we look at two distinct MCs: $MC3$ and $MC20$. Both are made of μ-events that have exclusively tried to send spam to innocent victims thanks to the Windows Messenger service, using UDP packets. Both MCs have been observed over a large period of time, more than 600 days in both cases. Even if they, conceptually, look similar, there are important differences between $MC3$ and $MC20$. First, the targeted ports are not identical: in $MC3$, UDP packets are being sent to three different UDP ports, namely 1026, 1027 and 1028, while in $MC20$ packets are sent exclusively to the 1026 UDP port. Then, as illustrated in Fig.4 where we can see the cumulative distribution (CDF) of sources IP addresses (grouped by /8 blocks of addresses), we observe that $MC3$ is uniformly distributed in the IPv4 space. This result is absurde since large portions of the IPv4 space can not be allocated to individual machines (multicast, bogons, unassigned, etc.) and, in all these regions, it is impossible to find compromised machines sending spams. If we find these IPs in packets hitting our honeypots, it clearly means that these are spoofed IP addresses. Furthermore, the uniform distribution of all the IP addresses in that MC leads us to believe that all other IPs are also spoofed. On the other hand, $MC20$ has a constant distribution pointing exclusively to a single /8 block owned by an ISP located in Canada[3]. A likely explanation is that those spammers have also used spoofed addresses to send UDP messages to the Windows Messenger service, and they have been able to do so for 600 days without being disturbed!

To further validate these results, we also looked at the payloads of the UDP packets by computing a hash for each packet payload. What we discovered is quite surprising: all payloads sent by the sources have exactly the same message template, but the template was different for the two clouds. Fig.5 and

---

[3] Actually, a closer inspection of sources IP addresses reveals they were randomly chosen from only two distinct /16 blocks from this same /8 IP subnet.

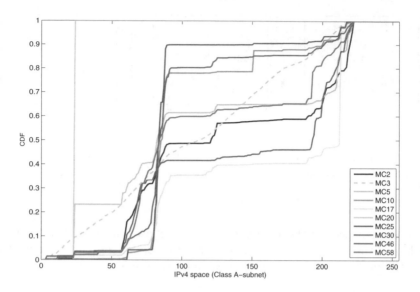

Fig. 4. CDF's of originating IP subnet distributions for the largest phenomena

```
SYSTEM  ALERT  - STOP! WINDOWS REQUIRES IMMEDIATE ATTENTION.
Windows has found CRITICAL SYSTEM ERRORS.

To fix the errors please do the following:
1. Download Registry Cleaner from: http://www.wfix32.com
2. Install Registry Cleaner
3. Run Registry Cleaner
4. Reboot your computer
FAILURE TO ACT NOW MAY LEAD TO DATA LOSS AND CORRUPTION!
```

Fig. 5. Spam template used in $MC3$

Fig.6 show the two different templates used by spammers of $MC3$ and $MC20$ respectively. Regarding $MC3$, we also observe many alternate URL's, such as: 32sys.com, Fix64.com, Key32.com, Reg64.com, Regsys32.com, Scan32.com, etc, whereas spammers in $MC20$ use apparently almost[4] always the same URL (www.registrycleanerxp.com).

This knowledge has been derived from the observation of the MCs automatically built by our method. This illustrates the richness and meaningfulness of the analyses that can be performed. At this point, there are still two questions left unanswered when we look at those two UDP spam phenomena:

---

[4] For $MC20$, only a few instances of spam messages were observed with a different URL: nowfixpc.com

```
Local System User
CRITICAL ERROR MESSAGE! - REGISTRY DAMAGED AND CORRUPTED.

To FIX this problem:
Open Internet Explorer and type:  www.registrycleanerxp.com
Once you load the web page, close this message window

After you install the cleaner program
you will not receive any more reminders or pop-ups like this.

VISIT www.registrycleanerxp.com IMMEDIATELY!
```

Fig. 6. Spam template used in $MC20$

i) Do all those UDP packets really use spoofed IP addresses, and how were they sent (e.g., from a single machine in the Internet or from a very large botnet)?
ii) Could it be that those two phenomena have in fact the same root cause, i.e., the same (group of) people running in parallel two different spam campaigns?

To answer the first question, we have extracted from the UDP packets the Time To Live (TTL) value of their IP headers. We have computed the distributions of these TTL values for both phenomena, grouped by targeted platform. The results, illustrated in Fig.7, seems to confirm our intuition about spoofed UDP packets, since these TTL distributions are too narrow to originate from a real population of physical machines. In both cases ($MC3$ and $MC20$), we observe that the TTL distributions have a width of about 5 hops, whereas TTL distributions for non-spoofed packets are normally much larger, certainly when sources are largely distributed. As a sanity check, we retrieved the TTL distributions for another phenomenon, which has been validated as a botnet of machines. As one can see in Fig.8, the TTL distributions are much larger (around 20 hops) than for spoofed UDP packets. Another finding visible in Fig.7 is the unusual initial value used for TTL's, which also indicates that those packets were probably forged using raw sockets, instead of using the TCP/IP protocol stack of the operating system.

Finally, trying to answer the last question (same root cause or not), we looked at one additional feature of the attacks. We generated a distribution of sources by grouping them based on the *day and hour of the week* they have been observed by our platforms (using the same universal time reference, which is GMT+1 in this case). As one can see in Fig.9, the result is very intriguing: although there is no privileged day or time interval in the week on which we observe a specific pattern, the UDP traffic created by $MC3$ (in dashed) and $MC20$ (in green) look apparently synchronized. Since both phenomena have lasted more than 600 days, it is quite unlikely that such correlation could be due to chance only. So, while we have no true evidence to verify this, we can reasonably assume that both phenomena have been orchestrated by the same people, or at least using the same software tool and sets of compromised machines.

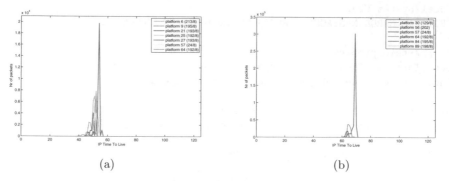

(a)   (b)

Fig. 7. TTL distribution of UDP packets for $MC3$ (a) and $MC20$ (b) (grouped by targeted platform)

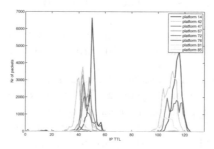

Fig. 8. TTL distribution of TCP packets for a phenomenon (MC28) attributed to a botnet targeting ports 445T and 139T (grouped by targeted platform)

MC10: P2P aberrations. $MC10$ is a very interesting, yet intriguing, cloud. Our technique has grouped together 138 μ-events that have been observed over a period of 573 days. All these events share a number of common characteristics that we have some difficulty to explain:

1. The vast majority of these μ-events target a single platform, located in China. A very few μ-events have also hit another platform in Spain.
2. The vast majority of these μ-events originate from Italy and Spain only.
3. All these μ-events exist during a single day.
4. All these μ-events target a single high TCP port number, most of them not being assigned to any particular protocol (e.g. 10589T, 15264T, 1755T, 18462T, 25618T, 29188T, 30491T, 38009T, 4152T, 46030T, 4662T, 50656T, 53842T, 6134T, 6211T, 64264T, 64783T, 6769T, 7690T)
5. these μ-events share a substantial amount of source addresses between them.
6. A number of high port numbers correspond to port numbers used by well known P2P applications (e.g., 4662/TCP, used by eDonkey P2P network).

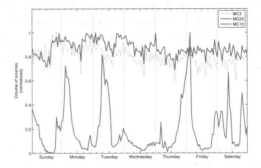

Fig. 9. Distribution of malicious sources grouped by weekdays. For each MC, a data point represents the accumulated number of sources observed for a given day and hour of the week.

This last remark leads us to hypothesize that this extremely weird type of attack traces may have something to do with P2P traffic aberrations. It can be a misconfiguration error or, possibly, the side effect of a deliberate attack against these P2P networks, as explained in [12,5], in which authors argued that it is possible to use P2P networks to generate DDoS attacks against any arbitrary victim.

Also, Figure 9 highlights the fact that these 138 μ-events are not randomly distributed over the hours of the week but that, instead, they seem to exist on a limited number of recurrent moments.

All these elements tend to demonstrate the meaningfulness of grouping all these, apparently different, attack events. Even if we are not able, at this stage, to provide a convincing explanation related to their existence, our method has, at least, the merit of having highlighted the existence of these, so far, unknown phenomena.

It is our hope that other teams will build upon this fundational result to help all of us to better understand these numerous threats our approach has identified.

6   Conclusions

In this document, we have presented the WOMBAT attack attribution method. We have explained its motivations, its principles, the various steps it was made of, as well as some of the interesting results it had delivered so far. We have applied that technique to 2 years of attack traces captured on 40 low interaction honeypots located all over the world. It is worth noting that the method could as easily be applied on completely different threats-related events. In fact, the interim Symantec report published mid October 2009 on the analysis of rogue AV web sites offers results of the application of this very same method to the problem of understanding the modus operandi of malicious users setting up rogue AV campaigns.

It is our hope that people will be interested in trying to understand the rationales behind the *Misbehaving Clouds* we have identified. We are eager to share as much information as possible with such interested parties. Similarly, we are looking forward in having other opportunities to apply this method to other security datasets that future partners would be willing to share with us.

References

1. Basseville, M., Nikiforov, I.V.: Detection of Abrupt Changes:Theory and Application. Prentice Hall, Englewood Cliffs (1993)
2. Beliakov, G., Pradera, A., Calvo, T.: Aggregation Functions: A Guide for Practitioners. Springer, Berlin (2007)
3. Collins, M.P., Shimeall, T.J., Faber, S., Janies, J., Weaver, R., De Shon, M., Kadane, J.: Using uncleanliness to predict future botnet addresses. In: IMC 2007: Proceedings of the 7th ACM SIGCOMM conference on Internet measurement, pp. 93–104. ACM, New York (2007)
4. Dacier, M., Pouget, F., Debar, H.: Attack processes found on the internet. In: NATO Symposium IST-041/RSY-013, Toulouse, France (April 2004)
5. Defrawy, K.E., Gjoka, M., Markopoulou, A.: Bottorrent: misusing bittorrent to launch ddos attacks. In: SRUTI 2007: Proceedings of the 3rd USENIX workshop on Steps to reducing unwanted traffic on the internet, Berkeley, CA, USA, pp. 1–6. USENIX Association (2007)
6. Jain, A.K., Dubes, R.C.: Algorithms for Clustering Data. Prentice-Hall advanced reference series (1988)
7. Kullback, S., Leibler, R.A.: On information and sufficiency. Annals of Mathematical Statistics 22, 79–86 (1951)
8. Leita, C., Pham, V.H., Thonnard, O., Ramirez Silva, E., Pouget, F., Kirda, E., Dacier, M.: The leurre.com project: collecting internet threats information using a worldwide distributed honeynet. In: 1st WOMBAT workshop, April 21st-22nd, Amsterdam, The Netherlands (April 2008)
9. Leita, C., Dacier, M.: Sgnet: a worldwide deployable framework to support the analysis of malware threat models. In: Proceedings of the 7th European Dependable Computing Conference (EDCC 2008) (May 2008)
10. Leurre.com, Eurecom Honeypot Project (September 2009), http://www.leurrecom.org/
11. Lin, J.: Divergence measures based on the shannon entropy. IEEE Transactions on Information Theory 37(1), 145–151 (1991)
12. Naoumov, N., Ross, K.: Exploiting p2p systems for ddos attacks. In: InfoScale 2006: Proceedings of the 1st international conference on Scalable information systems, p. 47. ACM, New York (2006)
13. Pang, R., Yegneswaran, V., Barford, P., Paxson, V., Peterson, L.: Characteristics of Internet Background Radiation. In: Proceedings of the 4th ACM SIGCOMM conference on the Internet Measurement (2004)
14. Pavan, M., Pelillo, M.: A new graph-theoretic approach to clustering and segmentation. In: Proceedings of IEEE Conference on Computer Vision and Pattern Recognition (2003)
15. Pham, V.-H.: Honeypot traces forensics by means of attack event identification. PhD thesis, TELECOM ParisTech (2009)

16. Pham, V.-H., Dacier, M.: Honeypot traces forensics: the observation view point matters. In: NSS 2009, 3rd International Conference on Network and System Security, October 19-21, Gold Coast, Australia (December 2009)
17. Pham, V.-H., Dacier, M., Urvoy Keller, G., En Najjary, T.: The quest for multi-headed worms. In: Zamboni, D. (ed.) DIMVA 2008. LNCS, vol. 5137, pp. 247–266. Springer, Heidelberg (2008)
18. Pouget, F., Dacier, M., Debar, H.: Honeypot-based forensics. In: Proceedings of AusCERT Asia Pacific Information Technology Security Conference 2004, Brisbane, Australia (May 2004)
19. Pouget, F., Dacier, M., Pham, V.H.: Leurre.com: on the advantages of deploying a large scale distributed honeypot platform. In: ECCE 2005, E-Crime and Computer Conference, Monaco, March 29-30 (2005)
20. Provos, N.: A virtual honeypot framework. In: Proceedings of the 12th USENIX Security Symposium, August 2004, pp. 1–14 (2004)
21. Shepard, R.N.: Multidimensional scaling, tree fitting, and clustering. Science 210, 390–398 (1980)
22. Thonnard, O., Dacier, M.: A framework for attack patterns' discovery in honeynet data. In: DFRWS 2008, 8th Digital Forensics Research Conference, Baltimore, USA, August 11- 13 (2008)
23. Thonnard, O., Dacier, M.: Actionable knowledge discovery for threats intelligence support using a multi-dimensional data mining methodology. In: ICDM 2008, 8th IEEE International Conference on Data Mining series, Pisa, Italy, December 15-19 (2008)
24. Thonnard, O., Mees, W., Dacier, M.: Addressing the attack attribution problem using knowledge discovery and multi-criteria fuzzy decision-making. In: KDD 2009, 15th ACM SIGKDD Conference on Knowledge Discovery and Data Mining, Workshop on CyberSecurity and Intelligence Informatics, Paris, France, June 28th - July 1st (2009)
25. Wheeler, D., Larsen, G.: Techniques for Cyber Attack Attribution. Institute for Defense Analyses (October 2003)
26. Yager, R.R.: On ordered weighted averaging aggregation operators in multicriteria decisionmaking. IEEE Trans. Syst. Man Cybern. 18(1), 183–190 (1988)
27. Yegneswaran, V., Barford, P., Paxson, V.: Using honeynets for internet situational awareness. In: Fourth ACM Sigcomm Workshop on Hot Topics in Networking, Hotnets IV (2005)

Biometrics and Security

Venu Govindaraju

Professor, Computer Science and Engineering
Director, Center for Unified Biometrics and Sensors
University of Buffalo (SUNY Buffalo), USA

Abstract. The science of Biometrics is concerned with recognizing people based on their physiological or behavioral characteristics. It has emerged as a vibrant field of research in today's security conscious society. In this talk we will introduce the important research challenges in Biometrics and specifically address the following topics: i) unobtrusive people tracking using a novel evolutionary recognition paradigm, ii) efficient indexing and searching of large fingerprint databases, iii) cancelability of templates where the task is to ensure that enrolled biometric templates can be revoked and new templates issued, and iv) fusion of fingerprints with other biometric modalities such as face where we will explore optimal trainable functions that operate on the scores returned by individual matchers.

A. Prakash and I. Sen Gupta (Eds.): ICISS 2009, LNCS 5905, p. 38, 2009.
© Springer-Verlag Berlin Heidelberg 2009

Remote Electronic Voting with Revocable Anonymity

Matt Smart and Eike Ritter

School of Computer Science
University of Birmingham, UK
{m.j.smart,e.ritter}@cs.bham.ac.uk

Abstract. We present a new remote, coercion-free electronic voting protocol which satisfies a number of properties previously considered contradictory. We introduce (and justify) the idea of revocable anonymity in electronic voting, on the grounds of it being a legal requirement in the United Kingdom, and show a method of proving the validity of a ballot to a verifier in zero knowledge, by extension of known two-candidate proofs.

1 Introduction

It is undoubtedly a challenge to design electronic voting systems that satisfy what is an ever-growing list of requirements that are difficult to achieve simultaneously. Many governments have begun to adopt electronic voting with a view to improving voter turnout, with hardly any success. One of the driving factors for electronic voting is *remote voting*—the requirement that a citizen can vote from any location. This is unfortunately very difficult to achieve whilst minimising the potential for voter coercion. Further, how is it possible to satisfy voter privacy (anonymity) whilst also allowing the voter to verify that her vote has been counted? Can we assure ballot correctness for any number of candidates?

An especially important property in electronic voting is *anonymity* (privacy)—the notion that no voter should be linkable to their ballot. In this work, we introduce *revocable anonymity* to electronic voting — the notion that it should be possible to link one's identity to one's ballot, but *only* with the agreement of a Judge and a quorum of mutually distrusting parties.

In the UK, it is a legal requirement that it should be possible for the election authorities to link a ballot to its voter [2, p. 106]. To our knowledge, no work has previously considered this notion (equivalent to revocable anonymity in electronic voting), but it seems important to do so (note that some other protocols may be able to achieve this with modification [16,6], but give no detail as to how to do so, and would seemingly not provide a sufficient solution—we discuss this later). One can envisage a situation in which, since voters are entirely anonymous, an attacker can vote on behalf of people who should be unable to vote, but, for whatever reason, are still on the electoral roll. In a 2005 postal vote scandal in Birmingham, UK, "possibly well over 2,000 of the votes cast"

A. Prakash and I. Sen Gupta (Eds.): ICISS 2009, LNCS 5905, pp. 39–54, 2009.

were fraudulent and illegitimate for one ward alone [26]. We feel that permitting anonymity revocation in extreme circumstances is fundamental to reducing election fraud such as this.

1.1 Related Work

In our experience, there is no work which provides revocable anonymity in electronic voting, and little work which provides large-scale, coercion-resistant, remote electronic voting ([6] is a good example, but does not seem scalable). We here discuss how previous authors have satisfied some of the important properties of e-voting without revocable anonymity, and our strategy to achieve them.

Many electronic voting protocols [24,10,16,9,28] rely on anonymous channels, or anonymous and untappable channels [19], to satisfy some security properties. When considering voting over the Internet (an inherently insecure medium), one needs to think about how an anonymous channel could be implemented in the first place.

Attempts have been made to achieve anonymous channels with mix networks [4,22,18,24,3,13], which provide effective anonymity, but can often be slow, inefficient, complex and subject to single points of failure (in the case of decryption mixes). Indeed, it has been argued [27] that for an Internet-based voting protocol, there is no way to reliably implement an anonymous communication channel over the Internet. Volkamer and Krimmer [27] suggest that IP address tracking or trojan horse viruses alone mean that any attempt at an anonymous channel would always suffer from some weakness.

Thankfully, in our work, we do not need to use anonymous *or* untappable channels (which are, when from voter to talliers, a very strong assumption), relying instead on various designated verifier proofs to satisfy voter verifiability whilst maintaining coercion-resistance and privacy.

In our work, we follow the scheme of many previous protocols using homomorphic encryption to ensure universal verifiability and unlinkability of ballots [1,7,8,11,28,16], which naturally lends itself to threshold cryptography, affording us a greater level of assurance against corrupted talliers. These protocols, along with some of those already mentioned, require, for remote voting, that the voter is not observed at the "very moment of voting" [18]. Indeed, Benaloh and Tuinstra state that "physical separation of the voter from possible coercive agents is fundamental to any uncoercible election protocol" [1, p. 550].

Lee *et al.* [18], amongst others, suggest the use of a *tamper-resistant randomiser*—smart card—and non-voter-observation at the point of voting, to guarantee coercion-resistance. An alternative is to have every voter use a public voting booth which either uses a smart card, as above, or a paper ballot which is optically processed by machine [4,22,21,5,20].

We note that any protocol providing a list of voters' identities with encrypted ballots could provide revocable anonymity, given the collusion of all parties needed to perform decryption. However, such a list clearly violates full coercion-resistance, as the fact that a voter has voted successfully can be determined by anyone. Juels *et al.* [16] and implementations thereof [6] involve talliers only keeping a list of votes at the end of the election (discarding the previous stage's encrypted credentials), thus severing the direct link between voter and vote. Revocation of anonymity would require a highly inefficient Plaintext Equivalence Test between the credential supplied with a vote and every credential on the voter list, followed by a collusion with the registrar. Lee *et al.* [18] would allow for revocation, *but* subject to collusion of the administrator, the entire mix and n talliers. The nature of usage of the bulletin board in the protocol also suggests that full coercion-resistance is not possible, as the fact that Alice has voted is plainly visible. Prêt à Voter [22] and similar schemes do not offer revocation at all, since Alice's choice of ballot paper is random, and as any identifying information is destroyed (by Alice), she cannot be linked to her ballot. In any case, no other protocol discusses revocable anonymity at all, to our knowledge. We note that revocable anonymity is a concept which has been considered at great length in other fields, such as digital cash [14,15,17].

In digital cash, it is particularly important that it should be possible to link an electronic coin to the person who spent it once the transaction has occurred (for example, that coin may have been spent twice, or spent illegally). It is similarly important to be able to link a person's identity to all coins available to him (for example, to protect against money laundering). One manner in which this can be done is to encode an encrypted copy of the coin owner's identity into every coin. Requiring two or more parties to perform encryption, including a judge [15], ensures that a user's anonymity won't be revoked unless there is sufficient legal cause. In our work, we protect the voter's identity using a similar mechanism.

1.2   Our Contribution

In this work, we introduce a remote electronic voting protocol which satisfies several properties considered important in electronic voting, leading to several contributions:

- A secure voting protocol allowing a quorum of authorities to link a ballot to its voter (revocable anonymity), whilst achieving coercion-resistance and legitimate voter privacy
- A novel method of allowing the voter to achieve coercion-resistance without anonymous channels or tamper-resistant devices, through designated-verifier signatures
- An extension of previous schemes to prove ballot validity for two-candidate elections, to multiple-candidate elections

The protocol we present achieves the above properties, as well as the standard electronic voting properties (completeness, uniqueness, coercion-resistance, fairness, and legitimate-voter privacy), while having no need for anonymous or untappable channels (or implementations thereof).

Protocol Schema. We present a two-phase protocol, where voters do not need to synchronise between phases they are actively involved in. Our reasoning for

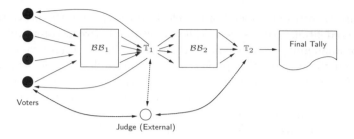

Fig. 1. A schematic for our protocol

splitting into two phases is to preserve the anonymity of the legitimate voter, henceforth referred to as Alice. In the first phase, voters receive eligibility tokens with designated verifier signatures, and form ElGamal encryptions of ballots, submitting them to a bulletin board. A member of a semi-trusted tallier group re-encrypts Alice's vote.

In the second phase, Alice receives a designated verifier proof of re-encryption (along with some other fake proofs), and her re-encrypted vote is posted to another bulletin board with an encrypted version of her identity. Alice can then check her vote has been included, or contact a Judge otherwise.

Once all votes are posted to the second bulletin board, a tally is calculated and announced. A simple schematic diagram of the protocol is given in Figure 1.

1.3   Structure

In §2, we define a number of preliminaries, including the terminology used, and a number of primitives which we make use of. In §3, we give the participants, trust model and threat model for our work. We present our protocol in §4, and the requirements we have satisfied in §5. Finally, we conclude.

2   Preliminaries

In this paper, we assume the availability of the following cryptographic primitives. Note that we are working in the formal model, not in provable security. Therefore we make the assumption that the cryptography in the primitives below is perfect.

2.1   Threshold ElGamal Encryption Scheme

We use a standard ElGamal encryption scheme under a q-order multiplicative subgroup $G_q = \langle g \rangle$ of $\mathbb{Z}_p^*$, generated by an element $g \in \mathbb{Z}_p^*$, where p and q are suitably large primes, and $q|(p-1)$. All agents a in the protocol have a private key s_a of which only they have knowledge. Each agent has a corresponding public key $h_a = g^{s_a}$ where g is a known generator of the subgroup. Public keys are common knowledge to all users. For more information on the encryption scheme we use, the reader is directed to the appropriate paper. We use a (t, n)-threshold decryption scheme analogous to that of Cramer et $al.$ [8]. For brevity we do not discuss this here.

2.2 Strong Designated Verifier Signature Scheme

We adopt the designated verifier signature scheme of Saeednia et $al.$ [23] due to its efficient nature, but others would be acceptable. We use designated verifier signatures to enable a prover (Bob, or any one of the first-round talliers in our case) to prove a statement to a verifier (Alice) by proving the validity of a signature. However, Alice is unable to prove the signature's validity to $anyone$ else, on the grounds that she could have produced it herself [23, p. 43]. For brevity we do not discuss the scheme here, but direct the reader to the appropriate paper instead [23].

2.3 Proof of Equality of Discrete Logarithms

In order to prevent an attack in our voting scheme (voting for several candidates or for one candidate multiple times with the same ballot), we require that the voter demonstrates to a verifier that her vote is of the correct form (without revealing what the vote is).

As we discuss later, a voter's vote is of the form $(x, y) = (g^\alpha, h_{\mathbb{T}_2}^\alpha g^{M^{i-1}})$ where $\alpha \in_R \mathbb{Z}_q$, M is the maximum number of voters and i represents the position in the list of candidates of the voter's chosen candidate. Alice needs to prove, in zero knowledge, that she is sending to the bulletin board some value for y where the exponent of g is in $\{M^0, \ldots, M^{L-1}\}$ where L is the number of candidates. If we did not have such a proof, any voter could spoil the election by adding spurious coefficients to the exponent, thereby voting several times.

We extend the technique of Cramer et $al.$ [8], who use a non-interactive proof of equality of discrete logarithms to prove the validity of a ballot in a two-candidate election. We extend the two-candidate scenario to L candidates, providing a proof for the relation given by

$$\log_g x = \log_{h_{\mathbb{T}_2}}(y/g^{M^0}) \vee \ldots \vee \log_g x = \log_{h_{\mathbb{T}_2}}(y/g^{M^{L-1}})$$

In Figure 2, we give a generalised adaptation (**G-PEQDL**) of the above proof of equality of discrete logarithms scheme where Alice votes for candidate k ($1 \leq k \leq L$) with $(x, y) = (g^\alpha, h^\alpha g^{M^{k-1}})$. This is the only place where we extend one of the primitives we use. We provide a more detailed explanation (and proof) of the G-PEQDL in [25].

2.4 Designated Verifier Re-encryption Proofs

The properties of the ElGamal encryption scheme allow re-encryption (randomisation) of ciphertexts. Given a ciphertext (x, y), another agent is able to generate a re-encryption $(x_f, y_f) = (xg^\beta, yh^\beta)$, where $\beta \in_R \mathbb{Z}_q^*$.

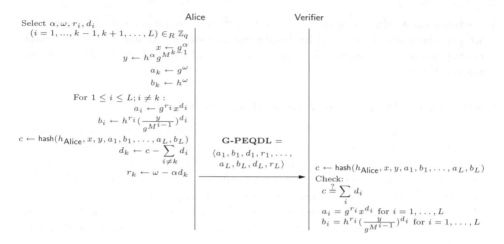

Fig. 2. Our generalised non-interactive proof of ballot validity for a vote for candidate k

In our protocol, we use an ElGamal re-encryption to preserve the voter's anonymity. However, the voter needs to have some conviction that her vote has been counted (individual verifiability). We achieve this via a *Designated Verifier Re-encryption Proof* (DVRP) based on Alice's keypair: such a proof convinces Alice that a given re-encrypted ciphertext is equivalent to that she generated, whilst not convincing any third party[1]. We adopt the scheme used by Lee *et al.* [18,12], such that the prover, P (the agent that does the re-encryption) demonstrates to Alice that (x_f, y_f) is equivalent to (x, y) in such a manner that the original message m (encrypted in (x, y)) is not revealed, and this proof cannot convince any other entity. The reader is directed to the appropriate papers for more details.

3   Protocol Model

3.1   Participants

Our protocol is modelled with 5 kinds of participants. A participant (agent) is an interactive polynomial-time random computation. All agents are able to communicate via a network, which is not secure or anonymous in any way.

The participants are as follows:

– **Voters.** The protocol allows M voters $v_i \in \{v_0, v_1, ..., v_{M-1}\}$ to vote. Alice is an honest voter who wishes to vote anonymously. She is able to vote many times, but *once* unobserved. Eligible voters' public keys are publicly known.

---

[1] Note that in order to fully protect against Alice's private key being stolen from her, we could give her, during in-person registration, a new public/private keypair $(s_{\text{Alice}-v}, h_{\text{Alice}-v})$, which acts as a session key for Alice's vote. This pair could then be used for the DVRP. However, such a modification is not strictly necessary.

- **First Round Bulletin Board/First Round Talliers.** Our protocol uses two separate *bulletin boards*. A standard bulletin board is a public broadcast channel with memory. The first bulletin board we use is writable only by *voters*. All voters send an encrypted vote and signed proof of validity to this board, which we denote as $\mathcal{BB}_1$.

  The *first-round talliers* $\mathbb{T}_1$ are a *semi-trusted* group of agents[2], each possessing an ElGamal secret key $s_{\mathbb{T}_1}$ in its entirety, which any one of them can use to remove the first layer of encryption on Alice's vote[3]. We assume that each instance would be busy enough, and that votes would be batched before sending to $\mathcal{BB}_2$, so that timing attacks would be ineffective. Our justification for having multiple members of $\mathbb{T}_1$ is to prevent a bottleneck of computational power, but if this problem were ignored, we could equally substitute the group for a single entity.

  The first round talliers are responsible for ensuring that Alice's vote is valid according to the set of valid possible votes, not coerced, and not a double-vote. They are unable to see Alice's actual vote token. $\mathbb{T}_1$ also encrypts Alice's identity, should anonymity revocation be required. They issue Alice with vote validity tokens during registration.
- **Second Round Bulletin Board/Second Round Talliers.** The second bulletin board $\mathcal{BB}_2$ is viewable by all users of the protocol, and writable only by $\mathbb{T}_1$. It lists only the re-encrypted (valid) votes in a random permutation. The votes themselves, (x, y), are encrypted with the public key of the second round talliers.

  The *second-round talliers* are a group of agents (disjoint from $\mathbb{T}_1$) who decrypt the ballots listed on the second round bulletin board using threshold ElGamal with a shared key $s_{\mathbb{T}_2}$. The second round talliers will also publish the final tally.
- **Anonymity Teller Group.** As well as each being separate groups $\mathbb{T}_1, \mathbb{T}_2$, the tallier groups form part of a larger group which deals only with the voter's anonymity. This group contains an equal number of members of $\mathbb{T}_1$ and $\mathbb{T}_2$ and is simply denoted $\mathbb{T}$. As such, it has a public key $g^{s_{\mathbb{T}}}$ and associated private key $s_{\mathbb{T}}$, where the private key is distributed amongst all members as before. In this case, to decrypt, a quorum of a size t_{id}, greater than the size of either $\mathbb{T}_1$ or $\mathbb{T}_2$, will need to collude to decrypt. Note that this decryption is only ever needed when a voter's identity needs to be traced, as our protocol is optimistic. Further, a voter's anonymity cannot be revoked without the agreement of the quorum *and* the Judge.
- **Judge.** The Judge is an entity of the protocol that is rarely used. She has two purposes:
  1. If Alice cannot find her re-encrypted vote on the bulletin board, she asks the Judge for verification.

---

[2] We discuss our need for trusting $\mathbb{T}_1$ later in this Section.

[3] The size of $\mathbb{T}_1$ would need to be determined empirically depending on the size of the electorate. Since each member of the group has a copy of the same key, the size only affects how much of a bottleneck (in terms of computational power) $\mathbb{T}_1$ is.

2. The Judge also authorises anonymity revocation (having been presented with appropriate evidence of the need for revocation) in order to deliberately link a ballot to a voter, by applying her private key for a decryption.

Note that the Judge is only used in a minority of cases, i.e., where a voter's identity needs to be revealed, or Alice cannot find her vote on the bulletin board. The Judge, understandably, is trusted. We note that she could equally be formed from a coalition of mutually distrusting parties, disjoint from $\mathbb{T}_1/\mathbb{T}_2$, and selected by the electoral authorities. However, we see the Judge more in terms of a physical arbiter of justice in a court of law.

(Partially) Trusting $\mathbb{T}_1$. The purpose of the first-round talliers is to check the eligibility of Alice to vote and to re-encrypt Alice's vote before it is posted to the second bulletin board. To achieve anonymity, we need to *partially* trust $\mathbb{T}_1$. This means that we trust that $\mathbb{T}_1$:

- will not reveal the link between Alice's ballot (x, y) and her re-encrypted ballot (x_f, y_f), except by request of the Judge;
- will make valid encryptions of voter identities when forming $\overline{\mathsf{id}}$ tags;
- will act honestly in communications with the Judge (no other honest communications are required than those stated here);
- will only sign and post to $\mathcal{BB}_2$ ballots which are valid

Note therefore that $\mathbb{T}_1$ *at no point* has access to Alice's unencrypted vote. We further do not trust $\mathbb{T}_1$ to reliably send communications—if messages do not arrive as expected, the voter can detect this.

We believe that the trust we have placed in $\mathbb{T}_1$ is the minimum assumption necessary to assure the properties we wish to satisfy. We further discuss our decision in [25].

3.2 Trust Model

We make the following assumptions in our protocol:

1. All parties trust that $\mathbb{T}_1$ will not reveal the link between a ballot (x, y) and its re-encryption (x_f, y_f)
2. All parties trust that $\mathbb{T}_1$ will perform valid encryptions of each voter's identity, to afford anonymity revocation
3. The Judge and $\mathbb{T}_2$ trust that $\mathbb{T}_1$ will only sign and post to $\mathcal{BB}_2$ ballots which are valid
4. The Judge trusts that $\mathbb{T}_1$ will accurately and honestly send any data requested by it, to the Judge
5. All participants trust that the Judge will only authorise revocation of anonymity in appropriate circumstances
6. Alice trusts that she will receive one (and only one) valid voting token, along with several invalid ones, from the first-round talliers during registration.

7. Alice trusts the Judge to honestly state whether votes have been counted
8. All parties trust that voter identities will be stored correctly (and securely) on the second-round bulletin board

Note that we have already assumed that: $\mathbb{T}_1$ will batch votes before sending to $\mathcal{BB}_2$, to prevent timing attacks; Alice can vote once unobserved; and a t-sized quorum of $\mathbb{T}_2$ will not collude to break fairness or decrypt ballots until voting is over.

3.3 Threat Model

In this section, we consider the potential threats that could affect our protocol, based on the attacker's capabilities. We address how these threats are managed in §4. As to the assumptions we make about the attacker's strength based on the strength of the cryptography we use, we assume perfect cryptography.

Note that in our protocol, the attacker can assume the role of any entity (except the Judge). He is able to corrupt up to $t-1$ talliers where collusion is required to decrypt messages (and t is the threshold size for that quorum). All channels are public, so the attacker can:

1. Read messages
2. Decrypt and read any message m, subject to having the correct decryption key s for an encrypted message $(g^\alpha, g^{\alpha s}m)$
3. Intercept messages
4. Inject bad ballots in the first phase, and spurious messages generally
5. Temporarily block messages (although we assume resilient channels for liveness)

4 Protocol

Our voting protocol has four stages:

Stage 1: Ballot Validity Tokens
The protocol begins with Alice registering *in person* to vote (this would be with $\mathbb{T}_1$). At this point, she receives a *random number of* values δ_i, which are generated *at the point of registration*. Each has a designated verifier signature $\mathsf{DVSign}_{\mathbb{T}_1}(\delta_i)$ paired with it, which has been generated by a member of $\mathbb{T}_1$. However, only one of these signatures is valid (clearly, only the voter with the correct private key can verify this fact). Alice hence receives a string

$$\langle (\delta_0, \mathsf{DVSign}_{\mathbb{T}_1}(\delta_0)), (\delta_1, \mathsf{DVSign}_{\mathbb{T}_1}(\delta_1)), \ldots, (\delta_{n-1}, \mathsf{DVSign}_{\mathbb{T}_1}(\delta_{n-1})) \rangle$$

The coercion-resistance Alice enjoys increases with $|n|$ (i.e., the probability that the attacker can guess the correct δ value decreases with $|n|$).

Note that Alice would be able to generate designated verifier signatures at her liberty. Alice is able to calculate which of the signatures is valid for the value

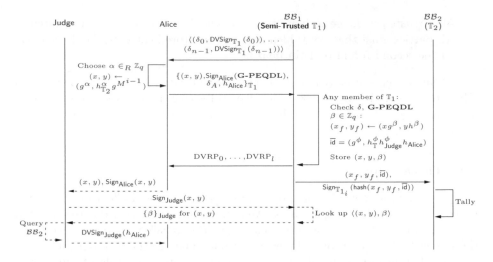

Fig. 3. Our protocol. Dashed lines indicate a non-compulsory part of the protocol (complaints). Note that the first communication ($\mathbb{T}_1 \to$ Alice) is in-person.

paired with it, and the tallier stores, on a private electoral roll (accessible only to $\mathbb{T}_1$) the valid δ value for Alice with her name. If Alice votes under coercion, since she received a random number of δ values, an observer cannot force her to use all values (she could conceal one or more, or arbitrarily insert values). Hence she simply votes using invalid δ values.

If she later votes without coercion[4], she sends the correct δ value with her vote as a 'proof' of validity. Upon checking for eligibility, the talliers simply check Alice's submitted δ value against the correct one stored on the private electoral roll . If she were to send a value for which the DV-Signature was incorrect when sent to her, this would alert the first-round talliers that her vote was made under coercion, which would alter their response to her. However, a coercer would not be able to distinguish a valid δ value from an invalid one, as he has no way of determining whether Alice herself made the designated verifier signature, or indeed whether the signature is valid.

Stage 2: Encrypted Vote Posting

As with other voting protocols using homomorphic encryption, we choose the form of the ballot in such a way that decryption of all ballots multiplied together leads to a simple tally of votes. A vote for the ith candidate is given as $g^{M^{i-1}}$, where M is the maximum number of voters.

Voter Alice selects a value $\alpha \in_R \mathbb{Z}_q$, and encrypts her vote for candidate i using the public key of the *second round talliers*, to give $(x, y) = (g^\alpha, h_{\mathbb{T}_2}^\alpha g^{M^{i-1}})$. She groups this with the correct δ value δ_A, and her public key h_{Alice}. Finally, she calculates the Generalised Proof of Equality of Discrete Logarithms (see §2.3) for

---

[4] We assume that Alice is able to vote unobserved, but she only needs to do this once.

her ballot (x, y) to prove that the vote is of correct form, and produces a standard ElGamal signature on this. This tuple $\langle (x, y), \mathsf{Sign}_{\mathsf{Alice}}(\textbf{G-PEQDL}), \delta_A, h_{\mathsf{Alice}} \rangle$ is encrypted with the public key of the first-round talliers, and posted to the first round bulletin board, $\mathcal{BB}_1$.

Stage 3: Validity Checking

Once Stage 2 is complete, any member $\mathbb{T}_{1_i}$ of $\mathbb{T}_1$ removes the first layer of encryption on each vote on the first-round bulletin board. That tallier then:

1. verifies that the vote is legitimate, by ensuring that the δ value given is the one stored with Alice's name on the private electoral roll[5]. Note that because the votes themselves are encrypted for $\mathbb{T}_2$, the first-round talliers cannot see *how* a voter votes — merely *that* a voter has attempted to vote.
2. verifies the G-PEQDL supplied with the ballot (x, y) to determine that Alice's vote is a single vote for a single valid candidate in the election

Once the validity of a ballot is assured, and any invalid ballots are disposed of, $\mathbb{T}_{1_i}$ re-encrypts (x, y) with a random factor β to give (x_f, y_f). That member also encrypts Alice's public key by doing the following:

– Select a random $\phi \in_R \mathbb{Z}_q$
– Using the joint public key for both sets of talliers $h_{\mathbb{T}}$, and the Judge's public key, form $\overline{\mathsf{id}} = (g^\phi, h_{\mathbb{T}}^\phi h_{\mathsf{Judge}}^\phi h_{\mathsf{Alice}})$.

The tallier then continues. He:

3. generates a signature on $\mathsf{hash}(x_f, y_f, \overline{\mathsf{id}})$, and concatenates this with $(x_f, y_f, \overline{\mathsf{id}})$ to form the final message string.

The tallier responsible for the re-encryption sends Alice a designated-verifier re-encryption proof (DVRP) that her vote has been included on the public bulletin board as (x_f, y_f), along with a number of other correct DVRPs, which are not valid for Alice (only she will be able to determine this). Note that if Alice's sent δ value were invalid, the tallier would send Alice only invalid DVRPs, meaning that an attacker could not determine whether her vote was invalid simply by observing messages received by Alice. As before, Alice would be free to insert seemingly valid DVRPs into the communication.

The tallier will then personally store the values $\langle (x, y), \beta \rangle$, and mark on the private electoral roll that Alice has voted (for example, by adding a signature of her public key). This information will never be released, except to the Judge as proof that Alice's vote was counted. The tuple $\langle x_f, y_f, \overline{\mathsf{id}}, \mathsf{sign}_{\mathbb{T}_1}(\mathsf{hash}(x_f, y_f, \overline{\mathsf{id}})) \rangle$ is posted to the second-round talliers' bulletin board. Alice is able to check the second bulletin board to ensure her vote appears and the signature on it is valid, but cannot convince anyone else of this fact (nor can she decrypt the re-encrypted vote). Any entity can check that a vote on the bulletin board is valid by verifying the signature for the hash of that vote.

---

[5] We presume that the private electoral roll is made inaccessible (or unconvincing) to coercers. We could accomplish this with designated verifier signatures.

Stage 4: Tallying

Once all DVRPs have been sent to their respective voters, it is simple for the second-round talliers $\mathbb{T}_2$ to decrypt votes. First, each $\langle (x_f, y_f), \overline{\mathsf{id}} \rangle$ is checked against its signed hash. Those not matching are ignored in tallying. A quorum of t talliers jointly decrypt a product

$$(X, Y) = (\prod_{j=1}^{l} x_{f_j}, \prod_{j=1}^{l} y_{f_j})$$

(without any single member having access to the private key, as discussed in §2.1), and then post the product to a publicly viewable place. The quorum threshold-decrypt the resulting tally, giving $g^{r_1 M^0 + r_2 M^1 + \ldots + r_L M^{L-1}}$, and $r_1, \ldots, r_L$ as the final tally. Note that any party can verify that any vote must have been correct, by comparing each published hash to the values given with it.

Anonymity Revocation

We have built into our protocol the ability to recover a voter's identity after the voting process is complete, but only with the co-operation of the Judge and a quorum of $\mathbb{T}$, the anonymity group. When Alice's vote is submitted to $\mathcal{BB}_2$, part of it is a token $\overline{\mathsf{id}} = (g^\phi, h_\mathbb{T}^\phi h_{\mathsf{Judge}}^\phi h_{\mathsf{Alice}})$ If, in the tallying phase of the protocol, any ballot is found to be illegal (or if, for any other reason, anonymity has to be revoked), a quorum of members of the *anonymity tallier group* $\mathbb{T}$ need to collude (note that the t_{id} value for this threshold decryption should be higher than the size of either $\mathbb{T}_1$ or $\mathbb{T}_2$).

$$\frac{h_\mathbb{T}^\phi h_{\mathsf{Judge}}^\phi h_{\mathsf{Alice}}}{g^{\phi s_\mathbb{T}}} = h_{\mathsf{Judge}}^\phi h_{\mathsf{Alice}}$$

The Judge must now be sent the token, with appropriate evidence justifying anonymity revocation. The Judge can then divide by $g^{\phi s_{\mathsf{Judge}}}$ to give the voter's identity.

Voter Complaints

A disadvantage of using designated-verifier re-encryption proofs is that Alice cannot prove the validity of the proof she receives from the first-round talliers that her vote has been re-encrypted as (x_f, y_f), which she may need to do if she cannot find her re-encrypted vote on $\mathcal{BB}_2$.

A solution we might adopt would be for Alice to receive a 1-out-of-L re-encryption proof [12], which is requested by Alice after all votes are posted to the board. However, such a proof is quite laborious and would allow an attacker to see that Alice's vote was counted. Instead, Alice sends her original (x, y) to the Judge. The Judge requests the stored β from the first-round talliers, and can then use these to check that Alice's vote was counted. If Alice's vote is counted, the Judge sends her a designated verifier signature for her public key, h_{Alice}. Otherwise, she makes the designated verifier signature invalid. Only Alice can determine this fact, and can again insert valid signatures arbitrarily. If Alice's vote is shown to have not been counted, we could also allow her to collude with the Judge to submit a vote a second time—in this manner, if her vote is again not counted, the Judge can take further action.

5 Properties of the Protocol

We now present the properties which our protocol satisfies. The explanations of how we satisfy each property are beyond the scope this paper and are provided in [25]. We use the Dolev-Yao model and hence assume that the cryptographic operations presented in §2 are perfect; in other words the intruder is not able to break any of the these cryptographic schemes but is able to intercept, change and delete all messages. We assume resilient channels to obtain liveness properties.

1. **Eligibility:** Only eligible voters should be able to vote.
2. **Uniqueness:** Only one vote per voter should be counted
3. **Receipt-Freeness:** The voter should be given no information which can be used to demonstrate to a coercer how *or if* they have voted, *after* voting has occurred
4. **Coercion-Resistance:** It should not be possible for a voter to prove how they voted or even if they are voting, even if they are able to interact with the coercer during voting
5. **Verifiability**
   (a) **Individual Verifiability:** A voter should be able to verify that their vote has been counted correctly
   (b) **Universal Verifiability:** Any observer should be able to verify that all votes have been counted correctly
6. **Fairness:** No-one can gain any information about the result of the tally until the end of the voting process and publication of votes
7. **Vote Privacy:** Neither the authorities nor any other participant should be able to link any ballot to the voter having cast it, *unless* the protocol to revoke anonymity has been invoked
   (a) **Revocable Anonymity:** It should be possible for an *authorised entity* (or collaboration of entities, for us) to reveal the identity of any *single* voter by linking his vote to him.
8. **Remote Voting:** Voters should not be restricted by physical location

It should be noted that even in the event that $\mathbb{T}_1$ were not trusted and became compromised, vote privacy, fairness, and individual verifiability (in so much that Alice can ensure her vote is counted), are still satisfied—these are not dependent on trusting $\mathbb{T}_1$. Receipt-freeness and coercion-resistance are satisfied in that Alice still cannot show *how* she votes.

The assumptions we make on $\mathbb{T}_1$ make it unnecessary to require assumptions made in other approaches on remote electronic voting, e.g. anonymous, often untappable channels [24,9,10,11,7], availability of a trusted Smart-Card or 'randomiser' to perform re-encryptions and proofs thereof [18,11,9], or the assumption that the voter cannot be observed at all during voting. It should be noted that using a Smart-Card to re-encrypt instead of $\mathbb{T}_1$ would affect other properties, such as eligibility and remote voting.

6 Conclusion

We have presented an election protocol providing what we believe to be the first scheme for revocable anonymity, whilst also allowing the voter coercion-free remote voting and verifiability, as well as legitimate-voter privacy. We require no untappable channels, and achieve an efficient 1-out-of-L scheme, integrating an extension of two-candidate discrete proofs of logarithm equality to L parties.

Our protocol also satisfies *remote voting*: as long as the voter is connected to the Internet, they are able to vote from any location, under the assumption that they can vote unobserved once, and register in person at any point before the election. This, we argue, is a very natural assumption to make.

We envisage that, given the remote nature of our protocol, it could be implemented across the Internet. Future work will concentrate on removing the need to trust any single party (except the Judge) at all, and on enhancing the remote-voting nature of the protocol—we might consider how to ensure that the machine the voter votes from can be trusted by the voter. One option might be to allow the user to vote only through a signed applet.

Acknowledgements

We would like to thank Mark Ryan and Tom Chothia for their helpful comments on earlier versions of this paper.

References

1. Benaloh, J., Tuinstra, D.: Receipt-Free Secret-Ballot Elections (Extended Abstract). In: Proceedings of the Twenty-Sixth Annual ACM Symposium on the Theory of Computing, Montreal, pp. 544–553. ACM, New York (1994)
2. Blackburn, R.: The Electoral System in Britain. Macmillan, London (1995)
3. Boneh, D., Golle, P.: Almost Entirely Correct Mixing with Applications to Voting. In: Proceedings of the ACM Conference on Computer and Communications Security, Washington DC, pp. 68–77. ACM, New York (2002)
4. Chaum, D., Ryan, P.Y.A., Schneider, S.: A Practical, Voter-verifiable Election Scheme. In: di Vimercati, S.d.C., Syverson, P.F., Gollmann, D. (eds.) ESORICS 2005. LNCS, vol. 3679, pp. 118–139. Springer, Heidelberg (2005)
5. Chaum, D., van de Graaf, J., Ryan, P.Y.A., Vora, P.L.: High Integrity Elections. Cryptology ePrint Archive, Report 2007/270 (2007), http://eprint.iacr.org/
6. Clarkson, M.R., Chong, S., Myers, A.C.: Civitas: Toward a Secure Voting System. In: Proceedings, 2008 IEEE Symposium on Security and Privacy, pp. 354–368. IEEE, Los Alamitos (2008)

7. Cramer, R., Franklin, M., Schoenmakers, B., Yung, M.: Multi-Authority Secret-Ballot Elections with Linear Work. In: Maurer, U.M. (ed.) EUROCRYPT 1996. LNCS, vol. 1070, pp. 72–83. Springer, Heidelberg (1996)
8. Cramer, R., Gennaro, R., Schoenmakers, B.: A Secure and Optimally Efficient Multi-Authority Election Scheme. In: Fumy, W. (ed.) EUROCRYPT 1997. LNCS, vol. 1233, pp. 103–118. Springer, Heidelberg (1997)
9. Fan, C.-I., Sun, W.-Z.: An efficient multi-receipt mechanism for uncoercible anonymous electronic voting. Mathematical and Computer Modelling 48, 1611–1627 (2008)
10. Fujioka, A., Okamoto, T., Ohta, K.: A Practical Secret voting Scheme for Large Scale Elections. In: Zheng, Y., Seberry, J. (eds.) AUSCRYPT 1992. LNCS, vol. 718, pp. 244–251. Springer, Heidelberg (1993)
11. Hirt, M.: Multi-Party Computation: Efficient Protocols, General Adversaries and Voting. PhD thesis, ETH Zurich (2001)
12. Hirt, M., Sako, K.: Efficient Receipt-Free Voting Based on Homomorphic Encryption. In: Preneel, B. (ed.) EUROCRYPT 2000. LNCS, vol. 1807, pp. 539–556. Springer, Heidelberg (2000)
13. Jakobsson, M., Juels, A., Rivest, R.L.: Making Mix Nets Robust for Electronic Voting by Randomised Partial Checking. In: Proceedings of the 11th USENIX Security Symposium, Berkeley, pp. 339–353. USENIX Assoc. (2002)
14. Jakobsson, M., M'Raihi, D., Tsiounis, Y., Yung, M.: Electronic Payments: Where Do We Go From Here? In: Baumgart, R. (ed.) CQRE 1999. LNCS, vol. 1740, pp. 43–63. Springer, Heidelberg (1999)
15. Jakobsson, M., Yung, M.: Revokable and Versatile Electronic Money (Extended Abstract). In: CCS 1996: Proceedings of the 3rd ACM Conference on Computer and Communications Security, pp. 76–87. ACM Press, New York (1996)
16. Juels, A., Catalano, D., Jakobsson, M.: Coercion-Resistant Electronic Elections. In: WPES 2005: Proceedings of the 2005 ACM Workshop on Privacy in the Electronic Society, pp. 61–70. ACM, New York (2005)
17. Kügler, D., Vogt, H.: Off-line Payments with Auditable Tracing. In: Blaze, M. (ed.) FC 2002. LNCS, vol. 2357. Springer, Heidelberg (2003)
18. Lee, B., Boyd, C., Kim, K., Yang, J., Yoo, S.: Providing receipt-freeness in mixnet-based voting protocols. In: Lim, J.-I., Lee, D.-H. (eds.) ICISC 2003. LNCS, vol. 2971, pp. 245–258. Springer, Heidelberg (2004)
19. Okamoto, T.: Receipt-Free Electronic Voting Schemes for Large Scale Elections. In: Christianson, B., Lomas, M. (eds.) Security Protocols 1997. LNCS, vol. 1361, pp. 25–35. Springer, Heidelberg (1998)
20. Rivest, R., Smith, W.: Three Voting Protocols: ThreeBallot, VAV, and Twin. In: Proceedings of Electronic Voting Technology Workshop, 2007, Boston, MA, pp. 1–14 (2007)
21. Ryan, P.Y.A.: Prêt à Voter With a Human-Readable, Paper Audit Trail. Technical Report CS-TR: 1038, Newcastle University (2007)
22. Ryan, P.Y.A., Schneider, S.A.: Prêt à Voter with re-encryption mixes. In: Gollmann, D., Meier, J., Sabelfeld, A. (eds.) ESORICS 2006. LNCS, vol. 4189, pp. 313–326. Springer, Heidelberg (2006)
23. Saeednia, S., Kremer, S., Markowitch, O.: An Efficient Strong Designated Verifier Signature Scheme. In: Lim, J.-I., Lee, D.-H. (eds.) ICISC 2003. LNCS, vol. 2971, pp. 40–54. Springer, Heidelberg (2004)
24. Sako, K., Kilian, J.: Receipt-Free Mix-Type Voting Scheme: A practical solution to the implementation of a voting booth. In: Guillou, L.C., Quisquater, J.-J. (eds.) EUROCRYPT 1995. LNCS, vol. 921, pp. 393–403. Springer, Heidelberg (1995)

25. Smart, M., Ritter, E.: Remote Electronic Voting with Revocable Anonymity. Technical Report CSR-09-06, School of Computer Science, University of Birmingham (2009), ftp://ftp.cs.bham.ac.uk/pub/tech-reports/2009/CSR-09-06.pdf
26. Stewart, J.: A Banana Republic? The Investigation into Electoral Fraud by the Birmingham Election Court. Parliamentary Affairs 59(4), 654–667 (2006)
27. Volkamer, M., Krimmer, R.: Secrecy forever? Analysis of Anonymity in Internet-based Voting Protocols. In: Proceedings, First International Conference on Availability, Reliability and Security, ARES 2006, Vienna, pp. 340–347. IEEE, Los Alamitos (2006)
28. Weber, S.G., Araújo, R., Buchmann, J.: On Coercion-Resistant Electronic Elections with Linear Work. In: Proceedings, 2007 2nd International Conference on Availability, Reliability and Security, Vienna, pp. 908–916. IEEE, Los Alamitos (2007)

On Secure Implementation of an IHE XUA-Based Protocol for Authenticating Healthcare Professionals*

Massimiliano Masi, Rosario Pugliese, and Francesco Tiezzi

Università degli Studi di Firenze, Viale Morgagni, 65 - 50134 Firenze, Italy
masi@math.unifi.it, {pugliese,tiezzi}@dsi.unifi.it

Abstract. The importance of the Electronic Health Record (EHR) has been addressed in recent years by governments and institutions. Many large scale projects have been funded with the aim to allow healthcare professionals to consult patients data. Properties such as confidentiality, authentication and authorization are the key for the success for these projects. The Integrating the Healthcare Enterprise (IHE) initiative promotes the coordinated use of established standards for authenticated and secure EHR exchanges among clinics and hospitals. In particular, the IHE integration profile named XUA permits to attest user identities by relying on SAML assertions, i.e. XML documents containing authentication statements. In this paper, we provide a formal model for the secure issuance of such an assertion. We first specify the scenario using the process calculus COWS and then analyse it using the model checker CMC. Our analysis reveals a potential flaw in the XUA profile when using a SAML assertion in an unprotected network. We then suggest a solution for this flaw, and model check and implement this solution to show that it is secure and feasible.

1 Introduction

In recent years, the exchange of Electronic Health Records (EHRs) among clinics and hospitals has become an interesting field of research and study for academia and the industry. An EHR is a set of sensitive data containing all healthcare history of a patient (e.g. medical exams or prescriptions).

Two important concepts in EHR management are security and interoperability: the content of an EHR cannot be disclosed to unauthorized people without an explicit patient consent and has to be accessible by heterogeneous systems. These requirements impose that any software participating in an EHR exchange must adhere to common specifications.

Integrating the Healthcare Enterprise (IHE) [1] is a worldwide initiative founded for promoting the coordinated use of established standards to improve information sharing in an healthcare scenario. To achieve security and interoperability, many profiles for integrating different systems have been proposed by IHE. These profiles can be combined for building healthcare applications by using a Service Oriented Computing (SOC) approach and OASIS standards such as SAML [2], ebXML [3], and WS-Trust [4].

---

* This work has been supported by the EU project Sensoria, IST-2005-016004.

A. Prakash and I. Sen Gupta (Eds.): ICISS 2009, LNCS 5905, pp. 55–70, 2009.
© Springer-Verlag Berlin Heidelberg 2009

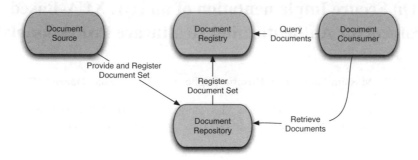

Fig. 1. The XDS model

IHE specifications are by now used to build nationwide projects with the aim of sharing patient healthcare data, such as the French GIP-DMP [5] or the Austrian ARGE-ELGA [6] EHR projects.

A typical EHR transmission is made by exploiting an ebXML registry/repository model (called in IHE jargon Cross Enterprise Document Sharing, XDS), as depicted in Figure 1. A document source (typically a medical device) provides and registers documents for a given patient to a repository that extrapolates metadata and feeds a registry. A document consumer (a workstation used by an healthcare professional) queries the registry for documents related to the patient. The registry searches in its metadata and replies with a set of links. These links are used by the consumer for retrieving documents from the repository.

Confidentiality and auditing is achieved using Transport Layer Security (TLS)) [7] and logging as defined in the Audit Trail and Node Authentication (ATNA) profile [1]. Any node participating in ATNA owns an host X.509 certificate for attesting machine's identity. Requisites of each profile can be merged (i.e. *grouped*) together for building a complete infrastructure. For instance, XDS grouped with ATNA provides a secure and audited data exchange through TLS channels using a registry/repository model.

Healthcare professionals authentication is one of the basic requirements for the access of person related health data at regional, national and also multinational level. Authentication is defined by IHE in the Cross Enterprise User Assertion (XUA) integration profile. The XUA specification covers the use of a SAML authentication assertion issued by an identity provider to be injected using WS-Security [8] during the documents queries. Due to local government complexities where each nation / hospital / clinic have its own authentication method, the assertion issuance process is leaved open. The WS-Trust standard is only suggested, but not proposing a specific profile or a set of messages to be exchanged potentially leads to weak implementations.

Because of the impact that the IHE specifications are having, formal models of protocols and standards are needed. A large body of work has been already made on analyzing WS-Trust protocols, see e.g. [9,10,11,12], where message-level authentication [13] properties are verified. By relying on them, in this paper we aim at formalizing and implementing a protocol combining WS-Trust and IHE profiles. More specifically, our protocol is built on an XDS transaction grouped with ATNA and authenticated by an

```
<saml:Assertion><saml:Issuer> issuer-identity </saml:Issuer>
    <ds:Signature> ... </ds:Signature>
    <saml:Subject><saml:NameID> username </saml:NameID>
        <saml:SubjectConfirmation Method="#bearer">
            <saml:SubjectConfirmationData> ...</saml:SubjectConfirmationData>
        </saml:SubjectConfirmation>
    </saml:Subject>
    <saml:Conditions NotBefore="ts1" NotOnOrAfter="ts2">
        <saml:AudienceRestriction><saml:Audience> registry-address </saml:Audience>
        </saml:AudienceRestriction>
    </saml:Conditions>
    <saml:AuthnStatement  AuthnInstant="ts3"> ...
    </saml:AuthnStatement>
    <saml:AttributeStatement> ... </saml:AttributeStatement>
</saml:Assertion>
```

Fig. 2. Excerpt of a sample SAML token (using the *bearer* method)

XUA SAML assertion. To our best knowledge, this is the first tentative to formalize protocols derived from IHE specifications.

The process for issuing a SAML token is a delicate task: if an assertion is stolen, a malicious attacker can re-use it and have access to unauthorized healthcare data. One could suggest to use TLS for authenticating channels during the issuance. In fact, IHE supports TLS by means of ATNA for compatibility with legacy non-WS standards such as Dicom [14] and Health Level 7 version 2 [15]. However, given the possibility by XUA to choose any issuance process, the use of TLS should be discouraged in favor of WS-Security. Moreover, as argued in [11], if a secure transport layer in web service communications is used, intermediaries cannot manipulate the messages on their way; this does not comply with the requirements of SOC. For these reasons, our proposal does not rely on TLS.

It is worth noticing that in the IHE security model, applications should also avoid heavy use of encryption, because the impact on performance of the current encryption algorithms is excessive [1]. Indeed, IHE applications can even run on medical devices with a reduced computational power.

The work presented in this paper consists of three main contributions. First, we fill the gap left open by XUA by proposing a protocol (Section 2) for issuing the SAML token according to the IHE and OASIS dictates. Second, we formally specify the protocol (Section 3) using the calculus COWS [16]. We then analyze (Section 4) the formal model with the model checker CMC and show that a potentially severe security flaw exists in the SAML assertion format specified by XUA. Third, we provide an implementation of the protocol with our revised assertion format (the implementation is only sketched in Section 5, the interested reader is referred to [17]). We conclude by touching upon comparisons with related work and directions for future work (Section 5). A list of all acronyms used in the paper is reported in Table 3 at page 68.

2   An XUA-Based Protocol

As previously discussed, XUA does not address the authentication mechanisms of the local network. Instead, it leverages on the abstraction layer introduced by SAML. The SAML OASIS standard is a set of specification documents defining *assertions* (or tokens) and a *protocol* to exchange them. A SAML authentication assertion is an XML document issued by a *Security Token Service (STS)*[1] that contains statements about an authentication procedure performed by an underlying authentication mechanism (such as Kerberos) for a *subject*. An example is shown in Figure 2. The SAML token is then used by the service requester to interact with the services listed in the AudienceRestriction element.

The contacted *service provider* uses the assertion for authenticating the requester by verifying the digital signature of the trusted issuer. SAML subjects can be confirmed with the method listed in the SubjectConfirmation element. Here, we are interested in two methods named *bearer* [2] and *holder-of-key (HoK)* [18]. The bearer subject confirmation method tells the service provider that the subject of the assertion is the presenter (i.e. the bearer) of the assertion. In the holder-of-key method, *STS* binds an identity for the subject (or for the requester) as X.509 data. By this means, we set the subject of the assertion as the healthcare professional with confirmation data as the ATNA certificate of the requesting machine. The service provider can compare such data with the X.509 identity carried in the TLS transaction.

By means of the formal investigation presented in Section 4, we discovered a security flaw due to the format of the SAML assertion. XUA explicitly says that the bearer subject confirmation method shall be supported. However, in large scale networks it is unrealistic to assume that each node is trusted. Compromised nodes may exist and if one is able to obtain a SAML assertion issued for another, authorized node, with the bearer method it can re-use the assertion to gain access to secret resources. In fact, the service provider has no knowledge if the presenter of the assertion was the original requester. With the holder-of-key method, requester identity is bound as subject confirmation data and digitally signed by *STS*. The service provider can now detect if the bearer is the node which the assertion was intended for by checking if the identity set by *STS* matches the one presented in the communication channel by means of ATNA.

In [11], the feeling of the authors is that it looks like impossible to authenticate correctly the request for a security token issue in a two step protocol as it is instead suggested in the WS-Trust specification. Since our aim is to propose a secure and authenticated holder-of-key assertion issuance, we designed a challenge-response WS-Trust protocol in four message exchanges.

Our model involves an XDS transaction grouped with ATNA and XUA for retrieving documents for a patient with id *Susan*. The protocol that we propose, written in a notation commonly used for describing security protocols, is shown in Table 1 and is graphically depicted in Figure 3.

Notation $\{M\}_{dKey}$ stands for the symmetric encryption of message M using the derived key *dKey*, $\{M\}_{K^+_{STS}}$ for the encryption of M using the public key of *STS* and $\{[M]\}_{K^-_{STS}}$ for the signature of M using *STS*'s private key (where [M] is the hash code of M). *ts*, *ts'*, *ts1* and *ts2* are timestamps.

The consumer C initiates the protocol by sending the message (1) for requesting a token to *STS*. It sends its identity C, a unique message identifier *msgId1*, using WS-Addressing [19], and the identity of the Security Token Service *STS*. Notation UT(*user*,

---

[1] For the sake of simplicity, we assume an STS that is directly able to authenticate users, i.e. it plays also the role of the identity provider.

Table 1. The proposed XUA protocol

$C \rightarrow STS$	: $C, msgId1, STS, \mathrm{UT}(user, salt, int), ts1, \mathrm{RST}(REG)$	(1)
$STS \rightarrow C$	: $STS, C, msgId2, msgId1, \mathrm{RSTR}(ctx, \{STS, n, ts, ctx\}_{dKey})$	(2)
$C \rightarrow STS$	: $msgId3, msgId2, STS, ts2, \mathrm{RSTR}(ctx, \{n+1, C, msgId3, msgId2, ctx\}_{K_{STS}^+})$	(3)
$STS \rightarrow C$	: $C, STS, msgId4, msgId3, \mathrm{RSTRC}(\mathrm{RSTR}(\{[STS, ts', user, REG]\}_{K_{STS}^-}))$	(4)
$C \rightarrow REG$	: $C, REG, msgId5, \{[STS, ts', user, REG]\}_{K_{STS}^-}, \text{'Susan'}$	(5)
$REG \rightarrow C$	: $REG, C, msgId6, msgId5, docLinks$	(6)

salt, int) stands for the WS-Security Username Token Profile 1.1 [20] and contains the username, a random number which acts as a cryptographic salt, and an integer, respectively. RST(*REG*) is the WS-Trust 1.3 *Request Security Token* where the registry address *REG* is the ultimate recipient of the token.

Once received the message, *STS* unpacks the value of the username token, unpacks the RST(*REG*) element (*REG* must be in the *STS*'s list of valid assertion targets) and computes the derived key *dKey*. The key is computed by *STS* by concatenating the password of the user (which is given as input by the real human sitting in front of the workstation and is known by *STS* by means of the underlying authentication mechanism) with the salt and then hashed using the SHA-1 algorithm. The result of this operation

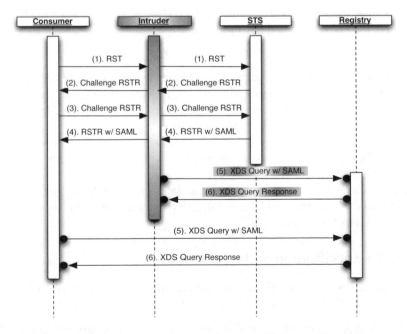

Fig. 3. The WS-Trust protocol for SAML token issuance. Messages (5) and (6) are over TLS channels. An intruder can steal the SAML token in message (4) and, if the subject confirmation method is *bearer*, can perform an unauthorized authenticated query.

is also hashed using SHA-1. This process is repeated until the total number of hash operations equals the iteration count *int*. Then, *STS* encrypts the challenge composed by its identity, a nonce *n*, a new timestamp *ts* and the WS-Trust `context` element *ctx* of the challenge (i.e. an identifier defined by WS-Trust used for correlating the messages involved in the token issuance). Indeed, *STS* challenges the requester in order to be sure on its identity and attesting its availability. RSTR is the WS-Trust *Request Security Token Response* element that contains the challenge data.

When message (2) is received by *C*, it computes *dKey* using the same algorithm as the *STS* and decrypts the message (indeed, it is the only participant able to do it). *C* performs the WS-Addressing checks: message (2) must contain the identifier *msgId1* indicating that (2) is in response to (1). It also checks if the request comes from a participants whose identity is included in the RSTR, by means of TLS mutual authentication, for instance. *C* now trusts that the challenge really comes from *STS*. Then, it adds 1 to the nonce and encrypts it, together with the message identifiers and the context, using the *STS* public key. The reply is in message (3).

After receiving the message, *STS* decrypts the content of the RSTR, checks if the nonce is equal to the one that it sent (plus one) and if the context is the same. If it is able to perform all these operations, then it can attest the identity of the user sitting in front of *C*. Thus, it issues the SAML assertion (it is signed by *STS* according to the SAML Signature profile, as enveloped signature) and sends it to *C*, via message (4). The assertion is:

$$\{[STS, ts', user, REG]\}_{K_{STS}^-}$$

where the confirmation method is *bearer*. In fact, if we would have used the *holder-of-key* method, the assertion would be as follows:

$$\{[C, STS, ts', user, REG]\}_{K_{STS}^-}$$

The assertion then contains the requester's identity as ATNA X.509 certificate, here simply represented by *C*, the issuer identity, a timestamp, the user name and the audience restriction list. We omit for simplicity all the details introduced by the SAML specification (e.g. the assertion time range validity).

Once *C* has obtained a security token, it can finally query the registry *REG* to retrieve the links to the repositories containing the EHR data that it is looking for. The query is message (5), which contains the SAML assertion.

Finally, once received message (5), *REG* validates the token. Using the *STS*'s public key it verifies the signature and, if it is valid, delivers the requested resource (i.e. the links *docLinks*) to *C* via message (6).

3   COWS Specification of the Protocol

In this section, first we report the syntax and the informal semantics of COWS[2], then we present the COWS specification of the XUA protocol in Section 2. Our specification

---

[2] For the sake of simplicity, we present here a fragment of COWS without linguistic constructs for dealing with forced termination, since such primitives have not been used in the protocol specification. We refer the interested reader to [16,21] for the presentation of the full language and for many examples illustrating COWS peculiarities and expressiveness.

Table 2. COWS syntax

$s ::=$	(services)
nil | $u.u!$ $<u, \dots, u>$ | $p.o?$ $<u, \dots, u>.s$	(empty activity, invoke, receive)
| $s_1 + s_2$ | $s_1 \| s_2$ | $[n\sharp] s$ | $[X] s$	(choice, parallel, name & var. delim.)
| $* s$ | $A(u, \dots, u)$ | let $A(u, \dots, u) = s$ in s' end	(replication, call, let definition)

reflects many real-world implementation details. Algorithms, field names and message flows are taken from OASIS standards.

3.1 COWS Syntax and Informal Semantics

COWS [16] is a formalism specifically devised for modelling (and analysing) service-oriented applications; in fact, its design has been influenced by the principles underlying the OASIS standard for orchestration of web services WS-BPEL [22]. The syntax of COWS, written in the 'machine readable' format accepted by the interpreter and the model checker CMC [23] that we use for the analysis, is presented in Table 2. It is defined using the following notational conventions: *variables* (ranged over by X, Y, ...) start with capital letters; *names* (ranged over by n, m, ..., p, p', ..., o, o', ...) start with digits or lower case letters; *identifiers* (ranged over by u, u_1, u_2, ... and used as non-terminal symbol only) are either variables or names; *service identifiers* (ranged over by A, A', ...) start with capital letters and each of them has a fixed non-negative arity. Names are used to represent communicable values, partners and operations.

Invoke and *receive* are the basic communication activities provided by COWS. Besides input and output parameters, both activities indicate an *endpoint*, i.e. a pair composed of a partner name p and an operation name o, through which communication should occur. An endpoint p.o can be interpreted as a specific implementation of operation o provided by the service identified by the logic name p. An invoke p.o! $<u_1, \dots, u_n>$ can proceed as soon as all arguments $u_1, \dots, u_n$ are names (i.e. have been evaluated). A receive p.o? $<u_1, \dots, u_n>.s$ offers an invocable operation o along a given partner name p. Partner and operation names can be exchanged in communication (although dynamically received names cannot form the endpoints used to receive further invocations). This makes it easier to model many service interaction and reconfiguration patterns.

A *choice* can be used to pick out one receive activity among those leading its arguments that are enabled for execution.

Execution of *parallel* terms is interleaved, except when a communication can be performed. In this case, if more than one matching receives are ready to process a given invoke, only one of the receives with greater priority (i.e. the receives that generate the substitution with 'smaller' domain, see [16,21]) is allowed to progress.

The *delimitation* operators are the *only* binders of the calculus: $[n\sharp] s$ and $[X] s$ bind n and X, respectively, in the scope s. Name delimitation can be used to generate 'fresh' private names (like the restriction operator of π-calculus), while variable delimitation can be used to regulate the range of application of the substitution generated by an inter-service communication. This takes place when the arguments of a receive and of a concurrent invoke along the same endpoint match and causes each variable argument of the receive to be replaced by the corresponding name argument of the invoke within the whole scope of variable's declaration. In fact, to enable parallel terms to share the state (or part of it), receive activities in COWS do *not* bind variables.

The *replication* operator $* s$ permits to spawn in parallel as many copies of s as necessary. This, for example, is exploited to model persistent services, i.e. services which can create multiple instances to serve several requests simultaneously.

Finally, the *let* construct permits to re-use the same 'service code', thus allowing to define services in a modular style; let $A(u, \ldots, u) = s$ in s' end behaves like s', where calls to A can occur. A service *call* $A(u'_1, \ldots, u'_n)$ occurring in the body s' of a construct let $A(u_1, \ldots, u_n) = s$ in s' end behaves like the service obtained from s by replacing the formal parameters $u_1, \ldots, u_n$ with the corresponding actual parameters $u'_1, \ldots, u'_n$.

3.2 Protocol Specification

Due to lack of space we only present the relevant part of the COWS specification of the XUA-based protocol and refer the interested reader to [17] for the overall specification.

To effectively take part to the protocol, each participant has to be able to call some internal functions, defined in some basic libraries provided by the programming language used to specify the service. These functions implement algorithms, such as SHA for hashing, RSA for public-key cryptography and AES for symmetric key cryptography, necessary to properly manage the data to be sent and received. An internal function can be rendered in COWS as a term of the following form[3]:

$$
\begin{aligned}
*(\; &\texttt{p.req?}\langle inputData_1\rangle \; . \; \texttt{p.resp!}\langle inputData_1, outputData_1\rangle \\
+ \; &\texttt{p.req?}\langle inputData_2\rangle \; . \; \texttt{p.resp!}\langle inputData_2, outputData_2\rangle \\
+ \; &\ldots + \texttt{p.req?}\langle inputData_n\rangle \; . \; \texttt{p.resp!}\langle inputData_n, outputData_n\rangle \;)
\end{aligned}
$$

where p indicates the partner name of the considered participant, while req and resp indicate the operations used to call the function and to receive the result, respectively. To guarantee that the result $outputData_i$ is properly delivered to the caller, it is sent back together with the correlated $inputData_i$. In this way, if the same function $f(\cdot)$ is concurrently called, then the results will not be mixed up. Thus, in the example below

$$(\texttt{p.req!}\langle 100\rangle \; | \; [\texttt{X}] \; \texttt{p.resp?}\langle 100, \texttt{X}\rangle \; . \; s_1) \; | \; (\texttt{p.req!}\langle 250\rangle \; | \; [\texttt{Y}] \; \texttt{p.resp?}\langle 250, \texttt{Y}\rangle \; . \; s_2)$$

where we have two calls, the pattern-matching-based communication of COWS ensures that, irrespective of the execution order, the occurrences of variable X in s_1 will be replaced by $f(100)$, while the occurrences of Y in s_2 will be replaced by $f(250)$.

Each protocol participant P is rendered in COWS as a pair of service definitions of the form $A(\ldots) = P$ within a let construct:

```
P(p,... ) =
        [hashReq♯] [hashResp♯] [encReq♯] [encResp♯] [decReq♯] [decResp♯] ...
      ( sha1(p, hashReq, hashResp)
        | rsa1_5_PublicKey(p,encReq,encResp,decReq,decResp)
        | ... other internal functions ...
        | P_behaviour(p,hashReq,hashResp,encReq,...) ) )

      P_behaviour(p,hashReq,hashResp,encReq,...) = s_P
```

---

[3] These COWS terms play a role similar to that of functions in the applied π-calculus [9,24].

where p is the participant partner name and s_P is the COWS term modelling the participant's behaviour. Name delimitations are used here to make the functions sha1, rsa1_5_PublicKey, ... internal by declaring that hashReq, hashResp, encReq, ... are private operation names known to P_behaviour and to the internal functions, and only to them.

The term representing the consumer's behaviour is[4]

```
sts.rst!<c,msgId1,sts,user,salt,1000,timestamp1,uri,rst_req>
| [MsgId2] [Challenge] [Y] (
c.rstr?<Y,c,MsgId2,msgId1,Challenge>. c.fault!<Y,differentFrom,sts>
+ c.rstr?<sts,c,MsgId2,msgId1,Challenge>.
( -- Calculate the aes128 key based on his password
  c.hashReq!<pwd,salt,1000>
  | [DKey] c.hashResp?<pwd,salt,1000,DKey>.
  ( -- Decrypt the Challenge
    c.decReq!<DKey,Challenge>
    | [Nonce] [Created] [Context] [X](
      c.decResp?<DKey,Challenge,X,Nonce,Created,Context>.
        c.fault!<X,differentFrom,sts,for,Context>
      + c.decResp?<DKey,Challenge,sts,Nonce,Created,Context>.
        ( -- Encode the response
          c.encReq!<gen_key,Nonce,1,c,msgId3,MsgId2,Context>
          | [EncData] c.encResp?<gen_key,Nonce,1,c,msgId3,MsgId2,Context,EncData>.
            ( -- Encode the generated key with sts public key
              c.encReq!<stsPubKey,gen_key>
              | [EncKey] c.encResp?<stsPubKey,gen_key,EncKey>.
                ( -- Send the response to sts
                  sts.rstrr!<msgId3,MsgId2,sts,timestamp2,EncKey,EncData>
                  | [MsgId4] [SAMLTimestamp] [Signature]
                    -- Receive token back
                    c.rstrc?<c,sts,msgId3,MsgId4,SAMLTimestamp,user,uri,Signature>.
                    ( -- Query reg for the resource identified by uri
                      reg.storedQuery!<c,reg,sts,msgId5,SAMLTimestamp,user,uri,
                                       Signature,"Susan"> ) ) ) ) ) ) )
```

As expected, the consumer starts by invoking STS, by executing the invoke activity along the endpoint sts.rst and by sending the request security token data. This invocation corresponds to message (1) in Table 1, where the iteration number *int* is 1000 and the registry address specified in the RST is uri. Then, the consumer waits for message (2), by means of the two receive activities along c.rstr. Notice that, in accordance with the WS-Addressing standard and due to the pattern-matching mechanism regulating the COWS communication, only messages that carry the name msgId1 can be accepted by the consumer. Moreover, the identity of STS, i.e. sts, must be contained in the message, otherwise a fault is raised (represented by the invoke activity along the endpoint c.fault)[5]. Once message (2) is received, the consumer calculates the derived key by exploiting its internal hashing function (using operation hashReq and hashResp) and, similarly, decrypts the challenge (using operation decReq and decResp). Then, pattern-matching and the choice operator are used again to check the presence of the STS's identity within the challenge. Now, the consumer can prepare the response for STS, by

---

[4] The string -- indicates that the rest of the line is a comment (and is ignored by CMC).

[5] Notice that if both receives along c.rstr match an incoming message, hence the first argument is sts, due to the prioritized semantics of COWS only the second receive (which generates a smaller substitution) can progress.

encrypting the challenge data, where the nonce has been incremented by 1 (this is represented by the couple Nonce, 1). Differently from the abstract description of message (3) shown in Table 1, the COWS specification follows the concrete approach used in the implementation (based on XML encryption): thus, the AES algorithm is used to encrypt the data rather than RSA. The used symmetric key gen_key, supposed to be calculated by the consumer, is in its turn encrypted with RSA by using the STS's public key and attached to the message. Finally, when the message containing the token arrives (receive along c.rstrc), the consumer invokes the storedQuery operation (the XDS feature for querying Susan's documents) provided by the registry.

The term representing the *STS* behaviour is

```
* [C] [MsgId1] [User] [Salt] [Iteration] [Timestamp1] [URI] [RST]
  sts.rst?<C,MsgId1,sts,User,Salt,Iteration,Timestamp1,URI,RST>.
  ( -- Retrieve the User's password
    sts.getPwd!<User>| [Pwd] sts.getPwdResp?<User,Pwd>.
    ( -- Calculate the derived key
      sts.hashReq!<Pwd,Salt,Iteration>
    | [DKey] sts.hashResp?<Pwd,Salt,Iteration,DKey>.
      ( -- Create the challenge
        sts.encReq!<DKey,sts,nonce1,created1,contextId>
      | [Challenge] sts.encResp?<DKey,sts,nonce1,created1,contextId,Challenge>.
        ( -- Send the challenge to the consumer
          C.rstr!<sts,C,msgId2,MsgId1,Challenge>
        | -- Receive the challenge response
          [MsgId3] [Timestamp2] [EncKey] [EncData]
          sts.rstrr?<MsgId3,msgId2,sts,Timestamp2,EncKey,EncData>.
          ( -- Decrypt the encoded key
            sts.decReq!<stsPrivateKey,EncKey>
          | [Gen_key] sts.decResp?<stsPrivateKey,EncKey,Gen_key>.
            ( -- Decrypt the encoded data
              sts.decReq!<Gen_key,EncData>
            | [MsgId3] sts.decResp?<Gen_key,EncData,nonce1,1,C,MsgId3,
                                    msgId2,contextId>.
              -- Now, the consumer is authenticated
              ( -- Create a token SAML
                sts.hashReq!<sts,samlTimestamp,User,URI>
              | [SAMLhash] sts.hashResp?<sts,samlTimestamp,User,URI,SAMLhash>.
                ( -- Sign the hash code
                  sts.sign!<stsPrivateKey,SAMLhash>
                | [Signature] sts.signResp?<SAMLhash,Signature>.
                  ( -- Send the token
                    C.rstrc!<C,sts,MsgId3,msgId4,samlTimestamp,
                             User,URI,Signature> ) ) ) ) ) ) ) ) )
```

The replication operator * at the beginning of the term specifies that STS is a persistent service, i.e. it is capable of creating multiple instances to serve several requests simultaneously. Thus, when it receives a message along the endpoint sts.rst, corresponding to message (1) of the protocol, it creates an instance initialized with the received data. The instance, by means of operations getPwd and getPwdResp, retrieves the user's password from a private database. Using the password, it can derive a symmetric key to encrypt the challenge, by exploiting again its internal functions. Invoke along C.rstr and the subsequent receive along sts.rstrr permit sending and receiving message (2) and (3), respectively. Now, by using stsPrivateKey, STS can decipher the symmetric key generated by the consumer, which is then used to decrypt the challenge response.

Notice that, pattern-matching in the communication along sts.decResp permits checking that the response contains the incremented nonce and the context; this guarantees
that the sender of the message is really the consumer acting on behalf of the authorized
user. Therefore, STS creates the token, by exploiting its internal functions, and sends it
to the consumer.

Finally, the term representing the registry's behaviour is

```
* [Cust] [STS] [MsgId5] [TS] [User] [Uri] [Signature]
  reg.storedQuery?<Cust,reg,STS,MsgId5,TS,User,Uri,Signature,"Susan">.
  -- Validate the token
  ( -- Calculate the hash code of the token data
    reg.hashReq!<STS,TS,User,Uri>
    | [CalculatedHash] reg.hashResp?<STS,TS,User,Uri,CalculatedHash>.
      (  -- Retrieve the STS's public key
        reg.getKey!<STS>
        | [PubKey] reg.getKeyResp?<STS,PubKey>.
          ( -- Check the signature by using PubKey
            reg.check!<PubKey,Signature>
            | [Hash] reg.checkResp?<Signature,Hash>.
            [compare♯]
              ( -- Compare the hash codes
                reg.compare!<CalculatedHash>
                | [X] ( reg.compare?<X>. reg.attackDetected!<Cust>
                      + reg.compare?<Hash>. reg.deliveringResource!<Cust> ) ) ) ) )
```

When the registry receives a consumer's query, by means of the receive activity along the
endpoint reg.storedQuery, it validates the token within the message. To this purpose,
we assume that the registry has a private database storing the public keys of all trusted
STSs, and can interact with it by calling the operations getKey and getKeyResp. Instead, to check the validity of the signature, it calls function signChecker by means
of check and checkResp. After calling such function, the registry obtains the hash
code of the signature (and stores it in the variable Hash); by comparing it with the recalculated hash code (stored in the variable CalculatedHash) using the private operation compare, it can either detect that an attack has been performed (this is signaled by
the activity reg.deliveringResource! < Cust >) or state that the token is valid. In
this last case, the activity reg.deliveringResource! < Cust > is used to signal that
the registry is ready to deliver the resource to the consumer. In fact, we do not model here
message (6), since the flaw we are interested to capture concerns the previous message
exchanges.

4   Protocol Analysis

As shown in Figure 3 we have to deal with two types of communication channels:
TLS protected channels for communicating with the registry and untrusted channels
for communicating with the STS. We assume the intruder as any authorized user in the
network (i.e. it owns an ATNA host certificate). Therefore, it can start any mutual authenticated TLS transaction with the registry and it can look in any message exchanged
bySTS. Basically, we consider the intruder model introduced by [25] for TLS channels
and the well-known Dolev-Yao model [26] as regards the communication with STS
along untrusted channels. We focus on an intruder that intercepts the message sent by

STS containing the SAML token issued for the consumer (message (4)) and re-uses the token (without modifying it) for an its own query to the registry (message (5), sent by the intruder). This is rendered in COWS as

```
Intruder(i, c, sts, user, uri, reg) =
  [MsgId4] [TS] [Signature]
  c.rstrc?<c,sts,msgId3,MsgId4,TS,user,uri,Signature> .
    ( i.underAttack!<>
      | --Forwards the message to the consumer
        c.rstrc!<c,sts,msgId3,MsgId4,TS,user,uri,Signature>
      | --Performs the attack
        reg.storedQuery!<i,reg,sts,msgId5,TS,user,uri,Signature,"Susan"> )
```

Once the intruder has caught message (4) (receive activity along c.rstrc), besides forwarding the message to the consumer and querying the registry, it enables the invoke activity i.underAttack! <>. This activity is only used during the analysis to signal that the system is under attack. Notably, the intruder's query differs from the consumer's one for the first argument only, which is i instead of c.

The analysis of the protocol is carried out by exploiting CMC [23], a software tool that permits model checking SocL formulae over COWS specifications. SocL [27] is an action- and state-based, branching time, temporal logic specifically designed to express properties of service-oriented systems. Here, we are interested to look for the presence of security flaws in the protocol, which can be expressed in SocL as follows:

```
AG [request(samlToken,requestedBy,c)]
   not EF (systemUnderAttack(i) and deliveringResource(to,i))
```

This formula means that it holds *globally* (operator AG) that *if* (operator [·]) a SAML token has been requested by the consumer (action request(samlToken, requestedBy, c)), then it does *not* (operator not) hold that *eventually* (operator EF) the system will be under attack by intruder i (predicate systemUnderAttack(i)) and, at the same time, the registry will deliver the resource to i (predicate deliveringResource(to, i)).

The previous formula is stated in terms of *abstract* actions and predicates, meaning that, e.g., a token is requested or a resource is ready to be delivered, while the COWS specification is stated in terms of *concrete* actions, i.e. communication of data tuples along endpoints. To verify an abstract property over a concrete specification, CMC permits to specify a set of *transformation rules*, such as

```
Action *.rst<$requestor,*,*,*,*,*,*,*,*>
              -> request(samlToken,requestedBy,$requestor)
 State $attacker.underAttack! -> systemUnderAttack($attacker)
 State *.deliveringResource! <$X> -> deliveringResource(to, $X)
```

The first rule maps a concrete action involving the operation rst to the abstract action request(samlToken, requestedBy, $requestor), where the (meta-)variable $requestor will be replaced with the actual requestor during the on-the-fly model checking process, while the symbol * is a wildcard. Similarly, the second and third rules map the actions involving operations underAttack and deliveringResource to the corresponding state predicates. We refer the interested reader to [27] for a complete account of abstraction rules.

As already mentioned in the Introduction, CMC returns FALSE when checking the above SocL formula over the abstracted COWS specification. In fact, the system can perform the following sequence of (abstract) actions:

request(samlToken,requestedBy,c); *internal actions*; challenge(samlToken); *internal actions*; challengeResp(samlToken); *internal actions*; response(samlToken,requestedBy,c); request(registryQuery,requestedBy,i); *internal actions*

and reach a state where both predicates systemUnderAttack(i) and delivering-Resource(to,i) hold.

Now, let us modify the COWS specification to model the use of the *holder-of-key* confirmation method rather than the *bearer* method. With respect to the specification presented in Section 3, the main difference is that in the new STS specification the invoke sts.hashReq! < sts, samlTimestamp, User, URI >, used to generate the hash code of the SAML token data, is replaced with sts.hashReq! < sts, samlTimestamp, User, C, URI >. This time the result returned by CMC when checking the previous formula over the protocol specification is TRUE. In fact, the registry can detect that the intruder's query is fake by comparing the intruder's identity with the identity contained in the SAML token by means of ATNA credentials.

5 Concluding Remarks

We have presented our initial experience on the analysis of protocols for building health-care applications. Our long term goal is to develop a general methodology based on formal methods for studying such protocols and to show its feasibility for the analysis of real-world scenarios, whereas an analysis without formal techniques is sometime unfeasible due to the complexity of healthcare applications.

Specifically, we have considered a Web Service security protocol for obtaining an XUA SAML authentication assertion, using the WS-Trust OASIS standard. To the best of our knowledge, our work is the first tentative to provide a formal study for IHE specifications. This kind of protocols are obtaining an ever increasing relevance since they are used to exchange patients' healthcare data and are widely adopted. We have revealed a potential flaw in the specification and we have also proposed a solution. Afterwards, we have implemented the 'revised' protocol using WS-Trust 1.3, SAML 2.0, WS-Security and the WS-Security Username Token Profile 1.1. We have also used the Axis2 library (available at http://ws.apache.org/axis2) and the JBoss application server (http://www.jboss.org). Our Java implementation consists of four services: the *Document Consumer* and *Document Registry*, a *Document Repository* and a *Security Token Service*. All the XDS services are given as a courtesy of the Tiani "Spirit" company located in Vienna, Austria (http://www.tiani-spirit.com). The modified STS is available as Axis2 service at http://office.tiani-spirit.com:41081/SpiritIdentityProvider/services/STS09. A more detailed account of the implementation together with the COWS sources can be found in [17].

Table 3. List of acronyms

ATNA	Audit Trail and Node Authentication
ebXML	Electronic Business using eXtensible Markup Language
EHR	Electronic Health Record
HoK	holder-of-key
IHE	Integrating the Healthcare Enterprise
RST	Request Security Token
RSTR	Request Security Token Response
SAML	Security Assertion Markup Language
SOC	Service Oriented Computing
STS	Security Token Service
TLS	Transport Layer Security
XACML	eXtensible Access Control Markup Language
XDS	Cross Enterprise Document Sharing
XUA	Cross Enterprise User Assertion

Related Work. Web Services analysis with the use of formal methods is not a novel research field. Microsoft Research proposes the TulaFale specification language [10,9] for security analysis of web services. TulaFale uses CryptoVerif [28] as model checking engine. The main focus is on SOAP Message Rewrite attacks that we do not consider in our work since our signatures are defined by the SAML standard. In [10] the authors analyze WS-Trust for a secure exchange of a Security Context Token while we consider WS-Trust for issuing a SAML token.

The SAML 1.0 and 2.0 specifications have been studied e.g. in [12,29,30]. However, they concentrate on the SAML Protocol and Profiles [31] to obtain SAML Authentication assertion, while we focus on WS-Trust. The work closest to ours is [12] where the SAML-based Single Sign-On for Google Apps is analyzed with the tool AVISPA [32]. A flaw in the Google implementation is found, where a fake Service Provider can potentially access a Google resource without the password of the user. Similarly to our scenario, the flaw discovered is in the format of the SAML assertion, that lacks the Audience list. In XUA, the Audience list must be contained in the assertion and refer to the registry, hence this kind of attack cannot occur.

Future Work. As the above mentioned works and ours witness, to simply adopt WS-Security and WS-Trust does not guarantee absence of security flaws. Due to the widespread diffusion of such standards, especially in EHR, it is then worthwhile pursuing this line of research. Therefore, in the near future we plan to continue our formal methods-based investigation of the security issues that can arise in healthcare environments, such as XACML-based authorization processes, patient consent and confidentiality, as specified in the IHE profiles[6].

---

[6] IHE profiles strictly follow international guidelines such as Health Insurance Portability and Accountability Act (HIPAA) and EU commissions reports.

References

1. The IHE Initiative: IT Infrastructure Technical Framework (2009), http://www.ihe.net
2. OASIS Security Services TC: Assertions and protocols for the OASIS security assertion markup language (SAML) v2.02 (2005)
3. OASIS/ebXML Registry Technical Committee: ebXML business process specification schema technical specification v2.0.4 (2006), http://www.ebxml.org
4. OASIS Web Services Security TC: WS-Trust 1.3 specification (2007)
5. GIP DMP: Dossier Médical Personnel A French Project, http://www.d-m-p.org
6. ARGE-ELGA: Die Arbeitsgemeinschaft Elektronische Gesundheitsakte, http://www.arge-elga.at
7. Dierks, T., Rescorla, E.: The Transport Layer Security (TLS) Protocol Version 1.2. Technical Report RFC 5246, IETF (August 2008)
8. OASIS Web Services Security TC: Web service security: SOAP message security (2006)
9. Bhargavan, K., Fournet, C., Gordon, A.D., Pucella, R.: TulaFale: A Security Tool for Web Services. CoRR abs/cs/0412044 (2004)
10. Bhargavan, K., Corin, R., Fournet, C., Gordon, A.D.: Secure sessions for web services. In: SWS, pp. 56–66. ACM, New York (2004)
11. Kleiner, E., Roscoe, A.W.: On the relationship between web services security and traditional protocols. In: Mathematical Foundations of Programming Semantics, MFPS XXI (2005)
12. Armando, A., et al.: Formal Analysis of SAML 2.0 Web Browser Single Sign-On: Breaking the SAML-based Single Sign-On for Google Apps. In: FMSE. ACM, New York (2008)
13. Lowe, G.: A hierarchy of authentication specifications, pp. 31–43. IEEE, Los Alamitos (1997)
14. ACR-NEMA: Digital imaging and communications in medicine, dicom (1995)
15. Health Level Seven organization: Hl7 standards (2009), http://www.hl7.org
16. Lapadula, A., Pugliese, R., Tiezzi, F.: A calculus for orchestration of web services. In: De Nicola, R. (ed.) ESOP 2007. LNCS, vol. 4421, pp. 33–47. Springer, Heidelberg (2007)
17. Masi, M., Pugliese, R., Tiezzi, F.: On secure implementation of an IHE XUA-based protocol for authenticating healthcare professionals (full version), http://rap.dsi.unifi.it/cows/
18. OASIS Security Services TC: SAML v2.0 Holder-of-Key Assertion Profile (March 2009)
19. Gudgin, M., Hadley, M., Rogers, T.: Web Services Addressing 1.0 - Core. Technical report, W3C, W3C Recommendation (May 2006)
20. OASIS Web Services Security TC: Username token profile v1.1 (2006)
21. Lapadula, A., Pugliese, R., Tiezzi, F.: A Calculus for Orchestration of Web Services (full version). Technical report, Dipartimento di Sistemi e Informatica, Univ. Firenze (2008), http://rap.dsi.unifi.it/cows
22. OASIS WSBPEL TC: Web Services Business Process Execution Language v2.0 (2007)
23. ter Beek, M.H., Gnesi, S., Mazzanti, F.: CMC-UMC: A framework for the verification of abstract service-oriented properties. In: Shin, S.Y., Ossowski, S. (eds.) 2009 ACM Symposium on Applied Computing (SAC), pp. 2111–2117. ACM, New York (2009)
24. Abadi, M., Fournet, C.: Mobile values, new names, and secure communication. In: POPL, pp. 104–115 (2001)
25. Broadfoot, P., Lowe, G.: On distributed security transactions that use secure transport protocols. In: 16th Computer Security Foundations Workshop, pp. 63–73. IEEE, Los Alamitos (2003)
26. Dolev, D., Yao, A.: On the security of public key protocols. IEEE Transactions on Information Theory 29(2), 198–208 (1983)

27. Fantechi, A., Gnesi, S., Lapadula, A., Mazzanti, F., Pugliese, R., Tiezzi, F.: A model checking approach for verifying COWS specifications. In: Fiadeiro, J.L., Inverardi, P. (eds.) FASE 2008. LNCS, vol. 4961, pp. 230–245. Springer, Heidelberg (2008)
28. Blanchet, B.: CryptoVerif: Computationally sound mechanized prover for cryptographic protocols. In: Dagstuhl seminar Formal Protocol Verification Applied (October 2007)
29. Groß, T.: Security analysis of the saml single sign-on browser/artifact profile. In: ACSAC, pp. 298–307. IEEE, Los Alamitos (2003)
30. Hansen, S., Skriver, J., Nielson, H.: Using static analysis to validate the saml single sign-on protocol. In: WITS, pp. 27–40. ACM, New York (2005)
31. OASIS Security Services TC: Profiles for the OASIS Security Assertion Markup Language (SAML) v2.0 (2005)
32. Armando, A., et al.: The AVISPA Tool for the Automated Validation of Internet Security Protocols and Applications. In: Etessami, K., Rajamani, S.K. (eds.) CAV 2005. LNCS, vol. 3576, pp. 281–285. Springer, Heidelberg (2005)

On the Untraceability of Anonymous RFID Authentication Protocol with Constant Key-Lookup

Bing Liang[1], Yingjiu Li[1], Changshe Ma[1,3], Tieyan Li[2], and Robert Deng[1]

[1] School of Information Systems, Singapore Management University, 80 Stamford Road,
Singapore, 178902
[2] Institute for Infocomm Research, A*STAR Singapore
[3] School of Computer, South China normal University, Guangzhou, China, 510631
liangb02@gmail.com, {yjli,changshema}@smu.edu.sg,
litieyan@i2r.a-star.edu.sg, robertdeng@smu.edu.sg

Abstract. In ASIACCS'08, Burmester, Medeiros and Motta proposed an anonymous RFID authentication protocol (BMM protocol [2]) that preserves the security and privacy properties, and achieves better scalability compared with other contemporary approaches. We analyze BMM protocol and find that some of security properties (especial untraceability) are not fulfilled as originally claimed. We consider a subtle attack, in which an adversary can manipulate the messages transmitted between a tag and a reader for several continuous protocol runs, and can successfully trace the tag after these interactions. Our attack works under a weak adversary model, in which an adversary can eavesdrop, intercept and replay the protocol messages, while stronger assumptions such as physically compromising of the secret on a tag, are not necessary. Based on our attack, more advanced attacking strategy can be designed on cracking a whole RFID-enabled supply chain if BMM protocol is implemented. To counteract such flaw, we improve the BMM protocol so that it maintains all the security and efficiency properties as claimed in [2].

Keywords: RFID, Anonymous, Authentication, Privacy.

1 Introduction

Radio Frequency Identification (RFID) technology has been applied in a range of industries such as libraries [12], automatic payment [15], animal tracking [15], supply chains [8] and E-passport [16]. An RFID system generally incorporates three components: tag, reader and back-end database. Typically, a reader can interrogate with a tag and send the tag's information to database for verification. There are two main kinds of tags: active tags which are battery-powered [14] and passive tags without battery, which are powered by the electromagnetic field established by the reader's antenna. As the cost of active tags is much higher than the passive ones, only passive tags are considered to be suitable for large-scale applications such as supply chain management.

Privacy and scalability are two important perspectives in RFID protocols. On the aspect of privacy, if the tag is not managed carefully, the privacy of its carrier will be inferred by a malicious party. In some cases, the tags can release the information about an individual's medication record, banknote's serial number, culture preference,

A. Prakash and I. Sen Gupta (Eds.): ICISS 2009, LNCS 5905, pp. 71–85, 2009.
© Springer-Verlag Berlin Heidelberg 2009

location information, and etc.. In other cases, a company's sensitive information such as product price, and supply chain routine can be obtained by the company's opponent, which may lead to the financial loss of the company. In all, privacy is one of the most essential security consideration in RFID system.

Besides the privacy concern, scalability is another important issue in designing an RFID authentication protocol. RFID users usually have a high requirement of the proceeding time. In the survey of [4], more than half the people in the investigation consider efficiency of the RFID authentication process quite important, far more important than those people who consider security important. In [2], Burmester, Medeiros and Motta (BMM) proposed an RFID authentication protocol with constant key-lookup to balance the privacy requirement and scalability. To the best of our knowledge, this protocol is one of the most scalable solutions that preserve privacy as claimed (please see Section 7 for more details about related works). In this paper, we identify the shortcoming in BMM protocol [2] and propose an improved protocol accordingly. We argue that the improved protocol provides stronger privacy than the BMM protocol, while the performance of the improved protocol is the same as the BMM protocol. Our contributions in this paper are summarized below:

1. We analyze the BMM-protocol and find a subtle flaw, by which we can break the privacy property, namely untraceability. Exploiting this flaw, we design an easy-to-launch attack under a weak adversary model. Under our attack, an adversary can easily trace a tag in a supply chain party. Thus, one by one, we can trace such a tag in a whole supply chain if the BMM protocol is implemented.
2. To improve the protocol, we propose an anonymous RFID authentication protocol that can fulfill all privacy claims of [2], including defense against eavesdropping attack, spoofing attack, replay attack, de-synchronization attack, tracing attack and compromising attack.

The organization of this paper is as follows: In Section 2, we introduce the notation that will be used in this paper. In Section 3, we review the BMM protocol. In Section 4, we elaborate on our attack. In Section 5, an example on cracking the whole supply chain is presented. Further, in Section 6, we propose the improved protocol and analyze its security properties. In Section 7, we introduce the related works on RFID authentication. In Section 8, we conclude the paper.

2   Notation

If $A(\cdot, \cdot, ...)$ is a randomized algorithm, then $y \leftarrow A(x_1, x_2, ...; cn)$ means that y is assigned the unique output of the algorithm A on inputs $x_1, x_2, ...$ and coins cn. Let g be a pseudorandom function (PRF) [7]. If S is a set, then $s \in_R S$ indicates that s is chosen uniformly at random from S. If $x_1, x_2, ...$ are strings, then $x_1\|x_2\|\cdots$ denotes the concatenation of them. If x is a string, then $|x|$ denotes its bit length in binary code. Let ε denote the empty string. If S is a set, then $|S|$ denotes its cardinality (i.e. the number of elements of S). If ctr is a counter which starts from n_1 and ends with n_ℓ, then $ctr(j)$ denotes its jth value, i.e. $ctr(j) = n_j$, where $1 \leqslant j \leqslant \ell$. Let IV be an initial vector for the PRF g.

3   The BMM Protocol

In this section, we review the BMM protocol, (which is shown in Figure 1).

In the RFID system constructed by BMM protocol, there is a set-up procedure which initializes the reader and every tag. Then, they will engage in a protocol to identify the tag. The whole RFID system is described as follows.

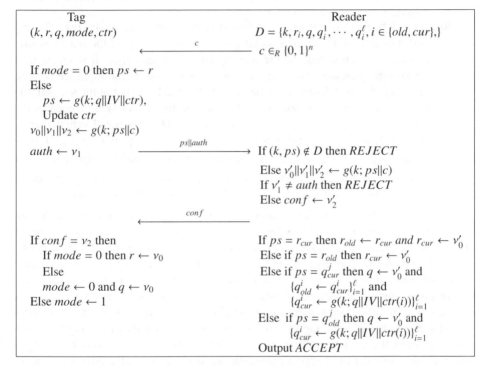

Fig. 1. BMM Protocol

Setup: When creating a new tag T, the system generates a secret key k, a pseudonym seed q, a one-time pseudonym r, a counter $ctr = 1$, and a flag $mode = 0$. Then it sets up the initial state information of the tag T as the tuple $(k, q, r, ctr, mode)$. The system also associates the tag T with its identity ID_T in the reader's database by initiating a tuple $(r_{old}, r_{cur}, q^1_{old}, \cdots q^\ell_{old}, q^1_{cur}, \cdots q^\ell_{cur}, k, q, ID_T)$, where $r_{old} = r_{cur} = r$ and $q^j_i = g(k; \|q\|IV\|ctr(j))$, for $i = \{old, cur\}$, and $j = 1, \cdots \ell$.

The BMM Protocol: It runs in three rounds:

Round 1. First, the reader starts the protocol by sending a challenge c to the tag. Upon receiving c, the tag first checks its $mode$ state: if $mode = 0$, it sets the pseudonym $ps = r$; otherwise, it computes $ps = g(k; q\|IV\|ctr)$ and updates the counter $ctr = ctr + 1$. Then, the tag calculates $v_0\|v_1\|v_2 = g(k; ps\|c)$. Here, v_0 is used to replace the pseudonym r; $auth = v_1$ is used to authenticate itself to the reader, and v_2 is used to authenticate the reader.

Round 2. The tag sends the message $ps\|auth$ to the reader. Upon receiving $ps\|auth$, the reader requests to its back-end database to look up the tuple $(r_{old}, r_{cur}, q_{old}^1, \cdots$ $q_{old}^{\ell}, q_{cur}^1, \cdots q_{cur}^{\ell}, k, q_0, ID_T)$ such that $r_i = ps$ or $q_i^j = ps$, where $i = \{old, cur\}$ and $j = 1, \cdots \ell$, through using ps as an index. If the tag is de-synchronized within ℓ times, we can find the tuple in constant time by $2\ell + 2$ indexes. If the tuple is found, the reader calculates $v_0'\|v_1'\|v_2' \leftarrow g(k; ps\|c)$ and accepts the tag if $auth = v_1'$. Otherwise, the tag is rejected. If a tag is accepted, the reader prepares a confirmation message $conf \leftarrow v_2'$.

Round 3. The reader sends the confirmation message $conf$ to the tag. The tag authenticates the reader by checking whether $conf = v_2$. If the reader is successfully authenticated, the tag then updates its pseudonym: if $mode = 0$, it updates the pseudonym $r = v_0$; if $mode = 1$, it updates pseudonym seed $q = v_0$ and keep the pseudonym r unchanged. If the reader is not authenticated, the tag sets $mode = 1$ and does nothing else. On the reader side, it updates the tuple $(r_{old}, r_{cur}, q_{old}^1, \cdots, q_{old}^{\ell}, q_{cur}^1, \cdots q_{cur}^{\ell}, k, q_0, ID_T)$ associated with the tag as follows. If $ps = r_{cur}$, it updates $r_{old} = r_{cur}$ and $r_{cur} = v_0'$. If $ps = r_{old}$, it only updates $r_{cur} = v_0'$. If $ps = q_{old}^j$ for some j between 1 and ℓ, it updates $q = v_0'$ and $q_{cur}^j = g(k; \|q\|IV\|ctr(j))$ for $j = 1, \cdots \ell$. If $ps = q_{cur}^j$ for some j between 1 and ℓ, it updates $q = v_0'$, $q_{old}^j = q_{cur}^j$ and $q_{cur}^j = g(k; \|q\|IV\|ctr(j))$ for $j = 1, \cdots \ell$.

Burmester, Medeiros and Motta claimed that it can *"support anonymity with constant key-lookup cost; however, it suffers from entrapment attacks"* [2]. To preserve the privacy of a queried tag, an adversary that eavesdrops over the protocol should not be able to figure out the identifier of the tag with higher likelihood than a pure random guess. The same should also apply to an unauthorized reader that attempts to query the tag. In other words, the protocol should ensure "tag anonymity", in terms of session unlinkability: an adversary should not be able to link together two or more protocol sessions involving the same tag (regardless whether the identity of the tag is known or not) to track the activities of the tag. To achieve this, any two protocol exchanges involving the same tag must appear reasonably random such that the adversary cannot differentiate it with non-negligible probability from two protocol exchanges involving two different tags.

Unfortunately, there exist some flaws in the updating procedures in the design of BMM protocol. The flaws can be subsequently exploited to launch a simple attack to trace a tag in a series of protocol runs.

4   Attacking the BMM Protocol

In this section, we describe a three-run interleave attack and show how to use it to track a tag. Our attack is easy to launch as it requires a weak adversary model as depicted below.

4.1   The Adversary Model

In typical RFID security scenarios, adversaries with different levels of power are modeled to analyze different RFID authentication protocols [10]. We consider adversaries with three levels of power as follows:

- **Level-1 (Passive attack):**
  Able to perform passive eavesdropping and intercept messages over legitimate protocol sessions.
- **Level-2 (Active attack with protocol participation & protocol disruption):**
  Able to communicate with a legitimate tag or reader by following the steps specified under the protocol and to replay, corrupt, block or inject (replace)messages.
- **Level-3 (Active attack with secret compromise):**
  Able to capture a legitimate tag and extract its secrets through physical layer attack and side channel attacks.

It is reasonable to assume that a higher level adversary also possesses the abilities of all levels preceding it, i.e. a level-3 adversary has the abilities of level-1 and level-2 adversaries, as well as the set of additional abilities of physical layer attacks and side channel attacks. As we will be showing in next subsection, our attack requires a relatively weak adversary model (*w.r.t.*, a level-2 adversary), where an adversary has limited ability to communicate with a legitimate tag following protocol steps.

Different kinds of attacks can achieve variable goals. Eavesdropping attacks can track a tag successfully if the tag's responses keep same. Attackers can communicate with trusted readers and trusted tags through spoofing and replay attack. De-synchronization attacks can interrupt regular communications between trusted readers and tags through blocking, modifying and injecting messages. Denial of Service (DoS) attacks mean that a legitimate reader is flooded with useless messages so that it cannot communicate with legitimate tags normally.

4.2 Three-Run Interleave Attack

We first give the intuition behind our attack. We observe that the state information (index) 'r' in the tag always keeps unchanged in the protocol executions when $mode = 1$ and $conf = v_2$ (see Figure 1). It means that the tag will reply with the same response in the next interrogation. Our attack follows this observation and uses a 'three-run interleave' technique to push the tag into the state of $mode = 1$ and $conf = v_2$.

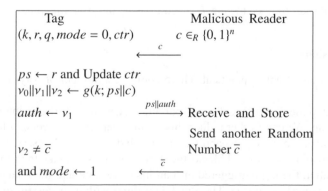

Fig. 2. First Run of The Attack

As mentioned in Section 4.1, we assume a level-2 adversary as the malicious reader, denoted by $\mathcal{R}^M$. We denote a legitimate tag by $\mathcal{T}$ and a trusted reader by $\mathcal{R}^T$. The attack consists of three runs, during which $\mathcal{T}$ is interrogated by $\mathcal{R}^M$ twice and by $\mathcal{R}^T$ once. We present the attack in detail as follows.

1. **First Run: $\mathcal{R}^M$ interrogates $\mathcal{T}$**
   This first run of our attack is illustrated in Figure 2. During the first protocol run, $\mathcal{R}^M$ interrogates $\mathcal{T}$ with an incomplete protocol execution. We assume that $\mathcal{R}^M$ can launch attacks after several legitimate communications between $\mathcal{R}^T$s and $\mathcal{T}$, so we can consider the initial status of $\mathcal{T}$ as $mode = 0$. After sending a challenge c, $\mathcal{R}^M$ receives the reply message $ps\|auth = r\|v_1$ from $\mathcal{T}$. As $\mathcal{R}^M$ does **not** share any secret with $\mathcal{T}$, it cannot compose the correct confirmation message for $\mathcal{T}$. Instead, $\mathcal{R}^M$ sends a random value $\bar{c}$ to $\mathcal{T}$. At the tag's side, $\bar{c}$ cannot be verified against $conf$, so $\mathcal{T}$ changes its status into an attacked state with $mode = 1$. To this end, $\mathcal{R}^M$ stores the reply '$r\|v_1$' and continues to the next step.

   Note that if $\mathcal{R}^M$ sends queries to a tag continuously, he/she can only obtain the unlinkable information $ps\|auth$. Therefore, to get useful information, which can link the same tag by comparing 'r', the adversary intentionally involves a trusted reader $\mathcal{R}^T$ in the second run.

2. **Second Run: $\mathcal{R}^T$ interrogates $\mathcal{T}$**
   The second run of our attack is shown in Figure 3. During the second protocol run, $\mathcal{T}$ is put forward and interrogated by a trusted reader $\mathcal{R}^T$ with a complete protocol execution, while $\mathcal{R}^M$ does nothing. Note that in the first run of our attack, $\mathcal{T}$ toggles its $mode$ in $\mathcal{T}$ to '1'; therefore, after $\mathcal{T}$ receives the confirmation message from the legitimate reader, its $mode$ is changed into '0'. As now, $\mathcal{T}$ only updates q into v_0 but keeps r unchanged.

3. **Third Run: $\mathcal{R}^M$ interrogates $\mathcal{T}$**
   During the third protocol run, $\mathcal{R}^M$ interrogates with $\mathcal{T}$ again as in the first run for tracing the same tag $\mathcal{T}$ that has been interrogated in the first run. To achieve this, $\mathcal{R}^M$ sends the same challenge c to the tag and expects a repeated reply by $\mathcal{T}$. Recall that in the second run, a successful protocol run between $\mathcal{R}^T$ and $\mathcal{T}$ toggles $\mathcal{T}$ to a secure status $mode = 0$. Following the protocol, $\mathcal{T}$ shall reply with $ps\|auth = r\|v_1$, which is the same authentication information as that in the first run. It is thus easy for the attacker to trace the tag $\mathcal{T}$ by comparing the $ps\|auth$ values.

4.3   Discussions

We stress that our attack is practical. There could be a number of ways to launch such an attack.

Recall that in the first protocol run of our attack, a malicious reader interrogates with a legitimate tag. We can further reduce this requirement if the adversary has minimum eavesdropping and blocking capabilities: in the first run, the adversary eavesdrops the first two protocol messages and blocks the third messages to make the protocol incomplete. Thereafter, the tag is triggered into an insecure state and the reader updates the status for the record of this tag. The attack continues with a successful second run and an incomplete third run (same as that of the first run). By comparing the eavesdropped

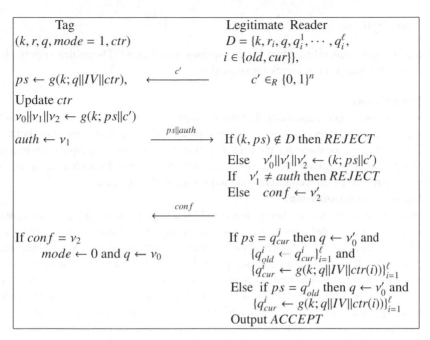

Fig. 3. Step Two of The Attack

messages in the first run and the third run, the adversary can trace the tag. Such an adversary is more stealthy as no active interrogation between a malicious reader and a legitimate tag is needed[1].

In summary, the attack can be extended, but not limited to the following forms:

$\diamond \; \dashrightarrow \mathcal{R}^M \dashrightarrow \mathcal{R}^T \dashrightarrow \mathcal{R}^M \dashrightarrow$

$\diamond \; \dashrightarrow \mathcal{R}_{\mathcal{A}}^T \dashrightarrow \mathcal{R}^T \dashrightarrow \mathcal{R}_{\mathcal{A}}^T \dashrightarrow$

$\diamond \; \dashrightarrow \mathcal{R}^M \dashrightarrow \mathcal{R}^T \dashrightarrow \mathcal{R}_{\mathcal{A}}^T \dashrightarrow$

$\diamond \; \dashrightarrow \mathcal{R}_{\mathcal{A}}^T \dashrightarrow \mathcal{R}^T \dashrightarrow \mathcal{R}^M \dashrightarrow$

Where $\mathcal{R}_{\mathcal{A}}^T$ denotes an adversary's presence in an interrogation between a trusted reader and a legitimate tag.

5   Cracking a Whole Supply Chain by Using the Basic Attack

Based on the basic three-run interleave attack, more advanced attacking strategies are designed to crack an RFID-enabled supply chain that implements the BMM protocol.

---

[1] Note that in the third run, a different challenge c'' could be used by a trusted reader to challenge the tag. As long as the r value is not updated in the second run, the ps value is still the same as the one in the first run.

5.1 Assumptions

We need to make several reasonable assumptions about an RFID-enabled supply chain before we elaborate on our attacking strategies.

1. *Trusted Zone:*
   We consider a geographically distributed supply chain, in which each party in the supply chain may receive tagged articles, process these articles, and ship them out. For simplicity, we consider the area as a trusted zone inside a supply chain party, and public zone outside. An adversary is not able to interact with a legitimate tag in a trusted zone, but can interrogate with a tag in the public zone.

2. *One-time Authentication:*
   While tagged articles are being processed by a supply chain party, the authentication is performed only once (*e.g.*, typically at the entry point of the trusted zone). This is reasonable as authentication procedure is much more expensive and time-consuming than identifier scanning procedure. As the area inside a supply chain party is considered as a trusted domain, indeed no additional authentication is necessary. While multiple scanning for identifying the tags is still allowed to facilitate other operations (which are not security related). This is to guarantee that only one successful session of authentication protocol is conducted in a trusted zone so that once the articles are shipped out to the public zone, the adversary can launch the tracing attack.

3. *Sticky Adversary:*
   We assume that an adversary may possess multiple readers at multiple locations or equivalently possess one reader at multiple instant locations. In other words, we assume an ubiquitous adversary who is able to stick on the targeted articles in the public zone along a supply chain.

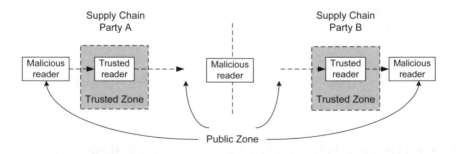

Fig. 4. An Example for Cracking Supply Chain System

With these assumptions, we illustrate how to crack a supply chain system as in Figure 4, where two supply chain parties are involved. In an attack, the adversary can setup malicious readers in the public zones near each supply chain party. Furthermore, two attacking strategies are given below.

5.2   Attacking Strategies

Case 1: Tracing a Single Tag along Supply Chain

Suppose an adversary targets on a particular article with an RFID tag $\mathcal{T}$. Before it arrives at supply chain party A, a malicious reader can launch its attack by interrogating with $\mathcal{T}$ and obtaining a ps value ($ps = r$) specific to this tag. Inside the domain of party A, $\mathcal{T}$ is authenticated once and processed in some other ways. At last, the article attached with $\mathcal{T}$ is shipped out. Once again, a malicious reader scans all outbound articles and find this particular tag with the pseudonym ps. Following on, the adversary repeats the attacks at various transportation locations visited by this article. Eventually, a list of visited sites of the article, $[\cdots \to A \Rightarrow B \Rightarrow C \Rightarrow D \Rightarrow E \cdots \to]$, are recorded, which enables the total visibility of this article (in the supply chain, which is serious breach of its privacy). The tracing attack is illustrated in Figure 5.

Case 2: Tracing Multiple Tags and Constructing Supply Chain Map

Suppose an adversary, for the purpose of obtaining commercial secret, targets on a manufacture who supplies its goods to various distributors, retailers, *etc.*, via complex supply chain paths. To construct such a map, he/she needs to trace all the goods attached with tags along their supply chains. As such, the adversary first builds a database for all the tags scanned immediately after the goods are shipped out. Suppose 100 tags are being scanned and recorded in the database, as shown in Figure 6. For each record of the database, $\sqrt{}$ (or $\times$) represents whether the tag is scanned at certain locations or not. 'ps' denote the pseudonyms of a tag, for simplicity, $|ps| = 32$. As long as the adversary

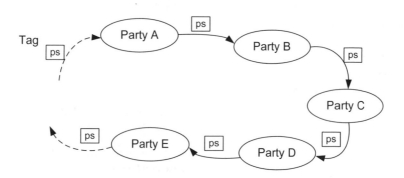

Fig. 5. Tracing A Single Tag along its Supply Chain

Tag	ps	Location 1	Location 2	Location 3	Location 4	Location 5	$\cdots$
Tag 1	09310A78	$\sqrt{}$	$\sqrt{}$	$\times$	$\times$	$\sqrt{}$	$\cdots$
Tag 2	38901D43	$\times$	$\sqrt{}$	$\sqrt{}$	$\sqrt{}$	$\sqrt{}$	$\cdots$
$\vdots$	$\cdots$	$\cdots$	$\cdots$	$\cdots$	$\cdots$	$\cdots$	$\cdots$
Tag 100	9A7B2811	$\sqrt{}$	$\times$	$\sqrt{}$	$\sqrt{}$	$\times$	$\cdots$

Fig. 6. The Adversary's Database

has enough resources to monitor all potential locations via a number of supply chains, it will finally draw a complete map for all delivery paths.

We assume that there are L possible locations for each tag, and the number of total tags is N. An attacker only needs to set up a database with size of $O(L \times N)$. He/she can efficiently query the information of a tag in polynomial time.

6   Improving the BMM Protocol

We observe that the main reason that the BMM protocol is vulnerable to our three-run interleave attack is that the pseudonym 'r' shared between the legitimate tag and the trusted reader is not properly updated. Intuitively, we solve the problem by updating the pseudonym r at both side after the third protocol message is sent even if the *mode* is 1 for the tag.

6.1   Improved Protocol

Our improved protocol is shown Figure 7. In the first round, our protocol is the same as the BMM protocol except that we separate the result $g(k; ps\|c)$ into four parts v_0, v_1, v_2 and v_3. The new part v_3 is used to update r when the tag's *mode* = 1, and other parts are

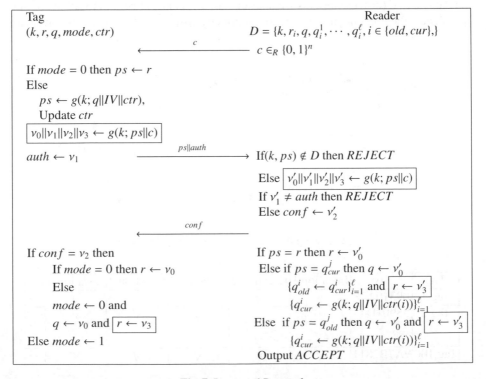

Fig. 7. Improved Protocol

kept the same as those of the original BMM protocol. In the second round, the reader also needs to divide the result of $g(k; ps\|c)$ into four parts v'_0, v'_1, v'_2 and v'_3. Here, v'_3 is used to update the reader when the received $ps = q_i^j, i \in \{old, cur\}, j = 1, 2 \cdots \ell$, and the reader keeps other operations the same as BMM protocol. In the third round, after receiving the confirmation message in the protocol, we update the status of r at the tag's side with $r \leftarrow v_3$ when '$mode = 1$' holds in the tag. In this round, we also update the status as described in the boxed parts at the reader in Figure 7. Since the pseudonym 'r' is updated whenever the $mode$ is 0 or 1, the response of the tag behaves randomly at every interrogation. Therefore, our three-run interleave attack is no longer feasible.

6.2   Security Analysis

We analyze the improved protocol regarding some important security properties. The essential objective of the protocol is to achieve mutual authentication between a reader and a tag without disclosing the tag's identity to a third party, and it is based on a classic challenge-response mechanism. Without the shared secret, no polynomial probabilistic time (PPT) adversary can generate the authentication messages transferred between the two parties.

Our improved protocol's main purpose is to protect the tags' privacy, which means to keep tags' anonymity and untraceablity. Our improved protocol prevents tags from *tracing attack*. The meaning of untraceability contains two aspects: 1) The outputs of a tag in any two sessions are unlinkable, and 2) The outputs of readers are independent from those of tags. First of all, we analyze the outputs of any two sessions of a tag. For any two session i *and* j, $i \neq j$ of a tag, let $ps(i)\|auth(i)$ and $ps(j)\|auth(j)$ denote the output of the session i and j, respectively.

$$ ps = \left\{ \begin{array}{ll} r, & mode = 0 \\ g(k; q\|IV\|ctr), & mode = 1 \end{array} \right\} $$

If $mode = 0$, then $ps = r$, and r is updated by a PRF $g(\cdot)$ in the tag after every successful protocol; otherwise, $ps = g(k; q\|IV\|ctr)$, the output of PRF $g(\cdot)$. Therefore, whether $ps = r$ or $ps = g(k; q\|IV\|ctr)$, $ps(i)$ and $ps(j)$ are independent as the output of a PRF are pairwise independent. The latter part of the tags' output is $auth = v_1$ which is a part of $g(k; ps\|c)$ ($g(\cdot)$ is a PRF). Therefore, $auth(i)$ and $auth(j)$ are independent and unlinkable. As a result, $ps(i)\|auth(i)$ is independent from $ps(j)\|auth(j)$.

Second, we illustrate the output of the reader is independent from the output of a tag. We consider the output of tag is $ps\|auth$ and the output of the reader is $conf$. ps is the input of the PRF $g(k; ps\|c)$, and $conf$ is the output of PRF $g(\cdot)$. As the input and output of a PRF are independent, ps is independent from $conf$. The $auth = v_1$ is the second part of the output $g(k; ps\|c)$, and $conf = v'_2$ is the third part of the output of the PRF $g(k; ps\|c)$. Therefore, $auth$ is independent from $conf$. In all, the output of tag $ps\|auth$ is independent from the output of the reader $conf$. Thus, the independence of outputs between different sessions of a tag and the independence of outputs between a reader and a tag guarantee the privacy of tags, and attackers cannot trace a tag by eavesdropping or active interrogations.

Based on challenge-and-respond technique, mutual authentication, PRF in both tag and reader, and update processes, Level-2 attacks cannot be applied here, for instance, *de-synchronization attack.* Because the trusted reader keeps not only the newly updated values, but also the old values corresponding to a former corrupted protocol run, if a tag is pushed de-synchronized with the legitimate reader by a malicious adversary, it can still be recognized by referring to the older record $q_{old}^i, i = 1, 2, \cdots, N$ in the database. By successful mutual authentication, the reader and tag can be re-synchronized again. As we argue in section 4.1, our improved protocol can prevent level-2 attack, so it can possess the ability of counteracting weaker attacks. To counteract Level-1 attacks, for example, *eavesdropping attack*, an adversary can only obtain the challenge c and pseudonyms $ps\|auth$ and v_2', which are generated by PRF, but nothing else. Level-1 adversaries cannot link the information together to trace a tag, either. To prevent Level-2 attackers, the challenge-and-respond technique protects the reader from Denial-of-Service (Dos) attack. In addition, since fresh random numbers are generated by both the reader and the tag for mutual authentication and both the tag and the reader update their states after a successful protocol run, simple *spoofing* and *replay attacks* have negligible success rate. In addition, unlike some tree-based RFID protocol [11], if some tags are compromised unfortunately, released information will not affect other tags' secrecy due to that tags do not share secrets in our protocol.

Nevertheless, the improved protocol does not incur any additional cost with respect to storage and computation. Therefore, the lightweightness of the BMM protocol is maintained. As stated in [2], the database stores limited numbers of q_i^j, when these numbers are used up, the BMM protocol suffers from an "entrapment attack". The "entrapment attack" means *"the tag is prevented from communicating with authorized readers and can only be interrogated by the adversary"* [2]. In conclusion, as mentioned in Section 3, the security analysis we conducted is limited to level-1 to level-2 adversaries, while level-3 adversary is more powerful and may bring more harmful attacks to the existing protocol.

7   Related Work

Numerous of papers addressing RFID security and privacy have been published recently (please refer to [8] for a detailed literature survey). Our concern in this paper is on RFID reader/tag (mutual) authentication, which has also been rigorously studied in the literature [3] [5], [6], [9], [11], [13], [17].

A number of RFID authentication protocols based on secure one-way hash functions have been proposed [18]. In one of the previous works, Ohkubo, Suzuki and Kinoshita (OSK) proposed using of hash chain to update the internal states [13]. The scheme needs to compute two different hash function values, one to update the tag's secret and the other one to compute the response that is transmitted to the reader during tag identification. This method incurs a large overhead at the reader's side due to the exhaustive search in the back-end database to identify the tag. To mitigate the high search cost, Avoine and Oechslin proposed an optimization of the scheme using a time-memory trade-off for the computation of OSK hash chains [1]. However, in the later works [5] and [6], the authors pointed out that the optimized scheme is still vulnerable to tag impersonation attack and suffers from low scalability in the presence of attacks. Dimitriou in [5] proposed a challenge-response protocol for tag-reader authentication. However, it is still possible for an adversary to de-synchronize tags , leading to a denial of service.

Pseudonym Random Function (PRF) has been used in the design of RFID protocols. In [17], Tsudik proposed YATRAP protocol for RFID authentication. It only needs a single key and a single pseudorandom function (PRF) in a tag, but it is vulnerable to de-synchronization and denial of service (DoS) attacks as the timestamps can be manipulated in this protocol. Then, Chatmon, van Le and Burmester's YATRAP+ and OTRAP [3] were proposed to address the problem of YATRAP. Their schemes were essentially designed mainly for privacy-preserving identification of tags without providing reader authentication.

To reduce protocol overhead, people used tree-structure in RFID protocols. Dimitriou proposed a tree-based privacy-preserving RFID identification scheme [6]. In [11], Molnar, Soppera, and Wagner proposed a tree based scheme with a high scalability of identifying tags. Under these schemes, each tag stores a group of secret keys that lie along the path of a key tree from root to leaf layer maintained by the back-end database. During RFID identification, a tag responds a group of values computed using the group of secret keys over a random challenge and the reader will use the group of responses to identify a tag. However, it is difficult to implement key updating because some keys are shared by different tags. Even worse, if one tag's secret is compromised, it may affect others and leak their secrets.

Next, we analyze the overhead of typical RFID protocols. Assume there are N tags in an RFID system. The hash-lock protocol in [18] requires an exhaustive search in the reader's database to identify a tag, so the overhead of this protocol is $O(N)$. In the OSK protocol [13], the reader has to calculate hash values with $O(N)$ complexity. Molnar and Wagner's method manages the keys of tags in [12] with a cost of $O(log(N))$. Although the cost is already much better than the exhaustive search in other protocols, it is still non-ignorable when the number of tags increases to unimaginable amount. At this time, the scalability is a headache of the database's administrator.

Therefore, we can see even if with the help of hash function, PRF, and tree structure, it is still a difficult problem to balance the security and scalability. Our improved protocol not only guarantees nearly all the security properties such that it protects tags from eavesdropping attacks, spoofing attacks, replay attacks, de-synchronization attacks, tracing attacks and compromising attacks, but also possesses constant key-lookup time in terms of exact match of an index in a database.

8   Conclusion

In this paper, we investigate the security and scalability of a newly proposed RFID authentication protocol by Burmester, Medeiros and Motta [2]. We found a subtle flaw in this protocol. Under a weak adversary model, an attacker can launch a three-run interleave attack to trace and identify a tag. Further on, complex attacking strategies can be constructed on cracking the whole supply chain using such an authentication protocol. We improve this protocol by eliminating the flaw in BMM protocol. We provide a security analysis on the improved protocol and claim that it meets its security requirements and that it is as efficient as the original protocol in each invocation.

Acknowledgment. This work is partly supported by A*Star SERC Grant No. 082 101 0022 in Singapore.

References

1. Avoine, G., Oechslin, P.: A scalable and provably secure hash-based RFID protocol. In: Third IEEE International Conference on Pervasive Computing and Communications Workshops, 2005. PerCom 2005 Workshops, pp. 110–114 (2005)
2. Burmester, M., de Medeiros, B., Motta, R.: Robust, anonymous RFID authentication with constant key-lookup. In: ASIACCS 2008: Proceedings of the 2008 ACM symposium on Information, computer and communications security, pp. 283–291. ACM, New York (2008)
3. Chatmon, C., van Le, T., Burmester, M.: Secure anonymous RFID authentication protocols. Technical Report TR-060112 (2006)
4. Czeskis, A., Koscher, K.: RFIDs and secret handshakes: defending against ghost-and-leech attacks and unauthorized reads with context-aware communications. In: Conference on Computer and Communications Security – ACM CCS, October 2008. ACM Press, New York (2008)
5. Dimitriou, T.: A Lightweight RFID Protocol to protect against Traceability and Cloning attacks. In: Conference on Security and Privacy for Emerging Areas in Communication Networks – SecureComm, Athens, Greece, September 2005. IEEE, Los Alamitos (2005)
6. Dimitriou, T.: A secure and efficient RFID protocol that could make big brother (partially) obsolete. In: IEEE International Conference on Pervasive Computing and Communications, pp. 269–275 (2006)
7. Goldreich, O., Goldwasser, S., Micali, S.: How to construct random functions. J. ACM 33(4), 792–807 (1986)
8. Juels, A.: RFID Security and Privacy: A Research Survey. IEEE Journal on Selected Areas in Communications 24(2), 381–394 (2006)
9. Juels, A., Pappu, R., Parno, B.: Unidirectional Key Distribution Across Time and Space with Applications to RFID Security. In: 17th USENIX Security Symposium, San Jose, CA, USA, July 2008, pp. 75–90. USENIX (2008)
10. Lim, T.-L., Li, T., Gu, T.: Secure rfid identification and authentication with triggered hash chain variants. In: ICPADS 2008: Proceedings of the 2008 14th IEEE International Conference on Parallel and Distributed Systems, Washington, DC, USA, pp. 583–590. IEEE Computer Society, Los Alamitos (2008)
11. Molnar, D., Soppera, A., Wagner, D.: A Scalable, Delegatable Pseudonym Protocol Enabling Ownership Transfer of RFID Tags. In: Preneel, B., Tavares, S. (eds.) SAC 2005. LNCS, vol. 3897, pp. 276–290. Springer, Heidelberg (2006)
12. Molnar, D., Wagner, D.: Privacy and Security in Library RFID: Issues, Practices, and Architectures. In: Pfitzmann, B., Liu, P. (eds.) Conference on Computer and Communications Security – ACM CCS, Washington, DC, USA, October 2004, pp. 210–219. ACM Press, New York (2004)
13. Ohkubo, M., Suzuki, K., Kinoshita, S.: Cryptographic Approach to "Privacy-Friendly" Tags. In: RFID Privacy Workshop, November 2003. MIT, MA (2003)
14. Rieback, M., Crispo, B., Tanenbaum, A.: RFID Guardian: A Battery-Powered Mobile Device for RFID Privacy Management. In: Boyd, C., González Nieto, J.M. (eds.) ACISP 2005. LNCS, vol. 3574, pp. 184–194. Springer, Heidelberg (2005)

15. Rieback, M., Crispo, B., Tanenbaum, A.: The Evolution of RFID Security. IEEE Pervasive Computing 5(1), 62–69 (2006)
16. Rotter, P.: A Framework for Assessing RFID System Security and Privacy Risks. IEEE Pervasive Computing 7(2), 70–77 (2008)
17. Tsudik, G.: YA-TRAP: Yet Another Trivial RFID Authentication Protocol. In: International Conference on Pervasive Computing and Communications – PerCom 2006, Pisa, Italy, March 2006. IEEE Computer Society Press, Los Alamitos (2006)
18. Weis, S., Sarma, S., Rivest, R., Engels, D.: Security and Privacy Aspects of Low-Cost Radio Frequency Identification Systems. In: Hutter, D., Müller, G., Stephan, W., Ullmann, M. (eds.) Security in Pervasive Computing. LNCS, vol. 2802, pp. 454–469. Springer, Heidelberg (2004)

Biometric Identification over Encrypted Data Made Feasible

Michael Adjedj[1,2], Julien Bringer[1], Hervé Chabanne[1,3], and Bruno Kindarji[1,3]

[1] Sagem Sécurité, Osny, France
[2] Université Bordeaux I, UFR de Mathématiques, Bordeaux, France
[3] Institut Telecom, Telecom ParisTech, Paris, France

Abstract. Realising a biometric identification scheme with the constraint of storing only encrypted data is an exciting challenge. Whereas a recent cryptographic primitive described by Bringer *et al.* and named Error-Tolerant Searchable Encryption achieves such a goal, the associated construction is not scalable to large databases. This paper shows how to move away from the model of Bringer *et al.*, and proposes to use Symmetric Searchable Encryption (SSE) as the baseline for biometric identification. The use of symmetric cryptography enables to achieve reasonable computational costs for each identification request.

This paper also provides a realistic security model for this problem, which is stronger than the one for SSE. In particular, the construction for biometric identification is resilient to statistical attacks, an aspect yet to be considered in the previous constructions of SSE.

As a practical example, parameters for the realisation of our scheme are provided in the case of iris recognition.

Keywords: Identification, Biometrics, Searchable Encryption.

1 Introduction

Biometric recognition systems are based on the unicity of some biological trait every human being carries along. For instance, it is possible to verify if a given individual is the one he claims to be (*Authentication*), or to find someone's identity using his biometrics (*Identification*).

In most cases, identification is done by comparing a new acquisition of the biometric trait (a biometric **template**) with a database that is stored on a server. The server can be outsourced, and we do not want it to learn more information than it ought to. If the database is not encrypted, or if the server first decrypts the data before comparing the traits, this leads to privacy leakage, as the server then learns personal information on the people that use the biometric system.

One of the inherent problems of working with some biometric templates is their fuzziness. Two captures by the same sensor, of the same biometric trait of the same person, are in most cases significantly different. The standard way to deal with this fuzziness is to use a matching function, which is able to tell whether two templates come from the same biometric trait.

A. Prakash and I. Sen Gupta (Eds.): ICISS 2009, LNCS 5905, pp. 86–100, 2009.

Using only traditional matching algorithms, the server has to execute $\mathcal{O}(N)$ matching comparisons to find a match among N biometric samples. This is infeasible in a satisfactory computation time for large databases. Unfortunately, matching algorithms that compare encrypted templates are rare – and expensive.

Moreover, doing an identification implies to look for the template among a collection that is the closest to the one presented at a sensor. Instead of doing all the traditional operations in the encrypted domain, we choose to do both the matching and the search at the same time. Combining encryption with search capabilities is a cryptographic primitive called **searchable encryption**.

To the best of our knowledge, the only construction that achieves biometric identification with encrypted biometric data is [5,6]. However the privacy of this construction is based on the use of a Private Information Retrieval protocol [8] and asymmetric cryptography; and such a protocol's computational complexity is always (at least) linear in the size of the database. To avoid this pitfall, we focus in this paper on symmetric cryptography.

Recent works on Symmetric Searchable Encryption [2,3,7,9,12,17] provide schemes with constant-time access to servers; the price to pay is a leakage of the **search pattern**: the server can tell whether a word was queried twice and can even recover links between documents and words. This enables to infer relations between requests and for instance to determine, after a statistical survey, the queried word. We formalize this advantage in the adversarial model stated in Section 4.2. In particular, Condition 3 is a barrier to statistical attacks. To cope with this classical weakness, we introduce a way to protect the access pattern on the server's side.

This paper solves the issue of preserving privacy in a biometric identification system. As opposed to previous work, the computational cost for this purpose is quite low, making use of recent advances in the fields of similarity searching and secure querying on a remote server. In the end, we perform biometric identification over a wholly encrypted database, in such a way that the server does not have an advantage over the users' privacy.

2   Basic Concepts

For a given biometric, let B be the set of all possible biometric features, *i.e.* data captured by a biometric sensor. Consider a user $\mathcal{U}$, his biometric trait is noted β. From a measurement of β using a sensor, the so-called **biometric template** is computed after feature extraction and is noted b ($b \in B$). A matching algorithm is a function $m : B \times B \to \mathbb{R}$, which computes a similarity score between two templates. Let b and b' be the results of two measurements from the same biometric. Then, with a high probability, their matching score $m(b, b')$ is **small**. We say that b and b' constitute a **matching pair**. Otherwise, when they are from different biometrics, with a high probability, their matching score is **large**. In practice, some thresholds are chosen λ_{min}, λ_{max} and the score is considered **small** (resp. **large**) if it is smaller (resp. greater) than λ_{min} (resp. λ_{max}). Depending on the values fixed for λ_{min} and λ_{max}, errors eventually occur: 1. The system declares two templates obtained from different users as a matching pair; this is called a False Acceptance (**FA**). 2. The system states that two templates extracted from the same user do not match; this is the False Reject case (**FR**).

At registration, a user chooses a pseudonym, also called an **identity**. A **biometric identification system** recognizes a person among others. On input b_{new}, the system returns a set of identities (corresponding to a templates set $\{b_{ref}\}$), such that all matching scores between b_{new} and the b_{ref}'s are small. This means that b_{new} and b_{ref} possibly correspond to the same person.

We restrict ourselves to the case where biometric templates are in the Hamming space $B = \{0, 1\}^n$ with the Hamming distance d (e.g. IrisCode [10]). Two templates b, b' of a same user $\mathcal{U}$ are with a high probability at distance $d(b, b') < \lambda_{min}$. Similarly, when b and b' comes from different users, they are with a high probability at distance $d(b, b') > \lambda_{max}$. In this case, and in the rest of the paper, the matching algorithm consists in evaluating a Hamming distance.

3   Useful Tools

3.1   Locality-Sensitive Hashing

For two different inputs with a small matching score, *i.e.* close in the sense of the Hamming distance, Locality-Sensitive Hash families output, with a high probability, the same value. We use them to decrease disparities between two similar templates.

Definition 1 (Locality-Sensitive Hashing [14]). *Let (B, d_B) be a metric space, U a set of smaller dimensionality. Let $r_1, r_2 \in \mathbb{R}$, $p_1, p_2 \in [0, 1]$ such that $p_1 > p_2$.*

*A family $H = \{h_1, \ldots, h_\mu\}$, $h_i : B \to U$ is (r_1, r_2, p_1, p_2)-**LSH**, if*

$$\forall h \in H, \ x, x' \in B \begin{cases} Pr[h(x) = h(x') \,|\, d_B(x, x') < r_1] > p_1 \\ Pr[h(x) = h(x') \,|\, d_B(x, x') > r_2] < p_2 \end{cases}$$

Some examples of LSH families are given in [5,13,14]. Another example of practical use is given in Section 5.1.

Remark 1. With regard to Definition 1, LSH hash functions have no cryptographic property. *Per se*, the security of our construction does not rely on the use of LSH functions.

3.2   Symmetric Searchable Encryption – SSE

Searchable Encryption is described as follows.

- A client $\mathcal{U}$ has a collection of documents consisting of sequences of words.
- He encrypts the whole collection along with some indexing data.
- He stores the result on a (remote) server.

The server should be able to return all documents which contain a particular keyword, without learning anything about the aforementioned keyword.

Let $\Delta = \{\omega_1, \cdots, \omega_d\}$ be the set of d distinct words (typically a dictionnary). A *document* $D \in \Delta^*$ is a sequence of words of Δ. The *identifier* $id(D)$ is a bitstring that uniquely identifies the document D (e.g. its memory address). A *collection* $\mathcal{D} = (D_1, \cdots, D_n)$ is a set of n documents. $\mathcal{D}(\omega)$ denotes the lexicographically ordered list of identifiers of documents which contains the word ω.

For efficiency reasons, we only focus on the **symmetric** searchable encryption paradigm.

Definition 2 (Symmetric Searchable Encryption Scheme [9]). *A Symmetric Searchable Encryption scheme is a collection of four polynomial-time algorithms* Keygen, BuildIndex, Trapdoor, Search *such that:*

Keygen (1^ℓ) *is a probabilistic key generation algorithm, run by the client to setup the scheme. It takes a security parameter ℓ and returns a secret key K.*

BuildIndex $(K, \mathcal{D})$ *is a (possibly probabilistic) algorithm run by the client to compute the index $\mathcal{I}_\mathcal{D}$ of the collection $\mathcal{D}$. It takes as entry a secret key K and a collection of documents $\mathcal{D}$. The index returned allows the server to search for any keyword appearing in $\mathcal{D}$.*

Trapdoor (K, ω) *is a deterministic algorithm which generates a trapdoor T_ω for a given word ω under the secret key K. It is perfomed by the client whenever he wants to search securely for all the documents where ω occurs.*

Search $(\mathcal{I}_\mathcal{D}, T_w)$ *is run by the server to search in the entire collection $\mathcal{D}$ for all the documents identifiers where the queried word ω appears. It returns $\mathcal{D}(\omega)$.*

These primitives give a functional aspect of what Symmetric Searchable Encryption provides. The associated security model is described in [9], and briefly depicted in Appendix A.1. The goal is to achieve *Adaptive Indistinguishability*, a security property stating that an adversary does not get information on the content of the registered documents. More precisely, if two different collections are registered, with constraints on the number of words per document, an adversary cannot distinguish between two sequences of search requests.

Remark 2. A noticeable construction of a scheme adaptively indistinguishable was also provided in [9] (cf. Appendix A.2), and inspired our identification data structure. Although this scheme is proved secure in their model, this does not cover statistical attacks where an adversary tries to break the confidentiality of the documents or the words based on statistics about the queried words and the index (cf. Remark 5).

4   Fast and Secure Biometric Identification

Our construction does not simply mix a SSE scheme with a LSH family. Indeed, we ensure the security of our biometric identification protocol against statistical attacks, which is an improvement with respect to a direct combination of SSE with LSH.

4.1 Our Idea in a Nutshell

Our Biometric Identification process has two phases: a **search phase** which carries out every request on the database $\mathcal{DB}$ and sends back to the sensor client $\mathcal{SC}$ the search result, an **identification phase** which treats data extracted from search results to proceed to the identification. The search phase is constructed following the principle of the SSE scheme from [9]. The following entities interact:

- Human users $\mathcal{U}_i$: a set of N users who register their biometrics.
- Sensor client $\mathcal{SC}$: a device that captures the biometric data and extracts its characteristics to output the biometric template. It also sends queries to the server to identify a user.
- The server: replies to queries sent by $\mathcal{SC}$ by providing a set of search results and owns a database $\mathcal{DB}$ to store the data related to the registered users.

Remark 3. We consider that $\mathcal{SC}$ is honest and trusted by all other components. In particular, $\mathcal{SC}$ is the only entity which is in possession of the cryptographic key material used in the protocol. To justify this assumption, we emphasize that the object of this paper is to provide a solution to the secure storage of reference templates, but not to provide an end-to-end architecture. See Remark 6 for details on key management.

We provide the three following methods:

1. `Initialize`(1^ℓ): It produces the parameters $\mathcal{K}$ of the system, according to a security parameter ℓ. $\mathcal{K}$ must contain secret keys sk used to encrypt the identities, and K used in the SSE scheme.
2. `Enrolment`$(b_1, \ldots, b_N, ID_1, \ldots, ID_N, \mathcal{K})$: It registers a set of users with their biometric characteristics. For a user $\mathcal{U}_i$, it needs a biometric sample b_i and his identity ID_i. This returns an index $\mathcal{I}$.
3. `Identification`$(\mathcal{K}, b)$: It takes as input a newly captured template b and it returns a set of identities for which the associated templates are close to b. See Conditions 1 and 2, Section 4.2.

Definition 3. *In our proposal,* keywords *are evaluations of LSH functions on templates, concatenated with the index of the considered function, i.e. $h_i(b)\|i$, for $i \in [1, \mu]$ where b is the captured template of a user.*

Identifiers are the encryptions of the identities of the registered users. We have, $\mathrm{id}(\mathcal{U}_i) = \mathcal{E}_{sk}(ID_i)$ *for $i \in [1, N]$ where $\mathcal{E}_{sk}$ is an encryption function with the secret key sk, and ID_i is the identity of the user $\mathcal{U}_i$.*

The interaction between the server and $\mathcal{SC}$ defines the identification view, required for the security experiments. It consists of the encrypted identities of the registered users, and informations sent by $\mathcal{SC}$ when a user $\mathcal{U}$ is being identified.

Definition 4 (Identification View). *The* identification view *under the secret keys K and sk is defined as*

$$IdV_{K,sk}(b') = (\mathcal{I}, T_{h_1(b')\|1}, \ldots, T_{h_\mu(b')\|\mu}, \mathcal{E}_{sk}(ID_1), \ldots, \mathcal{E}_{sk}(ID_N))$$

where b' is a freshly captured template from $\mathcal{U}$.

4.2   Security Requirements

We assume that the Hamming space $B = \{0,1\}^n$ is such that $n \geq \ell$, where ℓ is the security parameter. A function f is said to be negligible if for all non-constant polynomial P, and for all sufficiently large k, we have $f(k) < \frac{1}{|P(k)|}$. In the sequel, a probability is negligible if it is negligible in ℓ.

First of all it is important that the scheme actually works, *i.e.* that the retrieval of the identity of a registered user gives the correct result. This can be formalized by the two following conditions.

Condition 1 (Completeness). *The system is* complete *if for all $b' \in B$, the result of* Identification(b') *contains the set of identities for which the associated templates b_i are close to b' (ie. $d(b', b_i) < \lambda_{min}$), except for a negligible probability.*

Condition 2 (Soundness). *The system is* sound *if, for each template b' such that $d(b', b_i) > \lambda_{max}$,* Identification$(b')$ *is the empty set $\emptyset$, except with negligible probability.*

To avoid statistical attacks, we do not want the database to infer relations between different identities. This is modeled by the following condition.

Condition 3 (Adaptive Confidentiality). *An identification system achieves adaptive confidentiality if the advantage* $\text{Adv}_{\mathcal{A}} = |\Pr(b_0 = b'_0) - \frac{1}{|B|}|$ *of any polynomial-time adaptive adversary is negligible in the next experiment, where $\mathcal{A} = (\mathcal{A}_1, \mathcal{A}_2)$ is an opponent taking the place of the server, and $\mathcal{C}$ is a challenger at $\mathcal{SC}$'s side.*

1. $\mathcal{K}$	$\xleftarrow{R}$	Initialize(1^{ℓ})	$(\mathcal{C})$
2. $b_1, \ldots, b_N$	$\longleftarrow$	B	$(\mathcal{A})$
3. $\mathcal{I}_1$	$\longleftarrow$	Enrolment$(b_1, \ldots, b_N)$	$(\mathcal{C})$
4. $b, IdV_{K,sk}(b)$	$\longleftarrow$	$\mathcal{A}_1^{\texttt{Identification}}(\mathcal{I}_1)$	$(\mathcal{A})$
5. b_0	$\xleftarrow{R}$	B	$(\mathcal{C})$
		such that $\forall i \in [1, N], d(b_0, b_i) > \lambda_{max}$	
6. $\mathcal{I}_2$	$\longleftarrow$	Enrolment$(b_0, b_1, \ldots, b_N)$	
6'. $b, IdV_{K,sk}(b)$	$\longleftarrow$	$\mathcal{A}_1^{\texttt{Identification}}(\mathcal{I}_1, \mathcal{I}_2)$	$(\mathcal{A})$
7. b'_0	$\longleftarrow$	$\mathcal{A}_2(\mathcal{I}_1, \mathcal{I}_2, b, IdV_{K,sk}(b), IdV_{K,sk}(b_0))$	

Enrolment$(b_1, \ldots, b_N)$ *stands for* Enrolment$(b_1, \ldots, b_N, ID_1, \ldots, ID_N, K, sk)$.

In this game, the attacker is allowed to set a templates database $b_1, \ldots, b_N$ of its choice (2.). Then the challenger creates the database by enrolling the whole collection (3.), and the adversary can make a polynomial number of identifications (using the method Identification) of the templates of his choice (4.). The challenger then picks a random template b_0 (5.) and it recreates the database $\mathcal{I}_2$ (6.). The attacker is allowed once again to make a polynomial number of identifications from the templates of its choice (6'.) and he is challenged to retrieve the initial template b_0 (7.), given the knowledge of $\mathcal{I}_1, \mathcal{I}_2$, and the views of the identifications.

This condition expresses the confidentiality of the enrolled templates, even if the adversary has access to the index and to identification views, which may give him the possibility to construct a statistical model on it.

Condition 4 (Non-adaptive Indistinguishability). *We say that a biometric identification system achieves indistinguishability if the advantage* $\mathsf{Adv}_{\mathcal{A}} = |\Pr(e = e') - \frac{1}{2}|$ *of any polynomial-time adversary* $\mathcal{A} = (\mathcal{A}_1, \mathcal{A}_2)$ *is negligible in the following game:*

$$
\left|
\begin{array}{lll}
1.\ b_1, \dots, b_N & \stackrel{R}{\longleftarrow} B & (\mathcal{C}) \\
2.\ b^{(0)}, b^{(1)} & \longleftarrow \mathcal{A}_1(\mathcal{C}(IdV_{K,sk})) & (\mathcal{A}) \\
3.\ e & \stackrel{R}{\longleftarrow} \{0,1\} & (\mathcal{C}) \\
4.\ e' & \longleftarrow \mathcal{A}_2(IdV_{K,sk}(b^{(e)})) & (\mathcal{A})
\end{array}
\right.
$$

where $\mathcal{A}_1(\mathcal{C}(IdV_{K,sk}))$ *stands for the fact that the adversary accesses to the identification view produced when* $\mathcal{C}$ *executes a polynomial number of identification requests, without knowing the input randomly chosen by the challenger.*

This experiment is executed as follows: The challenger first creates a set of templates $b_1, \dots, b_N$ (1.), and executes a polynomial number of identification requests. The adversary has access to all the identification views (2.). The attacker then chooses two templates for which he believes he has an advantage (2.), and the challenger picks at random one of them and executes its identification (3.). The attacker is finally challenged to determine which template the challenger chose (4.).

4.3 Our Identification Protocol

<u>Initialize</u>(1^{ℓ}):

- We choose an IND-CPA symmetric encryption scheme $(\mathcal{G}, \mathcal{E}, \mathcal{D})$.
- We use the Symmetric Searchable Encryption scheme from [9] (see Appendix A.2 for the construction detail) out of which we pick the functions (Keygen, Trapdoor, Search) and adapt them to our needs.
- We fix a threshold $0 < \lambda \leq \frac{1}{2}$.
- Let $H = (h_1, \dots, h_{\mu})$ be a $(\lambda_{min}, \lambda_{max}, p_1, p_2)$- LSH family, $\mu \geq \ell$.
- Let $K = \mathtt{KeyGen}(1^{\ell})$, and $sk = \mathcal{G}(1^{\ell})$.
- Let π_K be the pseudo-random permutation indexed by the key K used in the SSE scheme.

Output $\mathcal{K} = (h_1, \dots, h_{\mu}, K, sk, \lambda)$.

<u>Enrolment</u>$(b_1, \dots, b_N, ID_1, \dots, ID_N, \mathcal{K})$: Consider N users $\mathcal{U}_1, \dots, \mathcal{U}_N$ to be enrolled. Their template are denoted by b_i, and their identity ID_i, $i \in [1, N]$. We recall that in our construction, the words we consider are the $h_i(b)\|i$, $i \in$

<u>Enrolment</u>$(b_1, \ldots, b_N, ID_1, \ldots, ID_N, \mathcal{K})$:

- Initialization:
  - build $\Delta = \{h_i(b_k) || i; \quad i \in [1, \mu], \ k \in [1, N]\}$
  - for each $\omega_{i_k} \in \Delta$, build $\mathcal{D}(\omega_{i_k})$ the set of identifiers of users $\mathcal{U}_{k'}$ such that $h_i(b_{k'}) || i = \omega_{i_k}$
  - compute $\mathtt{max} = \max_{\omega \in \Delta}(|\mathcal{D}(\omega)|)$ and $m = \mathtt{max} \cdot |\Delta|$
- Build look-up table T:
  - for each $\omega_i \in \Delta$
    for $1 \leq j \leq |\mathcal{D}(\omega_i)|$
      set $\mathtt{T} [\pi_K(\omega_i \,\|\, j)] = \mathcal{E}_{sk}(ID_{i,j})$
  - if $m' = \sum_{\omega_i \in \Delta} |\mathcal{D}(\omega_i)| < m$,then set the remaining $(m - m')$ entries of T to random values.
- Output $\mathcal{I} = \mathtt{T}$

Fig. 1. Enrolment Procedure

$[1, \mu]$, $b \in B$, where h_i is one of the chosen LSH functions, and b is a reference template from a registered user.

We alter the `BuildIndex` algorithm of the SSE scheme into `Enrolment` to take into account the need for identification (cf. Figure 1).

Remark 4. Our scheme stores identifiers encrypted by an IND-CPA scheme so that no relation between the entries could be found by observing the index $\mathcal{I}$. This prevents inferring statistics from the $\mathcal{DB}$ content. Proposition 3 formalizes this intuition.

<u>Identification</u>$(\mathcal{K}, b')$:
Search phase: When a user $\mathcal{U}$ wants to be identified, $\mathcal{SC}$ captures his biometric trait in a template b'. $\mathcal{SC}$ evaluates each LSH function on b' to compute $\omega_{k_i} = h_i(b') || i, i \in [1, \mu]$ and sends to the server the trapdoors:

$$T_{\omega_{k_i}} = \mathtt{Trapdoor}(K, \omega_{k_i}) = (\pi_K(\omega_{k_i} || 1), \ldots, \pi_K(\omega_{k_i} || \mathtt{max}))$$

The server executes the `Search` algorithm on the different trapdoors $T_{\omega_{k_i}}$ – each call to $\mathtt{Search}(t_1, \ldots, t_{\max})$ returns $\mathtt{T}[t_1], \ldots \mathtt{T}[t_{\max}]$ – and sends to $\mathcal{SC}$ the array $\mathcal{ID}(b')$ which corresponds to all the search results:

$$\mathcal{ID}(b') = \begin{bmatrix} \mathcal{E}_{sk}(ID_{k_1,1}) & \cdots & \mathcal{E}_{sk}(ID_{k_1,\max}) \\ \vdots & \ddots & \vdots \\ \mathcal{E}_{sk}(ID_{k_\mu,1}) & \cdots & \mathcal{E}_{sk}(ID_{k_\mu,\max}) \end{bmatrix}$$

where each row is made of the output of $\mathtt{Search}(T_{\omega_{k_i}})$. It may happen that a virtual address $\pi_K(h_i(b') || i || j)$ is invalid, in this case the server sends NULL instead of an identifier.

Identification phase: $\mathcal{SC}$ decrypts all received identifiers and determines the number of occurrences of each identity to output the list of the ones that appear more than $\lambda\mu$ times, *i.e.* the list of identities $\{ID(\mathcal{U}_l)\}$ that verify this inequality: $\sum_{i=1}^{\mu}\sum_{j=1}^{\max} \mathbb{1}_{ID(\mathcal{U}_l)}\left(ID_{k_i,j}\right) > \lambda\mu$, where $\mathbb{1}$ is the indicator function. If the result is still ambiguous after that the identity that appeared the most was selected, an empirical rule is applied.

4.4   Security Properties

We use Shannon's entropy, $\mathcal{H}_2(\lambda) = \lambda \cdot log\frac{1}{\lambda} + (1 - \lambda) \cdot log\frac{1}{1-\lambda}$

Proposition 1 (Completeness). *Provided that H is a $(\lambda_{min}, \lambda_{max}, p_1, p_2)$-LSH family, for $1 - p_1 \leq \frac{1}{4\mathcal{H}_2(\lambda)+c}$, with $c \geq 1$, our scheme is complete.*

Proposition 2 (Soundness). *Provided that H is a $(\lambda_{min}, \lambda_{max}, p_1, p_2)$-LSH family, for $p_2 \leq \frac{1}{2^{\frac{1}{\lambda}+c}}$, with $c \geq 1$, our scheme is sound.*

The proofs of Propositions 1 and 2 are given in Appendix B. The underlying idea is that computing the μ LSH functions separates the close and the distant template pairs.

Proposition 3 (Adaptive Confidentiality). *Provided that the underlying encryption scheme $(\mathcal{G}, \mathcal{E}, \mathcal{D})$ is a IND-CPA secure scheme, our construction ensures the templates confidentiality.*

Sketch of Proof. The adversary $\mathcal{A}$ is allowed to execute some identification requests. If $\mathcal{A}$ is able to reconstruct the template b_0, then he can infer links between the enrolled b_i and the associated identification result $\mathcal{ID}(b_0)$.

Due to the IND-CPA security of $(\mathcal{G}, \mathcal{E}, \mathcal{D})$, a simulator can simulate the array $\mathcal{ID}(b)$ during the second enrolment phase in the following way: when it receives for the first time a set of trapdoors $\{T_{h_1(b||1)}, \ldots, T_{h_\mu(b||\mu)}\}$, for a template b, it picks up a random array of size $\mu \cdot \mathtt{max}$ and stores the correspondence between the trapdoors and this array. When the adversary sends the same trapdoors, the same result is sent back by the simulator. This way, an adversary who can make links between informations contained in the array $\mathcal{ID}(b)$, can also infer links between random identifiers, which is impossible. Thus the property. □

Proposition 4 (Non-Adaptive Indistinguishability). *Provided that π_K is a pseudo-random permutation depending on a secret key K, and that $(\mathcal{G}, \mathcal{E}, \mathcal{D})$ is semantically secure, our construction ensures the non-adaptive indistinguishability.*

Sketch of Proof. This property is mainly a consequence of the semantic security of the SSE scheme we consider. Indeed, for π_K a pseudo-random permutation, a simulator can simulate the trapdoors sent by the sensor client during an identification, and it can also simulate the server's response because of the semantic security of the symmetric encryption scheme used. □

Remark 5. We emphasize that the aforementioned properties define an adequate description of what resistance against statistical attacks would be.

A scheme, that would be no more than a combination of the SSE scheme described in [9] with the use of LSH functions, would not be resistant against these methods. An adversary is, in that setting, able to retrieve – and compare – the identifiers of the users enrolled, and thus infer knowledge on the identity of a user that did not proceed to identification.

Similarly, if the identifiers are not encrypted, an attacker who observes the views of identification can gather statistics on the identification of the different users. This enables him to link the identity of users - as some are more likely to be identified than others - with the response of the server. Moreover, he can manage a very general statistical attack in that case: by learning the relation between identities and keywords (i.e. LSH values of biometric data), he can even reconstruct unknown templates.

Note that our technique to thwart statistical attacks is quite general and can be reused in other contexts.

5   Practical Considerations

5.1   Choosing a LSH Family

To explain that our scheme meets the usual needs for a practical deployment of a biometric identification system, let us consider the case of biometric iris recognition as a practical example. A well-known method to represent iris is to use Daugman's IrisCode [10] algorithm. The outcome is a 4096-bit vector, where half of them carry information held in the iris, and the other part is a "mask" of the significant bits.

In [13], a method to increase the efficiency of iris identification is described. By applying specific projection functions into $\{0, 1\}^{10}$, the search among an iris dataset can be accelerated. The projected values of an iriscode serve in a pre-filtering step. Experiments successfully reported in [13] on a UAE database, containing $N = 632500$ iris records, show that it decreases the number of necessary matching to 41 instead of N to achieve identification. The authors determine a biometric template b as a candidate for b' if b and b' give the same evaluations with at least three functions; see [13] for more details. Their functions can be in fact considered as a $(\lambda_{min}, \lambda_{max}, (1 - \frac{\lambda_{min}}{2048})^{10}, (1 - \frac{\lambda_{max}}{2048})^{10})$-LSH family and we can thus apply our construction without degrading their results. This shows the actual practicality of our scheme.

The family is made by $\mu = 128$ hash functions, which each extracts a 10-bit vector. Our parameter λ can be set to $\lambda = \frac{3}{128}$. According to traditional matching algorithms, we can choose $\lambda_{min} = 0.25 \cdot 2048 = 512$ and $\lambda_{max} = 0.35 \cdot 2048 = 716.8$, which gives the probabilities $p_1 \simeq 0.056$ and $p_2 \simeq 0.013$ (with the notations of Definition 1). The probability of Identification(b') *not* returning a template close to b' is given by $\sum_{i=0}^{\lfloor \lambda \mu \rfloor} \binom{\mu}{i} p_1^i (1 - p_1)^{\mu-i} \simeq 0.066$ and the other probability to consider is, for b' far from all the b_i, $\Pr[\text{Identification}(b') \neq$

$\emptyset] = \sum_{i=\lceil \lambda \mu \rceil}^{\mu} \binom{\mu}{i} p_2^i (1 - p_2)^{\mu-i} \simeq 0.095$. Note that those probabilities are small, and not negligible, but they can be considered attractive for practical uses (as asserted by the results from [13]).

5.2 Implementation

To check further the feasibility of our scheme, we implemented our scheme and conduced a first empirical evaluation on the ICE 2005 database [15,16] which contains 2953 images from 244 different eyes. The results are similar to those deduced in the previous section from the results of [13]. For instance, the probability that the genuine identity is not in the outputted list of candidates is below 10%.

Remark 6. In addition to this performance consideration, it is important to notice that the deployment of the scheme is quite simple as only the client needs to know the secret keys. So management of the keys is reduced to a distribution to the clients that are allowed to run identification requests onto the remote server.

For a similar reason, the scheme only uses classical cryptographic schemes; therefore it does not suffer of the same weaknesses [1] as some other biometric protection schemes.

5.3 Complexity

We here evaluate the computational complexity of an identification request on the server's side as well as on $\mathcal{SC}$. We note $\kappa(op)$ the cost of operation op.

- On the server's side: assuming that we organize the look-up table in a *FKS* dictionnary [11], a search is made in constant time and the server has μ searches to achieve.
- On $\mathcal{SC}$'s side:

$$\kappa(identification) = \kappa(trapdoors) + \kappa(count)$$
$$= \mu.\texttt{max}.\left[\kappa(hash) + \kappa(encryption) + \kappa(decryption)\right]$$

$\kappa(hash)$ is the computational complexity to evaluate a LSH function, and $\kappa(encryption)$ is the one to apply the pseudo-random permutation π_K. The final count needs to compute the number of occurences of each identity, it can be made in computation time linear in the size of the final array, hence the term $\mu.\texttt{max}.\kappa(decryption)$ (remember that before counting, $\mathcal{SC}$ has to decrypt the search results). If the chosen hash functions map $\{0,1\}^*$ to $\{0,1\}^m$ (for $m \in \mathbb{N}^*$) and assuming that images of these functions are equally distributed, the `max` value can be bounded by $\mathcal{O}(\frac{N}{2^m})$, where N is the number of registered users. So the overall complexity is $\mathcal{O}\left(\mu \frac{N}{2^m}\right) \cdot \left[\kappa(hash) + \kappa(encryption) + \kappa(decryption)\right]$. A traditional identification algorithm would cost $\mathcal{O}(N)$ matching operations; with the parameters given in Section 5.1, our solution is 8 times more efficient, with the additional benefit of the encryption of the data.

Remark 7. The complexity of the construction initially proposed in [6] was globally the same at the client level (modulo the use of asymmetric cryptography rather than symmetric schemes in our case). It consists in computing the LSH images of the freshly acquired template, and in preparing μ PIR queries associated to the hashes. While this computation is costly, it is still doable in reasonable time. However on the server side, $\mathcal{S}$ must compute the PIR replies, and cannot do it in less than a linear time in the database's size (2^m). Indeed, no matter what PIR scheme is used, $\mathcal{S}$ always needs to process the whole database before sending its reply; here we enable secure biometric identification with only μ constant-time operations at $\mathcal{S}$'s side.

Acknowledgements

The authors thank the referees for their comments. This work is partially supported by funding under the Seventh Research Framework Programme of the European Union, Project TURBINE (ICT-2007-216339).

References

1. Ballard, L., Kamara, S., Reiter, M.K.: The practical subtleties of biometric key generation. In: van Oorschot, P.C. (ed.) [18], pp. 61–74
2. Bellare, M., Boldyreva, A., O'Neill, A.: Deterministic and Efficiently Searchable Encryption. In: Menezes, A. (ed.) CRYPTO 2007. LNCS, vol. 4622, pp. 535–552. Springer, Heidelberg (2007)
3. Boneh, D., Di Crescenzo, G., Ostrovsky, R., Persiano, G.: Public Key Encryption with Keyword Search. In: Cachin, C., Camenisch, J.L. (eds.) EUROCRYPT 2004. LNCS, vol. 3027, pp. 506–522. Springer, Heidelberg (2004)
4. Boneh, D., Kushilevitz, E., Ostrovsky, R., Skeith III, W.E.: Public Key Encryption That Allows PIR Queries. In: Menezes, A. (ed.) CRYPTO 2007. LNCS, vol. 4622, pp. 50–67. Springer, Heidelberg (2007)
5. Bringer, J., Chabanne, H., Kindarji, B.: Error-tolerant searchable encryption. In: IEEE International Conference on Communications, 2009. ICC 2009, June 2009, pp. 1–6 (2009)
6. Bringer, J., Chabanne, H., Kindarji, B.: Identification with encrypted biometric data. CoRR abs/0901.1062 (2009) Full version of [5]
7. Chang, Y.C., Mitzenmacher, M.: Privacy Preserving Keyword Searches on Remote Encrypted Data. In: Ioannidis, J., Keromytis, A.D., Yung, M. (eds.) ACNS 2005. LNCS, vol. 3531, pp. 442–455. Springer, Heidelberg (2005)
8. Chor, B., Kushilevitz, E., Goldreich, O., Sudan, M.: Private Information Retrieval. J. ACM 45(6), 965–981 (1998)
9. Curtmola, R., Garay, J., Kamara, S., Ostrovsky, R.: Searchable Symmetric Encryption: Improved Definitions and Efficient Constructions. In: CCS 2006: Proceedings of the 13th ACM conference on Computer and communications security, pp. 79–88. ACM, New York (2006)
10. Daugman, J.: High Confidence Visual Recognition of Persons by a Test of Statistical Independence. IEEE Trans. Pattern Anal. Mach. Intell. 15(11), 1148–1161 (1993)

11. Fredman, M.L., Komlós, J., Szemerédi, E.: Storing a Sparse Table with O(1) Worst Case Access Time. ACM 31 (1984)
12. Goh, E.-J.: Secure Indexes. Cryptology ePrint Archive, Report 2003/216 (2003), http://eprint.iacr.org/2003/216/
13. Hao, F., Daugman, J., Zielinski, P.: A Fast Search Algorithm for a Large Fuzzy Database. IEEE Transactions on Information Forensics and Security 3(2), 203–212 (2008)
14. Indyk, P., Motwani, R.: Approximate Nearest Neighbors: Towards Removing the Curse of Dimensionality. In: Symposium on the Theory of Computing (1998)
15. Liu, X., Bowyer, K.W., Flynn, P.J.: Iris Recognition and Verification Experiments with Improved Segmentation Method. In: Fourth IEEE Workshop on Automatic Identification Advanced Technologies (AutoID), Buffalo, New York, October 17-18 (2005)
16. National Institute of Standards and Technology (NIST). Iris Challenge Evaluation (2005), http://iris.nist.gov/ICE
17. Sedghi, S., van Liesdonk, P., Doumen, J.M., Hartel, P.H., Jonker, W.: Adaptively Secure Computationally Efficient Searchable Symmetric Encryption. Technical Report TR-CTIT-09-13 (April 2009)
18. van Oorschot, P.C. (ed.): Proceedings of the 17th USENIX Security Symposium, San Jose, CA, USA, July 28-August 1. USENIX Association (2008)

A   Security Model Associated to Symmetric Searchable Encryption

The following model for Symmetric Searchable Encryption was proposed in [9]. We briefly state the requirements and provide the construction given by the authors to comply with the model.

A.1   Security Model for Symmetric Searchable Encryption

A **history** H_q is an interaction between a client and a server over q queries, consisting of a collection of documents $\mathcal{D}$ and q keywords $\omega_1, \cdots, \omega_q$. Let $\mathcal{D}$ be a collection of n documents $(D_1, \cdots, D_n)$, and let Enc be an encryption function. If the documents of $\mathcal{D}$ are stored encrypted by Enc, and $H_q = (\mathcal{D}, \omega_1, \cdots, \omega_q)$ is a history over q queries, an adversary's **view** of H_q under the secret key K is defined as

$$V_K(H_q) = (id(D_1), \ldots, id(D_n), \text{Enc}_K(D_1), \ldots, \text{Enc}_K(D_n), \mathcal{I}_\mathcal{D}, T_{\omega_1}, \ldots, T_{\omega_q})$$

The History and the View of an interaction determine what did an adversary obtain after a client executed the protocol; an estimation of the information leaked is given by the Trace. Let $H_q = (\mathcal{D}, \omega_1, \ldots, \omega_q)$ be a history over q queries. The **trace** of H_q is the sequence

$$Tr(H_q) = (id(D_1), \ldots, id(D_n), |D_1|, \ldots, |D_n|, \mathcal{D}(\omega_1), \ldots, \mathcal{D}(\omega_q), \Pi_q)$$

where Π_q is a symmetric matrix representing the access pattern, *i.e.* $\Pi_q[i,j] = 1$ if $\omega_i = \omega_j$, and $\Pi_q[i,j] = 0$ otherwise.

For such a scheme, the security definition is the following.

Definition 5 (Adaptive Indistinguishability Security for SSE [9]). *A SSE scheme is said to be adaptively indistinguishable if for all $q \in \mathbb{N}$ and for all probabilistic polynomial-time adversaries $\mathcal{A}$, for all traces Tr_q of length q, and for all polynomially sampleable distributions*

$$\mathcal{H}_q = \{H_q \ : \ Tr(H_q) = Tr_q\}$$

(i.e. the set of all histories of trace Tr_q), the advantage $\mathtt{Adv}_{\mathcal{A}} = \left|\Pr\left[b' = b\right] - \frac{1}{2}\right|$ of the adversary is negligible.

$\mathrm{Exp}_{\mathcal{A}}^{IND}$

1. K	$\leftarrow \mathtt{Keygen}(1^k)$	$(\mathcal{C})$
2. $(\mathcal{D}_0, \mathcal{D}_1)$	$\leftarrow \mathcal{A}$	$(\mathcal{A})$
3. b	$\xleftarrow{R} \{0,1\}$	$(\mathcal{C})$
4. $(\omega_{1,0}, \omega_{1,1})$	$\leftarrow \mathcal{A}(\mathcal{I}_b)$	$(\mathcal{A})$
5. $T_{\omega_{1,b}}$	$\leftarrow \mathtt{Trapdoor}(K, \omega_{1,b})$	$(\mathcal{C})$
6. $(\omega_{i+1,0}, \omega_{i+1,1}) \leftarrow \mathcal{A}(\mathcal{I}_b, T_{\omega_{1,b}}, \ldots, T_{\omega_{i,b}})$ *for $i = 1, \ldots, q-1$*		$(\mathcal{A})$
7. $T_{\omega_{i+1,b}}$	$\leftarrow \mathtt{Trapdoor}(K, \omega_{i+1,b})$	$(\mathcal{C})$
8. b'	$\leftarrow \mathcal{A}(V_K(H_b))$	$(\mathcal{A})$

In this experiment, the attacker begins by choosing two collections of documents (2.), which each contains the same number of keywords; then the challenger follows by flipping a coin b (3.), and the adversary receives the index of one of the collections $\mathcal{D}_b$; he then submits two words $(\omega_{1,0}, \omega_{1,1})$ (4.) and receives the trapdoor for $\omega_{1,b}$ (5.). The process goes on until the adversary has submitted q queries (6. and 7.) and he is challenged to output b (8.).

A.2   SSE Construction

The algorithms that implement the Symmetric Searchable Encryption in [9] are depicted in Figure 2. The scheme is proven indistinguishable against adaptive adversaries.

For this construction, a pseudo-random permutation noted π_K is used, where K is the secret key of the system. The security of this scheme rests on the indistinguishability of this pseudo-random permutation which ensures the indistinguishability of the sent data.

B   Detailed Proofs

B.1   Proof of Proposition 1

Let $\mathcal{U}$ be a registered user to be identified, with reference template b and identity $ID(\mathcal{U})$. Let b' be a freshly captured template such that $d(b, b') < \lambda_{min}$. The scheme is complete if the probability for $ID(\mathcal{U})$ not to be returned is negligible, *i.e.* if $ID(\mathcal{U})$ appears less than $\lambda\mu$ times in $\mathcal{ID}(b')$.

Let us consider the event E_i : "$\mathcal{E}_{sk}(ID(\mathcal{U}))$ does not appear in row i of $\mathcal{ID}(b')$". E_i happens if and only if $h_i(b')||i||j \neq h_i(b)||i||j$, which happens with probability $1 - p_1$. Then, the probability for the scheme not to be complete is given

---

<u>**Keygen**</u>(1^k): Generate a random key $K \xleftarrow{R} \{0,1\}^k$

<u>**BuildIndex**</u> $(K, \mathcal{D})$:

- Initialization:
    - scan $\mathcal{D}$ and build Δ, the set of distinct words in $\mathcal{D}$.
    - for each $\omega \in \Delta$, build $\mathcal{D}(\omega)$
    - compute $\texttt{max} = \max_{\omega \in \Delta}(|\mathcal{D}(\omega)|)$ and $m = \texttt{max} \cdot |\Delta|$
- Build look-up table **T** :
    - for each $\omega_i \in \Delta$
        for $1 \le j \le |\mathcal{D}(\omega_i)|$
            set $\texttt{T}\,[\pi_K(\omega_i \parallel j)] = \texttt{id}(D_{i,j})$
    - if $m' = \sum_{\omega_i \in \Delta} |\mathcal{D}(\omega_i)| < m$, then set the remaining $(m - m')$ entries of **T** to identifiers of documents $\texttt{id}(D_r)$, $r \in \{1, \ldots, n\}$ such that the same identifier holds for the same number of entries.
- Output $\mathcal{I}_{\mathcal{D}} = \texttt{T}$

<u>**Trapdoor**</u> (K, ω): Output $T_\omega = (\pi_K(\omega \parallel 1), \ldots, \pi_K(\omega \parallel \texttt{max}))$

<u>**Search**</u> $(\mathcal{I}_{\mathcal{D}}, T_\omega)$: For $1 \le i \le \texttt{max}$: retrieve $\texttt{id} = \mathcal{I}_{\mathcal{D}}\,[T_\omega[i]]$

Fig. 2. Adaptively secure SSE construction [9]

by: $\Pr\left[ID(\mathcal{U}) \text{ appears in less than } \lfloor \lambda\mu \rfloor \text{ positions }\right] = \sum_{i=0}^{\lfloor \lambda\mu \rfloor} \binom{\mu}{i} p_1^i (1 - p_1)^{\mu-i}$. But, considering $1 - p_1 \le \frac{1}{4^{\mathcal{H}_2(\lambda)+c}}$, we have: $(1 - p_1)^{\mu-i} \le \frac{1}{4^{(\mathcal{H}_2(\lambda)+c)(\mu-i)}} \le \frac{1}{4^{(\mathcal{H}_2(\lambda)+c)(\frac{\mu}{2})}} = \frac{1}{2^{\mu(\mathcal{H}_2(\lambda)+c)}}$.

Thus,
$$\sum_{i=0}^{\lfloor \lambda\mu \rfloor} \binom{\mu}{i} p_1^i (1 - p_1)^{\mu-i} \le \sum_{i=0}^{\lfloor \lambda\mu \rfloor} \binom{\mu}{i} (1 - p_1)^{\mu-i} \le (\lfloor \lambda\mu \rfloor + 1) \cdot \frac{2^{\mu \mathcal{H}_2(\lambda)}}{2^{\mu(\mathcal{H}_2(\lambda)+c)}} \le$$
$(\lfloor \lambda\mu \rfloor + 1) \cdot \frac{1}{2^{c\mu}}$ which is negligible. This proves the result. □

B.2   Proof of Proposition 2

Let b' be a freshly captured template such that $d(b, b') > \lambda_{max}$ for any registered template b. The system returns an identity if and only if one identity appears in at least $\lceil \lambda\mu \rceil$ entries. This implies that for at least $\lceil \lambda\mu \rceil$ LSH functions h, we have, $h(b) = h(b')$. Given a hash function, and regarding the definition of a LSH family, this occurs with a probability p_2. So, $\Pr[\texttt{Identification}(b') \ne \emptyset] = \sum_{i=\lceil \lambda\mu \rceil}^{\mu} \binom{\mu}{i} p_2^i (1 - p_2)^{\mu-i} \le 2^\mu \cdot p_2^{\lambda\mu}$. If $p_2 \le \frac{1}{2^{\frac{1}{\lambda}+c}}$, this probability is negligible too. This gives the result. □

Correcting and Improving the NP Proof for Cryptographic Protocol Insecurity*

Zhiyao Liang and Rakesh M. Verma

Computer Science Department, University of Houston,
Houston Texas 77204-3010, USA
zliang@cs.uh.edu, rmverma@cs.uh.edu

Abstract. We improve the NP proof for the insecurity problem, partly motivated by an error in the NP proof of the influential paper "Protocol insecurity with a finite number of sessions and composed keys is NP-complete" by Rusinowitch and Turuani [1]. We enhance several different aspects of the proofs with a complete presentation, and we prove stronger results that fix the non-trivial error. Besides fixing the error, our proof framework has reusable structure and proves several results that are neither covered nor proved in [1] and its sequels, including the important fact that the attacker does not need to generate nonces in an attack, which the proof of [1] relies on. We show a sharper result that the complexity of the derivation problem is in square time. Furthermore, we extend the scope of the NP complexity to cover the scenarios where a fixed number of role instances are assumed, and delayed decryption is allowed. These are new results since the NP result of assuming a fixed number of role instances does not seem to be obtainable by a reduction from the NP result of assuming a fixed number of sessions, and [1] and its sequels cannot handle delayed decryption.

Keywords: Cryptographic protocols, secrecy, insecurity, NP.

1   Introduction

The influential paper "Protocol insecurity with a finite number of sessions and composed keys is NP-complete" [1], which can also be found at [2], proves that the NP-completeness of checking secrecy when the number of sessions of a protocol run is bounded by fixed number.[1] We believe this is among the most important complexity results of checking cryptographic protocols. We are motivated to have a thorough understanding of the proof of [1], not only for the interest in the complexity theory of checking cryptographic protocols, but also

---

* Research is done at the University of Houston, supported in part by NSF grants CCF 0306475 and CNS 0755500. Current address of the first author: LDCSEE Department, West Virginia University, Morgantown, WV 26506, USA.

[1] The word "fixed" is more precise than "bounded" or "finite", as discussed in [3], since the bound n of the number of sessions in a run should not be a part of an input instance in order to establish the non-deterministic polynomial (NP) time result.

A. Prakash and I. Sen Gupta (Eds.): ICISS 2009, LNCS 5905, pp. 101–116, 2009.

because we may improve the design of deterministic algorithms. For instance, the performance of deterministic protocol checker may not be better than guessing a minimal attack on the protocol, which is a notion addressed in [1].

This paper is organized as follows: In the rest of Section 1 we present related work and our contributions. Section 2 includes the modeling. In Section 3 we present an error of [1]. We present a series of enhanced results that are generally applicable in Section 4. In Section 5 we accomplish the improved NP proof and discuss the differences between our approach and the approach of [4].

In this paper, for a definition, observation, lemma or theorem, if it is marked with a *, then it is provided by this paper, not by [1] or its sequels; otherwise, it is mentioned here with the same statement and number as in [1] or [4].

1.1 Related Work

In [5] an NP-procedure is claimed. We do not focus on the work of [5] for two reasons: (1) In [5] encryption keys must be atomic, while in [1] encryption keys are more generally allowed to be composite. Extending atomic keys to composite keys is non-trivial for the following reasons: By assuming atomic keys, the attacker's computation to derive a message from a set of terms E can be organized in two stages, to analyze terms in E as much as possible and then to construct terms. But, if composite keys are allowed, this two-stage computation, which some proofs rely on, is not valid. Further discussion of this issue can be found in [6]. Also, a composite key could be any term, which can make the analysis significantly more complex. (2) The proof in [5] of the NP result is sketchy. In [7] there is an NP-complete result of checking secrecy with a bounded number of role instances. The proof of [7] assumes atomic keys, and the size of each message in a run is assumed to be less than a certain number K. Bounding the message size could make the NP proof considerably simpler, and the Directed Acyclic Graphs (DAGs) are not needed to represent terms, while the proofs of [1] rely on DAGs. A detailed explanation of why DAGs are needed, including an example, is in [8]. There is an NP-proof in [9], but that proof assumes only atomic keys and does not have as many details as [1].

The approach of [1] is extended in the subsequent papers [10] [11] [12], written by Chevalier, Küsters, Rusinowitch, and Turuani, to cover the NP complexity of checking secrecy beyond free term algebra when XOR operator, Diffie-Hellman exponentiation, and commuting public key encryption are allowed.

We noticed a non-trivial error of [1] in proving that in a normal attack (minimal attack) the size of the substitution for the variables can be polynomially bounded. We presented this error with a counter-example in a technical report [13]. We do not think this error is avoided or fixed in the subsequent papers [10], [11] and [12] after studying them. We also noticed that several aspects of the modeling and proofs of [1] can be improved or clarified. Some of these aspects are improved in the sequels of [1], such as the definition of normal attack, while some are not, such as the absence of the proof to show that the attacker does not need to generate nonces.

After this research was completed last year, we emailed our work to Rusinowitch and Turuani, the authors of [1], who reviewed our work and pointed us to another recent paper [4], in which a different proof approach is given that can avoid the error; however, in that paper the presentation, which emphasizes a set of so called oracle rules mixed with standard attacker rules, is designed for considering commuting operators. This makes it significantly hard for us to verify and interpret the NP proof just for the standard Dolev-Yao model assuming free term algebra, and especially for our concerns including fixing the error.

More detailed proofs and discussions of this research can be found in [8].

1.2 Contributions of This Paper

We present a complete proof system and make the following contributions.

(1) We present the error in the proof of the main theorem in [1] stating that the substitution size of a normal attack can be polynomially bounded. We prove this result by proving several stronger lemmas based on Lemma 4 of [1].

(2) Our modeling and NP proof uniformly cover the two scenarios of assuming a fixed bound on sessions or a fixed bound on role instances, while the second scenario is not covered in [1] and its sequels. One helpful feature of our work is that we improve the definition of a minimal attack.

(3) We allow delayed decryption in a protocol by introducing the concept of "dynamic roles" in the modeling, which enables our NP proof to cover the scenario where delayed decryption is allowed. Delayed decryption is not mentioned in [1] and cannot be handled convincingly in the sequels of [1].

(4) We prove that the attacker does not need to generate nonces, an assumption that the proofs of [1] and its sequels rely upon, and is mentioned as obvious in the Summary of [1], but the proof is nontrivial. Understanding this assumption is important, since there are situations where the attacker does need to generate different nonces for an attack such as when disequality test of two terms are allowed in a protocol and when message sizes are bounded, which has been addressed in several papers [14] [7] [15].

(5) We prove several generally applicable results on term derivation and substitution that are not covered in [1] and its sequels. Based on these results, we build a reusable proof structure for both an improved proof of Lemma 4 of [1] and the proof of the fact that the attacker does not need to generate any nonce.

(6) We show that the derivation problem has a quadratic time complexity.

2 Modeling

We choose our modeling and notations to be as consistent as possible with those of [1] and its sequels. In order to clarify and enhance the proof and to broaden the scope of the NP complexity, we improve the definitions of protocol run and normal attack. These improved notions capture the essential meaning of their counterparts in [1] and its sequels. Using our model, the established results of [1] are still valid without the need to change their statements, and the error can also be exactly described.

Atom is the set of atomic ground terms, i.e., constants (*ground* means variable free). *Var* is the set of variables. A **term** can have variables. A symmetric encryption has the form $\{x\}_y^s$ where y can be any term. An asymmetric encryption has the form $\{x\}_k^p$, where k belongs to *Keys* which is the set of asymmetric keys (public keys and private keys). Each asymmetric key is atomic. K_a and K_a^- represent the public key and private key an agent a. A bijection $.^{-1}$ on Keys maps a public (private) key to its corresponding private (public) key. A symmetric key is allowed to be a composite term. $\langle .,. \rangle$ represents a pair. A *list* has the form $\langle x, y, z \cdots \rangle$, which is the same as $\langle x, \langle y, \langle z \cdots \rangle\rangle\rangle$. When a list is encrypted or is a message in a protocol, its enclosing brackets are removed. The following grammar defines terms:

$$term \quad ::= \quad Atoms \mid Vars \mid \langle term, term \rangle \mid term_{Keys}^p \mid term_{term}^s$$

We will indicate which terms are variables of a protocol in the proofs when necessary, often a lower case symbol is used to represent a variable.

The set of **subterms** of a term t, denoted as $Sub(t)$, is defined as follows:

$Sub(t) = \{t\}$ if t is atomic; $\qquad Sub(\langle x, y \rangle) = Sub(x) \cup Sub(y) \cup \{\langle x, y \rangle\}$;
$Sub(x_y^s) = Sub(x) \cup Sub(y) \cup \{x_y^s\}; \quad Sub(x_y^p) = Sub(x) \cup \{y\} \cup \{x_y^p\}$.

The function Sub can obviously be extended to apply to a set of terms or other definitions where terms are involved, such as a role or a protocols defined below.

The Directed Acyclic Graph (**DAG**) representation of a set E of terms is a graph $(\mathcal{V}, \mathcal{E})$ with labeled vertexes and edges, where

- $\mathcal{V} = Sub(E)$, i.e. the vertices are labeled one-to-one with subterms of E;
- if a vertex v is labeled with $\{x\}_y^{s/p}$, or a pair $\langle x, y \rangle$, then two edges $v \rightarrow_{left} v_l$ and $v \rightarrow_{right} v_r$ are in $\mathcal{E}$, where v_l and v_2 are labeled with x and y.

The DAG-representation of a term is unique. The number of edges in a DAG is no more than two times the number of vertexes. The **DAG size** of a set of terms E, which is denoted as $|E|_{DAG}$, is the number of distinct subterms of E and is also the number of vertexes in the DAG representation of E. It is straightforward to extend the definition of DAG size to apply to structures based on terms, for example, $|P|_{DAG}$ for a protocol (introduced later) P is the number of different subterms appearing in P.

A **Replacement** δ is a set of single replacements $\{[t_1 \leftarrow t_1'), \cdots [t_n \leftarrow t_n']\}$, for some $n \geq 1$. When δ is applied to a term G, $\delta(G)$ returns a term G' where for each subterm t of G, if $[t \leftarrow t']$ appears in δ, then every occurrence of t in G is replaced by t' in G'. A **substitution** is a special replacement that only replaces variables by ground terms. For two replacement δ and γ, $\delta\gamma(t)$ means $\delta(\gamma(t))$. A **ground replacement** only replaces ground terms by ground terms.

An **act** is either a *send act* that has the form "$+Msg$" for some term Msg, or a *receive act* that has the form "$-Msg$" for some term Msg. A **role** is a sequence of acts that are supposed to be executed by the same agent. The variables appearing in a role are divided to *self-chosen* variables and *others-chosen* variables, that should be clear from the context. In a role, the message where an others-chosen variable x first appears, must be a received message. Note that variables in [1] correspond to others-chosen variables here.

A **protocol** is a set of roles, and a special set S_0 of ground atomic terms, which is the **initial knowledge** of the attacker.

Informally, a protocol is often described as a sequence of message exchanges between agents, called the *communication sequence* (CS). A set of roles can be parsed from the communication sequence. For example, Table 1 shows the communication sequence between A and B, which is similar to the fixed version of the public key Needham-Schroeder protocol [16]. The term k is initially known to a but unknown to b. The nonces n_a and n_b are (number generated once) generated by a and b respectively. Tables 2 and 3 show a's role and b's role respectively. In a's role, the set of self-chosen variables is $\{a, n_a, k, b\}$, and the set of others-chosen variables is $\{n_b\}$. In b's role, the set of self-chosen variables is $\{b, n_b\}$, and the set of others-chosen variables is $\{a, n_a, k\}$.

Table 1. A protocol's CS	**Table 2.** a's role	**Table 3.** b's role
1. $a \Rightarrow b$: $\{a, \{n_a\}_k^s\}_{K_b}^p$	1. $+ \{a, \{n_a\}_k^s\}_{K_b}^p$	1. $- \{a, \{n_a\}_k^s\}_{K_b}^p$
2. $b \Rightarrow a$: $\{b, n_b, \{n_a\}_k^s\}_{K_a}^p$	2. $- \{b, n_b, \{n_a\}_k^s\}_{K_a}^p$	2. $+ \{b, n_b, \{n_a\}_k^s\}_{K_a}^p$
3. $a \Rightarrow b$: $\{a, n_b, k\}_{K_b}^p$	3. $+ \{a, n_b, k\}_{K_b}^p$	3. $- \{a, n_b, k\}_{K_b}^p$
4. $b \Rightarrow a$: $\{b, n_a\}_{K_a}^p$	4. $- \{b, n_a\}_{K_a}^p$	4. $+ \{b, n_a\}_{K_a}^p$

The following derivation rules can be applied to a set of terms, by replacing the LHS terms with the RHS terms. These rules, called the **attacker's rules**, describe the attacker's internal computation to analyze and construct terms.

Decomposition rules:

$L_d(\langle x, y \rangle) : \langle x, y \rangle \to x, y, \langle x, y \rangle$;
$L_d(\{x\}_k^p) : \{x\}_k^p, k^{-1} \to \{x\}_k^p, k^{-1}, x$;
$L_d(\{x\}_y^s) : \{x\}_y^s, y \to \{x\}_y^s, y, x$.

Composition rules:

$L_c(\langle x, y \rangle) : x, y \to x, y, \langle x, y \rangle$;
$L_c(\{x\}_k^p) : x, k \to x, k, \{x\}_k^p$;
$L_c(\{x\}_y^s) : x, y \to x, y, \{x\}_y^s$.

For a rewrite rule $L_d(t)$ or $L_c(t)$, t is called the **principle term** of the rule. The relation between two sets of terms M and M', denoted as $M \to M'$ means there exists a rule $l \to r$ such that l is a subset of M and M' is obtained by replacing l by r in M. $\to^*$ is the reflexive and transitive closure of $\to$.

Let E be a set of terms and let t be a term such that there is E' with $E \to^* E'$ and $t \in E'$. Then we say that t is forged from E and it is denoted as $t \in \mathbf{forge}(E)$. A **derivation** D is a sequence $E_0 \to_{r_1} E_1 \to_{r_2} \cdots \to_{r_n} E_n$, where E_i for $0 \le i \le n$ is a set of terms, and r_i is an application of a rewrite rule described above; and if $t \in E_n$ and $t \notin E_{n-1}$, with $n > 0$, then t is called a *goal* of D. If r_i, for $1 \le i \le n$, has the form $LHS_i \to RHS_i$, for two sets of terms LHS_i and RHS_i, then $LHS_i \subset E_{i-1}$ and $E_i = E_{i-1} \cup RHS_i$. A shortest derivation from E with goal t is denoted as $Deriv_t(E)$.

For example, given a set of terms $E_0 = \{K_a, \{x\}_{\langle c,d \rangle}^s, c, \{d\}_{K_a^-}^p\}$, if the attacker knows E_0, then $x \in forge(E_0)$, since there is a derivation $E_0 \to_{L_d(\{d\}_{K_a^-}^p)} E_1 = E_0 \cup \{d\} \to_{L_c(\langle c,d \rangle)} E_2 = E_1 \cup \{\langle c, d \rangle\} \to_{L_d(\{x\}_{\langle c,d \rangle}^s)} E_3 = E_2 \cup x$.

A **run**, of a protocol P, is defined by a tuple $(\mathcal{P}, \pi, \sigma)$, explained as follows:

- $\mathcal{P}$ is set of *prefixes* of copies of roles where each role copy has its independent scope of variables, i.e. variables are (implicitly) renamed per role copy. These role copies are executed by regular agents, not the attacker, while the attacker's behaviors are covered by the attacker's rules.
- π is a function mapping each act of the role copies of $\mathcal{P}$ to a positive integer, and if e_1 and e_2 are two acts in the same role copy and e_1 appears before e_2 in the role then $\pi(e_1) < \pi(e_2)$.
- σ is a substitution replacing the variables in $\mathcal{P}$ to ground terms. Especially, for each self-chosen variable x in a role, $\sigma(x)$ is an atom.

For an integer i we define $\mathcal{S}_{<i} = \{t \mid t$ is the (message) term sent in an act e of a role copy in $\mathcal{P}$, and $\pi(e) < i\}$. $\mathcal{S}_{\leq i}$ is defined similarly. $\mathcal{S}_i$ ($\mathcal{R}_i$) denotes the set of terms sent (received) in some act e with $\pi(e) = i$. A *condition* must be satisfied: For each act e in $\mathcal{P}$ where a message t is received, $\sigma(t) \in forge(S_0 \cup \sigma(\mathcal{S}_{<\pi(e)}))$. Each (prefix) role copy in $\mathcal{P}$ is called a **role instance** of the run, and the ground instances of its messages are implied by σ.

An **attack** on a protocol P is a run $(\mathcal{P}, \pi, \sigma)$ where $Secret \in forge(S_0 \cup \sigma(\mathcal{S}_{\leq end}))$ where end is the largest $\pi(e)$ for some act e, and $Secret$ is a special atom. A **minimal attack**, or a **normal attack**, on a protocol P is an attack $(\mathcal{P}, \pi, \sigma)$ such that among all of the attacks on P with the same $\mathcal{P}$ and π, this attack has the smallest $|\sigma|_{DAG}$. In [11] and [4], minimal attack is defined based on $|\sigma|_{DAG}$, which simplifies the corresponding definition in [1]. Note that here we do not require a minimal attack to have the smallest $|\sigma|_{DAG}$ among all possible attacks (with different $\mathcal{P}$), like the corresponding definitions in [1] and its sequel [11]. In [4] the minimal attack is defined similarly to be the one with minimal size of σ among all attacks with the same π. However, our definition seems to express more exactly our idea of the relaxation on the definition of normal attack, which is important to prove the NP complexity of both cases of bounding the number of sessions and bounding the number of role instances.

Given a term t, $Var(t)$ means the set of variables appearing in term t, and $Atoms(t) = \{g \mid g \in Sub(t)$ and g is an atomic, ground term$\}$. $Var()$ and $Atoms()$ can be easily extended to apply to a set of terms, or some structure based on terms such as P or $\mathcal{P}$. Given a protocol P, for a term t, $SV_P(t)$ and $OV_P(t)$ are the set of self-chosen and others-chosen variables of P appearing in t. $SV_P()$ and $OV_P()$ can also be similarly applied to a set of terms or some term-based structure. Given a $\mathcal{P}$, we define $\mathcal{C} = \{\sigma(y) \mid y \in SV_P(\mathcal{P})\}$.

2.1   Modeling Discussion

Our model emphasizes the notion of roles since we believe it is essential. A protocol in [1] is described as a set of rules, where each rule receives a message and then sends a message. These rules can be easily translated to or from roles.

Our model does not describe the common behavior of the attacker and regular agents to generate fresh terms (nonces), which is the style of the modeling of [1] and its sequels. In [1] it is mentioned that any term dynamically generated in a run by the attacker can be considered generated before a run and included in the attacker's initial knowledge S_0. Since the attacker can generate unboundedly many nonces in a run, and the DAG size of S_0 is considered a part of the problem's input size, justifying this definition of S_0 for the correctness of the NP proof depends crucially on a fact that the attacker only needs to generate a polynomially bounded number of nonces for an attack. The nonces generated by regular agent in a run does not cause concern since these nonces are polynomially bounded when the number of sessions or role instances is bounded.

The notion of session deserves special consideration. A protocol run has one *session* means that in the run each role of the protocol cannot be executed more than once, i.e., a role cannot have more than one role instance. This precise interpretation of the notion of session is also mentioned in [9]. Similarly the scenario where a protocol run is bounded by n sessions, for a fixed number n, which is assumed by [1] and its sequels, means that each role cannot have more than n role instances in a run. Suppose a protocol has m roles, then assuming a bound of n sessions is a case of assuming a bound of $n \times m$ role instances. Also, assuming less than n role instances is a case of assuming less than n sessions. We do not see the NP complexity of assuming a fixed bound of role instances can be reduced to the one of assuming a fixed bound of sessions, or the other way, since the if and only if condition in the reduction cannot be established.

Intuitively the function π maps the acts of the role instances in a run to their (relative) occurring time. Our model allow two acts (also called events in the literature) of two role instances to occur at the same time in a run, which agrees with the Strand Space model [17]. If we require that two different acts in a run must occur at two different time points, then the acts in a run are interleaved into a linear trace according to their occurring time, which is a feature of the trace based models such as [18] and [6]. The model of [1] is also a trace based model. While it is intuitive that the two kinds of models are equivalent in terms checking cryptographic protocols, we think the style of Strand Space is naturally closer to our understanding of a protocol run.

Sometimes in a role, an agent receives an encryption without knowing the decryption key and does not know the enclosed plain text (such an encryption is called a *blind encryption*); however, at some later act the agent obtains the decryption key (or other needed information) and can decrypt an encryption that is received earlier in the role and then know the plain text. We call this behavior as *delayed decryption*. For example, for the protocol presented in Table 1, after b receives the first message, b cannot decrypt $\{n_a\}_k^s$ and know n_a since b cannot know k. After b receives the third message, b knows k and can decrypt decrypt $\{n_a\}_k^s$, a blind encryption received earlier, and then knows n_a.

In [11], the authors suggested that a protocol with delayed decryption is translated to another one without delayed decryption. However, there is no discussion on the procedure of such a "translation", and doing so will significantly modify a protocol, and may violate the design meaning of the protocol, especially when authentication security goals are of interest. In [19], the authors suggest representing each blind encryption in a message as a single variable in a role, and to

Table 4. b's role with length 1

1. $- \{a, x\}^p_{K_b}$

Table 5. b's role with length 2

1. $- \{a, x\}^p_{K_b}$
2. $+ \{b, n_b, x\}^p_{K_a}$

Table 6. b's role with length 3

1. $- \{a, \{n_a\}^s_k\}^p_{K_b}$
2. $+ \{b, n_b, \{n_a\}^s_k\}^p_{K_a}$
3. $- \{a, n_b, k\}^p_{K_b}$

attach an explicit equivalence test to a message where the blind encryption can be decrypted. However, it is not clear that the proof system of [1] and its sequels can handle explicit equality test.

We suggest each prefix of a role can be considered as an individual role where a blind encryption is represented as a variable or as an explicit encryption depending on the length of the role prefix. We call the prefixes of roles thus described as **dynamic roles**, which allows seamless handling of delayed decryption in our proof system. For example, Tables 4, 5, and 6 represent b's role with length 1, 2, and 3 respectively. b's role with length 4 is shown in Table 3.

3   The Error

The error of [1] is in the proof of Theorem 1, as stated below. We first present Definition 6 and Lemma 4 of [1], which are correct, for discussing Theorem 1.

Definition 6. For a protocol P, let t and t' be two terms and θ a substitution. Then t is a θ-match of t' if $t \notin OV_P(P)$ and $\theta(t) = t'$. This is denoted by $t \sqsubseteq_\theta t'$.

Lemma 4. Given a normal attack $(\mathcal{P}, \pi, \sigma)$ on a protocol P, for each x in $OV_P(\mathcal{P})$, there exists a term t such that $t \in Sub(\mathcal{P} \cup S_0)$, and $t \sqsubseteq_\sigma \sigma(x)$.

Theorem 1. If σ is the substitution in a normal attack $(\mathcal{P}, \pi, \sigma)$, then we have for all $x \in OV_P(\mathcal{P})$, $|\sigma(x)|_{DAG} \leqslant |\mathcal{P} \cup S_0|_{DAG}$.

Proof of Theorem 1 in [1]:   Given a set of variables U, we shall write $\overline{U} = \{\sigma(x) | x \in U\}$. Let $\mathcal{SP} = Sub(\mathcal{P} \cup S_0)$. For a certain variable $x \in OV_P(\mathcal{P})$, let us build by induction a sequence of sets $E_i \subseteq \mathcal{SP}$ and a sequence of sets V_i of others-chosen variables such that $|\sigma(x)|_{DAG} \leqslant |E_i, \overline{V_i}|_{DAG}$, starting from $i = 0$. Note that $|E_i, \overline{V_i}|_{DAG}$ means $|E_i \cup \overline{V_i}|_{DAG}$.

Basis: Let (E_0, V_0) be $(\emptyset, \{x\})$. So, $|\sigma(x)|_{DAG} \leqslant |E_0, \overline{V_0}|_{DAG}$ and $E_0 \subseteq \mathcal{SP}$.

Induction step: Assume that we have built (E_i, V_i) such that $|\sigma(x)|_{DAG} \leqslant |E_i, \overline{V_i}|_{DAG}$ and $E_i \subseteq \mathcal{SP}$, let us define E_{i+1} and V_{i+1}: If $V_i \neq \emptyset$, we choose any $x_{i+1} \in V_i$. Then there exists some $t_{i+1} \sqsubseteq_\sigma \sigma(x_{i+1})$ such that $t_{i+1} \in \mathcal{SP}$, according to Lemma 4. Note that it is guaranteed that $t_{i+1} \notin OV_P(\mathcal{P})$ and $x_{i+1} \notin Var(t_{i+1})$. We define $E_{i+1} = E_i \cup \{t_{i+1}\}$ and $V_{i+1} = Var(t_{i+1}) \cup V_i - \{x_{i+1}\}$. Since $t_{i+1} \in \mathcal{SP}$, $E_{i+1} \subseteq \mathcal{SP}$. Now the proof needs to show that

$$|\sigma(x)|_{DAG} \leqslant |E_{i+1}, \overline{V_{i+1}}|_{DAG} \tag{1}$$

In order to prove (1), the proof reaches a result that

$$|E_i, \overline{V_i}|_{DAG} \leqslant |\delta(E_i), \overline{V_i}|_{DAG} \leqslant |E_{i+1}, \overline{V_{i+1}}|_{DAG} \qquad (2)$$

where $\delta = \{[y \leftarrow \sigma(y)] \mid y \in Var(t_{i+1})\}$. Then by (2), and by the induction assumption $|\sigma(x)|_{DAG} \leqslant |E_i, \overline{V_i}|_{DAG}$, (1) is proved. This iteration process will terminate since there are only finitely many variables. At the end, say at the eth step, $V_e = \emptyset$, and $E_e \subseteq \mathcal{SP}$. Then we have $|\sigma(x)|_{DAG} \leqslant |E_e|_{DAG} \leqslant |\mathcal{P} \cup S_0|_{DAG}$. Theorem 1 is proved.

The error: The first inequality of (2), $|E_i, \overline{V_i}|_{DAG} \leqslant |E_i\delta, \overline{V_i}|_{DAG}$, cannot be proved, which can be intuitively explained as follows: in general, for a term t and a replacement δ, it is not always true that $|t|_{DAG} \leq |\delta(t)|_{DAG}$.

It is enough to show the problem of the proof of Theorem 1 in [1] by a **counterexample** to the iteration process of the proof where (2) is violated, as follows: Suppose in a protocol there are three others-chosen variables x_1 x_2 and x_3, and three constants (atoms) a b and c. Suppose in a normal attack, the three variables have the following instantiation:

- $\sigma(x_1) = \{\langle a, b \rangle\}^s_{\langle a,b \rangle};\quad \sigma(x_2) = \langle a, b \rangle;\quad \sigma(x_3) = b.$

Suppose in the protocol we can find the following three terms:

- $t_1 = \{\langle a, x_3 \rangle\}^s_{x_2};\quad t_2 = \langle a, x_3 \rangle;\quad t_3 = b.$

Note that $t_1 \sqsubseteq_\sigma \sigma(x_1)$ and $t_2 \sqsubseteq_\sigma \sigma(x_2)$ and $t_3 \sqsubseteq_\sigma \sigma(x_3)$.

Now let us start the process of updating E_i and V_i for the variable $x = x_1$, starting from $E_0 = \emptyset$ and $V_0 = \{x_1\}$, as shown by the following table:

i	x_i	t_i	E_i	V_i	$Sub(E_i, \overline{V_i})$	$\|E_i, \overline{V_i}\|_{DAG}$
0			$\emptyset$	$\{x_1\}$	$\{\ \{\langle a, b \rangle\}_{\langle a,b\rangle}, \langle a, b \rangle, a, b\ \}$	4
1	x_1	t_1	$\{t_1\}$	$\{x_2, x_3\}$	$\{\ \{\langle a, x_3 \rangle\}_{x_2}, \langle a, x_3 \rangle, a, x_3, x_2, \langle a, b \rangle, b\ \}$	7
2	x_2	t_2	$\{t_1, t_2\}$	$\{x_3\}$	$\{\ \{\langle a, x_3 \rangle\}_{x_2}, \langle a, x_3 \rangle, a, x_3, x_2, b\ \}$	6
3	x_3	t_3	$\{t_1, t_2, t_3\}$	$\emptyset$	$\{\ \{\langle a, x_3 \rangle\}_{x_2}, \langle a, x_3 \rangle, x_2, x_3, a, b\ \}$	6

Note that $|E_1, \overline{V_1}|_{DAG} = 7 > 6 = |E_2, \overline{V_2}|_{DAG}$, and (2) is violated.

4   Enhanced Results on Term Substitution and Derivation

The results presented in this section are generally applicable and we use them to construct an improved proof of Lemma 4, and similarly to prove that the attacker does not need to generate nonces for an attack.

The following observation captures our intuition that in a derivation no new atoms are generated.

Observation* 1: For a set of terms E and a term $t \in forge(E)$, $Atoms(t) \subseteq Atoms(E)$.

Proof. Since each composition or decomposition rule does not introduce any new atom (we do not model the attacker's behavior of generating nonces), for any derivation $E_0 \to_{r_1} E_1 \to_{r_2} \cdots E_h$, it is obvious that $Atoms(E_i) = Atoms(E_i+1)$, for $0 \leq i \leq h$. Since $t \in forge(E)$, there is a derivation $D = E \to_{r_1} E_1 \to_{r_2} \cdots E_h$, such that $t \in E_h$. So $Atoms(t) \subseteq Atoms(E_h) = Atoms(E)$. $\square$

In a protocol run, a certain set of atoms is the source of all atoms appearing in any message, as shown in the following observation.

Observation* 2: Given a protocol P, and a run (P, π, σ) of P, for each variable x in $OV_P(\mathcal{P})$, $Atoms(\sigma(x)) \subseteq Atoms(\mathcal{P} \cup S_0 \cup \mathcal{C})$. Recall that $\mathcal{C} = \sigma(SV_P(\mathcal{P}))$.

Proof. Let $G = Atoms(\mathcal{P} \cup S_0 \cup \mathcal{C})$. We prove by induction on i the *fact* that $Atoms(\sigma(\mathcal{R}_i)) \subseteq G$ and $Atoms(\sigma(\mathcal{S}_i)) \subseteq G$, which implies this observation since x must appear in some S_i or R_i. By the definition of protocol, for each term r in R_i, $\sigma(r) \subseteq forge(S_0 \cup \mathcal{S}_{<i})$. Then by Observation* 1, $Atoms(\sigma(r)) \subseteq G$. Therefore, $Atoms(\sigma(R_i)) \subseteq G$. For each s in $\mathcal{S}_i$, since each self-chosen variable is instantiated by an atom, $Atoms(\sigma(SV_P(s))) = \sigma(SV_P(s)) \subseteq C$. When $i = 1$, $OV_P(s) = \emptyset$. By a property of a protocol run, for each x in $OV_P(s)$, x must appear in some term that is received earlier in the run. For the induction step, by the induction assumption, $Atoms(\sigma(OV_P(s)) \subseteq G$. So $Atoms(\sigma(s)) = Atoms(s) \cup Atoms(\sigma(SV_P(s))) \cup Atoms(\sigma(OV_P(s))) \subseteq G$. $Atoms(\sigma(S_i)) \subseteq G$. $\square$

A way to describe a substitution, which is essential to define a protocol run, is by composing a ground replacement with another substitution, as follows:

Observation* 3: Consider a term T, two substitutions σ and σ', a ground replacement $\delta = [t \leftarrow t']$, such that the following conditions are satisfied:
1. There is no term g such that $g \in Sub(T)$ and g is not a variable and $\sigma(g) = t$.
2. Let $V_t = \{x | x \in Var(T)$ and $t \in Sub(\sigma(x))\}$. For a variable y, if $y \in V_t$, then $\sigma'(y) = \delta(\sigma(y))$; otherwise $\sigma'(y) = \sigma(y)$.

Then, $\sigma'(T) = \delta(\sigma(T))$ holds.

Proof. Condition 1 implies that if $t \in Sub(\sigma(T))$, i.e., t occurs in $\sigma(T)$, then t must occur as a subterm of $\sigma(x)$, for some $x \in Var(T)$. When δ is applied to $\sigma(T)$, the only changes to $\sigma(T)$ are made by replacing each occurrence of $\sigma(x)$ with $\delta(\sigma(x))$, for $x \in V_t$. $\sigma'(T)$ changes T in two aspects: Replacing the occurrences of each variable x in V_t with $\delta(\sigma(x))$, and replacing the occurrences of each variable y, for $y \notin V_t$, with $\sigma(y)$. So $\sigma'(T) = \delta(\sigma(T))$. $\square$

If $t \in forge(E)$, it is not necessarily true that $\delta(t) \in forge(\delta(E))$, although it is a convenient way to describe the relationship between two protocol runs. Lemma* 1 shows that in certain scenario such a relationship can be established.

Lemma* 1: For a set of terms E, a term t, a replacement $\delta = [w \leftarrow w']$ with two terms w and w'. If (1) w is not an asymmetric key, and (2) there is a derivation from E with a goal t without applying $L_d(w)$, then $\delta(t) \in forge(\delta(E) \cup \{w'\})$.

Proof. Since there is a derivation $D = E_0 \to_{r_1} E_1 \to_{r_2} E_2 \cdots \to_{r_h} E_h$, where $E_0 = E$, $t \in E_h$, and $L_d(w)$ does not appear, we want to construct a derivation D' from $E'_0 = \delta(E) \cup \{w'\}$ with a goal $\delta(t)$. D' has the form $D' = E'_0 \to_{r'_1}$

$E'_1 \rightarrow_{r'_2} E'_2 \cdots \rightarrow_{r'_h} E'_h$, and the ith derivation rule r'_i in D' is defined as follows:

- If r_i is the rule $L_c(w)$, then $r'_i = L_\emptyset$ (doing nothing) and $E'_{i-1} = E'_i$.
- Otherwise, let $r_i = L_{c/d}(T_i)$ for some term T_i, then $r'_i = \delta(r_i) = L_{c/d}(\delta(T_i))$.

We justify that D' is a valid derivation by showing two facts: (i) Let r'_i be of the form $LHS'_i \rightarrow RHS'_i$, then $LHS'_i \subseteq E'_{i-1}$. For (i), we prove a stronger fact that $E'_i = \delta(E_i) \cup \{w'\}$. (ii) r_i is applicable, i.e., with concerns like a rule of decrypting an encryption cannot be applied to a pair, also only an asymmetric key can be used to construct an asymmetric encryption. These two facts can be proved together by induction on i in D', checking each possible form of r'_i, observing that in D the corresponding facts are satisfied. Note that the conditions (1) and (2) of this lemma are needed to ensure that L'_i is always applicable. $\qquad\square$

It follows that Lemma 1 is also valid when we require that $\delta = [K_g \leftarrow K_f;\ K_g^- \leftarrow K_f^-]$, for some asymmetric key pairs $K_g\ K_g^-$, and $K_f\ K_f^-$.

Now we can prove that the attacker does not need to generate nonces in a run, by establishing the relationship between two runs, where one includes a nonce of the attacker, but the other does not.

Theorem* 1: Consider a protocol P, and a nonce n_I created by the attacker, i.e. $n_I \in S_0$ and n_I does not appear in the roles of P. Assume $\mathcal{I}$ is the attacker's name and $\mathcal{I} \in S_0$. If there an attack $(\mathcal{P}, \pi, \sigma)$ to P, then after n_I is removed from S_0, there is also an attack $(\mathcal{P}, \pi, \sigma')$, for some σ'

Proof. Let π map the acts in $\mathcal{P}$ from 1 to k. Let $Secret$ be a secret term that is leaked after the attack $(\mathcal{P}, \pi, \sigma)$, i.e. $Secret \in forge(\sigma(\mathcal{S}_{\leq k}) \cup S_0)$. Let $V_{n_I} = \{y | y \in Var(\mathcal{P})$ and $n_I \in Sub(\sigma(y))\}$. Let $\delta = [n_I \leftarrow \mathcal{I}]$, and $S'_0 = \delta(S_0) = S_0 - n_I$. We define σ' as follows: For a variable $y \in Var(\mathcal{P})$, if $y \notin V_{n_I}$, then $\sigma'(y) = \sigma(y)$, otherwise $\sigma'(y) = \delta(\sigma(y))$. We need to prove that for each r in R_i, $\sigma'(r) \in forge(\sigma'(\mathcal{S}'_{\leq i-1}) \cup S'_0)$, for $1 \leq i \leq k$, in order to justify that $(\mathcal{P}, \pi, \sigma')$ is a valid protocol run. Since $r \in forge(\sigma(\mathcal{S}'_{\leq i-1}) \cup S_0)$, and n_I is not an asymmetric key, and $n_I \in S_0$ implies that n_I can be trivially derived from $\sigma(\mathcal{S}_{\leq i-1}) \cup S_0$ without applying any derivation rule, by Lemma* 1, $\delta(\sigma(r)) \in forge(\delta(\sigma(\mathcal{S}_{\leq i-1}) \cup S_0) \cup \{\mathcal{I}\}) = forge(\delta(\sigma(\mathcal{S}_{\leq i-1})) \cup S'_0)$. So $\delta(\sigma(R_i)) \subseteq forge(\delta(\sigma(\mathcal{S}_{\leq i-1})) \cup S'_0)$; call it *fact 1*. Since n_I is an atom that is not a subterm in $\mathcal{P}$, there is no $g \in Sub(\mathcal{P})$ such that $\sigma(g) = n_I$ and $g \notin Var(\mathcal{P})$. Therefore, we can apply Observation* 3 to prove that $\sigma'(R_i) = \delta(\sigma(R_i))$ and $\sigma'(S_i) = \delta(\sigma(S_i))$; call it *fact 2*. Based on *fact 1* and *fact 2*, it follows that $\sigma'(R_i) \subseteq forge(\sigma'(\mathcal{S}_{\leq i-1})) \cup S'_0)$. Finally, we have to prove that $Secret \in forge(\sigma'(\mathcal{S}_{\leq k}) \cup S'_0)$. Note that $Secret \neq n_I$. Since $Secret \in forge(\sigma(\mathcal{S}_{\leq k}) \cup S_0)$ and n_I is not an asymmetric key and n_I is trivially derivable from S_0, it follows from *fact 2* and Lemma* 1 that $Secret = \delta(Secret) \in forge(\delta(\sigma(\mathcal{S}_{\leq k}) \cup S_0) \cup \{\mathcal{I}\}) = forge(\sigma'(\mathcal{S}_{\leq k}) \cup S'_0)$. $\qquad\square$

Similarly, the attacker does not need to dynamically generate asymmetric keys in a run, since its public key and private key are sufficient for an attack. Corollary* 1 straightforwardly follows from Theorem* 1 by a similar proof.

Corollary* 1: If there is an attack on a protocol P, then there is also an attack where the attacker does not generate nonces or asymmetric keys.

We are motivated to improve proof of Lemma 4 in [1], which is the key lemma to prove the NP result, for better structure and clarity. Based on the observations and lemmas developed in this section, we present in [8] an improved proof of Lemma 4, using Lemma* 1 and Observation* 3, with a proof structure similar to the proof of Theorem* 1.

In [11] and [4] it is shown that the derivation problem, can be solved in deterministic polynomial time. We show a sharper result below.

Theorem* 2: Given a set of terms E and a term t, let $m = |E, t|_{DAG}$, to decide that $t \in forge(E)$ (derivation problem) can be solved in $O(m^2)$ time.

Proof. $t \in forge(E)$ if and only if there is a shortest derivation from E for the goal t, denoted as $Deriv_t(E)$. It is simple to prove, as in [1], that for each derivation rule $L_{c/d}(w)$ in $Deriv_t(E)$, $w \in Sub(E \cup \{t\})$. So there are at most m derivation rules applied in $Deriv_t(E)$. Assume $Sub(E \cup \{t\})$ has its enhanced DAG representation, so that each subterm can directly reach its parent term and its children terms (top level subterms), and a key can directly reach its inverse key. We construct a process with at most m iterations, corresponding to the length of $Deriv_t(E)$. Initially all terms in G are marked with Y, and all other terms are marked with N. In the ith iteration, for each term $w \in Sub(E \cup \{t\})$ that is marked with N, we check if $L_c(w)$ is applicable: If each child node of w is marked with Y, then mark t as Y'. Also, for each term marked with Y, we check if $L_d(w)$ applicable, i.e., w must be composite, and if w is an encryption the decryption key is marked with Y. Then we check if $L_d(w)$ is useful: If some child term g of w is obtainable after applying $L_d(w)$, and if g is marked with N, mark g by Y'. Finally in the iteration all terms labeled by Y' (temporary) change their labels to Y. The process ends if $i > m$, or if t is marked with Y. $t \in forge(E)$ if and only if t is marked with Y in the end. Since the cost of each iteration is $O(m)$, and there are $O(m)$ iterations, the total time cost is $O(m^2)$.   □

5   Fixing the Error and Improving the NP Proof

In this section we show that results stronger than Lemma 4 and Theorem 1 in [1] can be proved based on Lemma 4 and an iterative process, which is in the spirit of the proof of Theorem 1 in [1].

The following lemma captures our intuition that leads to the fix of the error. It shows that in a run there must be a variable such that the size of its instance is bounded by the size of the protocol.

Lemma* 2: Consider a normal attack $(\mathcal{P}, \pi, \sigma)$ on a protocol P. If $OV_P(\mathcal{P}) \neq \emptyset$, then there is a variable x such that $x \in OV_P(\mathcal{P})$ and $\sigma(x)$ has a σ match t (denoted as $t \sqsubseteq_\sigma \sigma(x)$), where $t \in Sub(\mathcal{P} \cup S_0)$, and $OV_P(t) = \emptyset$.

Proof. By Lemma 4 $\sigma(x)$ always has a σ match t in $Sub(\mathcal{P} \cup S_0)$. Therefore, for the sake of contradiction, we assume in a normal attack, for each others-chosen variable x, for each t such that $t \sqsubseteq_\sigma \sigma(x)$, $OV_P(t) \neq \emptyset$. Now we go through an iterative process to show it is impossible. At every step of the process, say the ith step, $1 \leq i$, a variable x_i and a term t_i are considered. At the first step, step 1, x_1 is chosen to be any variable in $OV_P(\mathcal{P})$, and t_1 is any term such that $t_1 \sqsubseteq_\sigma \sigma(x_1)$, and $t_1 \in Sub(\mathcal{P} \cup S_0)$. By lemma 4, such a t_1 always exists. The $i + 1^{th}$ step, for $i \geq 1$, continues this process by choosing any variable x_{i+1} such that $x_{i+1} \in OV_P(t_i)$, and then by choosing t_{i+1} to be any term such that $t_{i+1} \sqsubseteq_\sigma \sigma(x_{i+1})$, and $OV_P(t_{i+1}) \neq \emptyset$. Such x_{i+1} and t_{i+1} exist by the contradictory assumption and Lemma 4. Since $t_i \notin OV_P(\mathcal{P})$ and $OV_P(t_i) \neq \emptyset$, t_i must be a composite term and x_{i+1} is a strict subterm of t_i. So $|\sigma(x_{i+1})|_{DAG} < |\sigma(t_i)|_{DAG}$. Since $\sigma(x_i) = \sigma(t_i)$, $|\sigma(x_i)|_{DAG} = |\sigma(t_i)|_{DAG}$ follows; hence, $|\sigma(x_i)|_{DAG} > |\sigma(x_{i+1})|_{DAG}$. It means that $|\sigma(x_i)|_{DAG} > |\sigma(x_j)|_{DAG}$, for $i < j$. So x_i and x_j are two different variables, for $i \neq j$. Since $OV_P(\mathcal{P})$ is finite, the process cannot continue forever. Let k be the last step of this process. Then $OV_P(t_k) = \emptyset$ (otherwise the process continues to the $k+1$ step) which is a contradiction, and the lemma is proved. $\square$

It can be proved very similarly that the size of the instance of each others-chosen variable can be bounded by the protocol size:

Corollary* 2: Given a normal attack $(\mathcal{P}, \pi, \sigma)$ to a protocol P, let G and G' be any two disjoint sets of others-chosen variables and $G \cup G' = OV_P(\mathcal{P})$, assuming $OV_P(\mathcal{P}) \neq \emptyset$, and $G \neq \emptyset$, then there is a variable x in G such that $\sigma(x)$ has a σ match t, i.e. $t \sqsubseteq_\sigma \sigma(x)$, such that $t \in Sub(\mathcal{P} \cup S_0)$ and $OV_P(t) \subseteq G'$.

Based on the above two results, we can prove the following lemma, which is stronger than Lemma 4 of [1].

Lemma* 3: In a normal attack $(\mathcal{P}, \pi, \sigma)$ on a protocol P, for every variable x in $OV_P(\mathcal{P})$, and for every term y such that $y \in Sub(\sigma(x))$, there is a term t such that $t \in Sub(\mathcal{P} \cup S_0)$ and $t \notin OV_P(\mathcal{P})$, and $y = \sigma(t)$.

Proof. We choose a sequence of variables x_i, for $1 \leq i$, such that $x_i \in OV_P(\mathcal{P})$, and a sequence of sets of variables V_j, for $0 \leq j$, such that $V_j \subseteq OV_P(\mathcal{P})$, $V_0 = OV_P(\mathcal{P})$. x_i, for $1 \leq i$, is chosen to satisfy the following condition: There is a term t_i, $t_i \in Sub(\mathcal{P} \cup S_0)$, and $t_i \notin OV_P(\mathcal{P})$, and $\sigma(t_i) = \sigma(x_i)$ (i.e, $t_i \sqsubseteq_\sigma \sigma(x_i)$), and $OV_P(t_i) \subseteq (OV_P(\mathcal{P}) - V_{i-1})$. Then $V_i = V_{i-1} - \{x_i\}$. This process ends when $V_i = \emptyset$. By Corollary* 2, at the ith step, the corresponding t_i always exists. We prove by induction that for each x_i, the fact stated in this lemma is true. Basis: when $i = 1$, directly implied by Lemma* 2, which is a special case of Corollary* 2, x_1 can always be found to satisfy this lemma. For the induction step, we assume the lemma holds for all x_j that $1 \leq j < i$. Let $G_i = \{g | g \in Sub(t_i), g \notin OV_P(t_i)\}$. Then $Sub(\sigma(x_i)) = Sub(\sigma(t_i)) = \sigma(G_i) \cup Sub(\sigma(OV_P(t_i)))$. For any term y such that $y \in \sigma(G_i)$, the lemma is satisfied since $y \sqsubseteq_\sigma \sigma(y)$. For any y such that $y \in Sub(\sigma(OV_P(t_i)))$ the fact is also satisfied, because $OV_P(t_i) \subseteq (OV_P(\mathcal{P}) - V_{i-1})$, and each variable in $OV_P(t_i)$ is some x_j for $j < i$ that satisfies the lemma by the induction assumption. $\square$

Now we prove Theorem* 3, which is stronger than (implies) Theorem 1.

Theorem* 3: For a normal attack $(\mathcal{P}, \pi, \sigma)$ on a protocol P, $|\sigma(\mathcal{P} \cup S_0))|_{DAG} \leq |\mathcal{P} \cup S_0|_{DAG}$.

Proof. Let $G = S_0 \cup \{g | g \in Sub(\mathcal{P}), g \notin OV_P(\mathcal{P})\}$. It follows that $Sub(\sigma(\mathcal{P} \cup S_0)) = \sigma(G) \cup Sub(\sigma(OV_P(\mathcal{P})))$. For each term y in $Sub(\sigma(OV_P(\mathcal{P})))$, by Lemma* 3, there is a term t such that $t \in G$, and $\sigma(t) = y$. therefore, $Sub(\sigma(OV_P(\mathcal{P}))) \subseteq \sigma(G)$. So, $Sub(\sigma(\mathcal{P} \cup S_0)) = \sigma(G)$. Now we can prove that $|\sigma(\mathcal{P} \cup S_0))|_{DAG} = |Sub(\sigma(\mathcal{P} \cup S_0))|_{card} = |\sigma(G)|_{card} \leq |G|_{card} \leq |Sub(\mathcal{P} \cup S_0)|_{card} = |\mathcal{P} \cup S_0|_{DAG}$. Here $|S|_{card}$ means the cardinality of the set S.   □

Now we have a unified NP proof for fixed sessions and role instances.

Theorem* 4: Checking whether a cryptographic protocol has a secrecy failure is in NP, for both scenarios in a run, assuming the number of sessions has a fixed bound, and assuming the number of role instances has a fixed bound.

Proof. A non-deterministic algorithm can guess an attack $(\mathcal{P}, \pi, \sigma)$ on P such that $\mathcal{P}$ satisfies the bound on sessions or role instances. Let $|P|_{DAG} = l$. When the number of sessions is bounded by n, for some constant n, then $|\mathcal{P}|_{DAG} < l \times n$, which is also true when the number role instances is bounded by n. Since in a run we proved that the attacker's initial knowledge S_0 does not contain dynamically generated nonces and keys, as justified by Theorem* 1, and (by convention) S_0 contains only the names and public keys of the agents who participate in the run, and some shared keys, and the attacker's own public key and private key, it follows that $|S_0|_{DAG}$ is linear in $|\mathcal{P}|_{DAG}$. So, in both scenarios, $|\mathcal{P} \cup S_0|_{DAG} = O(l)$. Thanks to the way a normal attack is defined, by Theorem* 3, the algorithm can always guess a σ such that $|\sigma(\mathcal{P} \cup S_0))|_{DAG} \leq |\mathcal{P} \cup S_0|_{DAG} = O(l)$. Note that the requirement of a minimal attack is first handled by Lemma 4 in the proof. In order to verify that the guessed attack is really a run, the algorithm verifies the satisfiability of the *condition* that each received message in the attack is derivable from the set of previously sent messages together with S_0. There are at most $l \times n$ acts of receiving messages in the attack, in both scenarios. To check the *condition* for each received message has a polynomial time cost, or more exactly $O(l^2)$ by Theorem* 2. Therefore, to check the condition for all received messages can be computed in a polynomial time $(n \times l \times O(l^2) = O(l^3))$. So the algorithm is non-deterministic polynomial w.r.t. l, which is $|P|_{DAG}$.   □

Comparison with the Proof of [4].   In [4] there is a different approach that can avoid the error of [1]. The difference between that approach and our approach is the following: In [4], Lemma 4 of [1] is not addressed. Instead, Proposition 3.14, which is stronger than Lemma 4, is proved by a proof very similar to the proof of Lemma 4 in [1]. Proposition 3.14 in [4] basically corresponds to our Lemma* 3. In comparison, we prove Lemma* 3 using Lemma 4. The approach of [4] appears to be more direct to reach a result that is stronger than Lemma 4. Our approach actually follows the proof direction of [1], that is, to obtain Lemma 4 first, and then based on Lemma 4 to construct the NP proof using some iterative processes. Since we are not fully satisfied with the proof of Lemma 4 in [1], which is similarly used in [4] to prove Proposition 3.14, our efforts to build improved and reusable proof structure are not redundant. Besides, in our more comprehensive treatment for building the proof system, we have proved some new and generally applicable results that are not covered by the proof system of [1] and its sequels, like Lemma* 2 and Corollary* 2. It is interesting to see that we can follow the proof direction of [1] to reach the goal of fixing the error and broaden the scope of the NP complexity. More detailed discussion of the two different approaches are included in [8].

6 Summary

We improve the NP proof for the insecurity problem based on a influential paper [1], and its sequels. Our work improves the research of proving the NP complexity of the insecurity problem in scope, since the NP complexity can cover both scenarios of bounding sessions and role instances and delayed decryption can be handled; in proof structure, since we prove different results, such as proving the NP complexity of bounding sessions and role instances, and proving Lemma 4 and that the attacker does not need to generate nonces; and in depth since we build several enhanced results that are generally applicable, and we fix an error of [1]. The error is in the proof of Theorem 1 of [1], which is seemingly due to an incorrect reasoning step assuming that $|E|_{DAG} \leq |E\sigma|_{DAG}$, for a set of terms E and a substitution σ.

Since this research significantly enhanced our understanding of NP proofs of checking protocols, it has important implications for our current and future research on cryptographic protocols and cybersecurity, which include designing model checking and theorem proving algorithms.

Acknowledgment

We highly appreciate the discussion with Dr. Mathieu Turuani and Dr. Michael Rusinowitch and thank them for their review and supportive comments on our technical report [13], and the information on [4]. We thank Dr. Vitaly Shmatikov very much for his comments on and encouragement for this research.

References

1. Rusinowitch, M., Turuani, M.: Protocol insecurity with a finite number of sessions, composed keys is NP-complete. Theor. Comput. Sci. 1-3(299), 451–475 (2003)
2. Turuani, M.: Web page, http://www.loria.fr/~turuani/
3. Liang, Z., Verma, R.M.: Complexity of checking freshness of cryptographic protocols. In: Sekar, R., Pujari, A.K. (eds.) ICISS 2008. LNCS, vol. 5352, pp. 86–101. Springer, Heidelberg (2008)
4. Chevalier, Y., Küsters, R., Rusinowitch, M., Turuani, M.: Complexity results for security protocols with Diffie-Hellman exponentiation and commuting public key encryption. ACM Transactions on Computational Logic (TOCL) 9(4) (2008)

5. Amadio, R.M., Lugiez, D., Vanackère, V.: On the symbolic reduction of processes with cryptographic functions. Theor. Comput. Sci. 290(1), 695–740 (2003)
6. Millen, J.K., Shmatikov, V.: Constraint solving for bounded-process cryptographic protocol analysis. In: ACM Conference on Computer and Communications Security, pp. 166–175 (2001)
7. Durgin, N.A., Lincoln, P., Mitchell, J.C.: Multiset rewriting and the complexity of bounded security protocols. Journal of Computer Security 12(2), 247–311 (2004)
8. Liang, Z., Verma, R.M.: Correcting and Improving the NP Proof for Cryptographic Protocol Insecurity. Technical Report UH-CS-09-10, Computer Science Department, University of Houston (September 2009), http://www.cs.uh.edu/preprint
9. Tiplea, F.L., Enea, C., Birjoveanu, C.V.: Decidability and complexity results for security protocols. In: Verification of Infinite-State Systems with Applications to Security, pp. 185–211. IOS Press, Amsterdam (2006)
10. Chevalier, Y., Küsters, R., Rusinowitch, M., Turuani, M.: Deciding the security of protocols with Diffie-Hellman exponentiation and products in exponents. In: Pandya, P.K., Radhakrishnan, J. (eds.) FSTTCS 2003. LNCS, vol. 2914, pp. 124–135. Springer, Heidelberg (2003)
11. Chevalier, Y., Küsters, R., Rusinowitch, M., Turuani, M.: An NP decision procedure for protocol insecurity with XOR. Theor. Comput. Sci. 338(1-3), 247–274 (2005)
12. Chevalier, Y., Küsters, R., Rusinowitch, M., Turuani, M.: Deciding the security of protocols with commuting public key encryption. Electronic Notes in Theoretical Computer Science 125(1), 55–66 (2005)
13. Liang, Z., Verma, R.M.: A note on an NP-completeness proof for cryptographic protocol insecurity. Technical Report UH-CS-08-15, Computer Science Department, University of Houston (October 2008), http://www.cs.uh.edu/preprint
14. Froschle, S.: The insecurity problem: Tackling unbounded data. In: IEEE Computer Security Foundations Symposium 2007, pp. 370–384. IEEE Computer Society, Los Alamitos (2007)
15. Liang, Z., Verma, R.M.: Secrecy checking of protocols: Solution of an open problem. In: Automated Reasoning for Security Protocol Analysis (ARSPA 2007), July 2007, pp. 95–112 (2007)
16. Lowe, G.: Breaking and Fixing the Needham-Schroeder Public-Key Protocol Using FDR. In: Margaria, T., Steffen, B. (eds.) TACAS 1996. LNCS, vol. 1055, pp. 147–166. Springer, Heidelberg (1996)
17. Thayer, F.J., Herzog, J.C., Guttman, J.D.: Strand spaces: Proving security protocols correct. Journal of Computer Security 7(1) (1999)
18. Paulson, L.C.: The inductive approach to verifying cryptographic protocols. Journal of Computer Security 6(1-2), 85–128 (1998)
19. Corin, R., Etalle, S.: An improved constraint-based system for the verification of security protocols. In: Hermenegildo, M.V., Puebla, G. (eds.) SAS 2002. LNCS, vol. 2477, pp. 326–341. Springer, Heidelberg (2002)

Formal Verification of Security Policy
Implementations in Enterprise Networks

P. Bera[1], S.K. Ghosh[1], and Pallab Dasgupta[2]

[1] School of Information Technology
[2] Department of Computer Science & Engineering
Indian Institute of Technology, Kharagpur 721302, India
bera.padmalochan@gmail.com, skg@iitkgp.ac.in, pallab@cse.iitkgp.ernet.in

Abstract. In enterprise networks, the management of security policies and their configurations becoming increasingly difficult due to complex security constraints of the organizations. In such networks, the overall organizational security policy (global policy) is defined as a collection of rules for providing service accesses between various network zones. Often, the specification of the global policy is incomplete; where all possible service access paths may not be covered explicitly by the *"permit"* and *"deny"* rules. This policy is implemented in a distributed manner through appropriate sets of access control rules (ACL rules) in the network interfaces. However, the implementation must be complete i.e., all service access paths across the network must be implemented as *"permit"* and *"deny"* ACL rules. In that case, the unspecified access paths in a given policy must be implemented as either *"permit"* or *"deny"* rules; hence there may exist multiple ACL implementations corresponding to that policy. Formally verifying that the ACL rules distributed across the network interfaces guarantees proper enforcement of the global security policy is an important requirement and a major technical challenge. The complexity of the problem is compounded by the fact that some combination of network services may lead to inconsistent *hidden access paths* in the network. The ACL implementations ignoring these *hidden access paths* may result in violation of one or more policy rules implicitly. This paper presents a formal verification framework for analyzing security policy implementations in enterprise networks. It stems from boolean modeling of the network topology, network services and security policy where the unspecified access paths are modeled as *"don't-care"* rules. The framework formally models the *hidden access rules* and incorporates them in the distributed ACL implementations for extracting a security implementation model, and finally formulates a QSAT (satisfiability of quantified boolean formulae) based decision problem to verify whether the ACL implementation conforms to the global policy both in presence and absence of the *hidden access paths*.

Keywords: Network security, Security Policy, Access control list (ACL), Formal Verification.

A. Prakash and I. Sen Gupta (Eds.): ICISS 2009, LNCS 5905, pp. 117–131, 2009.
© Springer-Verlag Berlin Heidelberg 2009

1   Introduction

The management of services and operations in today's organizations are becoming increasingly dependent on their enterprise local area network (enterprise LAN). An enterprise LAN consists of a set of network *zones* (logical group of network elements) corresponding to different departments or sections, connected through various interface switches (typically, Layer-3 switches). The network service accesses between these zones and also with the external network (e.g., Internet) are governed by a global network security policy of the organization. This global policy is defined as a collection of service access rules across various network zones where the services referred network applications conforming to TCP/IP protocol. For example, some of the known network services are *ssh, telnet, http* etc. In reality, the security policy may be incompletely specified; which explicitly states the *"permit"* and *"deny"* access rules between specific network zones keeping remaining service access paths as unspecified.

The global security policy is realized in the network by configuring the network interfaces with appropriate sets of access control rules (ACLs). One of the major challenges in network security management is ensuring the conformation of the distributed security implementations with the global security policy. The distributed ACL implementation may not satisfy the global policy due to following reasons: (1) There may exist some unblocked *hidden service access paths* in the network which are not explicitly stated in the global policy; as a result the ACL implementation may lead the network to some state which violate one or more policy rules implicitly; (2) The combination of the ACL rules do not conform the global policy although there is no *hidden access path* in the network.

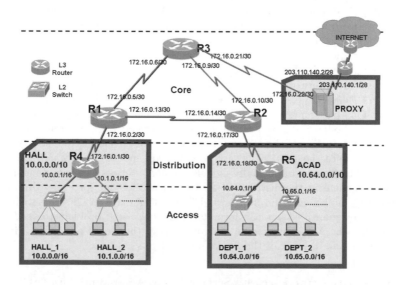

Fig. 1. A Typical Academic Network

Ensuring this satisfiability manually is difficult due to the complex security needs of present day networks (e.g. inclusion of *temporal service access rules*) and the presence of *hidden service access paths* in the network. The objective and the motivation behind the present work are presented with an example in the following section.

1.1   Objective and Motivating Example

A typical Academic network has been shown in Fig 1, which is deployed as hierarchical networking architecture consisting of *Core*, *Distribution* and *Access* layers. The network Access layer includes two network zones, namely, *HALL*(covers the student halls of residence) and *ACAD*(covers the academic departments). Moreover, the zones can be partitioned into sub-zones. For example, *HALL* is partitioned into *HALL_1*, *HALL_2* and so on. The *Core* includes three routers (R1, R2 and R3) and the distribution network consists of two routers (R4 and R5). The external access to Internet is realized through *PROXY* zone (consists of web proxy servers). The global security policy for the network is stated as follows:

*1. Internet (http) access is **NOT** allowed from **HALL***
*2. Internet (http) access is allowed from **ACAD***.

Now, let us consider the following implementation scenario: The ACL rule $\neg http$ (*HALL,PROXY*) is applied in the interface 172.16.0.1/30 of router R4 and $http(ACAD,PROXY)$ is applied in the interface 172.16.0.18/30 of router R5. This blocks all incoming *http* requests from *HALL* at R4 and allows the same from *ACAD* at R5. However, this does not strictly satisfy the intent (i.e., the global policy); because, there exist a *hidden http access path* from *HALL* to Internet (*PROXY* zone). One can access *ssh/telnet* from *HALL* to *ACAD* (which may be allowed from *HALL* as it is not explicitly stated in the global policy) and access Internet from there (which is allowed from *ACAD*). This *hidden access path* may be formally represented as follows:

$$\text{ssh(HALL,ACAD)} \wedge \text{http(ACAD,PROXY)} \Rightarrow \text{http(HALL,PROXY)} \quad (1)$$

$$\text{telnet(HALL,ACAD)} \wedge \text{http(ACAD,PROXY)} \Rightarrow \text{http(HALL,PROXY)} \quad (2)$$

While verifying the security implementations (the distribution of ACL rules to various switches), it is required to consider such hidden rules which capture the relation between known services. Therefore, a correct ACL implementation should restrict these hidden access paths consistently. The problem becomes more complex if the policy rules incorporate temporal constraints, e.g. *"http access from **HALL** is not allowed in week-days during 0800-1700 hours"*. Therefore it is required to verify the correctness at the various windows of time.

The combination of network services that can create hidden access paths needs to be known for verification. This constitutes a significant amount of domain knowledge in our verification problem. In order to accommodate new combinations of network services, our decision framework provides a formalism for specifying *hidden access rules*.

In the absence of *hidden access rules*, the task of verifying that the distributed ACL implementation conform the global security policies can be reduced to boolean satisfiability (SAT). On the other hand, when hidden access rules are considered, these rules can be applied transitively to discover the complex hidden access paths in the network, and the verification framework must examine all such paths. It will be shown that this verification problem can be modeled as the problem of checking the truth of a *Quantified Boolean Formula* (QBF), and can be solved in reasonable time using a QBF-SAT solver [15] [16].

The present work primarily focuses on the following issues:

– Specification of the global security policy using proposed security policy specification language, SPSL; which defines the security policy model;
– Extraction of implementation model from the distributed ACL implementations of the global policy;
– Formal modeling of *hidden access rules* and refinement of the implementation model by incorporating these rules;
– Boolean reduction of policy and implementation models and formulation of a quantified boolean satisfiability checking (QSAT) problem;
– Solving the satisfiability of the problem using appropriate QBF SAT solver.

Security policy model functionally reduces the explicit *"permit"* and *"deny"* service access rules into two boolean functions, $\mathcal{PT}$ *(V:service, S:source, D:dest, T:time)* and $\mathcal{PF}(V,S,D,T)$ which state whether the service V is allowed/denied between source S and destination D in time T respectively. The remaining access paths are modeled as *"don't care"* rules and also reduced into a boolean function *don't-care:$\mathcal{PX}$(V,S,D,T)*,where, $\mathcal{PX} = \neg\mathcal{PT} \wedge \neg\mathcal{PF}$. On the other hand, security implementation model captures the device specific access control rules [example:*Cisco ACL standard*] distributed across the interfaces of the network. Intuitively the implementation model completely define the service access paths across the network as either *"permit"* or *"deny"* ACL rules. Thus, the ACL implementation model define a boolean function, $\mathcal{AG}$ *(V:service, S:source, D:dest, T:time)*, which states whether the service V, is allowed between the source S and destination D, at time, T. The negation of $\mathcal{AG}$ trivially represents the blocked service access paths. The set of ACL rules and the network topology defines this function partially, but do not capture the *hidden access paths* between sources and destinations which are induced by the *hidden access rules*. Therefore we need to apply these rules to arrive at the correct definition of the function, $\mathcal{AG}$, which we refer as the final ACL implementation model, $\mathcal{M}_I$.

Given a policy model $\mathcal{M}_P$ [represented by the boolean functions $\mathcal{PT}$, $\mathcal{PF}$ and $\mathcal{PX}$] and a distributed ACL implementation model $\mathcal{M}_\mathcal{I}$, our objective is to check whether $\mathcal{M}_\mathcal{I}$ satisfies $\mathcal{M}_P$ or not. In the present work, this model checking problem is reduced into a boolean function F, say, $F = ((\mathcal{PT} \vee \mathcal{PX} \Rightarrow \mathcal{M}_\mathcal{I}) \wedge (\mathcal{PF} \vee \mathcal{PX} \Rightarrow \neg\mathcal{M}_\mathcal{I}))$ and its satisfiability is checked.

The rest of the paper is organized as follows. Section 2 presents the related work in network security analysis. In Section 3, the modeling of security policies using the proposed policy specification language, SPSL, has been described. The extraction of the ACL implementation model with formal modeling of hidden access rules has been presented in section 4. Section 5 presents QSAT based verification procedure along with verification results.

2   Related Work

Existing literatures on network security analysis primarily concentrate on inconsistency and redundancy checks but most of the works are not formally verified. Tools that allow user queries for the purpose of firewall analysis and management include Firmato [1] and Lumeta [2]. These tools can specify an abstract network access control policy and firewall rules that satisfy the policy but lacks in incorporating temporal constraints and hidden rule analysis. Liu et al [6] have given an algorithm specialized for finding redundancies. Uribe et al [3] focuses on high level modeling of firewall and network configurations that satisfy a given policy. But both of these tools can handle a specific set of problems and simple set of policy constraints. The notion of hidden access paths and the complexity it introduces into the analysis is not reported in any of these papers.

In order to arrive at a formal method for checking whether a set of ACL rules guarantee a global policy specification, it is necessary to evolve a language for specifying the policy requirements. Researchers have proposed different high level security policy specification languages, namely, HLFL [7], Firmato [1], FLIP [8] etc. FLIP [8], is one of the most recent conflict free firewall policy languages for network traffic access control, to enforce security and ensure seamless configuration management. In FLIP, security policies are defined as high level service oriented goals, which can be translated automatically into access control rules to be distributed to appropriate enforcement devices. FLIP guarantees that the rules generated are conflict-free. But, it does not address temporal policy constraints and hidden rule conflicts. We have proposed a high level language, namely, *Security Policy Specification Language (SPSL)* for specifying the global security policies of an organizational LAN. The language allows specifying explicit "permit" and "deny" service access rules and remaining service access paths are treated as *"don't care"* rules. The unique features of our language are easy-to-use constructs and methods for specifying temporal policy rules.

Formal methods have been used to address some specific problems in the area of network security. For example, the FIREMAN Toolkit [4] is capable of detecting inconsistencies and redundancies in single firewalls and in a network of firewalls. The set of all possible requests are formulated and model checking is used to divide the set into those which are accepted, those which are rejected, and those for which no rule applies. The tool can handle large sets of firewall rules since it uses an efficient BDD representation. The Network Policy Enforcement tool [11] is one of the recent tools in this line of work. Another recent work is proposed by Matousek, Rysavy, Rab, and Sveda [12] on formal models for network wide security analysis. They model the network topology with changing link states and deploys SAT-based bounded model checking of network security properties. Matsumoto and Bouhoula [5] proposes a SAT based approach for verifying firewall configurations with respect to security policy requirements. Again, the notion of hidden access paths and formalizing the verification problem in their presence has not been considered earlier.

3   Security Policy Specification

The security policy of a network defines a set of functional rules on flow of packets between different nodes in the network. Complexity of the policy depends on the size of the network, controlling parameters and dependency amongst the rules. The specification language must be expressive enough to represent complex security constraints correctly. We have proposed a security policy specification language, SPSL, for modeling the security policies. In the following section, the various constructs of the proposed language has been described.

3.1   Security Policy Specification Language(SPSL)

The main constructs of the SPSL can be classified as: (a) network topology constructs and (b) network services and policy rule constructs. The SPSL allows to specify explicit *"permit"* and *"deny"* service access rules across the network zones, whereas the *"don't care"* rules are derived from these rule sets during boolean reduction of the policy model.

Network topology specification: The proposed SPSL has the following constructs to describe the network topology.

Zone: A zone is a logical unit consisting of workstations, servers or other systems in the network, usually refers to a particular section of an organization. It is represented by IP address block(s) and it referred by the IP address block(s) or by a symbolic name. Further, a zone can be partitioned into multiple disjoint sub-zones.

> *Example 1: Zone Specification*
> Zone HALL_1 [10.0.0.0-10.0.255.255];
> Zone HALL_2 [10.1.0.0-10.1.255.255];
> Zone HALL [HALL_1, HALL_2];

Router: Routers are interconnection switches in the network. A router can be connected to a network zone or another router. It consists of set of interfaces.

Interfaces: An interface is the connecting link between a zone and a router or between multiple routers. Each interface is identified by an unique IP address.

> *Example 2: Router and Interface Specification*
> Interface int_R12 [172.16.0.13];
> Interface int_R13 [172.16.0.5];
> Interface int_R14 [172.16.0.2];
> Router R1 [Int_R12, Int_R13, Int_R14];

Network Service and Policy rule specification: The SPSL has the following constructs to specify the network services and policy rules.

Service: Network service is defined by a network protocol and a predicate associated with it. Each predicate defines the service port numbers or port ranges.

Example 3: Network Service Specification
```
service http = TCP [port = 80];
service ssh = TCP [port>20 AND port<23];
```

Policy Rule: A *policy rule* defines service access (*"permit"*/*"deny"*) path between a source and a destination zone under some constraints (optional). The static rules do not include temporal access constraints, whereas temporal rules include such constraints. SPSL models only time dependent constraints which can be combination of day and time range specifications. The source and destination can be zone containing single node, multiple nodes, union of multiple zones or a zone except a sub-zone. The rules on both *incoming* and *outgoing* packets from/to a zone can be specified through appropriate combination of the source and destination zone.

Example 4: Policy Rule Specification
```
deny ssh(HALL, ACAD);
permit telnet([HALL,DEPT_1], ACAD);
deny http(HALL,PROXY)[const=week_day(0800-1700)];
```

The specification generated from this phase defines the policy model, $\mathcal{M}_P$. In the SAT reduction phase, this policy model is reduced into three boolean functions $\mathcal{PT}$, $\mathcal{PF}$ and *"don't-care"*:$\mathcal{PX}$ which are described in section 5.

4   Security Implementation Model

Security policy of an enterprise LAN is implemented through a set of device specific access control rules (ACL) applied to various interfaces of the access switches (or routers) in a distributed manner. There are various device specific standards for specifying access control rules e.g. *Cisco standard ACL* [9]. Most of the standards are logically similar in the context of implementing basic security policy of a network. *Cisco standard ACL* has the feature to represent temporal constraints and is widely used in large scale networks. Here, the ACL file consists of an ACL configuration block and a set of ACL rules. The ACL rules represent the *"permit"* and *"deny"* service access paths between specified source and destinations. Set of ACL rules are logically combined into an *ACL-group*. The ACL configuration block holds the binding information of *ACL-groups* to router interfaces. The important property of this standard is that the ACL rules under each *ACL-group* are top down order dependent. In our approach, a model is extracted from the device specific *ACL implementation* corresponding to the global policy of the network. This process involves following phases; (a) Resolving inter-rule conflicts and topology dependency (b) Hidden access path analysis.

4.1   Resolving Inter-rule Conflicts and Topology Dependency

The proposed verification framework checks the statisfiability of the distributed ACL implementation with the global security policy through reduction of the rule bases into set of boolean formulas. So, it is required to represent the distributed ACL rule sets into a single ACL rule base which is inter-rule conflict-free and network topology independent without changing the ACL rule semantics. It firstly requires removal of inter-rule conflicts from the rule set associated to each router interface, and then merging of the conflict-free rule sets in a single rule base. The ACL inter-rule conflicts may occur due to rule component dependencies which are described as follows.

Rule subsuming conflict: Consider a pair of ACL rules P_1 and P_2 in the same *ACL-group* where P_1 precedes P_2;

P_1 : *permit* TCP X1, Y1 eq *ssh*;
P_2 : *deny* TCP X, Y eq *ssh*; such that $(X1 \subset X)$ and $(Y1 \subset Y)$.

Here, source and destination of P_1 are subsumed by the same of P_2. The pair of rules semantically means that *ssh* service accesses from any source in X to any destination in Y is denied except those where source and destination are X1 and Y1 respectively. To make these rules conflict-free, it is required to replace the rule P_2 with two new rules P_2' and P_2'' where,

P_2' : *deny* TCP (X-X1), Y eq *ssh*;
P_2'' : *deny* TCP X, (Y-Y1) eq *ssh*.

Similar type of conflict may occur between a pair of static and temporal service access rules under the same ACL group with identical *service* component.

Rule Overriding conflict: Consider a pair of ACL rules P_3 and P_4 in the same *ACL-group* where P_3 precedes P_4;

P_3 : *permit* TCP X,Y eq http;
P_4 : *deny* TCP X,Y eq http.

Here P_3 overrides P_4 because these rules contradict to each other. As the rule order is top down, resolving this conflict requires deletion of order-minor rule P_4 from the rule base.

On the other hand, consider a pair of rules P_5 and P_6,

P_5 : *permit* TCP X1, Y1 eq *ssh*;
P_6 : *permit* TCP X2, Y2 eq *ssh*;

such that, $((X1 \subset X2)$ and $(Y1 \subset Y2))$ or $((X2 \subset X1)$ and $(Y2 \subset Y1))$.

In such cases the order-major rule (P_5) overrides the order-minor rule (P_6). Resolving these conflicts require deletion of P_6 from the rule base.

The inter-rule conflict removal procedure resolves *rule subsuming* and *rule overriding* conflicts through selective *insertion/deletion* of rules *to/from* the rule sets associated to a each router interface. Once the conflicts from each rule set is resolved, the procedure removes the binding information (router and interface bindings) and merges the rule sets into a single rule base which is conflict-free and network topology independent. The *hidden access path analysis* procedure is applied on this rule base which is described in the following section.

4.2 Hidden Access Path Analysis

The hidden access paths may exist in a network due to the transitive access relationships between various known network services. In section 1.1, it has been shown how hidden *http* access paths may appear in a network through conflicting *ssh* and *telnet* services. The *hidden access paths* can be modeled through a set of formulas in predicate logic. For example, the hidden *http* access paths from any network zone X to any network zone Z can be formally represented as follows:

$$\forall X \forall Z, ((\exists Y, ssh(X, Y) \land http(Y, Z)) \Rightarrow http(X, Z)) \tag{3}$$

$$\forall X \forall Z, ((\exists Y, telnet(X, Y) \land http(Y, Z)) \Rightarrow http(X, Z)) \tag{4}$$

$$\forall X \forall Z, ((\exists Y \exists T, ssh(X, Y)[T] \land http(Y, Z)[T]) \Rightarrow http(X, Z)[T]) \tag{5}$$

$$\forall X \forall Z, ((\exists Y \exists T, telnet(X, Y)[T] \land http(Y, Z)[T]) \Rightarrow http(X, Z)[T]) \tag{6}$$

where, $X, Y, Z \in All\_Zone$ represent *network zones* and T represents arbitrary *time-constraint*. *All_Zone* is a set, *disjoint union* of distinct network zones.

The equations 3 and 4 represent *static hidden http access paths* whereas, equations 5 and 6 represent the *temporal hidden http access paths* with some time constraint T. The modelling and analysis of *hidden http access paths* in the ACL implementation has been carried out in this paper to prove the efficacy of the approach. Incidentally, Internet access through *http* is one of the major security concern in any enterprise network. However, the *hidden access paths* under other services can be formally modelled through similar approach.

For the proper assessment of the implementation with respect to the policy model, all such hidden access paths must be incorporated in the implementation model. In the present approach, the *hidden access rules* are reduced into quantified boolean formulas (QBF) and incorporated in the conflict-free ACL rule base to derive the refined implementation model $\mathcal{M}_\mathcal{I}$. The boolean reduction of the ACL implementation model is described in section 5.

5   QSAT Based Verification Procedure

In QSAT based approach, the verification problem is reduced into a quantified boolean formula (QBF) and its satisfiability is checked. Although satisfiability analysis is NP complete problem, still this technique is becoming popular today due to tremendous time tradeoffs of modern SAT [10] and QBF-SAT solvers [16] [17]. In the present work, the policy model is reduced into three boolean functions, $\mathcal{PT}$ *(V:service, S:source, D:dest, T:time)*, $\mathcal{PF}$ *(V,S,D,T)* and *don't-care:* $\mathcal{PX}$ *(V,S,D,T)*; where, $\mathcal{PX} = \neg \mathcal{PT} \land \neg \mathcal{PF}$. Whereas, the ACL implementation model must be complete and should not contain *"don't-care"* rules.

So, the implementation model is reduced into a boolean function, $\mathcal{AG}$ (V:service, S:source, D:dest, T:time) which represents the allowed service access paths between various network zones in specific time. The negation of $\mathcal{AG}$ trivially covers the service access paths which are not allowed. Then, the *hidden access rules* are incorporated in the model to reach the final implementation model, $\mathcal{M_I}$. Finally, the satisfiability of the formula $F = ((\mathcal{PT} \vee \mathcal{PX} \Rightarrow \mathcal{M_I}) \wedge (\mathcal{PF} \vee \mathcal{PX} \Rightarrow \neg\mathcal{M_I}))$ is checked using *quaffle* QBF-SAT solver [15].

5.1   Boolean Reduction of Models

In this phase, policy and implementation rule bases are functionally reduced into boolean clauses. There may exists two types of rules in the models: (a) Generic access control rules (*"permit"/"deny"*) which are common to both the models (b) Hidden access rules which are specific to the implementation model. The boolean reduction of the policy and implementation models are described in the following subsections respectively.

Policy Model Reduction: The policy model consists of a set of generic service access rules which represent the access paths to be allowed or blocked between specific source and destinations. The unspecified access paths are modeled as *"don't care"* rules. The policy model reduction process starts with mapping of the rule components into boolean variables. The rule components include *service (protocol, port number), source zone, destination zone, time-constraint* and *action*. A network zone can be specified as single IP address or range of IP addresses. So, the *source* and *destination* zones are mapped to 32 boolean variables. A range of IP addresses can be translated using disjunction ($\vee$) operator. Address ranges with masks can be reduced by bit-wise anding the masks with the base addresses. Similarly, protocol type and port numbers are mapped into appropriate boolean variables. In both the models, time constraints are modeled as disjunction of its valid periods. Each valid time period can contain *day of week, hours* and *minutes* etc. The components of a valid time period are mapped into a set of boolean variables. The functional mapping of rule components into boolean variables is depicted in Table 1.

After rule component mapping, the policy model reduction algorithm reduces the policy rules into two boolean functions $\mathcal{PF}$(V:service, S:source, D:dest, T:time), $\mathcal{PG}$(V,S,D,T) based on the *action* component (*"permit/1"* or *"deny/0"*). If the *action* is *"permit"*, then the rule is associated to $\mathcal{PT}$ as disjunction ($\vee$); otherwise, the rule is associated to $\mathcal{PF}$ as disjunction ($\vee$). Then the algorithm computes the boolean function *don't-care:*$\mathcal{PX}$(V,S,D,T) as $\mathcal{PX} = \neg\mathcal{PT} \wedge \neg\mathcal{PF}$. The policy model reduction algorithm is presented in Table 1 [refer **Algorithm1.**] Here, FP, FI, FS, FD and FT are boolean functions over the literals associated to the boolean variables corresponding to the rule components: *protocol, service port number, source, destination* and *time-constraint* respectively. Each literal can be a boolean variable or the negation of the variable. The reduced policy model $\mathcal{M_P}$ is represented by the boolean formulas, $\mathcal{PT}_{N+1}$, $\mathcal{PF}_{N+1}$ and $\mathcal{PX}$.

Table 1. Boolean Reduction Of Policy Model

Functional mapping of policy rule components into boolean variables
Protocol(P):FP(p_0, p_1)
PortNo(I):FI$(i_0, i_1, ..., i_7)$
Src_IP(SIP):FS$(s_0, s_1, ..., s_{31})$
Dst_IP(DIP):FD$(d_0, d_1, ..., d_{31})$
Time(T):FT$(dt_0, dt_1, dt_2, t_0, .., t_4)$
Action(g):$A(g)$

Algorithm1 :: Reduce_Pol_Model()
Input: Policy Rule Base $\{PR_1, PR_2, .., PR_N\}$
Output: Reduced Policy Model $\mathcal{M}_P$ $[\mathcal{PG}_{N+1}, \mathcal{PF}_{N+1}$ and $\mathcal{PX}]$
1. BEGIN
2. $\mathcal{PT}_1$=1/TRUE, $\mathcal{PF}_1 = 1/TRUE$
3.   FOR each policy rule PR_i (i=1 to N)
4. R_i = Reduce_Gen_Rule(PR_i)
5.   IF Action(R_i) = "permit" THEN
6. $\mathcal{PT}_{i+1} \Leftrightarrow (\mathcal{PT}_i \vee R_i)$
7. $\mathcal{PF}_{i+1} \Leftrightarrow \mathcal{PF}_i$
8.   END IF
9.   IF Action(R_i) = "deny" THEN
10. $\mathcal{PF}_{i+1} \Leftrightarrow (\mathcal{PF}_i \vee R_i)$
11. $\mathcal{PT}_{i+1} \Leftrightarrow \mathcal{PT}_i$
12.   END IF
13.   END FOR
14. $\mathcal{PX} \Leftrightarrow \neg\mathcal{PT}_{N+1} \wedge \neg\mathcal{PF}_{N+1}$
15. END

Procedure:: Reduce_Gen_Rule()
Input: A generic access control rule, PR_i or IR_i
Output: Boolean Reduction of the rule, PR_i or IR_i
1. BEGIN
2. $P_i \Leftrightarrow FP_i(p_o, p_1) \wedge$
3. $I_i \Leftrightarrow FI_i(i_0, i_1, .., i_7) \wedge$
4. $Serv_i \Leftrightarrow (P_i \wedge I_i) \wedge$
5. $SIP_i \Leftrightarrow FS_i(s_0, s_1, .., s_{31}) \wedge$
6. $DIP_i \Leftrightarrow FD_i(d_0, d_1, .., d_{31}) \wedge$
7. $T_i \Leftrightarrow FT_i(dt_0, dt_1, dt_2, t_0, .., t_4) \wedge$
8. $R_i \Leftrightarrow (Serv_i \wedge SIP_i \wedge DIP_i \wedge T_i)$
9. Return R_i
10. END

Implementation Model Reduction: This phase reduces the conflict-free generic ACL rule base into a boolean function, $\mathcal{AG}$(V:service, S:source, D:dest, T:time). The reduction algorithm starts with an initial model $\mathcal{AG}_0$ assigned to "TRUE". Then, it formulates boolean clause for each generic ACL rule [refer, *Reduce_Gen_Rule()* in the **Algorithm2**] and updates $\mathcal{AG}_0$ by incorporating the clause based on rule *action*. If the *action* is *"permit"*, the rule clause is associated to the model as disjunction [∨]; whereas for *"deny"* rules, the negation

Table 2. Boolean Reduction of Implementation Model

Algorithm2 :: `Reduce_Imp_Model()`
Input: ACL Rule Base $\{IR_1, IR_2, .., IR_N\}$
Output: Reduced Implementation Model $\mathcal{M_I}$
1. BEGIN
2. AG_1=1/TRUE
3.   FOR each generic ACL rule IR_i (i=1 to N)
4. FR_i = Reduce_Gen_Rule(IR_i)
5.   IF Action(FR_i)=''permit" THEN
6. $\mathcal{AG}_{i+1} \Leftrightarrow (\mathcal{AG}_i \vee FR_i)$
7.   ELSE
8. $\mathcal{AG}_{i+1} \Leftrightarrow (\mathcal{AG}_i \wedge \neg FR_i)$
9.   END IF
10.   END FOR
11. $\mathcal{M_I}$ =Reduce_hidden_rule($\mathcal{AG}_{N+1}$)
12. END
Procedure:: `Reduce_hidden_rule()`
Input: ACL Rule Model,$\mathcal{AG}_{N+1}$ and hidden rule set $\{HR_1, HR_2, .., HR_N\}$
Output: Refined Implementation Model incorporating the hidden rules
1. BEGIN
2. $M^0 = \mathcal{AG}_{N+1}$
3. FOR each hidden rule HR_i (i=1 to N)
4. M^i = Update_model_bool_hidden(M^{i-1}, HR_i)
5. END FOR
6. $\mathcal{M_I}$ =M^N
7. END
Procedure:: `Update_model_bool_hidden`(M^0, HR_1)
Input: Boolean model M^0 and hidden rule HR_1
$[HR_1 :: \forall X, \forall Z, \exists Y, ssh(X,Y) \wedge ssh(Y,Z) \Rightarrow ssh(X,Z)]$
Output: Updated model M^1 with reduction of hidden rule HR_1
1. BEGIN
2. $\forall X, \forall Z, \exists Y,$ IF $ssh(X,Y) \in M^0 \wedge ssh(Y,Z) \in M^0$ THEN
3. $M^1 \Leftrightarrow M^0 \vee ssh(X,Z)$
4.   Return M^1
5.   END IF
6. END
Reduced Boolean Clause:
$\forall X, \exists Y, \forall Z, \exists Serv_{ssh}, [Serv_{ssh} \wedge FS(X) \wedge FD(Y) \Rightarrow M^0] \wedge$
$[Serv_{ssh} \wedge FS(Y) \wedge FD(Z) \Rightarrow M^0] \Rightarrow [M^1 \Leftrightarrow M^0 \vee [Serv_{ssh} \wedge FS(X) \wedge FD(Z)]]$

of the clause is associated to the model as conjunction [∧]. In this way, the procedure formulates the generic ACL rule model, represented as $\mathcal{AG}_{N+1}$ [refer **Algorithm2** in Table 2]. Here, the `Reduce_Gen_Rule()` procedure functionally reduces the rule components into boolean as it does in policy model reduction.

After this step, the hidden rule reduction procedure models each hidden access rule into a quantified boolean formula and incorporates it in the generic ACL rule model, $\mathcal{AG}_{N+1}$. Initially, $\mathcal{AG}_{N+1}$ is assigned to a model M^0, then it is updated by the hidden access rules to produce intermediate models, M^1, M^2 and so on. Here, the `Update_model_bool_hidden()` procedure shows the reduction of one hidden access rule. The final boolean implementation model is represented by $\mathcal{M_I}$. The Implementation model reduction algorithm is presented in Table 2.

5.2 QBF SAT Solver and QSAT Query Formation

We have used *quaffle* QBF-SAT solver [15] [17] as the verification tool. It takes QSAT query in standard conjunctive normal form (CNF) and checks its satisfiability. The commonly used format for storing quantified CNF formulae (of QSAT problems) in ASCII files is *QDIMACS* [14].

The QSAT query for our problem can be stated as: *"Is the ACL implementation model ($\mathcal{M_I}$) satisfies the policy model ($\mathcal{M_P}$)"*. So, it is sufficient to check the satisfiability of the expression: $F = ((\mathcal{PT} \vee \mathcal{PX} \Rightarrow \mathcal{M_I}) \wedge (\mathcal{PF} \vee \mathcal{PX} \Rightarrow \neg\mathcal{M_I}))$. Here, the formula F is translated into CNF using standard algorithm for 3-CNF satisfiability [13]. The algorithm forms truth tables for every subexpression containing disjunctions of conjunctions and converts it into CNF applying De-Morgan's rules where each clause contains at most 3 literals. For example, equivalent CNF corresponding to the formula F can be represented as $(\neg\mathcal{PT} \vee \mathcal{M_I}) \wedge (\neg\mathcal{PF} \vee \neg\mathcal{M_I}) \wedge (\neg\mathcal{PX} \vee \mathcal{M_I}) \wedge (\neg\mathcal{PX} \vee \neg\mathcal{M_I})$. The formula F (in QDIMACS CNF format) is provided as input to *quaffle*. It checks the SAT or UNSAT of the formula.

5.3 Implementations and Verification Results

The SAT reduction algorithms presented in this paper are implemented in C programming language under Linux environment. Parsers have been developed for parsing the policy specification in SPSL and the device specific ACL implementation in a network. The framework has been verified with various test cases of implementations under defined policy specifications in an enterprise LAN. Some of the experimental results under the academic network [refer Fig 1] are shown in Table 3. It shows number of policy and ACL rules along with the variables and clauses in the reduced QSAT query under each test case. The result also shows SAT/UNSAT of the QSAT query along with the SAT reduction time and *quaffle* execution time. Here the number of policy and ACL rules are indicated by P and I respectively. The parameters V, Q and C indicate the number of variables, quantified variables and CNF clauses in the QSAT query respectively. T_{CR}, T_{SAT} and T_E indicate the ACL conflict removal time (in seconds), SAT reduction time(in seconds) and *quaffle* run time (in milliseconds) respectively. The SAT result implies that the implementation satisfies the policy whereas the UNSAT implies implementation does not satisfy the policy. The SAT reduction time indicates the time required to represent the policy and ACL rule bases into boolean models and to formulate the QSAT query. It is linearly dependent on the number of policy, ACL rules and hidden rules. Normally, hidden rule reduction time remains constant as the number of hidden rules is fixed in the model. On the other hand the ACL Conflict removal time is exponentially dependent on the ACL rule count as the procedure incorporates linear search on the ACL

Table 3. Verification Results

Test Cases	P	I	V	Q	C	quaffle Output	T_{CR}	T_{SAT}	T_E
TC1	10	10	80	21	159	SAT	2.84	7.16	1.19
TC2	23	25	88	24	198	UNSAT	4.57	8.17	0.88
TC3	23	28	88	24	201	SAT	4.63	8.34	0.75
TC4	38	38	94	28	231	UNSAT	5.21	9.33	1.17
TC5	45	32	94	22	215	SAT	5.11	8.47	0.93
TC6	45	45	90	25	245	UNSAT	5.76	9.17	1.12
TC7	56	52	98	25	260	UNSAT	5.55	9.56	1.12
TC8	56	56	101	25	263	SAT	5.12	8.57	0.95

rule base for finding conflicts. Typically, for large enterprise network, the number of policy and ACL rules lies within few hundreds. Further, the framework uses an efficient QBF-SAT solver, *quaffle*, which can process millions of clauses in a single run and produce the output in negligible time (usually, within a second). So, the framework will scale considerably well for standard enterprise LANs. The framework will help the network administrators in debugging the security implementations and the policy designers in making their policy specification correct and precise.

6   Conclusion

In today's complex enterprise network, there is an increasing requirement of validating the security implementation with the organizational security policy. This paper presents a formal verification framework to verify the access control based security implementations with respect to partially specified security policies for an enterprise LAN. The major contribution of the work lies in the analysis of the hidden service access paths, which plays a significant role in deriving correct security implementations in a network. The efficacy of the framework has been demonstrated through a case study. The proposed framework will facilitate in debugging of network security implementations efficiently and designing conflict free security policies in an enterprise network. Our future work is to address the security issues incorporating policy based routing and role based access control models in the implementation.

References

1. Bartal, Y., Mayer, A., Nissim, K., Wool, A.: Firmato: A Novel Firewall Management Toolkit. ACM Transaction on Computer Systems 22(4), 381–420 (2004)
2. Al-Shaer, E.S., Hamed, H.H.: Discovery of Policy Anomalies in Distributed Firewalls. In: Proceedings of IEEE INFOCOM 2004, Hong Kong, China, March 2004, pp. 2605–2626 (2004)

3. Uribe, T.E., Cheung, S.: Automatic Analysis of Firewall and Network Intrusion Detection System Configurations. In: ACM Workshop on Formal Methods in Security Engineering, Washington, DC, USA, October 2004, pp. 66–71 (2004)

4. Yuan, L., Mai, J., Su, Z., Chen, H., Chuah, C., Mohapatra, P.: FIREMAN: A Toolkit for Firewall Modeling and Analysis. In: 27th IEEE Symposium on Security and Privacy, Oakland, CA, USA (May 2006)

5. Matsumoto, S., Bouhoula, A.: Automatic Verification of Firewall Configuration with Respect to Security Policy Requirements. In: Proceedings of the International Workshop on Computational Intelligence in Security for Information Systems (CISIS 2008), Barcelona, Spain, October 2008, pp. 123–130 (2008)

6. Liu, A.X., Gouda, M.G.: Complete Redundancy Detection in Firewalls. In: Jajodia, S., Wijesekera, D. (eds.) Data and Applications Security 2005. LNCS, vol. 3654, pp. 193–206. Springer, Heidelberg (2005)

7. High Level Firewall Language, http://www.hlfl.org/ (Accessed on April 2009)

8. Zhang, B., Al-Shaer, E.S., Jagadeesan, R., Riely, J., Pitcher, C.: Specifications of A High-level Conflict-Free Firewall Policy Language for Multi-domain Networks. In: 12th ACM Symposium on Access control models and Technologies (SACMAT 2007), France, June 2007, pp. 185–194 (2007)

9. CISCO: Configuring IP access lists. CISCO white papers 23602 edition (July 2007)

10. Mahajan, Y.S., Fu, Z., Malik, S.: Zchaff 2004: An efficient SAT solver. In: Hoos, H.H., Mitchell, D.G. (eds.) SAT 2004. LNCS, vol. 3542, pp. 360–375. Springer, Heidelberg (2005)

11. Zhang, C.C., Winslet, M., Gunter, C.A.: On the Safety and Efficiency of Firewall Policy Deployment. In: 28th IEEE Symposium on Security and Privacy, Oakland, CA, USA, May 2007, pp. 33–50 (2007)

12. Matousek, P., Rab, J., Rysavy, O., Sveda, M.: A Formal model for Network-wide Security Analysis. In: Proceedings of 15th IEEE International Conference and Workshop on ECBS, Belfast, Ireland (2008)

13. Hofmeister, T., Schoning, U., Schuler, R., Watanabe, O.: A Probabilistic 3-SAT Algorithm further improved. In: Alt, H., Ferreira, A. (eds.) STACS 2002. LNCS, vol. 2285, pp. 192–202. Springer, Heidelberg (2002)

14. QDIMACS Standard Version 1.1., http://www.qbflib.org/qdimacs.html (Accessed on March 2009)

15. Yu, Y., Malik, S.: Yquaffle QBF solver, http://www.princeton.edu/chaff/quaffle.html (Accessed on March 2009)

16. Giunchinglia, E., Narrizzano, M., Tacchella, A.: QUBE: A System for deciding quantified boolean formulas satisfiability. In: International Joint Conference on Automated Reasoning (IJCAR), pp. 364–369 (2001)

17. Zhang, L., Malik, S.: Towards Symmetric treatment of Conflicts and satisfaction in quantified Boolean satisfiability. In: Van Hentenryck, P. (ed.) CP 2002. LNCS, vol. 2470, pp. 200–215. Springer, Heidelberg (2002)

Making Peer-Assisted Content Distribution Robust to Collusion Using Bandwidth Puzzles

Michael K. Reiter[1], Vyas Sekar[2], Chad Spensky[1], and Zhenghao Zhang[3]

[1] University of North Carolina, Chapel Hill, NC, USA
[2] Carnegie Mellon University, Pittsburgh, PA, USA
[3] Florida State University, Tallahassee, FL, USA

Abstract. Many peer-assisted content-distribution systems reward a peer based on the amount of data that this peer serves to others. However, validating that a peer did so is, to our knowledge, an open problem; e.g., a group of colluding attackers can earn rewards by claiming to have served content to one another, when they have not. We propose a puzzle mechanism to make contribution-aware peer-assisted content distribution robust to such collusion. Our construction ties solving the puzzle to possession of specific content and, by issuing puzzle challenges simultaneously to all parties claiming to have that content, our mechanism prevents one content-holder from solving many others' puzzles. We prove (in the random oracle model) the security of our scheme, describe our integration of bandwidth puzzles into a media streaming system, and demonstrate the resulting attack resilience via simulations.

1 Introduction

Many systems that distribute content with the help of peer-to-peer (P2P) overlays measure peer contribution and incentivize participation. Peers who contribute more are rewarded with better performance via higher priority in the distribution overlay (e.g., [1, 2, 3]) or priority service through server-assisted downloads (e.g., [4]), or with other mechanisms (e.g., discount coupons [4]). We refer to such systems as *contribution-aware* peer-assisted content distribution systems.

Unfortunately, mechanisms for demonstrating how much data a peer has served are vulnerable to a simple form of "shilling" [5,6], where colluding attackers report receiving service from each other without actually transferring content among themselves. In some systems, these attackers can degrade the system, e.g., by gaining a powerful position in the distribution overlay and then launching a denial-of-service attack [1, 2]. In others, this enables them to get higher priority service while contributing only a limited amount of upload bandwidth. Such attacks are not merely hypothetical, but occur frequently in widely used P2P systems (e.g., [3,7,8,9]). Fundamentally, what makes the problem difficult is that with today's network infrastructure, it is impossible for a third party to verify if a specific data transfer occurred between two colluding entities.

A. Prakash and I. Sen Gupta (Eds.): ICISS 2009, LNCS 5905, pp. 132–147, 2009.

We propose a *bandwidth puzzle* mechanism to make contribution-aware P2P content distribution robust to collusion attacks. With this mechanism, a *verifier* can confirm that claimed transfers of content actually occurred. For example, in P2P media streaming from a distinguished server (e.g., [1, 10, 2, 11]), or in P2P systems that have a distinguished node for tracking content-transfer transactions (e.g., [3,4,12]), this distinguished node can naturally play the role of the verifier.

There are two key insights behind our design. First, to those peers (or "provers") claiming to have some specific content, the verifier presents puzzles for which the solution depends on the content. That is, the solution is computationally simple for a prover who has the content, but more difficult for a prover who does not. Second, the verifier *simultaneously* presents these puzzles to all peers who currently claim to have the content, so as to make it difficult for a few peers who have the content to quickly solve both their own puzzles and puzzles for collaborators who do not. The verifier checks the puzzle solutions and also notes the time taken by the provers to report the solutions. Any peer whose solution is incorrect or whose solution time is greater than a threshold θ is a suspect for engaging in fake transactions. The verifier can either deny or revoke credits granted in these transactions.

Our design is lightweight and easy to implement in peer-assisted content distribution systems. Its security analysis, however, is more subtle than the design might at first suggest. An analysis must account for any strategy by which adversaries might allocate portions of each puzzle's search space so as to optimally utilize the time θ that each has to invest and, more importantly, the content bits that each possesses. We provide (in the random oracle model) a bound on the expected number of puzzles that a collection of adversaries can solve in θ time (using any such strategy), as a function of the number of content bits each possesses at the time the puzzles are issued and the numbers of hash computations and additional content bit retrievals that each adversary can perform in θ time. For example, this bound implies that for content of size n bits, an instance of our puzzle construction ensures that all adversaries claiming to have the content must download $\Omega(n)$ content bits to solve their puzzles in expectation, even if they retrieve up to n^ϵ bits on average before the puzzles are issued, for some constant $\epsilon < 1$. Moreover, this puzzle construction is efficient: It enables the verifier to construct each puzzle in $n \ln \frac{n}{n-n^\beta} + O(1)$ pseudorandom function computations in expectation and two hash function computations, for a configurable constant $0 < \beta < 1$, and to verify each puzzle in one comparison of hash function outputs. (Note that $\ln \frac{n}{n-n^\beta} = o(1)$, and so $n \ln \frac{n}{n-n^\beta} = o(n)$.) An honest prover invests $\frac{1}{2}n^{1+\alpha} \ln \frac{n}{n-n^\beta} + O(n^\alpha)$ time in expectation to solve this puzzle, for a configurable constant $\alpha > 0$ such that $\alpha + \beta > 1$.

We demonstrate the viability of bandwidth puzzles by integrating them into a functional multimedia streaming application. We find that a single verifier can scale to challenging thousands of peers simultaneously with puzzles, even while streaming content to other clients, and that puzzle distribution and solving introduce minimal jitter into the stream. We also show the benefits of bandwidth puzzles against attacks in a simulated large-scale P2P streaming deployment, where we show that puzzles improve the legitimate clients' stream quality 40-300%

(depending on the number of attackers) and reduce the attackers' quality by more than 2×. Moreover, the puzzle scheme limits the impact of such attacks by providing legitimate clients with performance nearly identical to the scenario when there are no attackers in the system.

To summarize, the contributions of this paper are: (i) the design of bandwidth puzzles (§4), a practical defense against a documented form of attack on P2P systems; (ii) analyses of our construction (in the random oracle model) that bounds the success attainable by adversaries against it (§5); (iii) implementation and evaluation of our construction in a functional streaming application (§6); and (iv) a demonstration of the benefits of puzzles on a simulated large-scale P2P streaming deployment (§7).

2   Related Work

Incentives in P2P systems: Several studies have demonstrated the limitations of P2P protocols in the presence of selfish or malicious users [13, 7]. Rewarding peer contributions can overcome these limitations (e.g., [1, 13]), but such mechanisms cannot prevent colluding attackers from *freely* granting each other credits for fake transactions. *Bilateral* (tit-for-tat) mechanisms such as BitTorrent appear robust to collusion attacks. However, several studies (e.g, [13, 14, 15, 16]) point out the limitations of bilateral mechanisms, and make the case for *global* mechanisms. By equating peers' debit and credit amounts for receiving and providing service, respectively, collusion can be made to yield no net gain (e.g., [4]). However, there are valid reasons to not equate the debit and credit amounts, such as asymmetries in upload and download bandwidth, and social considerations (e.g., [3]). Some global contribution-awareness schemes use pricing mechanisms (e.g., [17]), some of which are theoretically collusion-resistant (e.g., [16]). However, currency management presents practical challenges for these schemes. These challenges include bootstrapping new users in a Sybil-proof manner and ensuring rapid price convergence and sufficient liquidity in the presence of system churn. Bandwidth puzzles are a lightweight alternative to provide collusion resistance that avoids currency management challenges, by seeking instead to directly detect when collusion (including with Sybils) occurs.

Failure to report transactions or solve puzzles: Clients are responsible for reporting transactions and solving puzzles in order to grant uploaders credits for the transaction. This raises the possibility of downloaders failing to report transactions or solving the puzzles and thus not giving adequate credit to their uploaders. This problem is orthogonal to the collusion attacks we consider and can be addressed by using fair-exchange [4] or proof-of-service [18] mechanisms.

Client puzzles: Client puzzles (e.g., [19, 20, 21]) force clients to demonstrate proofs-of-work to a server. This is used to throttle the number of requests that a client can issue to defend against spam and denial-of-service attacks. Our bandwidth puzzle scheme is an adaptation of this approach, in order to "throttle" the reward that a client can receive for claimed content transfers, by tying puzzle solving to the content transferred and issuing puzzle challenges simultaneously.

Sybil attacks: Our adversary model – colluding attackers claiming to have contributed more resources than they actually have – is similar to a Sybil attack. Douceur [22] suggests that Sybils can be detected using simultaneous puzzle challenges similar to our work. These puzzles validate that each claimed "identity" owns some amount of computation resources. Bandwidth puzzles instead validate that each client has expended some amount of communication resources.

Proofs of data possession (PDP) and retrievability (POR): Our puzzle mechanism ties the puzzle solution to some specific content. In this respect, our construction is related to proofs of data possession (PDP) [23,24,25] and proofs of retrievability (POR) [26,27,28], that enable a user to verify that a remote store has not deleted or modified data the user had previously stored there. There are several conceptual differences between PDP/POR schemes and our puzzle scheme. First, PDP/POR focus only on the interaction between a single prover and verifier, and do not deal with multiple colluding adversaries. Second, PDP schemes minimize the communication between the prover and the verifier, without requiring that there be an asymmetry in the computation effort they expend. However, such an asymmetry and the ability to tune that asymmetry is crucial for our scheme. In particular, the solving cost must be sufficiently high — even with the claimed content — to prevent one prover with the content from solving puzzles for many others, and at the same time puzzle generation and verification must be very efficient since the verifier must do these simultaneously for many provers. Third, PDPs/PORs presume that the verifier no longer possesses the file about which it is querying. However, many settings in which we are interested (e.g., multimedia streaming of live events) lend themselves to having a verifier with access to the content being transferred.

3   System Model and Goals

Our system model consists of a designated *verifier* and untrusted *peers*, also called *provers*. Any node can be a verifier, if it can obtain the list of peers that purport to possess certain content and it has access to that content. We assume that peers report to the verifier the content they claim to have downloaded from others. P2P-assisted CDNs (e.g., [12], www.pandonetworks.com/cdn-peering), P2P assisted file-hosting (e.g., www.vipeers.com), and P2P streaming (e.g., [10, 1,2,29]) have a central node that can (or already does) serve this role.

Our goal is to enable the verifier to ensure that the claimed bandwidth expenditures to transfer that content actually occurred. The verifier does this by simultaneously presenting puzzles to the peers claiming to have certain content, and then recording the duration required by each prover to report its solution. We presume that the network latencies for sending puzzles and solutions between the verifier and the provers are stable over the timescales involved in puzzle solving [30]. On the basis of solution correctness and the puzzle-solving time, which it compares to a threshold θ, the verifier generates a list of peers suspected of not having the claimed content. The verifier can then take action to ensure that the uploaders in these suspicious transfers do not receive credits for them.

These puzzles should have properties typical of puzzle schemes: (i) Provers should be unable to precompute puzzle solutions, or use previous puzzle solutions to generate new puzzle solutions. (ii) The verifier should incur low computational costs to generate puzzles and check puzzle solutions, and should incur low bandwidth costs to send the puzzles and receive the solutions. (iii) The verifier should be able to adjust the difficulty of the puzzle, as appropriate.

Unlike previous puzzle constructions, however, bandwidth puzzles must also ensure that for colluding provers to solve their puzzles within time θ, the content each receives in doing so, on average (possibly before receiving the puzzle itself), is of size roughly proportional to the full content size. Were it not for the *simultaneity* in issuing puzzles, this would be impossible to achieve: each challenged prover could forward its puzzle to a designated solving prover who had the content, who could solve the puzzle and return it to the challenged prover. By (ii) above, the puzzle and solution would be small, implying that the bandwidth exchanged between the challenged prover and the solving prover would be small. Simultaneous puzzle challenges preclude such a strategy, since the solving prover is limited in the number of puzzles it can solve in time θ.

The above goal comes with three caveats. First, it is not possible for the verifier to ascertain which (if any) of the colluders actually has the content, even if it detects one or more of them as colluders via our scheme. For example, a prover with the content could invest its time in solving another prover's puzzle, at the expense of solving its own. Second, the content must not be substantially compressible. If it were, then provers could exchange the compressed version in lieu of the original, and our goal could not be achieved. As such, in the rest of this paper we treat the content as random, i.e., in which each bit is selected uniformly at random.[1] Third, due to churn, peers that previously downloaded content might no longer be available for solving puzzles. These peers could, however, aid collaborators that remain in the system by solving puzzles for them. Our scheme is most effective if most content exchanges for which a peer should be rewarded occur shortly after the initial distribution of the content, as would be appropriate for, e.g., streaming video of a live event. In this way, any content held by such "hidden" collaborators quickly becomes useless for solving puzzles.

4   The Construction

Let " $\leftarrow$ " denote assignment; " $x \xleftarrow{R} X$ " denote selection of an element from set X uniformly at random and its assignment to x; and "$||$" denote concatenation.

Security parameters: There are three security parameters that play a role in our construction. We use κ to denote the length of hash function outputs and keys to pseudorandom functions (see below). A reasonable value today might be $\kappa = 160$. The other two security parameters are denoted k and L, and together combine to dictate the difficulty of puzzle solving, and the costs that the verifier and prover incur in generating and solving puzzles, respectively.

---

[1] Note that this incompressibility requirement is already true for many of the popular formats (e.g., MPEG, DivX) in use today for transferring multimedia content.

Hash functions: We use two hash functions: $\mathsf{hash} : \{0,1\}^\kappa \times \{1\dots L\} \times \{0,1\}^k \to \{0,1\}^\kappa$ and $\mathsf{ans} : \{0,1\}^k \to \{0,1\}^\kappa$. (Hash functions typically take a single string as input; we can encode the three inputs to hash in an unambiguous fashion as a single string input.) To prove security of our construction in §5, we model hash as a random oracle, though collision-resistance of ans suffices.

Pseudorandom functions: A pseudorandom function family $\{f_K\}$ is a family of functions parameterized by a secret key $K \in \{0,1\}^\kappa$. Informally, it is infeasible to distinguish between an oracle for f_K where $K \xleftarrow{R} \{0,1\}^\kappa$, and an oracle for a perfectly random function with the same domain and range; see [31] for a formal definition. We use families $\{f_K^1 : \{1\dots L\} \to \{0,1\}^\kappa\}$ and $\{f_K^2 : \{1\dots k\} \to \{1\dots n\}\}$. We require that each f_K^2 be injective, and thus that $k \leq n$, where n is the content size in bits. We will discuss efficient implementations for f^2 below.

Pseudorandom functions and hash functions achieve their desired properties — indistinguishability from a random function in the first case, and collision-resistance in the second — with all but negligible probability as a function of κ.[2] For the rest of this paper, we assume that these properties hold, ignoring events that occur with probability negligible in κ.

Construction: The puzzle verifier generates puzzles to challenge a collection of provers simultaneously. Generally, we assume that the verifier generates one puzzle per prover, though there is no obstacle to sending multiple puzzles per prover. Each puzzle consists of a hash value $\hat{h}$ output from hash and, intuitively, a collection of *index-sets* $I_1 \dots I_L$. Each index-set is a set of k random content indices, i.e., uniformly random samples from $\{1\dots n\}$, without replacement. The verifier computes $\hat{h}$ as the hash of the content bits indexed by a randomly chosen index-set, appended together in an unambiguous order. Solving the

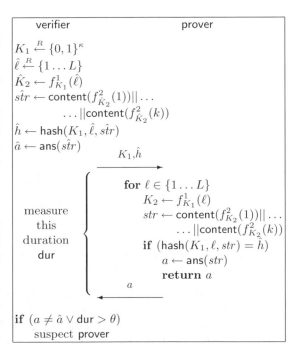

Fig. 1. One bandwidth puzzle

puzzle means finding which of the L index-sets has this property and, more specifically, the string that hashes to $\hat{h}$. This requires at most L computations

---

[2] A function $g(\cdot)$ is *negligible* if for any positive polynomial $p(\cdot)$, there is a κ_0 such that $g(\kappa) \leq 1/p(\kappa)$ for all $\kappa \geq \kappa_0$.

of hash for a prover who possesses the content, but could require substantially more for a prover who is missing some of the content indexed by the index-sets in the puzzle.

This construction, as described, would be inefficient. First, sending L index-sets of k indices each would require computation proportional to kL to generate the sets and then communication costs proportional to $kL \log_2 n$ to transmit them. To reduce these costs, the verifier generates index-sets pseudorandomly; see Fig. 1. First, it randomly selects a key K_1 for the family f^1 and an index $\hat{\ell} \xleftarrow{R} \{1 \dots L\}$ to denote the index-set from which the challenge $\hat{h}$ will be generated. Second, it generates a key $\hat{K}_2 \leftarrow f^1_{K_1}(\hat{\ell})$ from which it generates index-set $I_{\hat{\ell}} = \{f^2_{\hat{K}_2}(1) \dots f^2_{\hat{K}_2}(k)\}$. Note that the verifier never needs to generate the other $L-1$ index-sets, reducing its costs proportional to k alone. Simply sending K_1 and $\hat{h}$ suffices to enable the prover to search for $\hat{\ell}$, and incurs communication costs proportional only to κ. Because f^1 and f^2 are pseudorandom, the prover is unable to predict the index-sets better than random guessing prior to receiving K_1. Another way in which we reduce the communication costs is for the prover to return ans(str) for the string str satisfying $\hat{h} = \mathsf{hash}(K_1, \hat{\ell}, str)$, rather than str itself. As we will see, it is generally necessary for k (and hence str) to grow as a function of n, whereas there is no such need for κ (the size of ans outputs).

Finally, a subtle but important implementation challenge arises for f^2, because our security analysis in §5 requires that f^2 be injective. A natural approach to implement f^2, then, would be as a pseudorandom permutation (PRP) on $\{1 \dots n\}$, but known constructions of PRPs for small domains from ones for larger domains (e.g., AES) are relatively quite expensive (e.g., [32]). The approach we use here exploits the fact that for any given key K, f^2_K is evaluated in our construction on all of $1 \dots k$ anyway. Specifically, for a pseudorandom function family $\{f^3_K : \{1, 2, \dots\} \rightarrow \{1 \dots n\}\}$, we define $f^2_K(k')$ to be the k'-th *distinct* value in the sequence $f^3_K(1), f^3_K(2), \dots$; i.e., we "skip over" repeat outputs from f^3_K. For this implementation, we prove the following:

Theorem 1. *The construction of Fig. 1 has (i) expected puzzle generation cost of one* hash *computation, one* ans *computation, and* $n \ln \frac{n}{n-k} + O(1)$ *pseudorandom function computations, and (ii) expected puzzle solution cost (by an honest prover) of* $\frac{1}{2}L$ hash *computations, one* ans *computation, and* $\frac{1}{2}Ln \ln \frac{n}{n-k} + O(L)$ *pseudorandom function computations.*

Proof. The result follows by a "coupon collector" analysis. When generating $f^2_{K_2}(1) \dots f^2_{K_2}(k)$ for the ℓ-th index-set (i.e., $K_2 \leftarrow f^1_{K_1}(\ell)$), let X_i be a random variable denoting the number of computations of $f^3_{K_2}$ while having collected exactly $i-1$ *distinct* outputs of $f^3_{K_2}$. Then, X_i is geometrically distributed with parameter $p_i = 1 - \frac{i-1}{n}$, and $\mathsf{E}[X_i] = \frac{1}{p_i} = \frac{n}{n-i+1}$. So, the expected number of computations of $f^3_{K_2}$ is $\mathsf{E}\left[\sum_{i=1}^{k} X_i\right] = \sum_{i=1}^{k} \mathsf{E}[X_i] = \sum_{i=1}^{k} \frac{n}{n-i+1} = n\left(\sum_{i=1}^{n} \frac{1}{i} - \sum_{i=1}^{n-k} \frac{1}{i}\right) = n \ln \frac{n}{n-k} + O(1)$ since the harmonic number $H(n) = \sum_{i=1}^{n} \frac{1}{i}$ satisfies $H(n) = \ln n + \gamma + O(1/n)$ for γ a constant. Given this, the puzzle generation cost can be calculated by counting up the other operations, and the puzzle solving cost follows because the prover must generate $\frac{1}{2}L$ index-sets in expectation and invoke hash once per index-set to solve the puzzle.

Note that $\ln \frac{n}{n-k} = o(1)$ for any $k = o(n)$, e.g., $k = n^{\beta}$ for $0 < \beta < 1$, as discussed in §5. So, the cost of puzzle generation is sublinear in n.

5   Security

For proving the security of our construction, first recall that we assume that $\{f_K^1\}$ and $\{f_K^2\}$ are pseudorandom function families [31], and that ans is a collision-resistant hash function. The hash primitive is modeled as a random oracle in our proof, which enables us to quantify the security of our scheme as a function of the number of hash computations. That is, we cap the number q_{hash} of hash queries that any prover can complete in θ time, and then quantify the probability with which the prover returns $\hat{a}$ as a function of q_{hash}. Moreover, modeling hash as a random oracle enables us to exploit the property in our proof that one such computation provides no information about the computation of hash on any other value.

Of course, the probability that an adversarial prover succeeds in returning $\hat{a}$ within θ time (i.e., after making at most q_{hash} queries to hash) also depends on the number of content bits it receives before and during the puzzle-solving process. We model a prover's retrieval of content bits as calls to a random oracle content : $\{1 \dots n\} \rightarrow \{0, 1\}$. As discussed in §3, our construction requires that the content being exchanged have sufficient empirical entropy to be incompressible, as otherwise adversaries could "defeat" our verification by exchanging (in full) the compressed content. Thus, we model the content as a random string of length n, and track the number of bits that an adversary retrieves prior to returning a puzzle solution by the number of queries it makes to its content oracle.

Theorem 2. *Let* hash *and* content *be random oracles. Consider* A *collaborating adversaries, who are (i) collectively challenged to solve* P *puzzles; (ii) each permitted* q_{hash} *queries to* hash*; and (iii) collectively permitted* Aq_{pre} *queries to* content *before the distribution of the puzzles and* Aq_{post} *after. For any* s *and* $\hat{k}$ *satisfying* $1 \leq s \leq PL$ *and* $\log_2(q_{\mathsf{hash}} + L) + 2 \leq \hat{k} \leq k\left(1 - \frac{q_{\mathsf{pre}}}{n}\right) - 1$*, the expected number of puzzles that these adversaries can solve collectively is at most*

$$\frac{AP}{L}\left(\frac{sq_{\mathsf{post}}}{\hat{k} - \log_2(q_{\mathsf{hash}} + L) - 1} + 1\right) + Pn\Psi\left(s, PL, \frac{k}{n}\right) + P^2 L\Psi\left(k - \hat{k}, k, \frac{Aq_{\mathsf{pre}}}{n}\right)$$

where $\Psi(x, m, p) = \mathsf{P}\left[X \geq x\right]$ *for a binomially distributed r.v.* $X \sim \mathsf{B}(m, p)$.

The proof of this result is too lengthy to include here; the interested reader is referred to our companion technical report [33]. Very briefly, the second term of this sum accounts for the possibility that some $i \in \{1 \dots n\}$ appears in s or more index-sets, and the third term accounts for the possibility that the adversaries queried $k - \hat{k}$ or more indices in some index-set before the puzzles were issued.

The first term, then, bounds the number of puzzles the adversaries solve in expectation when neither of these events occur.

To see a consequence of Theorem 2, consider a constant number A of adversaries (i.e., constant as a function of n) challenged with a constant number P of puzzles (typically $P = A$) and that seek to each retrieve some $q_{\text{pre}} \leq n^\epsilon$ content bits on average, where $0 \leq \epsilon < 1$, before the puzzles are issued. Suppose that $q_{\text{hash}} = L$, and consider setting $L = n^\alpha$ for some $\alpha > 0$ and $k = n^\beta$ for some $0 < \beta < 1$ where $\alpha + \beta > 1$. Consider setting $\hat{k} = k - k(\delta + \frac{A q_{\text{pre}}}{n})$ for any constant $0 < \delta < 1$, in which case $\log_2(q_{\text{hash}} + L) + 2 \leq \hat{k} \leq k\left(1 - \frac{q_{\text{pre}}}{n}\right) - 1$ for sufficiently large n and we can show that $P^2 L \Psi\left(k - \hat{k}, k, \frac{A q_{\text{pre}}}{n}\right) \rightarrow 0$ as $n \rightarrow \infty$. Setting $s = (1 + \delta')\frac{PLk}{n}$ for $\delta' > 0$ implies $Pn\Psi\left(s, PL, \frac{k}{n}\right) \rightarrow 0$ as $n \rightarrow \infty$. For this value of s, Theorem 2 implies that $q_{\text{post}} = \Omega(n)$ for the adversaries to solve P (or any constant number of) puzzles in expectation. This, in our opinion, is a strong result: to solve the P puzzles in expectation, each adversary must retrieve, on average, an amount of the content roughly proportional to its size, even if each retrieves, on average, up to n^ϵ bits of the content before the puzzles are issued.

Examples of Theorem 2 for different values of A and n are shown in Fig. 2, which plots the minimum of P and that bound for $P = A$, $L = \frac{1}{12}n^{71/100}$, $k = \frac{1}{4}n^{3/10}$, $q_{\text{pre}} = n^{3/10}$, $q_{\text{post}} = n^{3/10}$, $s = 21An^{1/100}$, and $\hat{k}$ chosen optimally in the range $\log_2(q_{\text{hash}} + L) + 2 \leq \hat{k} \leq k\left(1 - \frac{q_{\text{pre}}}{n}\right) - 1$. For these parameters, presenting puzzles every $n = 2^{22}$ bits ≈ 520KB suffices to detect half of five collaborating adversaries in expectation, and

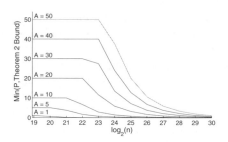

Fig. 2. An example of Theorem 2

presenting puzzles for each $n = 2^{25}$ bits ≈ 4MB suffices to detect half of 50 collaborating adversaries in expectation. Moreover, our bound is loose in several respects, and so the detection capability of this approach is even better than shown in Fig. 2.

6   Evaluation in a Media Streaming System

We implemented and evaluated a contribution-aware peer-assisted content distribution system augmented with bandwidth puzzles. The system is designed for streaming real-time media, e.g., a live broadcast of an event [10,1,2,29]. It uses a real-time transport protocol (RTP [34], jlibrtp.org) to stream media to a set of *seed* clients; these clients can then stream this to other clients over a P2P overlay. The server also acts as the verifier. In this role, it maintains a persistent TCP connection with each client (including the seeds) over which puzzle challenges and responses are communicated for each n bits of the media stream. Each client solves puzzles using a separate thread from that which handles the stream.

Our puzzle implementation uses AES to implement f^1 and f^3 (and hence f^2), and SHA-256 to implement hash and ans.

We evaluate our system on Emulab [35] using five classes of machines: 600MHz Pentium III with 256MB of memory (Class A); 850MHz Pentium III with 256MB of memory (Class B); 2GHz Pentium 4 with 512MB of memory (Class C); 3GHz 64-bit Xeon with 2GB of memory (Class D); and 2.4GHz Pentium Core 2 Duo with 2GB of memory (Class E). The server/verifier was a Class E machine. The server sends a 768Kbps stream[3] to 50 seed clients[4] over a 100Mb/s network. We also configured the network with wide-area parameters in certain tests, as described below. In all our experiments, we fixed $L = \frac{1}{12}n^{71/100}$ and $k = \frac{1}{4}n^{3/10}$, and so the security bounds in Fig. 2 are representative for our experiments.

Client heterogeneity and choice of n: We first examine the impact of n on puzzle-solving time and the advantage that faster computers have over slower ones, since the threshold θ must allow for slower computers to reliably solve their puzzles. Fig. 3 shows the ratio of the 95th percentile time for a Class-X machine ($X \in \{A, B,$ C, D, E\}) to the 50th percentile time for a Class-E machine. If the slowest clients that the server accommodates are of Class X, and the fastest are of Class E, then Fig. 3 shows the number of puzzles that the Class-E client

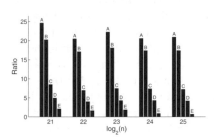

Fig. 3. Ratio of 95th percentile puzzle-solving time for Class-X machine ($X \in \{A,$ B, C, D, E\}) to 50th percentile puzzle-solving time for Class-E machine during live streaming experiments

can solve in θ time, if θ is set so that the Class-X client can solve one puzzle reliably.

Fig. 3 shows a large gap in puzzle-solving ability between the slowest and fastest machines. That said, the slowest machines would presumably not meet the minimum system requirements for viewing a live stream anyway; e.g., of the classes we consider, only D and E meet ESPN360's minimum requirements (see `espn.go.com/broadband/espn360/faq#21`). So, we discard Classes A and B (and conservatively include Class C) for the rest of our evaluation. Fig. 3 then shows that an attacker with a Class-E machine can successfully impersonate roughly seven Class-C machines, and so could inflate his claimed transfers by 7×. While not ideal, this provides a limit on the extent to which an adversary can game the system. Designing memory-bound extensions of our scheme to reduce the variability in solving time across different classes of machines [36, 21] is an interesting avenue for future work.

---

[3] For example, ESPN360 requires 400Kbps and recommends 768Kbps, see `espn.go.com/broadband/espn360/faq#21`

[4] As a point of comparison, the server in the popular P2P streaming system PPLive supports 25 seed clients at 400Kbps [11].

Having chosen to focus on machine classes C, D, and E, we further narrow our attention to puzzles for each $n = 2^{23}$ bits for the rest of our evaluation.

Application Impact: We now consider the impact on jitter of introducing puzzle solving into media streaming. Jitter [34] is an estimate of the statistical variance of the RTP (application layer) data packet interarrival time. Fig. 4 shows the distribution of jitter of the media stream at clients for a duration including 100 puzzle challenges, for different machine classes. Fig. 4 is a box-and-whiskers plot; each box shows the 25th percentile, median and 75th percentile values, and the whiskers extend to the 1st and 99th percentile values. As this figure shows, puzzles have little impact on jitter for any of Classes C–E.

Verifier Scalability: To test scalability, we fixed the number of clients to which a Class E server streams content at 50, but had it simultaneously generate and send puzzles to a number of clients (in addition to these 50) ranging from 0 to 10000. Due to limits on the number of available Emulab computers, we co-located the puzzle-receiving clients on a few machines,

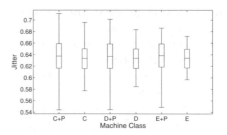

Fig. 4. Jitter per machine class. "+P" indicates with puzzles.

but still established an independent TCP connection to each one. We sampled the CPU and memory usage of the verifier (both user and system) during the tests at half-second intervals using `top`. Fig. 5(a) shows the distribution of CPU usage for the verifier in such a test. The verifier's median and even 75th percentile utilization is largely unchanged by challenging 10050 clients, and also sending the stream to 50 of them. The 99th percentile does increase, though it never reaches 100%. (Memory utilization exhibited moderate growth, and far less variance. It topped out at less than 75% in the 10050-client case.) We also confirmed the simultaneity of puzzle distribution in these tests: the time between sending the first puzzle and receiving an application-level acknowledgement from the last client to which a puzzle was sent (i.e., the 10050th) was at most 450ms. It is clear that even a moderately well-provisioned verifier machine scales beyond 10000 clients, and a machine with more cores and memory should easily scale far beyond that.

We also monitored one of the 50 clients receiving the media stream during these tests, to see the impact on its jitter as the number of puzzle-solving clients is increased. Fig. 5(b) shows that the median jitter at this client when the server challenges 10050 (including this one) is within 50% of the median jitter when this client is served in isolation. This suggests that increasing the number of puzzle-solving clients has little impact on individual clients' stream quality.

Wide-area effects: The primary concerns with streaming in a wide-area setting are latency and packet loss. Uniformly increased latency simply means that the verifier waits correspondingly longer to receive puzzle solutions. If there is

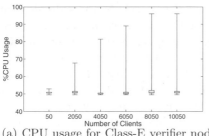

(a) CPU usage for Class-E verifier node

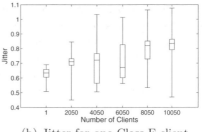

(b) Jitter for one Class-E client

Fig. 5. Scalability tests in which 50 clients receive stream from verifier, and a variable number of clients receive puzzle challenges from verifier

significant diversity across provers in the latencies to reach them, the verifier can send puzzles to more distant provers first, to increase simultaneity of distribution. (Geolocation by IP address can provide latency estimates that would be difficult for a prover to mislead.) Also, more puzzles or more difficult puzzles (i.e., by increasing n or L) can be used to minimize the effects of both latency variance across provers and transient latency variations per prover.

The more significant impact of wide-area streaming is the risk of increased packet loss. Distribution of puzzles over TCP helps to deliver puzzles and their solutions reliably, but the UDP-based RTP stream does not guarantee reliable delivery of stream packets. Consequently, during periods of high packet loss, an honest prover might be missing some of the content bits indexed in an index-set; if so, it searches through all possibilities for

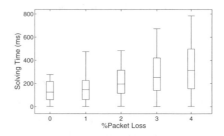

Fig. 6. Puzzle-solving time for a Class-E client as a function of packet loss

them. The effect of this searching on puzzle-solving time is shown in Fig. 6, where the network packet loss rate ranges from 0% to 4%. Even 2% represents an unusual packet loss rate that, e.g., justifies a "warning" indication at a real-time monitoring site like www.internetpulse.net; a 4% packet loss rate is "critical". This figure shows that even at 2% loss, nearly 75% of the puzzle-solving times experienced are within those observed with 0% loss, and the 99th percentile is within twice those observed with 0% loss. So, doubling θ during periods of 2% loss (as indicated at, e.g., www.internetpulse.net) should allow adequate puzzle-solving time, or θ could be permanently doubled with the cost of allowing adversaries more slack.

7   Benefits in a Peer-Assisted Streaming System

In this section, we show via simulation the benefits of using bandwidth puzzles in a contribution-aware peer-assisted streaming application (e.g., [10,1,2]).

Streaming Model: We assume that the multimedia stream is divided into discrete epochs of size 1000 units of simulation time where each unit corresponds to 100ms of real time. The content within each epoch is divided into suitably encoded *stripes* [10,1]. This encoding (e.g., [37]) has the property that a client can access the original content as long as it is able to download *at least* one stripe and it receives better performance (e.g., higher video quality) if it downloads more stripes. Each stripe is broken into 1MB *chunks* and peers download the chunks corresponding to each stripe using a suitable lookup mechanism.

Incentive Mechanism: We use an incentive scheme similar to Maze [3]. The streaming server, to which peers authenticate and periodically report transactions on a per-chunk basis, maintains a per-peer "points system". Each peer earns 1.5 points for every chunk uploaded and consumes 1 point per chunk downloaded. New peers are given initial points to allow some free downloads before they can contribute. Each peer queues incoming requests (i.e., asking it to upload some content) in increasing order of $rqsttime - 3\log\rho$, where $rqsttime$ is the request arrival time and ρ is the current number of points the requester has. (Intuitively, requests that arrived earlier and requests from peers with more points are served earlier.) Free-riders, i.e., with zero points, are denied service.

Adding bandwidth puzzles: In traditional contribution-aware systems, the server debits points from the downloader and credits points to the uploader on receiving a transaction report. In a system with bandwidth puzzles, handling transactions is slightly different. The server debits points from the downloader's account as before. However, it does not immediately credit the uploader for the transaction. Rather, at the end of each epoch, the server issues simultaneous puzzle challenges on a per-chunk basis in the role of the verifier; i.e., it iterates through the chunks for this epoch one by one, and challenges the clients that claimed to have received this chunk in the epoch. Upload credits are granted when the corresponding downloaders correctly answer their puzzle challenges.[5]

Attack Model: We specify attacks as a *collusion graph*, where each vertex is a malicious peer (actual or Sybil node). Each directed edge $x \to y$ represents an *fake uploader* relationship: peer x reports "fake" transactions on behalf of peer y, i.e., x requests the server to credit y for uploads even though y spends no bandwidth for the transfer. Each such x periodically reports fake transactions to the server in addition to its legitimate transactions (if any). We consider a scenario where attackers create fake identities that pretend to receive the stream. This helps attackers download more stripes (higher stream quality) and receive content directly from the seeds (higher priority service). For example, in a Star(200,19) graph, there are 200 nodes in the graph, organized in 10 "star" graphs. Each star has 19 leaf nodes representing the fake (Sybil) identities and the actual attacker is the center of the star. To model attackers' responses to puzzle challenges, we assume that a puzzle sent to a peer who does not have the

---

[5] Detecting downloaders that habitually refuse to solve puzzles is a separate problem that can be solved using fair-exchange or proof-of-service mechanisms; see §2.

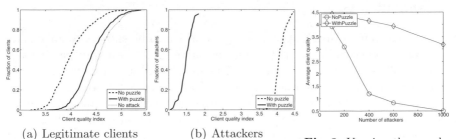

(a) Legitimate clients (b) Attackers

Fig. 7. Benefits in a P2P streaming system

Fig. 8. Varying the number of attackers

content or to a fake peer is solved with probability 0.1. In the Star(200,19) case, this means that in expectation $19 \times 0.1 = 1.9$ fake transactions get validated.[6]

Simulation Framework: We implemented an event-driven simulator modeling chunk exchanges, transaction reports, and puzzle challenges. We do not model network congestion effects and assume that the only bandwidth bottleneck is the upstream bandwidth bottleneck of the peers. The download requests at each peer are queued based on the requester's points as described above and served one at a time without preemption. Each streaming session lasts 50 epochs with all clients and attackers arriving at the start of the session. We assume that there are 10 stripes, each of size 2MB. In each epoch, the server bootstraps 5 seed nodes in the system with the 10 stripes for the next epoch. Some clients initially download stripes from these seed nodes and subsequently serve these to others. All exchanges and transaction reports occur at a 1MB chunk granularity.

Performance Benefits: We define the *user quality* to be the average number of stripes received by a client per epoch in the streaming session. Fig. 7(a) shows the CDF of the client quality in a streaming system with 100 legitimate clients under three scenarios: no attack, under a Star(200,19) attack without the puzzle scheme, and under a Star(200,19) attack with the puzzle scheme in place. We see that when the puzzle scheme is used the client quality with an attack is very close to a system without attackers. In Fig. 7(b), there is more than 2× reduction in the median attacker quality when bandwidth puzzles are used. Fig. 8 shows the average legitimate client quality as a function of the attack size. Each attack is of the form Star(X,19) where X is the number of attackers. As the number of attackers grows, the decrease in quality is less severe when the puzzle scheme is used. These results confirm that bandwidth puzzles can improve legitimate client performance and deter attackers in P2P streaming systems.

---

[6] Since 190 identities are fake, the attackers' resources correspond to $A = 10$. If the verifier issues puzzles per chunk ($\log_2(n) \approx 23$), the value of the bound in Theorem 2 for $A = 10$, $P = 200$, and, e.g., $L = \frac{5}{3}n^{71/100}$ and $q_{\text{post}} = n^{1/10}$ (and otherwise the same parameters used for Fig. 2) is consistent with setting the puzzle solving probability to be 0.1.

8   Conclusions

Peer-assisted content distribution systems continue to be subject to adversaries exploiting weaknesses in the underlying incentive mechanisms. In particular, a group of colluding adversaries can implement a "shilling" attack, i.e., by reporting service from one another without spending any actual resources, to get preferential service. Our work provides a simple, yet powerful primitive to thwart such collusion attacks in peer-assisted content distribution systems. It is based on simultaneously challenging peers with *bandwidth puzzles* to demonstrate that the purported data transfers actually took place. We quantify the security of our scheme in the random oracle model. We also showed via an implementation in a functional streaming system that our puzzles cost little in terms of scalability or perceived stream quality. Finally, we showed by simulation that bandwidth puzzles prevent colluding attackers from gaining undue advantage via shilling attacks and from impacting the performance of honest peers.

Acknowledgements. We are grateful to Katie Benedetto for useful discussions, and to the anonymous reviewers for their comments. This work was supported in part by NSF awards CT-0756998, CNS-0326472, and ANI-0331653, and Florida State University CRC award PG-022684.

References

1. Sung, Y., Bishop, M., Rao, S.: Enabling Contribution Awareness in an Overlay Broadcasting System. In: Proc. ACM SIGCOMM (2006)
2. Purandare, D., Guha, R.: BEAM: An Efficient Framework for Media Streaming. In: Proc. IEEE LCN (2006)
3. Lian, Q., Zhang, Z., Yang, M., Zhao, B.Y., Dai, Y., Li, X.: An empirical study of collusion behavior in the Maze P2P file-sharing system. In: Proc. ICDCS (2007)
4. Sirivianos, M., Park, J.H., Yang, X., Jarecki, S.: Dandelion: Cooperative Content Distribution with Robust Incentives. In: Proc. USENIX ATC (2007)
5. Dellarocas, C.: Immunizing online reputation reporting systems against unfair ratings and discriminatory behavior. In: Proc. ACM EC (2000)
6. Bhattacharjee, R., Goel, A.: Avoiding ballot stuffing in eBay-like reputation systems. In: Proc. ACM SIGCOMM P2P-ECON (2005)
7. Sirivianos, M., Park, J.H., Chen, R., Yang, X.: Free-riding in BitTorrent networks with the large view exploit. In: Proc. IPTPS (2007)
8. Liogkas, N., Nelson, R., Kohler, E., Zhang, L.: Exploiting BitTorrent for fun (but not profit). In: Proc. IPTPS (2006)
9. Adar, E., Huberman, B.A.: Free riding on Gnutella. First Monday 5 (2000)
10. Castro, M., et al.: SplitStream: High-bandwidth multicast in a cooperative environment. In: Proc. ACM SOSP (2003)
11. Huang, G.: Keynote: Experiences with PPLive. In: Proc. ACM SIGCOMM P2P-TV Workshop (2007)
12. Freedman, M.J., Freudenthal, E., Mazieres, D.: Democratizing content publication with Coral. In: Proc. NSDI (2004)
13. Feldman, M., Lai, K., Stoica, I., Chuang, J.: Robust Incentive Techniques for Peer-to-Peer Networks. In: Proc. ACM EC (2004)

14. Piatek, M., Isdal, T., Krishnamurthy, A., Anderson, T.: One hop reputations for peer to peer file sharing workloads. In: Proc. NSDI (2008)
15. Lai, K., Feldman, M., Stoica, I., Chuang, J.: Incentives for cooperation in peer-to-peer networks. In: Proc. P2P Econ (2004)
16. Aperjis, C., Freedman, M.J., Johari, R.: Peer-Assisted Content Distribution with Prices. In: Proc. CoNeXT (2008)
17. Belenkiy, M., et al.: Making P2P accountable without losing privacy. In: Proc. ACM WPES (2007)
18. Li, J., Kang, X.: Proof of service in a hybrid P2P environment. In: Proc. ISPA Workshops (2005)
19. Dwork, C., Naor, M.: Pricing via processing, or, combatting junk mail. In: Proc. CRYPTO (1993)
20. Juels, A., Brainard, J.: Client puzzles: A cryptographic defense against connection depletion attacks. In: Proc. NDSS (1999)
21. Dwork, C., Goldberg, A., Naor, M.: On memory-bound functions for fighting spam. In: Boneh, D. (ed.) CRYPTO 2003. LNCS, vol. 2729, pp. 426–444. Springer, Heidelberg (2003)
22. Douceur, J.: The Sybil attack. In: Proc. IPTPS (2002)
23. Ateniese, G., et al.: Provable data possession at untrusted stores. In: Proc. ACM CCS (2007)
24. Filho, D.L.G., Barreto, P.S.L.M.: Demonstrating data possession and uncheatable data transfer (2006), http://eprint.iacr.org/2006/150.pdf
25. Ateniese, G., Pietro, R.D., Mancini, L.V., Tsudik, G.: Scalable and Efficient Provable Data Possession (2008), http://eprint.iacr.org/2008/114.pdf
26. Juels, A., Kaliski Jr., B.S.: PORs: Proofs of retrievability for large files. In: Proc. ACM CCS (2007)
27. Bowers, K., Juels, A., Oprea, A.: Proofs of Retrievability: Theory and Implementation (2008), http://eprint.iacr.org/2008/175.pdf
28. Shacham, H., Waters, B.: Compact Proofs of Retrievability (2008), http://eprint.iacr.org/2008/073.pdf
29. Yin, H., et al.: Design and Deployment of a Hybrid CDN-P2P System for Live Video Streaming: Experiences with LiveSky. In: Proc. ACM Multimedia (2009)
30. Zhang, Y., Duffield, N., Paxson, V., Shenker, S.: On the Constancy of Internet Path Properties. In: Proc. IMW (2001)
31. Goldreich, O., Goldwasser, S., Micali, S.: How to construct random functions. J. ACM 33(4), 792–807 (1984)
32. Black, J., Rogaway, P.: Ciphers with arbitrary finite domains. In: Preneel, B. (ed.) CT-RSA 2002. LNCS, vol. 2271, pp. 114–130. Springer, Heidelberg (2002)
33. Reiter, M.K., Sekar, V., Spensky, C., Zhang, Z.: Making contribution-aware peer-assisted content distribution robust to collusion using bandwidth puzzles. Technical Report CMU-CS-09-136, Carnegie Mellon University (2009)
34. Schulzrinne, H., Casner, S., Frederick, R., Jacobson, V.: RTP: A transport protocol for real-time applications. IETF RFC 3550 (July 2003)
35. White, B., et al.: An Integrated Experimental Environment for Distributed Systems and Networks. In: Proc. OSDI (2002)
36. Abadi, M., Burrows, M., Manasse, M., Wobber, T.: Moderately hard, memory-bound functions. ACM TOIT 5, 299–327 (2005)
37. Goyal, V.K.: Multiple description coding: Compression meets the network. IEEE Signal Processing Magazine, 74–93 (September 2001)

An E-Cash Based Implementation Model for Facilitating Anonymous Purchasing of Information Products

Zhen Zhang[1], K.H. (Kane) Kim[1], Myeong-Ho Kang[1], Tianran Zhou[1],
Byung-Ho Chung[2], Shin-Hyo Kim[2], and Seok-Joon Lee[2]

[1] DREAM Lab, EECS Dept. University of California Irvine, CA, USA
zhen@dream.eng.uci.edu, khkim@uci.edu
[2] ETRI, Korea
shykim@etri.re.kr

Abstract. The rapid growing of online purchasing of information products poses challenges of how to preserve the customer's privacy during the online transactions. The current widely used way of online shopping does not consider the customer's privacy protection. It exposes the customer's sensitive information unnecessarily. We propose a new five-party implementation model called 5PAPS that provides much enhanced protection of the customer's privacy. The model combines the advantages of the e-cash techniques, the mix technique, the anonymous-honoring merchant model, and the anonymity-protecting payment gateway model. It is aimed for protecting the customer's anonymity in all applicable aspects. Security and anonymity issues of the model have been analyzed. The results show that the model is robust against varieties of common attacks and the customer's anonymity can be protected even in the presence of some collusion among the parties involved in the transactions. Experimental prototyping of the essential parts yields partial validation of the practical nature of the 5PAPS model, and it has also produced reliable estimates of the storage and messaging volume requirements present in sizable purchasing systems.

Keywords: Anonymous, purchasing, information product, encryption, e-cash, payment gateway, mix.

1 Introduction

A rapidly growing variety of information products such as e-books, software, music, and movies are becoming available for sale over the Internet in this century. The increasing popularity of online purchasing of information products poses challenges of how to preserve the customer's privacy. In contrast to the traditional purchasing mode involving cash payment, typical online purchasing systems require the customer to provide more personal information to verify themselves in the card-not-present situations. The examples of private information include credit card numbers, social security numbers, names, and billing addresses. Yet the customers have no control over the flow of their private information; nor do they have the rights to access and manage their sensitive payment or purchase records, because the data is normally stored in the servers operated by the merchant or the credit card company only.

A. Prakash and I. Sen Gupta (Eds.): ICISS 2009, LNCS 5905, pp. 148–162, 2009.

Therefore, the customer's privacy is unnecessarily exposed in the following ways.

Merchants know customer's payment details: Although merchants often employ access control and encryption mechanisms to protect the customer's payment information such as credit card numbers and customer's names, the potential number of merchants is quite large and thus the privacy risk here is quite high. Recent customer data breach incidents [6] suggest that the system currently in wide use may not be adequate.

Merchants know customer's Internet delivery addresses: Based on the current Internet infrastructure, the customer's Internet Protocol (IP) address is known to the information product providers. For customers using static IP addresses, the information may be used to trace to the real identity of the customer or at least reveal some personal information such as the customer's geographical location.

Banks / Credit card companies know the customer's purchase history: since the merchants send the customers' payment information to the banks / credit card companies directly, the banks / credit card companies usually have a full record of the customer's purchasing history. If the records are leaked to some malicious persons, they may be used against the customer. It therefore makes the e-commerce systems vulnerable targets for fraud and privacy stealing.

In this paper, we propose a new five-party implementation model that provides much enhanced protection of the customer's privacy in all the aspects mentioned above. The model is called here the five-party anonymous purchasing system (5PAPS). The main goal is to keep the customer anonymous whenever applicable, and let the customer reveal different parts of his/her sensitive information to different parties such that one party or two parties in collusion cannot produce information of which the leakage damages the customer's privacy. Our approach integrates the following three techniques in a new way to achieve the customer's anonymity.

E-cash techniques [1, 2, 3, 9, 10, 11, 12]: The e-cash techniques are employed to keep both merchants and banks / credit card companies from learning the real identities of the information product purchasers during the payment process. The e-cash is untraceable and therefore, the customer exposes nothing but the e-cash to the merchant and the banks / credit card companies know nothing about the customer's choice of products. In quite a few countries, traditional banks are not allowed to issue e-cash. In our 5PAPS model, a separate cyber-money company dedicated to issuing and clearing e-cash is employed.

The mix technique [5, 13]: The mix technique achieves the customer's anonymity at the networking level. It ensures that the customer's IP address is hidden from any communication peers. In addition, the mix technique preserves the customer's IP addresses during the downloading process.

The anonymity-honoring merchant: Here the merchant accepts inquiries and product orders from the customers who are using untraceable fictitious IPs or temporary (e.g., one-shot use) IDs. The merchant sends an invoice to the customer and the latter "sends" his/her payment instruction in an envelope on the face of which the invoice from the merchant is "pasted". The merchant then forwards the payment to the cyber-money company for clearing.

The payment gateway based technique [4]: Payment gateways (PGs) such as Paypal and Google Checkout serve the customers who wish to prevent their credit card and bank account information from being spread among the numerous merchants and instead keep such information in PG companies only. In the 5PAPS model, an enhanced version of PG, i.e., an anonymity-protecting PG, is employed. The PG based technique is used to prevent the cyber-money company from learning the customer's bank account information. When the customer wants to purchase e-cash by using credit card, the cyber-money company blindly forwards the sealed envelope containing the credit card authorization information to the PG which in turn forwards it to the bank/credit card company used by the customer.

After presenting the 5PAPS model, we discuss the security-enforcing properties of the model and show that the model is robust against varieties of attacks. We then analyze when the customer's anonymity can be compromised, especially under the severe collusion of multiple parties in the 5PAPS model. Such vulnerabilities can be easily tolerated in practice and thus the model is highly cost-effective.

Finally, as a partial validation of the practical nature of the 5PAPS model, a prototype implementation of a simple online purchasing and delivery system has been obtained. From this, we have been able to derive reliable estimates of the storage and messaging volume requirements present in sizable purchasing systems. Simple and yet effective extensions to reduce the requirements are also shown.

The remainder of the paper is organized as follows. Section 2 provides a brief review the related work. Section 3 then describes our 5PAPS model in detail. The security and anonymity issues of the 5PAPS model are then described in Section 4 and Section 5, respectively. In Section 6, we discuss the experimental prototyping and the storage and messaging volume requirements. Finally the paper is concluded in section 7.

2 Related Work

The most notable efforts aimed for achieving the customer's anonymity are the e-cash (also called e-coin) techniques [1, 2, 3, 9, 10, 11, 12]. The e-cash techniques attempt to emulate electronically the main features of the physical cash. E-cash systems were usually with the assumption that the same bank is responsible for giving out electronic coins and for accepting them later for deposit. The customer first uses a withdrawal protocol to purchase e-cash from the bank. By taking the advantage of the blind signature [1, 2, 3] technique, the withdrawal protocol allows the bank to sign and issue e-coins without knowing the content of the coins. Each coin shall represent a fixed amount of money, say 10 cents. The customer later pays the merchant with e-coins using a payment protocol. Since e-coins are untraceable, the merchant knows nothing about the customer from the payment process. Merchants then use a deposit protocol to clear the e-cash at the bank. Double-spending can be detected using online clearing [1] which verifies e-coins during the payment transaction. Off-line techniques have also been proposed to detect double-spending [2, 3, 11]. They ensure that if the customer uses an e-coin only once, his/her privacy is protected unconditionally. But if the customer reuses an e-coin, the bank can trace it to his/her account and prove that the customer has used the e-coin twice. Other work extends the basic e-cash schemes, considering issues such as divisibility [9, 10, 14] and efficiency [12]. One practical concern that has not been addressed by the e-cash techniques is that, the bank may not necessarily be the institution to issue and clear e-cash. It is preferable to separate the functionality of issuing/clearing e-cash from the responsibilities of banks.

In [4] the authors proposed a payment gateway (PG) based approach for preserving the customer's privacy during e-payment processing. The basic idea is to separate the customer's payment information and the order information. The payment information is encrypted by using the bank's public key and can be accessed by the bank only; while the order information is accessed by the merchant only. A PG is employed as a proxy, sitting between the bank and the merchant. It results that the customer's account details are kept secret from the merchant and his choices of goods are kept secret from the bank. In the PG based approach, because the payment information is sill traceable, the bank knows at least how frequently the customer purchases products online and how much money the customer spends during each transaction.

Finally, the mix techniques [5, 13] have been proposed to hide the networking address of the client when the client sends requests to the server. It also provides an indirect returning address that can be used for the server to reply the client without knowing the client's real network address.

3   The Five-Party Implementation Model: 5PAPS

We propose an integrated five-party implementation model that protects the customer's anonymity in online purchasing of information products (shown in Fig. 1). The model is called the five-party anonymous purchasing system (5PAPS). The model contains the following five parties,

- *Customer*: who wants buy information products offered by online merchants.
- *Anonymity-honoring Contents Shop/Merchant*: who offers information products such as e-books, software, games, mp3, movies, IP-TV, and reports online.
- *Cyber-money Company (CC)*: who is responsible for issuing and clearing e-cash.
- *Anonymity-protecting Payment Gateway (PG)*: who takes care of payment on behalf of the customer.
- *Bank*: who manages the accounts of all the other parties including the customer, the merchants, the cyber-money company, and the payment gateway. It takes care of money transfer among these parties.

To purchase information products, the customer first contacts the cyber-money company to purchase e-coins. The process involves the customer, the cyber-money company, the payment gateway, and the bank. Payments are made using conventional credit cards. After getting the e-cash, the customer then contacts the merchant to order the information products. The process is carried inside the cyber-money domain which includes the customer, the cyber-money company, and the merchant. Payments are made by using the e-cash.

The 5PAPS model provides secure communication channels such that all messages exchanged are encrypted and only the parties with the appropriate keys can decrypt and see the messages. Double-spending is prevented using an online clearing approach.

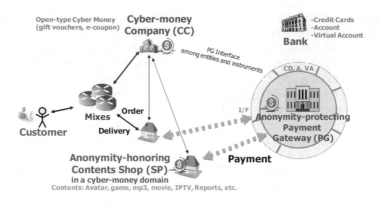

Fig. 1. The proposed five-party implementation model: 5PAPS

3.1 Primitives and Notations

The 5PAPS model makes use of the following.

- Asymmetric encryption/decryption algorithm (such as RSA [7])
  Pub-K: a public key
  Pri-K: a private key
  Pub-K(.): encrypt with the public key *Pub-K*
  Pri-K(.): decrypt with the private key *Pri-K*
  We use public/private key pairs of the mixes, the merchant, the payment gate-way, the cyber-money company, and the bank. They are denoted as $Pub\text{-}K_{mix\ i}$ /$Pri\text{-}K_{mix\ i}$ (for $i=1..m$), $Pub\text{-}K_{mr}$/$Pri\text{-}K_{mr}$, $Pub\text{-}K_{pg}$/$Pri\text{-}K_{pg}$, $Pub\text{-}K_{cc}$ / $Pri\text{-}K_{cc}$ and $Pub\text{-}K_b$ / $Pri\text{-}K_b$ respectively.
- Symmetric encryption/decryption algorithm (such as AES [8])
  K: a symmetric key
  $E_K(.)$: encrypt with the symmetric key *K*
  $D_K(.)$: decrypt with the symmetric key *K*
  The customer generates a symmetric key for each session. Thus the symmetric key is also called a session key. Session keys are denoted as K_i (for $i = 1, 2, …$).
- Blind signature [1, 2, 3]
  s(.) and *s'(.)*: *s'(.)* is a signing function and *s(.)* is the corresponding publicly known inverse function such that $s(s'(x)) = x$, where *x* is a binary string.
  blind(.) and *unblind(.)*: *blind(.)* is a blinding function and *unblind(.)* is its inverse, both known only to the customer, such that $unblind(s'(blind(x))) = s'(x)$

  The blind signature roughly means the signing function, *s'(.)*, is applied to a blinded value *x*. If the un-blinding function is applied to the blind signature, the outcome is exactly the same as directly applying the signing function, *s'(.)*, on *x*. The signature is blind in the sense that the signer knows nothing about the content of the envelope it signs; yet everyone is able to verify the signature.

  There are a number of blind signature techniques [1, 2, 3]. For the description of our model, we are using the blind RSA signature [1, 2]. Other blind signature techniques [3] can also be accommodated in our model easily.

- Mix [5]

$Pub\text{-}K_{mix\ i}$: the public key of Mix i

R_i (for $i = 0, 1,..$): random strings

A_{client}, A_{server}: the address of the client and the server respectively

K_1: a session key

Fig. 2 shows how to use a mix to hide the client's real address while enabling the client to send a request to the server and get the response. The client first sends the request to the mix together with its address encrypted by the mix's public key. The mix then forwards the request to the server, replacing the source address with its own address. The server sees the mix address instead of the client's address. For response, the server sends the reply together with the encrypted client's address back to the mix. The mix then decrypts to find the address of the client and forwards the response to the client.

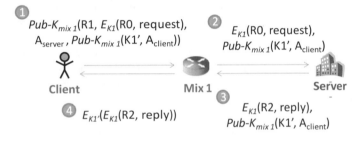

Fig. 2. Anonymous communication using a mix

If a single mix is employed, the mix is able to recognize and remember the fact that there was a correspondence between the client and the server. To mitigate the problem, a chain of mixes can be applied. Unless all the mixes collude, the secrecy of the correspondence is preserved. For convenience, we use the following notations for using a chain of m mixes:

$Pub\text{-}K_{mix\ 1\text{-}>m}(M) = Pub\text{-}K_{mix\ m}(R_m, .. Pub\text{-}K_{mix\ 1}(R_1, M)..)$, where M is a message

$Ret_{m\text{-}>1}(A) = Pub\text{-}K_{mix\ 1}(K_1', ..Pub\text{-}K_{mix\ m}(K_m', A)..)$, where A is an address

$Reply_{m\text{-}>1}(M) = E_{K1}(...E_{Km}(M)..)$

For denoting the IP addresses of the customer, the cyber-money company, the merchant, the payment gateway, and the bank, we use A_c, A_{cc}, A_{mr}, A_{pg}, and A_b respectively.

3.2 Protocol Details

The protocol has three phases described in the following.

3.2.1 E-Cash Purchasing Phase (Shown in Fig. 3)

Before the customer purchases any information product from a merchant, he/she shall first purchase e-cash from the cyber-money company. The initial step is to obtain the public keys of the respective parties to be involved in the purchasing of e-cash. The public keys can be obtained by asking for the certificates of all parties. Each party has its own certificate signed by a trust authority and the customer has already veri-fied the trust authority via some other source. A certificate usually includes the sub-ject name, the public key, and the policy for using the public key. The cyber-money company has its own certificate. It also collects the certificates of the payment gate-ways. The customer gets from the cyber-money company the certificates of the cyber-money company and the payment gateways. Of the payment gateways, the customer chooses one that can work with the bank / credit card companies which he/she uses. In case a chain of mixes are employed, the first mix shall also collect the certificates of all the mixes that will be used and return them to the customer upon a connection request. On completion of this step, the customer has the pubic keys from the cyber-money company, the payment gateway, the bank, and all the mixes. The case where a credit-card company is involved instead of a bank is not much different from the case where a bank is involved and not discussed in detail.

The second step in this phase is to generate a session key shared between the cus-tomer and the cyber-money company. Since the customer has already possessed all the public keys, this step can be easily accomplished by using the mix(es) as an in-termediary.

In the third step, the customer sends via mixes to the cyber-money company an e-cash request which includes a transaction number, a description of the product to purchase (i.e., the e-cash), and the price. The cyber-money company replies with the invoice. The customer then sends to the cyber-money company a message containing a payment part and an order part: *i*) the payment part is first encrypted by using the public key of the bank and enclosed in an envelope addressed to the bank, and then the envelope containing the encrypted payment part is encrypted by using the pubic key of the payment gateway and enclosed within an envelope addressed to the pay-ment gateway. The payment part contains the customer's credit card number, the payment amount, the hash code of the credit card information, the hash code of the invoice, the timestamp generated right before the payment part is sent, and a valid period after which the payment gets expired; *ii*) the order part contains the invoice, the blinded strings to be signed, the timestamp generated right before the order part is sent, and the valid period of the order. Note that only the bank can read the payment information. After receiving this message, the cyber-money company checks the invoice in the order part and forwards the payment part to the payment gateway to-gether with the amount of the payment and a payment identifier. The payment gate-way in turn forwards the payment part (after removing the envelope) to the bank together with the amount of the payment and a payment identifier. Then bank then decrypts and verifies the customer's payment information. If the payment is valid, the bank will pay the payment gateway by transferring money from the customer's bank account to the payment gateway's account. In the ideal case, the bank will leave no hint in the payment gateway's account regarding the source account of the transferred money and only the payment identifier that came from the payment gateway may be indicated. In such a case, the payment process shall keep the customer anonymous to the payment gateway, let alone to the cyber-money company. However, such anony-mous money transfer from the customer's bank account to the payment gateway's bank account requires modifications on the current bank practices. After the payment gateway gets paid by the bank, it then pays or gives a promissory note (using the payment identifier) to the cyber-money company. The payment process from the

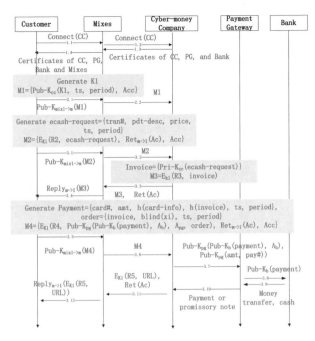

Fig. 3. Sequence diagram of e-cash purchasing phase

payment gateway to the cyber-money company does not reveal any information about the customer's real identity or his/her bank account. Once the cyber-money company gets paid or a promise by the payment gateway, it places on its web the signed e-coins encrypted by the session key and sends the URL to the customer. Finally, the customer can download via mixes the e-coins using the URL received from the cyber-money company.

3.2.2 Product Ordering Phase (Shown in Fig. 4)

Similar to the first two steps in the e-cash purchasing phase, the customer first gets the certificates of the merchant and all the mixes that will be used. Then the customer generates a session key to be shared with the merchant. In the third step, the customer sends via the mixes to the merchant a price confirmation request that includes a transaction number, a description of the products to purchase, and the published price. The merchant replies with an invoice. The customer then places an order which includes the invoice, n e-coins, where the value of n e-coins equals the price of the product, the timestamp generated right before the order is sent, and the valid period of the order. After receiving the order, the merchant checks the invoice and contacts the cyber-money company to verify the validity of the e-coins. If all e-coins are valid, the cyber-money company pays the merchant. The merchant then places on its web the information product encrypted with the session key and sends the URL to the customer.

3.2.3 Product Delivery Phase

In this phase, the customer downloads via the mixes the products from the merchant using the URL received during the ordering phase.

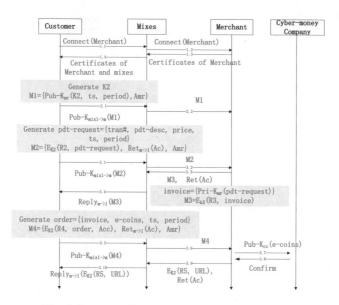

Fig. 4. Sequence diagram of product ordering phase

4   Security Analysis

- **Theorem 1** (security of message content): Assume there is no efficient algorithm to break RSA and AES, the contents of all the messages in the three phases are secure in the sense that only the parties with the appropriate keys are able to know the message contents.

  Note that in our protocol, all messages containing sensitive information are encrypted either using an RSA public key or an AES key, so only the party that hold the keys is able to read the messages.

  Particularly, in the 5PAPS model, all messages from and to the customer are transmitted via secure communication channels. Fig. 5 illustrates how to setup a secure communication channel between a customer and a server (i.e. the cyber-money company/merchant). The customer first requests the server's public key. It then generates randomly a session key tagged with a timestamp and a valid period. In the third step, the customer encrypts the session key with the server's public key and

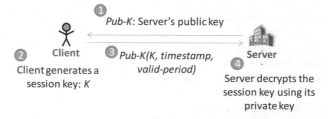

Fig. 5. Setup a secure communication channel between client and server

sends it to the server. Finally the server decrypts the message and obtains the session key. From then on, all the messages exchanged between the customer and the server are encrypted with the session key until the key expires. Note that no one except the server can decrypt the session key, so the communication is secure between the client and the server as long as the session key remains secure. This also prevents man-in-the-middle attacks as long as the server's public key remains secure.

- **Corollary 1** (confidentiality of payment)**:** Assume there is no efficient algorithm to break RSA, the customer's payment information remains confidential to all parties except the bank.

   As the customer's payment details are encrypted using the bank's public key, only the bank can decrypt it. Therefore, as long as the bank's private key remains secure, no eavesdropper in the communication network or any dishonest parties involved in the transactions can obtain the customer's payment information.

- **Theorem 2** (verifiability, unforgeability, untraceability and unlinkability of e-coin)**:** all e-coins obtained in the purchasing phase are verifiable, unforgeable, untraceable and unlinkable [1].

   Note that an e-coin takes the form of a pair of binary strings, $e\text{-}coin=\{x,\ Pri\text{-}K_{cc}(x)\}$. By checking whether $Pub\text{-}K_{cc}(Pri\text{-}K_{cc}(x))=x$, everyone can verify that the e-coin is formed using the cyber-money company's private key. Secondly, no one can forge e-coins; i.e. even with $e\text{-}coin_i=\{x_i,\ Pri\text{-}K_{cc}(x_i)\}\ i=1,2\ldots$, it is impractical for anyone except the cyber-money company to produce a new coin $e\text{-}coin=\{y,\ s'(y)\}$ such that $Pub\text{-}K_{cc}(s'(y))=y$ and $y{\neq}x_i$. Thirdly, each e-coin is untraceable, because the cyber-money company knows nothing about the correspondence between the signed matter $Pri\text{-}K_{cc}(x)$ and its blinded form $Pri\text{-}K_{cc}(blind(x))$. Finally, since e-coins contain no customer information, there is no relationship between any two coins from the same customer.

- Prevention of double-spending

The 5PAPS model prevents double-spending through online clearing. Duplications of e-cash may happen under two different types of scenarios: *i*) a customer tries to spend an e-coin twice. *ii*) a merchant attempts to cash the same e-coin twice. Online clearing is a simple way to detect double-spending. The cyber-money company keeps a list of all spent coins. Whenever the merchant receives e-coins from the customer, it immediately contacts the cyber-money company to confirm that the coins have not been previously spent. And if the coins are valid, the merchant immediately cashes the coins and the cyber-money company updates the list accordingly. Using the online approach, the two scenarios of double spending can be detected unambiguously. If the customer tries to spend a previously spent e-coin again, the merchant rejects the payment immediately. On the other hand, if the merchant tries to deposit a copy of the e-coin already deposited, the cyber-money company rejects the second deposit.

- Prevention of replay attacks

The 5PAPS model guarantees that no sensitive information can be reused. A timestamp and a valid period are attached to each message containing sensitive information, and the messages become obsolete after the first use [4]. This prevents the potential replay attacks.

5 Anonymity Analysis

5.1 Customer's Anonymity

During the product ordering phase, the customer's anonymity is protected by taking advantage of untraceable e-cash. The blind signature technique is used to ensure that there is no linkage between the contents of the e-coins and the customer's identity. In fact, the cyber-money company knows nothing about the correspondence between the $e\text{-}coin=\{x, Pri\text{-}K_{cc}(x)\}$ and the signed blinded content $Pri\text{-}K_{cc}(blind(x))$. Therefore, neither the merchant nor the cyber-money company can derive the customer's identity.

During the e-cash purchasing phase, the 5PAPS model separates the customer's payment details from the customer's order information. The payment details are encrypted by the bank's public key and thus accessible to the bank only, and the order information is never propagated to the bank. A payment gateway is employed to prevent the bank from learning anything about which merchants the customer deals with.

The IP address of the customer is protected by using a chain of mixes. The source address of any message originating from the customer will be replaced by the address of the first mix. In the opposite direction, every response message targeted for the customer goes through the mix chain in the reverse order and contain an encrypted return address $Ret_{m\text{-}>1}(A_c) = Pub\text{-}K_{mix\,m\text{-}>1}(A_c)$, where A_c is the customer's IP address.

5.2 Customer's Anonymity in the Collusion-Free Scenario

Assuming there is no collusion, Table 1, 2, 3 show the customer's anonymity with regard to different parties involved in the three phases, respectively. In the tables, "0" means the customer's privacy information described in the row is anonymous to the party shown in the column; while "1" means the information is known to the party.

Table 1. Customer's anonymity in e-cash purchasing phase

	1st mix	Other mixes	CC	PG	Bank
Customer's IP address (possibly reveals Customer's real identity)	1	0	0	0	0
Customer's payment details (including the credit card#, the name and the billing address)	0	0	0	0*	1
Customer's e-cash acquisition records	0	0	0	0	1**

* Assume the bank supports anonymous money transfer
** The bank doesn't know which CC the customer uses, but it knows how frequent the customer purchase e-cash and the amount of money the customer pays

Table 2. Customer's anonymity in product ordering phase

	1st mix	Other mixes	CC	Merchant
Customer's IP address (possibly reveals Customer's real identity)	1	0	0	0
Customer's payment details (including the credit card#, the name and the billing address)	0	0	0	0
Customer's order records	0	0	0	0

Table 3. Customer's anonymity in product delivery phase

	1st mix	Other mixes	Merchant
Customer's IP address (possibly reveals Customer's real identity)	1	0	0
Customer's order records	0	0	0

The results show that if there is no collusion among the four business units and the mixes, the customer's privacy is preserved in the maximum manner. In fact, only the bank knows the customer's detailed payment information and only the first mix knows the customer's IP address, both of which are inevitable. The customer's detailed order records stay anonymous to all parties, because the merchant knows nothing about the buyer's identity.

5.3   Customer's Anonymity in Collusion Scenarios

The threats on the customer's anonymity imposed by collusion are now discussed. Two kinds of collusion are considered. The first one is *trivial collusion* which means that a party knows some private information about the customer and this party leaks that information to some other parties. For example, if any party colludes with the first mix, then it will know the customer's IP address. Similarly, the bank also holds private information about the customer. Naturally, both the bank and the primary mixes must be strictly regulated and intensively audited by the government. The second kind is called *non-trivial collusion* and in this case, the pieces of information held by different parties in harmless manners are combined together and then some sensitive private information about the customer comes out. For example, as mentioned in Section 3.1, if all mixes collude, then the correspondence between the customer and the merchant is revealed. This correspondence will reveal information about the customer's purchasing patterns such as how frequently the customer purchase products from a particular merchant. In addition, traffic analysis techniques [15, 16] can be employed among colluding parties to derive private information about the customer. For example, if the

Table 4. Customer's anonymity under collusion in e-cash purchasing phase

	First+last mixes	First mix+CC	CC+PG+ Bank
Customer's correspondence with the CC (possibly reveals Customer's purchase patterns)	1	1	1
Customer's e-cash acquisition records	0	1	1

Table 5. Customer's anonymity under collusion in product ordering & delivery phases

	First+last mixes	First mix+Merchant
Customer's correspondence with the merchant (possibly reveals Customer's purchase patterns)	1	1
Customer's order records	0	1

first mix and the merchant collude, using techniques in [15], the correspondence between the customer and the merchant can also be revealed. In this section, we will focus on the non-trivial collusion. And we assume that IP addresses can be used to track down the real identity of the customer. Table 4, 5 show the customer's anonymity under non-trivial collusion in the three phases, respectively.

The results show that only in some extreme scenarios, for example, the mixes and the cyber-money company / merchant collude together, or the cyber-money company, the payment gateway, and the bank collude, there emerges new serious threats on the customer's anonymity. On the other hand, the results also implicitly show that the 5PAPS model can protect the customer's anonymity even in the presence of some collusion. For instance, in the product ordering phase, even if the merchant and the cyber-money company collude, the customer's payment information, order details and IP address are not revealed to them.

6 Experimental Prototyping and Estimates of Storage and Messaging Volume Requirements

We have built web-based e-store applications based on the Apache-Tomcat platform to demonstrate and partially validate our five-party implementation model. Among all the five parties, the customer, the cyber-money company and the merchant sites are implemented; while the payment-gateway and the bank sites are only simulated. The mix net has not been incorporated into the prototype yet. In the future work, we will continue to complete our prototyping of the 5PAPS model.

In the prototype, the communications among different parties follow the protocols presented in Section 3. The e-cash system is an online scheme based on RSA blind signature [1]. RSA with a key size of 1024 bits is used for asymmetric encryption and AES with a key size of 128 bits is used for symmetric encryption. For each coin, the binary string to be signed is of size 1024 bits.

The storage and networking overhead incurred by e-coins is non-trivial, and it affects the efficiency of the online shop. In fact, each e-coin represents a fixed amount of money, say 10 cents only. To purchase a product worth 100 dollars requires purchasing and paying 1000 e-coins. It means that we need to iterate the protocol for purchasing and depositing one e-coin 1000 times. The situation is even more significant, considering that the cyber-money company may deal with thousands of customers concurrently. In addition, the cyber-money company needs to remember all the coins that have been spent in order to detect double spending. We observe from our experimental work that each coin takes a size of 288 bytes. Assuming that each customer purchases products worth 1000 dollars in total every month, and there are 100,000 customers, the cyber-money company site may require an additional storage size of 288G bytes every month. It also means that for the e-coin acquisition phase and the product ordering phase, we will have an aggregated monthly network traffic of 288G bytes and 576G bytes, respectively.

Future work of the 5PAPS implementation model should focus on reducing the storage and message volumn requirements. On one hand, we can use divisible e-cash [9] [10] [14] or e-cash with multiple denominations [1] [17] to reduce the number of e-coins stored and transmitted by orders of magnitude. For example, to use multi-denomination e-cash, we can assigning different signing keys to different denominations. On the other hand, we can attach an expiration date to each e-coin such that history records of expired e-coins can be safely removed from the database of the cyber-money company. This can be achieved by updating the signing keys periodically. When the cyber-money company issues an e-coin, it explicitly tells the customer the coin's expiration time. When the expiration time arrives, the cyber-money company will use a new signing key and rejects any coins signed with the old key. It is the customer's responsibility to either spend or deposit the coins before they expire. The 5PAPS implementation model can easily accommodate these extensions.

7 Conclusion

In this paper, we proposed an integrated five-party implementation model 5PAPS that enables the customer to purchase information products anonymously. The model combines the advantages of the e-cash techniques, the mix technique, the anonymous-honoring merchant model, and the anonymity-protecting payment gateway model. It is aimed for protecting the customer's anonymity in all applicable aspects. An analysis of the security issues shows that our model is robust under varieties of common attacks. An analysis on the anonymity issues shows that the customer's anonymity can be best preserved even in presence of some collusion. An experimental prototyping work has produced hints on the significant storage and messaging volume requirements of the implementation model. We believe that the model is a good starting-point in realizing a secure e-commerce environment attractive to the people who want to preserve their privacy to a reasonable degree but much more research, especially, experimental research is needed.

Acknowledgement

This work was supported in part by the IT R&D program of MKE/KEIT, [2008-F-036-02, Development of Anonymity-based u-knowledge Security Technology] and in part by the University of California, Irvine.

References

1. Chaum, D.: Blind Signatures for Untraceable Payments. In: Advances in Cryptology Proceedings of Crypto 1982, pp. 199–203. Plenum Press, New York (1982)
2. Chaum, D., Fiat, A., Naor, M.: Untraceable Electronic Cash. In: Goldwasser, S. (ed.) CRYPTO 1988. LNCS, vol. 403, pp. 319–327. Springer, Heidelberg (1990)
3. Brands, S.: Untraceable Off-line Cash in Wallet with Observers. In: Stinson, D.R. (ed.) CRYPTO 1993. LNCS, vol. 773, pp. 302–318. Springer, Heidelberg (1994)
4. Ashrafi, M.Z., Ng, S.K.: Enabling Privacy-Preserving e-Payment Processing. In: Haritsa, J.R., Kotagiri, R., Pudi, V. (eds.) DASFAA 2008. LNCS, vol. 4947, pp. 596–603. Springer, Heidelberg (2008)
5. Chaum, D.: Untraceable Electronic Mail, Return Address, and Digital Pseudonyms. Communications of the ACM 24, 84–90 (1981)

6. The Boston Globe. Breach of data at TJX is called the biggest ever,
   http://www.privacy.org/archives/2007_03.html
7. Rivest, R., Shamir, A., Adleman, L.: A Method for Obtaining Digital Signatures and Public-Key Cryptosystems. Communications of the ACM 21(2), 120–126 (1978)
8. Daemen, J., Rijmen, V.: The Design of Rijndael: AES - The Advanced Encryption Standard. Springer, Heidelberg (2002)
9. Okamoto, T., Ohta, K.: Universal Electronic Cash. In: Feigenbaum, J. (ed.) CRYPTO 1991. LNCS, vol. 576, pp. 324–337. Springer, Heidelberg (1992)
10. Okamoto, T.: An efficient Divisible Electronic Cash Scheme. In: Coppersmith, D. (ed.) CRYPTO 1995. LNCS, vol. 963, pp. 438–451. Springer, Heidelberg (1995)
11. Ferguson, N.: Single Term Off-line Coins. In: Helleseth, T. (ed.) EUROCRYPT 1993. LNCS, vol. 765, pp. 318–328. Springer, Heidelberg (1994)
12. Camenisch, J., Hohenberger, S., Lysyanskaya, A.: Compact e-cash. In: Cramer, R. (ed.) EUROCRYPT 2005. LNCS, vol. 3494, pp. 302–321. Springer, Heidelberg (2005)
13. Danezis, G., Diaz, C.: A Survey of Anonymous Communication Channels. TechReport, Microsoft Research,
   http://research.microsoft.com/apps/pubs/default.aspx?id=70553
14. Chan, A., Frankel, Y., Tsiounis, Y.: Easy Come - Easy Go Divisible Cash. In: Nyberg, K. (ed.) EUROCRYPT 1998. LNCS, vol. 1403, pp. 561–575. Springer, Heidelberg (1998)
15. Murdoch, S.J., Danezis, G.: Low-cost traffic analysis of Tor. In: Proceedings of the 2005 IEEE Symposium on Security and Privacy, May 2005. IEEE CS, Los Alamitos (2005)
16. Danezis, G.: The traffic analysis of continuous-time mixes. In: Martin, D., Serjantov, A. (eds.) PET 2004. LNCS, vol. 3424, pp. 35–50. Springer, Heidelberg (2005)
17. Frankel, Y., Patt-Shamir, B., Tsiounis, Y.: Exact analysis of exact change. In: Proceedings of the 5th Israeli Symposium on the Thoery of Computing Systems (ISTCS), Ran-Gatan, Israel, June 17-19 (1997)

DROP: Detecting Return-Oriented Programming Malicious Code

Ping Chen[1], Hai Xiao[1], Xiaobin Shen[2], Xinchun Yin[2], Bing Mao[1], and Li Xie[1]

[1] State Key Laboratory for Novel Software Technology, Nanjing University
Department of Computer Science and Technology, Nanjing University, Nanjing 210093
{chenping,xiaohai}@sns.nju.edu.cn, {maobing,xieli}@nju.edu.cn
[2] College of Information Engineering, Yangzhou University, Yangzhou Jiangsu 225009, China
xcyin@yzu.edu.cn

Abstract. Return-Oriented Programming (ROP) is a new technique that helps the attacker construct malicious code mounted on x86/SPARC executables without any function call at all. Such technique makes the ROP malicious code contain no instruction, which is different from existing attacks. Moreover, it hides the malicious code in benign code. Thus, it circumvents the approaches that prevent control flow diversion outside legitimate regions (such as $W \oplus X$) and most malicious code scanning techniques (such as anti-virus scanners). However, ROP has its own intrinsic feature which is different from normal program design: (1) uses short instruction sequence ending in "ret", which is called gadget, and (2) executes the gadgets contiguously in specific memory space, such as standard GNU libc. Based on the features of the ROP malicious code, in this paper, we present a tool DROP, which is focused on dynamically detecting ROP malicious code. Preliminary experimental results show that DROP can efficiently detect ROP malicious code, and have no false positives and negatives.

1 Introduction

Return-Oriented Programming (ROP) is a technique which chains together existing instruction streams ending in a "ret" instruction, and then it perform arbitrary, Turing-complete computation without code injection. The instruction streams can be extracted from existing library/binary (e.g., standard GNU libc). Now it is not only available on the x86 platform [40], but also can be mounted on SPARC architecture [14].

ROP technique can be used to rewrite existing malicious code, and eventually become serious threats when used to compromise the computer, which we called as ROP attack. Similar to traditional attacks, such as remote code-injection attack, ROP attack leverages the software vulnerability to launch an attack. However, there are significant differences between ROP attack and traditional attack. ROP attack uses existing library/binary, and ROP malicious code contains only immediate data words and addresses which are pointed to the short instruction sequences in libc, rather than the instructions on which traditional attack relies. ROP malicious code breaks the assumption that preventing the attacker from executing injected code is sufficient to protect a computer, which is at the core of anti-virus software, and other defenses like Intel and AMD's $W \oplus X$ protections. In addition, although ROP attacks have common feature with traditional return-into-libc attacks [23, 27, 29], it is more difficult to defend ROP

A. Prakash and I. Sen Gupta (Eds.): ICISS 2009, LNCS 5905, pp. 163–177, 2009.

attacks for the following reasons: traditional return-into-libc attack uses libc functions, which can be wrapped or removed by the maintainers of libc. By contrast, ROP attack uses short instruction sequences, and each sequence is typically just two to five instructions length. It is non-trivial to remove the short instruction sequences, which exist in the libc or other library/binary widely.

Security tools have arm race with attack techniques. Attacks often use the software vulnerabilities to achieve their goals. Based on this observation, vulnerability detecting tools are leveraged to protect the vulnerability, such as buffer overflow and format string. Although several tools [13, 17, 18, 19, 39] can effectively defend a lot of existing vulnerabilities, none of them can assure that they have prevented all the software bugs. Besides, zero-day attacks become more serious than before, and they can compromise thousands of hosts in a few minutes. It is not sufficient that we only focus on detecting vulnerabilities, because it is too late to defend zero-day attacks. And we need to dynamically monitor the execution behavior of zero-day attacks. Based on the reasons mentioned above, there are a lot of defense tools which aim at detecting the malicious code according to its characteristics. Take remote code-injection attack for example, early works [22, 24, 34, 38, 42] aim at extracting the signature of the shellcode by pattern-based analysis, and the signature is the single, contiguous code sequence. As attackers are employing advanced evasion techniques such as polymorphism to circumvent the defense tools. Some works [15, 25, 32, 43] are further specific to these polymorphic attacks. For example, SigFree [43] is an attack blocker which audits whether the network packet contains instruction sequence and can be leveraged to detect some polymorphic shellcode. However, ROP attack will be resilient to all these defense tools mentioned above, as it has significant difference from traditional attacks, which assumes that malicious code contains instructions to achieve malicious purpose. Thus, these works will be blind to ROP payloads. Other tools [35, 36, 41, 45] use network emulation to detect the remote-injection code, and identify the execution behavior of polymorphic shellcode. Currently, network emulation solutions depend on discovery of instruction sequence, which does not exist in ROP malicious code, since ROP malicious code is totally combined by constant value and instruction address in libc or other existing library/binary. Thus it will be ineffective for ROP attacks. Moreover, based on the observation that most remote-injection attack will execute the code which is injected into the memory by the attacker, another detecting method $W \oplus X$ is used to detect shellcode. These techniques are deployed by the PaX [1] project as a patch for Linux. However, ROP attacks execute existing binary code in program, so it will not be detected by $W \oplus X$.

Although ROP attacks may circumvent many existing defense tools, and hide their malicious behavior in benign code. We find that ROP attack has its intrinsic feature. (1) ROP attack uses gadget ending in "ret" instruction which is used to jump to the next gadget, and the number of the instructions in the gadget is often less than five. By contrast, in benign program design, the pairs of "ret" instruction and "call" instruction represent the prologue and epilogue of the function. (2) "ret" instructions contiguously executed in ROP attacks and they pop up the addresses of the gadgets in existing library/binary. Whereas in normal program, "ret" instructions pop up the addresses which are not contiguously located in the same existing library/binary, that is to say, the distribution of addresses are dispersed. Based on the two differences between ROP attack and normal programs, we develop a tool named DROP, which dynamically detects ROP attack by checking whether the execution trace deviates from the normal execution route.

Our paper makes three major contributions:

- We select several gadgets from glibc-2.3.5 and leverage these gadgets to rewrite 130 x86 shellcode on milw0rm [28] by ROP technique.
- We statistically analyze a number of normal applications and ROP malicious code, and we point out the factors which represent the feature of ROP malicious code.
- We develop an effective tool to detect the ROP attack, with the best of our knowledge, our tool is the first one on detecting ROP attacks.

The rest of this paper is organized as follows: ROP attacks are described in section 2. In section 3, we present an overview of DROP. The design and implementation of DROP is illustrated at section 4. Section 5 provides the evaluation results of our tool. Section 6 examines its limitations, followed by a discussion of related work in section 7. Finally, section 8 concludes our work.

2   ROP Attack

In this section, we first describe the design of ROP malicious code. In practice, we extract several gadgets from glibc-2.3.5, and rewrite 130 x86 shellcode from milw0rm [28] by using these gadgets. Based on the experience of writing ROP malicious code, we point out the feature of ROP attacks.

2.1   Design of ROP Malicious Code

We extract 30 gadgets from glibc-2.3.5 based on the algorithm of finding useful instruction sequence [40]. All these gadgets contain no more than five instructions. We ignore the following "boring instructions" [40]. (1) *"pop ebp"* and *"leave"*, these two instructions ending in "ret" cannot be used in ROP shellcode. (2) *"unconditional jump"*, we ignore the code sequence *"jmp XXX; ret;"*, instead, we use the gadget *"pop %esp; ret;"* to perform the unconditional jump by changing the value of %esp.

Based on the gadgets we find in glibc-2.3.5, we rewrite 130 Linux x86 shellcode from milw0rm [28]. Adopting the ROP techniques proposed by Hovav Shacham [40], we also develop additional techniques to rewrite the ROP malicious code, and these techniques can improve the design of ROP malicious code.

- *Data Segment*: We put the "unconditional jump" gadget after the padding bytes('0x41') in the shellcode, and define the data segment next to the "unconditional jump". Then unconditionally jump to the next gadget which is close to the data segment. Just like in C Programming, we declare variables and constants at the beginning of the function, the data segment is used to store the temporary values or constant arguments of the system call. This technique avoids complicated calculation of the memory address used in ROP shellcode, especially when there are a lot of temporary values and constant arguments used by original shellcode.

- *Constant Value*: There are often some immediate values in shellcode, such as the system call number. In ROP shellcode, we cannot store them in memory directly, because it will bring NULL bytes to the shellcode. Alternatively, we store its negative values in the memory. Take "11(0xb)" for example, we store its negative value "-11(0xfffffff5)" in the memory, and use the gadget *"pop %edx; ret;"* to load -11 to %edx , then leverage the other two gadgets *"xor %eax, %eax; ret;"* and *"sub %edx, %eax; ret;"* to get the original immediate value 11.

- *Shortest Gadget Sequence*: We try to use the shortest gadget sequence to rewrite the original code. For example, if we want to load a value to memory, the gadget sequence mentioned by Hovav Shacham is *"pop %eax; ret; mov %eax, 0x18(%edx); ret"* [40], it contains two gadgets. By contrast, we use following gadget instead to achieve the same functionality. The difference is that we need to store the value subtracted by 10 in shellcode, and then pop it to %ecx.

```
pop    %ecx
add    $0xa,%ecx
mov    %ecx,(%edx)
ret
```

Figure 1 shows one example of the 130 ROP shellcode we rewrite. Figure 1 (a) shows the original shellcode, and Figure 1 (b) shows the ROP shellcode. These two kinds of shellcode have the same function: obtaining a command shell from which the attacker can control the compromised machine. In this example, glibc-2.3.5 is mapped at address 0x03000000, program stack is mapped at address 0x4fffff00, and in practice, we assume these addresses have already been obtained by the attacker.

0x31 , 0xc0, 0x50 ,   /* xor %eax, %eax;
                        push %eax
                        */
0x68, 0x2f, 0x2f, 0x73, 0x68, /* push$0x68732f2f;*/
0x68, 0x2f, 0x62, 0x69, 0x6e, /* push$0x6e69622f;*/
0x89, 0xe3,   /* mov %esp, %ebx;*/
0x50,   /* push %eax; */
0x53,   /* push %ebx;*/
0x89, 0xe1,   /* mov %esp ,%ecx;*/
0x31, 0xd2,   /* xor %edx, %edx;*/
0xb0, 0x0b,   /* mov $0xb, %al;*/
0xcd, 0x80;   /* int 0x80;*/
0x00
	0x9e, 0x7a, 0x03, 0x03 , /* xor %eax, %eax; ret; */
	0xe8, 0x7f, 0x02, 0x03, /* pop %edx; ret; */
	0x0c, 0xff, 0xff, 0x4f,
	0x10, 0x80, 0x02, 0x03, /*mov %eax, 0x18(%edx);ret;*/
	0xe8, 0x7f, 0x02, 0x03, /* pop %edx; ret; */
	0xf5, 0xff, 0xff, 0xff, /* -11 */
	0x9b, 0xa0, 0x06, 0x03, /* sub %edx, %eax; ret; */
	0x0d, 0xb1, 0x06, 0x03, /* pop %ebx; ret; */
	0x38, 0xff, 0xff, 0x4f, /* address of "/bin//sh" */
	0xe7, 0x7f, 0x02, 0x03, /* pop %ecx; pop %edx; ret;*/
	0x20, 0xff, 0xff, 0x4f,
	0x24, 0xff, 0xff, 0x4f,
	0xf5, 0xda, 0x08, 0x03, /* int 0x80; ret;*/
	0x38, 0xff, 0xff, 0x4f,
	0x12, 0x34, 0x56, 0x78,
	0x2f, 0x62, 0x69, 0x6e,
	0x2f, 0x2f, 0x73, 0x68, 0x00

(a)	(b)

Fig. 1. Example code: (a) original shellcode, and (b) the ROP shellcode

In Figure 1, we can see that except constant data *"/bin//sh"*, ROP malicious code is in the different shape from original code. The original code contains instructions, whereas ROP malicious code is consisted of the address of gadget and immediate data within libc. In addition, ROP malicious code leverages the gadgets ending in a "ret" instruction which pops up the address of the next gadget.

2.2 Features of ROP Malicious Code

Return-oriented Programming malicious code relies on existing code (e.g., libc) and contains no instructions. The organizational unit of a return-oriented attack is the gadget. Each gadget is an arrangement of words on the stack, and these words point to instruction sequences and immediate data words. When the gadget is invoked, it accomplishes several well-defined task, such as a load or an arithmetic operation [37].

Based on the practical experience of writing ROP malicious code, we find the feature of ROP malicious code as follows:

- ROP chains together gadgets (often contain no more than 5 instructions) which are already existing in the memory space, and each of these gadgets ending in "ret".
- ROP malicious code utilizes the contiguous gadget sequence.
- ROP technique hides the malicious code in benign code, as it only contains the immediate data or address value.

Formula in Table 1 is used to represent ROP malicious code. In this Formula, we define:

Definition 1 (Candidate Gadget). *Candidate Gadget refers to the instruction sequence ending in "ret". We defined the number of instructions in a Candidate Gadget as G_size. Candidate Gadget Set is briefly represented as G[1...n], G[i] represents the i_{th} Candidate Gadget in G set.*

Definition 2 (Contiguous Candidate Gadget Sequence). *Contiguous candidate gadgets are defined as the gadgets occur one after the other and they pop up the address within the same library/binary memory space. The Contiguous Candidate Gadget Sequence contains the contiguous candidate gadgets, and it is represented as S[1...k], S[i] represents the i_{th} Candidate Gadget in S set. The length of contiguous candidate gadget sequence is defined as S_length, and Max(S_length) represents the maximum value of S_length.*

Table 1. Expressions represent the ROP malicious code

$$G\_size = sizeof(G[i]) \ If \ Min\_Addr <= G[i].Addr <= Max\_Addr \&\& G[i] \in G;$$
$$S = \{S[i]|S[i].G\_size, S[i+1].G\_size <= T0 \&\& S[i]^1, S[i+1]^1 \in G\};$$
$$S\_length = \{length|length = sizeof(S)\};$$
$$ROP = Assert(Max(S\_length) >= T1);$$

[1] S[i] and S[i+1] are contiguous gadgets.

In Table 1, *Min_Addr / Max_Addr* is the start/end address of existing library/binary, where the gadgets are extracted from. *G_size* and *Max(S_length)* are the two factors which represent the feature of ROP malicious code. *T0* and *T1* are the thresholds of the *G_size* and *Max(S_length)*, respectively. To detect ROP malicious code, we need correctly choose the value of *T0* and *T1*.

3   Overview

Based on the differences between ROP malicious code and normal program, we implement a defense tool "DROP" to detect ROP malicious code. Based on the thresholds of G_size and $Max(S\_length)$, DROP monitors the program dynamically, intercepts the "ret" instruction, chooses the "ret" instruction which pops up the address in libc, and then checks whether the maximum length of contiguous candidate gadget sequence is more than $T1$ and each gadget has no more than $T0$ length. If so, DROP raises an alarm that the process executed contains ROP malicious code.

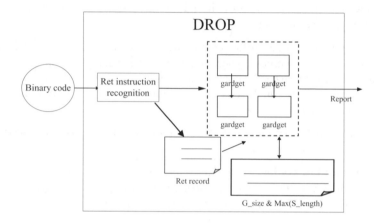

Fig. 2. Architecture of DROP

Figure 2 shows the architecture of our system. First, we recognize the "ret" instruction and determine whether it pops up the address within libc. If so, we record the address poped up by "ret" instruction. Second, we record the size of each *Candidate Gadget* (G_size). And we also record the length of contiguous gadget sequences (S_length). By referencing the thresholds of G_size and $Max(S\_length)$, we check whether ROP malicious code exists. Note that our system currently inspects the gadgets in the libc, it can be extended to other existing library/binary such as Linux Kernel.

4   Implementation Details

Our system is implemented on dynamical binary instrumentation tool Valgrind-3.4.0 [30]. DROP dynamically instruments the binary code and does statistical analysis to determine whether the execution route breaks the thresholds of G_size and $Max(S\_length)$, which are two main factors to separate the ROP malicious code from normal program.

Figure 3 shows the flow chart of DROP. First, DROP leverages Valgrind Core to translate the binary code into intermediate language VEX. Second, DROP recognizes the "ret" instruction represented by VEX. Third, DROP records the address poped up by "ret" instruction and checks whether the address is in libc. Then DROP counts the length of candidate gadget, which equals to the number of instructions between two

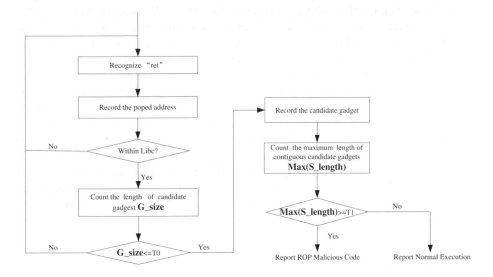

Fig. 3. Flow chart of DROP

"ret" instructions, and selects the candidate gadget whose length is no more than *T0*, that is to say, *G_size<=T0*. Finally DROP checks whether there are more than *T1* contiguous gadgets, in other words, *Max(S_length) >=T1*. If the binary execution meets the feature of ROP malicious code, DROP will report that there exists ROP malicious code.

There are two challenges to detect the ROP malicious code.

– *Ret Instruction Recognition.*

First we need to recognize the "ret" instruction and then record the address poped up by it. Valgrind translates binary code into intermediate language VEX, and Table 2 shows "ret" instruction represented by VEX in 32 bits architecture. There are four

Table 2. Ret Instruction Represented in VEX

```
[1]PUT(60) =0x804838A:I32;
[2]t3 =LDle:I32(t4);
[3]t5=Add32(t4,0x4:I32);
[4]PUT(16) =t5;
```

VEX statements which represent the "ret" instruction. The first statement is used to store the address of "ret" instruction in %eip(60), the second statement is used to pop up the address from the top of stack, then the third and fourth statements are used to regulate the value of %esp by adding 4 to it. In intermediate language VEX, *PUT* is used to write the value to the register, and *LDle* is used to load the value to the memory. We found the representation of "ret" instruction in VEX has following feature: (1) Using *LDle* to read the value from the top of stack; (2) Using the *Add32* expression , whose first operand is the same as the operand of *LDle* and second operand is 0x04; (3) The result of addition statement is the same as the right operand of *PUT* statement, and the register of *PUT* statement is %esp(16). We instrument the second VEX statement, which pops up the address from the top of stack, to record the address. When we identify the "ret" instruction, we check whether the address popped up by the "ret" instruction is in libc.

- *Contiguous candidate gadgets Recognition* . DROP recognizes the contiguous candidate gadgets as the following steps. First, when we find that the address poped up by "ret" instruction is in libc, DROP records the size of the candidate gadget ending in the "ret" instruction just recognized, and initiates the variable G_size as 0. Then DROP increases the G_size when executes one instruction, until encounters the next "ret" instruction. We select the candidate gadgets with the size G_size no more than $T0$. And then among these gadgets, we record the length of contiguous candidate gadget sequence and choose the maximum length of the contiguous candidate gadget sequence. If the maximum length is no less than $T1$, we raise an alarm that the program contains ROP malicious code.

5   Evaluation

In this section, we choosed a large number of normal programs and ROP malicious shellcode to determine the thresholds of the two factors which represent the feature of ROP: G_size and S_length. Based on the two factors, we evaluated the false positives and false negatives of DROP with hundreds of applications and several kinds of shellcode. Finally we test the performance overhead of DROP. The evaluation is performed on an Intel Pentium Dual E2180 2.00GHz machine with 2GB memory and Linux kernel 2.6.15. Tested programs are compiled by gcc-4.0.3 and linked with glibc-2.3.5.

5.1   Statistical Analysis of Normal Programs and Shellcode

We choose hundreds of applications to test the feature of normal programs' execution, and the sizes of these applications range from 10K to 100M. These tested programs cover major categories of common programs such as Database, Media Player, Web Server. Table 3 lists the statistical results of fifteen programs. Note that the rest of programs we analyzed also come up to the average statistical result listed in Table 3.

Table 3. Statistical result of normal program

Software	LOC (K)	Benchmark	The number of candidate gadget							Max(S_length)						
			$\leq=4$ [1]	$\leq=5$	$\leq=6$	$\leq=7$	$\leq=8$	$\leq=9$	$\leq=10$	$\leq=4$ [1]	$\leq=5$	$\leq=6$	$\leq=7$	$\leq=8$	$\leq=9$	$\leq=10$
slocate-2.7	89.2	Search patterns in 87K database	7	13	17	30	40	48	56	1	2	2	2	3	3	5
bzip2-1.0.5	236.6	Uncompress the 269K file	7	12	15	26	34	41	46	1	2	2	2	2	3	3
man-1.6c	248.5	Open the message catalog for ls	5	10	16	30	43	51	60	1	2	2	3	3	3	4
gzip-1.2.4	278.2	Uncompress the 55M file	1	4	8	19	25	31	34	1	2	2	2	2	3	3
bc-1.06	375.9	Finds primes between 2 and limits	5	9	11	21	27	33	39	1	2	2	2	2	2	4
ngircd-0.8.1	445.1	Validate and display configuration	8	15	19	30	38	44	53	1	2	2	2	2	2	4
zgv-5.8	479.5	View JPG file	8	17	25	49	64	78	88	1	2	2	3	3	3	3
gocr-0.46	823.6	Process JPG file	6	12	15	27	33	39	47	1	2	2	3	3	3	3
grep-2.5.1	904.1	Find pattern in 1.9 MB file	2	7	9	19	26	35	40	1	2	2	2	2	3	3
openssh-2.2.1	976.8	Login in using user name	11	21	25	30	42	43	52	1	2	2	2	2	3	5
tar-1.15.1	1149.0	Uncompress the 13.6M file	12	18	25	42	55	65	77	1	2	2	3	3	3	5
gcc-4.2.4	4060.4	Compile 1KB source code	5	10	12	23	33	41	46	1	2	2	2	3	3	5
httpd-2.2.0	9883.7	ab	19	31	91	118	144	163	174	2	2	2	2	3	4	5
python-2.5.2	13602.9	Process python file	12	18	25	41	56	65	72	1	2	2	2	2	4	5
php-5.2.5	24462.0	Process php file	13	21	28	53	73	93	108	1	2	3	3	4	4	6
Average			8	15	23	37	54	58	66	1	2	2	2	3	3	4

[1] **G_size=4,5,6,7,8,9,10**

In Table 3, columns 4-10 represent the number of candidate gadgets and the length of candidate gadget is *G_size*, and columns 11-17 represent the maximum length of contiguous gadget sequence *Max(S_length)*, and each gadget has the *G_size* length. From columns 4-10, we can see that the average number of candidate gadgets is 15 in normal programs, and each candidate gadget contains no more than 5 instructions. This number is relatively small, by contrast, most of ROP malicious code contain more than 15 gadgets. To find the common number of instructions in shellcode, we statistically analyze 130 x86 shellcode from milw0rm [28]. Figure 4 shows the number of instructions in the 130 shellcode. We can see 83 shellcode among 130 shellcode we study contain more than 15 instructions, nearly 63.4%. We also rewrite these 130 shellcode by ROP technique, and find that 87 ROP shellcode contain more than 15 gadgets, nearly 66.9%.

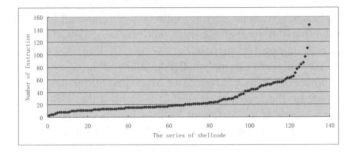

Fig. 4. The Number of Instructions in Shellcode

In addition, from columns 11-17, we can see that the larger the *G_size*, the longer the *Max(S_length)*. When *G_size* is no more than 5, the *Max(S_length)* is relatively stable and less than 2. On the contrary, based on the analysis of ROP malicious code, we find that the number of candidate gadgets is no less than 3. Malicious code uses system call to achieve malicious system operation, and the system call will be replaced by ROP technique with 3 gadgets at least. If these candidate gadgets are contiguous, the maximum length of contiguous candidate gadget sequence is more than 3. Based on the analysis of normal programs and ROP malicious code just mentioned above, we find that the threshold of *Max(S_length)* is about 3.

To further choose the thresholds of the two factors of ROP malicious code and make DROP have both low false positives and false negatives, we test a large number of normal programs and ROP malicious code which are monitored under DROP with

Table 4. The false positives and false negatives of DROP

T0 / T1	4	5	6	7	8	9	10
1	1.000/0.000	1.000/0.000	1.000/0.000	1.000/0.000	1.000/0.000	1.000/0.000	1.000/0.000
2	0.913/0.000	1.000/0.000	1.000/0.000	1.000/0.000	1.000/0.000	1.000/0.000	1.000/0.000
3	0.000/0.009	**0.000/0.000**	0.067/0.000	0.333/0.000	0.578/0.000	0.817/0.000	0.982/0.000
4	0.000/0.069	0.000/0.023	0.047/0.023	0.053/0.023	0.073/0.023	0.235/0.023	0.637/0.023
5	0.000/0.092	0.000/0.031	0.000/0.031	0.000/0.031	0.002/0.031	0.096/0.031	0.467/0.031
6	0.000/0.104	0.000/0.054	0.000/0.054	0.000/0.054	0.000/0.054	0.000/0.054	0.067/0.054

[1] False positives and false negatives of DROP are represented in the form of *x/y*, "x" represents the false positives, and "y" represents the false negatives.

the different thresholds of *G_size* and *Max(S_length)*. Table 4 shows the experimental results. And the thresholds of *G_size* and *Max(S_length)* are represented as *T0* and *T1*, respectively. We can see that when the value of *G_size* is increasing, it makes the false positives of DROP increase and false negatives decrease, on the contrary, when the value of *Max(S_length)* is increasing, it makes the opposite result.

From Table 4, we can see that the optimal thresholds of *Max(S_length)* and *G_size* are 3 and 5, respectively, because in this case, DROP has no false positives and false negatives. Note that the thresholds of *Max(S_length)* and *G_size* can be chosen by the user. In current implementation, we focus on x86 programs, and monitor the gadgets in libc. Thus, we select the thresholds of *Max(S_length)* and *G_size* as 3 and 5, respectively.

5.2   Analysis of False Positives and False Negatives

We choose 130 Linux x86 shellcode from milw0rm [28], and all these types of shellcode are rewritten by ROP to evaluate the effectiveness of DROP. Table 5 shows ten representative cases among 130 shellcode we tested. In Table 5, column 4 represents the number of instructions in original shellcode, and column 5 represents the number of gadgets in ROP shellcode we rewrote. We can see that DROP has no false negatives. Next we also measure the false positives of DROP. Note that DROP is based on the two factors which represent the feature of ROP malicious code, and the two character factors are determined by statistically analyzing hundreds of application mentioned in Section 5.1. We select additional hundreds of applications to analyze the false positives of DROP. Experimental result shows that DROP has no false positives. In addition, although so far, in practice, we have not constructed x86 ROP malicious code by using libc gadgets to circumvent DROP. In theory, however, DROP may have false negatives.

Table 5. ROP malicious code tested on DROP

Date of Shellcode	Size	Description	Instructions	Gadgets	Detected by DROP
2009-06-16	34 bytes	setreuid(),execve("/bin/sh",0,0) [11]	16	21	✓
2009-02-20	30 bytes	chmod("/etc/shadow",666) exit(0) [8]	11	8	✓
2009-02-04	34 bytes	killall5 shellcode [9]	13	15	✓
2009-01-16	30 bytes	PUSH reboot() [10]	12	8	✓
2008-11-19	86 bytes	edit /etc/sudoers for full access [7]	29	32	✓
2007-03-09	40 bytes	/sbin/iptables -F [6]	17	19	✓
2006-11-17	45 bytes	execve(rm -rf /) shellcode [3]	23	29	✓
2006-07-04	84 bytes	portbind (define your own port) [5]	47	84	✓
2006-04-03	25 bytes	execve("/bin/sh", ["/bin/sh", NULL]) [2]	11	8	✓
2006-01-21	5 bytes	normal exit w/ random return value [4]	3	3	✓

– *Multi-stage ROP malicious code.*
  Multi-stage shellcode reads the second stage payload and executes it. At the end of the first stage, it will subvert the control flow to the shellcode belonged to the second stage. At this moment, if the first stage shellcode executes "ret" instruction to jump to the second stage shellcode, it will pop up the address which is not in libc. Therefore, it may break the assumption that ROP malicious code contains no less than 3 contiguous address which are poped up by "ret" instructions within libc. In addition, if the first stage payload is short (less than 3 gadgets), it may make DROP ineffective. However, in practical analysis of shellcode, we have not found this kind of shellcode, because there is almost no chance for attacker to construct the first stage shellcode with less than 3 gadgets to read the second stage payload and jump to it.

– *Mutil-source ROP malcious code.*

Currently, we only monitor the gadgets in libc, if the ROP malicious code uses multi-source, such as the program text segment and Linux Kernel, and constructs the gadgets in interval. DROP will be blind to this kind of malicious code. In practice, it is hard to construct multi-source ROP malicious code, because it is non-trivial to simultaneously get the base address of the multi-source.

Although there are several methods which may be potentially circumventing DROP, as demonstrated, we believe our technique can be used to defend against ROP attacks. First, these attack techniques are not practical and hard to be implemented. Second, DROP is built based on the case study of normal programs and ROP malicious code, and our experimental results show that it has no false positives and negatives.

5.3 Performance Evaluation

We used the fifteen normal applications listed in Table 6 to measure the performance of our tool DROP. For each program, we tested the performance overhead when the program runs natively and under DROP.

Table 6. Performance Overhead of DROP

Prog.	LOC (K)	Benchmark	Native Run	Under DROP	Performance Overhead
slocate-2.7	89.2	Search patterns in 87K database	0.096s	0.593s	6.2X
bzip2-1.0.5	236.6	Uncompress the 269K file	3.357s	51.860s	15.4X
man-1.6c	248.5	Open the message catalog for ls	0.188s	1.234s	6.6X
gzip-1.2.4	278.2	Uncompress the 55M file	2.457s	10.839s	4.4X
bc-1.06	375.9	Finds primes between 2 and limits	0.125s	2.628s	21.0X
ngircd-0.8.1	445.1	Validate and display configuration	0.141s	0.625s	4.4X
zgv-5.8	479.5	View JPG file	0.145s	0.703s	4.8X
gocr-0.46	823.6	Process JPG file	0.136s	1.868s	13.7X
grep-2.5.1	904.1	Find pattern in 1.9 MB file	0.958s	9.753s	10.2X
openssh-2.2.1	976.8	Login in using user name	4.626s	14.803s	3.2X
tar-1.15.1	1149.0	Uncompress the 13.6M file	8.158s	15.463s	1.9X
gcc-4.2.4	4060.4	Compile 1KB source code	0.078s	0.748s	9.6X
httpd-2.2.0	9883.7	ab	1.019s	5.208s	5.1X
python-2.5.2	13602.9	Process python file	0.725s	4.188s	5.8X
php-5.2.5	24462.0	Process php file	0.612s	2.349s	3.8X
Average			1.521s	8.191s	5.3X

From Table 6, we can see the average performance slow down factor of DROP is nearly 5.3 times. With the best of our knowledge, the performance overhead of DROP is the relatively low Valgrind overhead. The performance overhead of DROP is mainly on the recognition of "ret" instruction and statistical analysis the length of contiguous gadget sequences (S_length). Note that we just propose the mechanism of detecting ROP malicious code, and we believe our method can be adopted by other binary dynamic instrumentation tools, such as PIN [26], and may get better performance.

6   Discussion

We implement DROP to detect ROP malicious code, and currently DROP is based on dynamic binary instrumentation tool Valgrind [30]. Different from vulnerability-based detection tools and malicious scanning tools, our tool aims at detecting ROP malicious code. DROP has following limitations:

- *Portability Limitation*. DROP only detect ROP malicious code written on x86 architecture, however, malicious code can be rewritten on other architecture by ROP technique. Thus it will be ineffective to detect ROP malicious code on other architectures. We believe that our detecting mechanisms can be deployed to other architectures, such as SPARC.
- *Detection Limitation*. There are two limitations. First, DROP detects ROP malicious code with the assumption that it contains at least three contiguous gadgets. However, some potential shellcode methods discussed in Section 5.2 may break this assumption, and make DROP not effective. Second, currently, DROP only detects the gadgets extracted from libc. However, some techniques may help attacker use other existing library/binary, such as Linux Kernel [21], to construct ROP malicious code. DROP will not be effective for this kind of ROP malicious code.

7   Related Work

7.1   Return-into-Libc Attack

ROP attack technique fits within the larger milieu of return-into-libc attack. However, there are some critical differences between ROP attack and traditional return-into-libc attacks. Traditional return-into-libc attack leverages libc functions, whereas ROP attack uses gadgets. One gadget contains no more than five instructions and it can be easily automatically extracted from the existing library/binary. Some original defense techniques against the traditional return-into-libc attack, such as Libsafe [13], will be ineffective for the ROP attacks. Besides, ROP attack can use other existing library/binary such as Linux Kernel, and makes it more challenging to detect ROP attack.

7.2   Defense Techniques Against Code Injection and Execution

$W \oplus X$ is a technique which ensures that no memory location in a process image is marked both writable ("W") and executable ("X"), typical defending tool is PAX [1]. It forbids memory pages both writable and executable. However, ROP attack does not execute the injected code, and thus cannot be detected by $W \oplus X$.

7.3   Malicious Code Scanners

Malicious Code Scanners [15,22,24,25,32,34,35,36,38,41,42,43,45] detect the context of input, and check whether there are malicious codes. Currently, several Malicious Code Scanners detect the malicious by using pattern matching. As ROP malicious code contains the address of gadgets or data, the string in malicious code is randomized, thus malicious code scanners will be ineffective for detecting ROP malicious code.

7.4   Integrity of Control Flow

Some existing tools can be deployed to prevent the control flow of program tampering. These tools monitor the sensitive control-flow objects such as return address and function pointer. There are several typical tools [12,17,18,19], and these tools may block the pre-condition of ROP attack : altering the control flow to the location ROP malicious code exists. Our tool is an alternative approach to detect ROP malicious code based on the assumption the control flow is tampered at least once.

7.5 Memory Tainting Techniques

Memory tainting is used to defend the memory maliciously read and written. This defense technique taints the memory location at bit/byte level, and detects whether the sensitive object is corrupted by outside inputs. TaintCheck [33] is a tool which can effectively detect the control-flow hijacking. Xu et al [44] proposed a dynamic taint analysis technique to check security-sensitive operations. Several tools aim at automatically detecting malicious behavior of malicious code from network using taint analysis,such as DAKADO [20], Vigilante [16] and VSEF [31]. All these tools mentioned above are effective for defending ROP attack, as they block the ROP malicious code to be injected into memory. Our tool is an alternative approach to detect ROP malicious code based on the assumption the malicious code can be successfully injected into memory.

8 Conclusion

In this paper, we have studied Return-Oriented Programming(ROP) and wrote several ROP malicious code by using this technique. In addition, we statistically analyzed a large number of normal programs and ROP malicious code, and investigated two factors that represent the feature of ROP: G_size and $Max(S\_length)$. Based on the observation, we found that there exist thresholds of the two factors, and can be leveraged to detect ROP malicious code by separating the ROP malicious code from normal programs. Our approach monitors program execution, and checks whether the execution comes up to the feature of ROP malicious code. We have implemented our approach in a system called DROP and applied it to analyze a number of normal programs and ROP malicious code on x86 architecture. Preliminary experimental results show that our approach is highly effective and practical, and has no false positives and negatives.

Acknowledgements

This work was supported in part by grants from the Chinese National Natural Science Foundation (60773171, 90818022, and 60721002), the Chinese National 863 High-Tech Program (2007AA01Z448), the Chinese 973 Major State Basic Program(2009CB320705), and the Natural Science Foundation of Jiangsu Province(BK2007136).

References

1. The pax project (2004), http://pax.grsecurity.net/
2. linux/x86 execve("/bin/sh", ["/bin/sh", null]). milw0rm (2006),
   http://www.milw0rm.com/shellcode/1635
3. linux/x86 execve(rm -rf /) shellcode. milw0rm (2006),
   http://www.milw0rm.com/shellcode/2801
4. linux/x86 normal exit w/ random (so to speak) return value. milw0rm (2006),
   http://www.milw0rm.com/shellcode/1435
5. linux/x86 portbind (define your own port). milw0rm (2006),
   http://www.milw0rm.com/shellcode/1979
6. linux/x86 /sbin/iptables -f. milw0rm (2007),
   http://www.milw0rm.com/shellcode/3445

7. linux/x86 edit /etc/sudoers for full access. milw0rm (2008),
   http://www.milw0rm.com/shellcode/7161
8. linux/x86 chmod ("/etc/shadow",666) & exit(0). milw0rm (2009),
   http://www.milw0rm.com/shellcode/8081
9. linux/x86 killall5 shellcode. milw0rm (2009),
   http://www.milw0rm.com/shellcode/8972
10. linux/x86 push reboot(). milw0rm (2009),
    http://www.milw0rm.com/shellcode/7808
11. linux/x86 setreuid(geteuid(),geteuid()),execve("/bin/sh",0,0). milw0rm (2009),
    http://www.milw0rm.com/shellcode/8972
12. Abadi, M., Budiu, M., Ligatti, J.: Control-flow integrity. In: Proceedings of the 12th ACM
    Conference on Computer and Communications Security(CCS), pp. 340–353. ACM Press,
    New York (2005)
13. Baratloo, A., Singh, N., Tsai, T.: Transparent run-time defense against stack smashing at-
    tacks. In: Proceedings of the Annual Conference on USENIX Annual Technical Conference,
    p. 21. USENIX Association, Berkeley (2000)
14. Buchanan, E., Roemer, R., Shacham, H., Savage, S.: When good instructions go bad: gen-
    eralizing return-oriented programming to risc. In: Proceedings of the 15th ACM Conference
    on Computer and Communications Security(CCS), pp. 27–38. ACM, New York (2008)
15. Cavallaro, L., Lanzi, A., Mayer, L., Monga, M.: Lisabeth: automated content-based signa-
    ture generator for zero-day polymorphic worms. In: Proceedings of the 4th International
    Workshop on Software Engineering for Secure Systems(SESS), pp. 41–48. ACM, New York
    (2008)
16. Costa, M., Crowcroft, J., Castro, M., Rowstron, A., Zhou, L., Zhang, L., Barham, P.: Vigi-
    lante: End-to-end containment of internet worm epidemics. ACM Transactions on Computer
    Systems (TOCS) 26(4), 1–68 (2008)
17. Cowan, C., Pu, C., Maier, D., Walpole, J., Bakke, P., Beattie, S., Grier, A., Wagle, P., Zhang,
    Q.: Stackguard: automatic adaptive detection and prevention of buffer-overflow attacks. In:
    Proceedings of the 7th Conference on USENIX Security Symposium, p. 5. USENIX Asso-
    ciation, Berkeley (1998)
18. Cowan, C., Barringer, M., Beattie, S., Kroah-Hartman, G., Frantzen, M., Lokier, J.: Format-
    guard: Automatic protection from printf format string vulnerabilities. In: Proceedings of the
    10th conference on USENIX Security Symposium, p. 2003 (2000)
19. Cowan, C., Beattie, S., Johansen, J., Wagle, P.: Pointguardtm: protecting pointers from buffer
    overflow vulnerabilities. In: Proceedings of the 12th Conference on USENIX Security Sym-
    posium, p. 7. USENIX Association, Berkeley (2003)
20. Crandall, J.R., Su, Z., Wu, S.F., Chong, F.T.: On deriving unknown vulnerabilities from zero-
    day polymorphic and metamorphic worm exploits. In: Proceedings of the 12th ACM Con-
    ference on Computer and Communications Security(CCS), pp. 235–248 (2005)
21. Hund, R., Holz, T., Freiling, F.C.: Return-oriented rootkits: Bypassing kernel code integrity
    protection mechanisms. In: Proceedings of 18th USENIX Security Symposium (2009)
22. Kim, H.A., Karp, B.: Autograph: toward automated, distributed worm signature detection.
    In: Proceedings of the 13th Conference on USENIX Security Symposium, p. 19. USENIX
    Association, Berkeley (2004)
23. Krahmer, S.: X86-64 buffer overflow exploits and the borrowed code chunks exploitation
    technique. Phrack Magazine (2005), http://www.suse.de/krahmer/no-nx.pdf
24. Kreibich, C., Crowcroft, J.: Honeycomb: creating intrusion detection signatures using hon-
    eypots. ACM SIGCOMM Computer Communication Review 34(1), 51–56 (2004)
25. Li, Z., Sanghi, M., Chen, Y., Kao, M.Y., Chavez, B.: Hamsa: Fast signature generation for
    zero-day polymorphic worms with provable attack resilience. In: Proceedings of the 2006
    IEEE Symposium on Security and Privacy, pp. 32–47 (2006)

26. Luk, C.K., Cohn, R., Muth, R., Patil, H., Klauser, A., Lowney, G., Wallace, S., Reddi, V.J., Hazelwood, K.: Pin: building customized program analysis tools with dynamic instrumentation. In: Proceedings of the 2005 ACM SIGPLAN Conference on Programming Language Design and Implementation, pp. 190–200. ACM, New York (2005)
27. McDonald, J.: Defeating solaris/sparc non-executable stack protection. Bugtraq (1999)
28. milw0rm: http://www.milw0rm.com/shellcode/linux/x86
29. Nergal: The advanced return-into-lib(c) exploits (pax case study). Phrack Magazine (2001), http://www.phrack.org/archives/58/p58-0x04
30. Nethercote, N., Seward, J.: Valgrind: a framework for heavyweight dynamic binary instrumentation. In: Proceedings of the 2007 PLDI Conference, vol. 42(6), pp. 89–100 (2007)
31. Newsome, J., Brumley, D., Song, D.: Vulnerability-specific execution filtering for exploit prevention on commodity software. In: Proceedings of the 13th Annual Network and Distributed System Security Symposium, NDSS (2006)
32. Newsome, J., Karp, B., Song, D.: Polygraph: Automatically generating signatures for polymorphic worms. In: Proceedings of the IEEE Symposium on Security and Privacy, pp. 226–241 (2005)
33. Newsome, J., Song, D.: Dynamic taint analysis for automatic detection, analysis, and signature generation of exploits on commodity software (2005)
34. Paxson, V.: Bro: a system for detecting network intruders in real-time. In: Proceedings of the 7th Conference on USENIX Security Symposium, Berkeley, CA, USA, p. 3 (1998)
35. Polychronakis, M., Anagnostakis, K.G., Markatos, E.P.: Network-level polymorphic shellcode detection using emulation. In: Büschkes, R., Laskov, P. (eds.) DIMVA 2006. LNCS, vol. 4064, pp. 54–73. Springer, Heidelberg (2006)
36. Polychronakis, M., Anagnostakis, K.G., Markatos, E.P.: Emulation-based detection of non-self-contained polymorphic shellcode. In: Kruegel, C., Lippmann, R., Clark, A. (eds.) RAID 2007. LNCS, vol. 4637, pp. 87–106. Springer, Heidelberg (2007)
37. Roemer, R., Buchanan, E., Shacham, H., Savage, S.: Return-oriented programming: Systems, languages, and applications (2009) (in review)
38. Roesch, M.: Snort - lightweight intrusion detection for networks. In: Proceedings of the 13th USENIX Conference on System Administration, pp. 229–238. USENIX Association, Berkeley (1999)
39. Ruwase, O., Lam, M.S.: A practical dynamic buffer overflow detector. In: Proceedings of the 11th Annual Network and Distributed System Security Symposium (NDSS), pp. 159–169 (2004)
40. Shacham, H.: The geometry of innocent flesh on the bone: return-into-libc without function calls (on the x86). In: Proceedings of the 14th ACM Conference on Computer and Communications Security (CCS), pp. 552–561. ACM, New York (2007)
41. Shimamura, M., Kono, K.: Yataglass: Network-level code emulation for analyzing memory-scanning attacks. In: Proceedings of the 6th International Conference on Detection of Intrusions and Malware, and Vulnerability Assessment, pp. 68–87 (2009)
42. Singh, S., Estan, C., Varghese, G., Savage, S.: Automated worm fingerprinting. In: Proceedings of the 6th Conference on Symposium on Opearting Systems Design & Implementation(OSDI), p. 4. USENIX Association, Berkeley (2004)
43. Wang, X., Pan, C.C., Liu, P., Zhu, S.: Sigfree: A signature-free buffer overflow attack blocker. IEEE Transactions on Dependable and Secure Computing 99(2) (2006)
44. Xu, W., Bhatkar, S., Sekar, R.: Taint-enhanced policy enforcement: a practical approach to defeat a wide range of attacks. In: Proceedings of the 15th Conference on USENIX Security Symposium (USENIX-SS 2006). USENIX Association, Berkeley (2006)
45. Zhang, Q., Reeves, D.S., Ning, P., Iyer, S.P.: Analyzing network traffic to detect self-decrypting exploit code. In: Proceedings of the 2nd ACM Symposium on Information, Computer and Communications Security, pp. 4–12. ACM, New York (2007)

A Framework for Behavior-Based Malware Analysis in the Cloud

Lorenzo Martignoni[1], Roberto Paleari[2], and Danilo Bruschi[2]

[1] Dipartimento di Fisica,
Università degli Studi di Udine
lorenzo.martignoni@uniud.it
[2] Dipartimento di Informatica e Comunicazione,
Università degli Studi di Milano
{roberto,bruschi}@security.dico.unimi.it

Abstract. To ease the analysis of potentially malicious programs, dynamic behavior-based techniques have been proposed in the literature. Unfortunately, these techniques often give incomplete results because the execution environments in which they are performed are synthetic and do not faithfully resemble the environments of end-users, the intended targets of the malicious activities. In this paper, we present a new framework for improving behavior-based analysis of suspicious programs. Our framework allows an end-user to delegate security labs, *the cloud*, the execution and the analysis of a program and to force the program to behave as if it were executed directly in the environment of the former. The evaluation demonstrated that the proposed framework allows security labs to improve the completeness of the analysis, by analyzing a piece of malware on behalf of multiple end-users simultaneously, while performing a fine-grained analysis of the behavior of the program with no computational cost for end-users.

1 Introduction

With the development of the underground economy, malicious programs are becoming very profitable products; they are used to spam, to perpetrate web frauds, to steal personal information, and for many other nefarious tasks. An important consequence of this lucrative motivation behind malware development is that these programs are becoming increasingly specialized and difficult to analyze: more and more often they attack very specific classes of users and systems and their code is continuosly updated to introduce additional features and specific modifications to thwart the analysis and eventually evade detection.

To counteract these new threats and to overcome the limitations of traditional malware analysis and detection techniques, security vendors and the research community are moving towards dynamic behavior-based solutions. This approach is becoming the primary method for security labs to *automatically* understand the behaviors that characterize each new piece of malware and to develop the appropriate countermeasures [1,2,3]. This technology is also used

A. Prakash and I. Sen Gupta (Eds.): ICISS 2009, LNCS 5905, pp. 178–192, 2009.

on end-users' hosts, to monitor the execution of suspicious programs and try to detect and block malicious behaviors in real-time [4,5,6].

Dynamic behavior-based analysis has two major disadvantages: incompleteness and non-negligible run-time overhead. Security labs analyze new malicious programs automatically in special environments (e.g., virtual machines) which allow very fine grained monitoring of the behavior of the programs. The automatic behavioral analysis of specialized malware becomes more and more difficult because the malicious behaviors manifest only in very specific circumstances. If the behavioral analysis is performed in inappropriate environments, like the synthetic ones used in security labs, the results are very likely to be incomplete. On the other hand, if the malicious program were analyzed directly on an end-user's machine, which is the intended target of the attack, the malicious behavior would have more chances to be triggered and it would be caught as it manifests. Unfortunately, the strict lightweight constraint required for end-users' systems does not allow a fine grained analysis of the behaviors of the programs [2,3]. Consequently, some malicious behaviors (e.g., the leakage of sensitive information) cannot be detected on end-users' machines. Current solutions address the incompleteness of dynamic analysis by systematically exploring all environment-dependent programs paths [7,8].

In this paper we propose a new framework for supporting dynamic behavior-based malware analysis, based on cloud computing, that blends together the computational power available in security labs (the cloud) with the heterogeneity of end-users' environments. The rationale of the framework are the two following assumptions. First, the security lab has no limit on the computational resources available and can exploit hardware features, in combination with recent advances in research, to further improve its computational capabilities [9,10,11]. Second, end-users' environments are more realistic and heterogeneous than the synthetic environments typically available in security labs and consequently are better suited for analyzing potentially malicious software. The proposed framework allows an end-user to delegate a security lab the execution and the analysis of a potentially malicious program and to force the program to behave as if it were executed directly in the environment of the former. The advantage is twofold. It allows the security lab to monitor the execution of a potentially malicious program in a *realistic end-user's environment* and it allows end-users to raise their level of protection by leveraging the computational resources of the security lab for fine-grained analysis that would not be feasible otherwise. Since each end-user's environment differs from the others and since the behavior of a program largely depends on the execution environment, through our framework, the security lab can improve the completeness of the analysis by observing how a program behaves in *multiple realistic end-users' environments*. Such in the cloud execution is made possible by a mechanism we have developed for forwarding and executing (a subset of) the system calls invoked by the analyzed program to a remote end-user's environment and for receiving back the result of the computation. As the execution path of a program entirely depends on the output of the invoked system calls, the analyzed program running in the security lab behaves as if it were executed directly in the environment of the user.

To evaluate the proposed approach, we have implemented a prototype for Microsoft Windows XP. Our evaluation witnessed that the distributed execution of programs is possible and the computational impact on end-users is negligible. With respect to the traditional analysis in the security lab, the analysis of malicious programs in multiple execution environments resulted in a significant relative improvement of the code coverage: with just four additional distinct end-users' environments we achieved an improvement of ∼15%.

To summarize, the paper makes the following contributions: (I) a new framework for dynamic behavior-based malware analysis in the cloud; (II) a working prototype of the above mentioned framework, that has also been integrated into an existing behavior-based malware detector; (III) an evaluation of the proposed framework, demonstrating the feasibility and the efficacy of our idea.

2   Overview

Imagine a malicious program, like the one shown in Fig. 1, that resembles the behavior of the BANCOS malware [12]. To ease the presentation we use high-level APIs of Microsoft Windows; nevertheless our approach works directly with the system calls invoked by these functions. The program polls the foreground window to check whether the user is visiting the website of a Brazilian bank. The existence of such a window is the *trigger condition* of the malicious behavior. If the bank website is visited, the program displays a fake authentication form to tempt the user to type his login and password. Finally, the program forwards the stolen credentials to a remote site.

The automatic analysis of such a piece of malware in a *synthetic execution environment*, like those available in a security lab, is very likely to give incomplete results. Such an environment is generated artificially and consequently it cannot satisfy all the possible trigger conditions of malicious programs. Furthermore, some malicious programs expect inputs from the user and then behave accordingly. As the analysis is performed automatically, user inputs are also artificial and that can prevent the triggering of certain behaviors. On the other hand, we have *realistic execution environments*, the systems of the end-users, which are more suited for analyzing a piece of malware like BANCOS, as they are the intended victims of the malicious activity. Indeed, in the system of a certain class of users, the users of Brazilian banks, our sample malicious program would manifest all its behaviors. Unfortunately, although such systems are more suited for the analysis, it is not reasonable to expect to use all their resources for detecting and stopping potentially malicious programs (fine grained analysis can introduce a slowdown by a factor of 20 [3,13]). Consequently, host-based detectors perform only very lightweight analysis and cannot detect certain malicious behaviors (e.g., to detect that sensitive information are being leaked using data-flow analysis).

2.1   Delegating the Analysis to the Cloud

In our framework the behavior-based analysis of a new suspicious program is performed in the cloud: the user U does not run directly on his system the

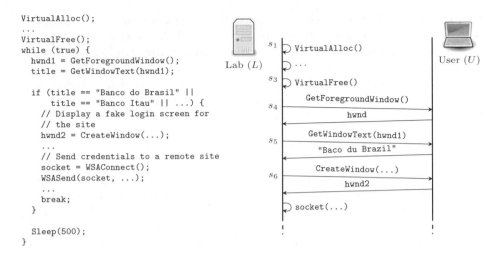

```
VirtualAlloc();
...
VirtualFree();
while (true) {
  hwnd1 = GetForegroundWindow();
  title = GetWindowText(hwnd1);

  if (title == "Banco do Brasil" ||
      title == "Banco Itau" || ...) {
    // Display a fake login screen for
    // the site
    hwnd2 = CreateWindow(...);
    ...
    // Send credentials to a remote site
    socket = WSAConnect();
    WSASend(socket, ...);
    ...
    break;
  }

  Sleep(500);
}
```

Fig. 1. Pseudo-code of a sample malicious program that resembles the BANCOS trojan

Fig. 2. Diagram of the execution of the sample malicious program in the security lab (L), by forcing the program to behave as in the environment of the end-user (U)

suspicious program, nor the malware detector, but he requests the security lab L to analyze the program on his behalf; in turn the latter requests the help of the former to mitigate the fact that its execution environment is synthetic. Our approach to overcome the limitations of the execution environment of L is based on the following assumption: a program interacts with the environment by invoking system calls, and the execution path taken by the program entirely depends on the output of these calls [14]. In our particular context, this assumption means that the triggering of a malicious behavior entirely depends on the output of the system calls invoked. It follows that, to achieve our goal, it is sufficient to force the system calls executed by the program in L to behave as they were executed in U. To do that, the system calls, instead of being executed in L, are executed in U, and L simulates their execution by using the output produced by U. It is worth noting that only a small subset of all the system calls executed by the program might actually affect the triggering of a malicious behavior. Examples of such system calls are (I) those used to access user's data (e.g., the file system and the registry), (II) those used to query particular system information (e.g., active processes, system configuration, open windows), and (III) those used to interact with the users (e.g., to process keyboard and mouse events). Therefore, the collaboration of U is needed only for these system calls, while the remaining ones can be executed directly in L.

Fig. 2 shows how our sample malicious program is executed and analyzed leveraging our framework. The scenario of the analysis is the following. The user U has received a copy of the program by email (or by another vector) and he executes the program. With a conventional behavior-based detector the program would be analyzed entirely on the host. With our framework instead, the program is not executed locally but it is submitted to the security lab L, that executes and analyzes the program with the cooperation of the user. The new analysis environment thus becomes $\langle L, U \rangle$. All the system calls executed by the program are intercepted. Our sample program initially executes some system calls $s_1, \ldots, s_3$ whose output does not depend on the environment (e.g., to allocate memory). These system calls are executed directly in L. Subsequently, the program tries to detect whether the user is browsing a certain website: it invokes $s_4 = $ GetForegroundWindow to get a reference to the window currently active on the desktop of the user. As the output of this call highly depends on the execution environment, L requests U to execute the call: L forwards s_4 to U, U executes s_4 and sends back the output to L. The program does not notice what is happening in the background and continues the execution. The next system call is $s_5 = $ GetWindowText, which is used to get the title of the foreground window. As one of its input arguments (hwnd1) is the output of a system call previously executed in U, s_5 is also executed in U. Supposing that the user in U is actually visiting a website targeted by the program, the trigger condition is satisfied and the program displays the fake login form to steal the user's credentials. As this activity involves an interaction with the user and such interaction is essential to observe the complete behavior of the program, the system calls involved with this activity are also forwarded to U, to get a realistic input. L can eventually detect that there is an illegitimate information leakage.

The in the cloud execution of a potentially malicious program does not expose the end-user to extra security risks. First, we confine the dangerous modifications the program could make to the system in the environment of the security lab. Second, more malicious behaviors can be detected and stopped, because the analysis performed in the lab is more thorough. Third, the execution of the program consumes less resources, as the user is in charge of executing a subset of all the system calls of the program. Forth, annoying popups are still redirected and shown to the user, but that would happen also if the program were executed normally.

2.2   Exploiting Diversity of End-Users' Environments

The proposed framework allows to monitor the execution of a potentially malicious program in multiple execution environments. Given the fact that end-users' environments are very heterogeneous (e.g., users use different software with different configurations, visit different web-sites), it is reasonable to expect that the completeness of the analysis improves with the increase of the number of different environments used.

To analyze a program in multiple execution environments, it is sufficient to run multiple instances of the analyzer, $L_1, \ldots, L_n$, such that each instance cooperates with a different environment $U_1, \ldots, U_n$ to execute the system calls that might affect the triggering of the malicious behaviors (i.e., the environments used are those of n of the potential victims of the malicious program, chosen according to some criteria). The security lab can thus observe how each analysis environment $\langle L_i, U_i \rangle$ affects the behavior of the program and can merge and correlate the behaviors observed in each execution.

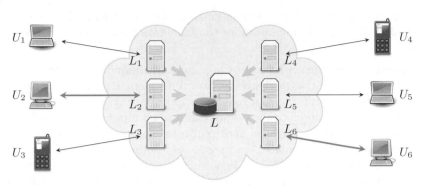

Fig. 3. Diagram of the execution of multiple instances of the analysis of a suspicious program in multiple execution environments $\langle L_1, U_1 \rangle, \ldots, \langle L_6, U_6 \rangle$. The central entity L aggregates the results of each analysis.

Fig. 3 shows how the analysis of our sample program is performed simultaneously in multiple execution environments $\langle L_1, U_1 \rangle, \ldots, \langle L_6, U_6 \rangle$. Each execution is completely independent from the others but the results of the analysis are collected and correlated centrally by L. As $U_1, \ldots, U_6$ are distinct environments, we expect the forwarded system calls to produce different output (e.g., to return different window titles) and thus to cause the various instances of the analyzed program to follow different paths. In the example, we have that the trigger condition is satisfied only in U_2 and U_6, but the web sites being visited are different (one user is visiting the web site of "Bancos do Brazil" and the other one the web site of "Banco Itau"). Therefore, the correlation of the results reveals that the program is effectively malicious and some of its trigger conditions.

3   Design and Implementation

The two parties participating to the in the cloud analysis of a program are the security lab, L for short, and the end-user (the potential victim), U for short. In this section we describe the components we have developed for these two parties to make such distributed execution possible. The current prototype implementation is specific for Microsoft Windows XP, but the support for other versions of the OS can be added with minimal efforts. At the moment, our prototype can successfully handle all the system calls involving the following system resources: file, registry keys, system and processes information, and some graphical resources.

3.1   Executing a Program in Multiple Environments

System calls hooking. To intercept the system calls executed by the analyzed program, we leverage a standard user-space hooking technique. We start the process we want to monitor in a suspended state and then inject a DLL into its virtual address space. The DLL hooks the functions `KiIntSystemCall` and `KiFastSystemCall`, two small function stubs used by Microsoft Windows for executing system calls [15,16]. This approach allowed to simplify the development and facilitated the integration of the framework into an existing malware detector.

System calls proxying. A user-space application cannot directly access the data structure representing a particular resource of the system (e.g., a file, a registry key, a mutex, a window) but it has to invoke the appropriate system calls to obtain an opaque reference, a *handle*, to the resource and to manipulate it. We exploit this characteristic of the operating system to guarantee a correct functioning of the analyzed program, and to simulate the existence of resources with certain properties that exists on a remote system, but do not in the system in which the program is executed. When a system call is invoked, we analyze the type of the call and its arguments to decide how to execute it: locally or remotely.

To differentiate between *local* and *remote* calls, we check if the system call creates a handle or if it uses a handle. To create a handle means to open an existing resource or creating a new one (e.g., to open a file), while to use a handle means to manipulate the resource (e.g., to read data from a open file). In the first case, we analyze the resource that is being opened and according to some rules (details follow) we decide whether the manipulation of the resource might influence the triggering of a malicious behavior. If not, we consider the resource and the system call *local* and we execute the call in L. Otherwise, we consider the resource and the system call *remote* and we forward and execute the latter in U. When we intercept a system call that uses a handle, we check whether the resource being manipulated (identified by the handle) is local or remote and we execute the call in L or U accordingly.

Fig. 4 represents the various components we have developed (highlighted) to intercept system calls and to execute them either locally or remotely. All system calls executed by the analyzed program P are intercepted. Local system calls are passed to the kernel as is, remote ones are forwarded to the system of the end-user. To execute a remote syscall in U, L serializes the arguments of the system call and sends them to U. The receiver deserializes the arguments, prepares the program state for the execution (i.e., by setting up the stack and the registers), and then executes the call. When the syscall returns, U serializes the output arguments and sends them back to L. Finally, L deserializes the output arguments, where the program expects them, and resumes the normal execution. The program P cannot notice when a system call is executed elsewhere, because it finds in memory the expected output.

On paper, the mechanism for serializing and proxying a system call looks simple; however, its implementation is very challenging. The Microsoft Windows system call interface, known as *native API*, is poorly documented. We put a lot of reverse engineering efforts to understand how to properly serialize all system calls and their arguments. After all, the Windows native API turned out to be well suited for proxying and to simulate the existence of resources that physically reside on a different system. No system call can operate concurrently on two resources, resources can always be distinguished, and system calls manipulating the same resource are always executed in the same environment.

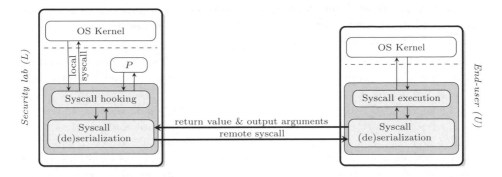

Fig. 4. System calls interception and remote execution (P is the analyzed program)

Choosing remote system calls. Remote system calls are selected using a whitelist. The whitelist contains a list of system calls names and a set of conditions on the arguments. Examples of the system calls we consider remote are: `NtOpenKey`, `NtCreateKey` (if the arguments indicate that the key is being opened for reading), `NtOpenFile`, `NtCreateFile` (if the arguments indicate that the file is being opened for reading), `NtQuerySystemInformation`, and `NtQueryPerformanceCounter`. The handles returned by these calls are flagged as remote, by setting the most significant bits (which are unused). Thus, we can identify subsequent system calls that access a remote resource and we have the guarantee that no overlap between handles referencing local and remote resources can occur.

GUI system calls. User's inputs and GUI resources often represent trigger conditions. For this reason it is important to let the analyzed program to interact with realistic user's inputs (i.e., GUI events) and resources. Although in Microsoft Windows all the primitives of the graphical user interfaces are normal system calls, to facilitate the proxying, we rely on Windows Terminal Services subsystem to automatically forward the user interface of the monitored application from the lab to the user's machine. In particular, our prototype uses *seamless* RDP (Remote Desktop Protocol) [17], that allows to export to a remote host the graphical interface of a single application instead of the entire desktop session. Therefore, if the analyzed program executed in the lab displays the user a fake login form and blocks for inputs, the form is transparently displayed in U and the received user's events (keystrokes and mouse clicks) are sent back to the program running in L.

The solution based on RDP allows only to forward a GUI to a remote system. However, the session in which the application is run belongs to L. Thus, attempts to query the execution environment would return the status of the environment in L. As an example let us consider the system calls associated with the API functions `GetForegroundWindow` and `GetWindowText`, used by our sample malware (Fig. 1) to check if the victim is visiting the website of a Brazilian bank. Without any special handling these system calls would return the windows of the session (on L). We want instead these calls to return information about the windows found in the remote environment. To do that, we execute them remotely as any other remote system call.

One-way isolation. One of the goal of our framework is to protect the system of the end-user from damages that could be caused by the analyzed program, without interfering with the execution of the program. The approach we adopt to achieve this goal is based on one-way isolation [18]: "read" accesses to remote system resources are allowed, but "write" accesses are not and are performed locally. That is, if the program executes a system call to create or to modify a resource we normally consider remote, we treat the resource as local and do not proxy the call. To guarantee a consistent program state, we also execute locally all subsequent system calls involving such resource.

In case the analyzed program turned out to be benign, system changes made in the lab environment could be committed to end-user's environment. Our prototype currently does not support this feature, nor does it support the correct isolation of a program that accesses a resource that is concurrently accessed by another.

3.2 An in the Cloud Behavior-Based Malware Detector

In order to demonstrate how our framework can naturally complement behavior-based malware detectors, we have integrated it in an existing detector [2], which is based on virtual machine introspection and is capable of performing fine grained information flow tracking and to identify data-flow dependencies between system calls arguments. The malware detector is built on top of a customized system emulator, which supports system calls interception and taint analysis with multiple taint labels. As our framework works directly inside the guest, the integration of the two components required only a trivial modification to allow the detector to isolate the system calls executed by the suspicious program from those executed by our prototype to proxy system calls and to ignore the latter.

To monitor the execution of a suspicious program in multiple end-users' environments it is sufficient to run multiple instances of the enhanced malware detector just described, where each instance collaborates with a different end-user's machine, and to merge the results. We have not yet addressed the problem of correlating the results of multiple analyses.

4   Evaluation

This section presents the results of testing our prototype implementation of the framework and presents a conceptual comparison of our approach with existing solutions that try to systematically explore all program paths. We evaluated the prototype with benign and malicious programs. The results of the evaluation on benign programs witness that our approach does not interfere with normal program execution and that it introduces a negligible overhead. Moreover, the evaluation demonstrates that the analysis of a piece of malware in multiple execution environments significantly improves the completeness of the results: with the collaboration of *just four* different execution environments we observed a ~15% relative improvement of the code coverage.

Table 1. List of tested benign programs, actions over which each program was exercised, and number of locally and remotely executed system calls (GUI system calls are not counted)

Program	Action	Local	Remote
ClamAV	Scan (remote) files with (remote) signatures	166,539	1,238
Eudora	Access and query (remote) address book	1,418,162	11,411
Gzip	Compress (remote) files	19,715	93
MS IE	Open a (remote) HTML document	1,263,385	10,260
MS Paint	Browse, open, and edit (remote) pictures	1,177,818	9,708
Netcat	Transfer (remote) files to another host	16,007	93
Notepad	Browse, open, and edit (remote) text files	929,191	7,598
RegEdit	Browse, view, and edit (remote) registry keys	1,573,995	13,697
Task Mgr.	List (remote) running processes	33,339	241
WinRAR	Decompress (remote) files	71,195	572

Experimental setup. The infrastructure used for the evaluation corresponds to the one described in Section 3.2, with the difference that, instead of performing behavior-based detection, we tracked the basic blocks executed in each run of the experiments. To simulate the lab environment we used a vanilla installation of Windows XP running inside the emulator, while as users' environments we used some other machines and we acted as the end-users.

Evaluation on benign programs. To verify that our framework did not interfere with the correct execution of the programs, we executed through our prototype multiple benign applications. The tested programs included both command line utilities and complex GUI applications. Table 1 reports the set of programs tested, together with the actions over which each program was exercised and with the number of local and remote system calls. We interacted with each program to perform the operations reported in the table. As we ran the experiments with the proxying of all supported system calls enabled, the numbers in the table indicate the total number of remotely executed calls and not only those involved with the described actions. For example, we used ClamAV to scan all the content of a directory. Through our framework the anti-virus transparently scanned a directory existing only in the simulated end-user's system, using a database of signatures which also existed only in the remote system.

We successfully executed all the actions reported in the table and verified that the resources that were accessed effectively corresponded to those residing on the system of the end-users. The number of system calls executed indicates that the programs used for the evaluation are quite complex and thus that our results are good representatives. We can conclude that: (I) system calls accessing remote resources do not interfere with system calls accessing local resources, (II) our framework does not interfere with the correct execution of programs, and (III) system calls proxying allows to transparently access system resources residing on remote hosts.

Performance overhead. We used a subset of the benign programs of Table 1 to evaluate the overhead introduced by our framework on the systems of the user and of the security lab. We observed that the number of remotely executed system calls depended on the type of applications and the actions exercised; consequently the overhead depended on these factors. On the system of the end-user, we measured a CPU, memory, and network usage that was roughly proportional to the number of remotely executed system calls. Nevertheless, in all cases, the resources consumed never exceeded the resources consumed when the same programs were executed natively on the system: on average we observed a 60% and 80% reduction of CPU and memory usage respectively. On the other hand, we noticed a slight increase of the resource usage in the system in the lab: on average we observed a 36% and 77% increase of CPU and memory usage respectively. We also measured that, on average, 956 bytes have to be transferred over the network to remotely execute a system call. For example, the execution of RegEdit required in total to transfer 1030Kb of data. In conclusion, our framework has negligible performance impact on the end-user and the impact on the security lab, without considering the overhead introduced by the analysis run on the framework, is sustainable and can be drastically reduced by improving the implementation (e.g., by compressing data before transmission).

Evaluation on malicious programs. We evaluated our framework against multiple malicious programs representing some of the most common and recent malware families. The goal of the evaluation was to measure whether the analysis of multiple executions of the same piece of malware, in different end-users' environments, gives more complete results then the analysis of a single execution of the program in an unrealistic environment (i.e., the vanilla installation of Windows XP).

To quantify the completeness of the results we measured the increase of code coverage. We initially executed batch each malicious program in the environment of the security lab and we recorded the set of unique basic blocks executed (excluding library code). Subsequently, we ran each malicious program multiple times through our prototype, each time in collaboration with a different end-user's environment, and again we recorded the set of unique basic blocks executed. Therefore, if b_0 represents the set of basic blocks executed in the environment of the security lab, and $b_i, i > 0$, represents the set of basic blocks executed with the collaboration of the ith end-user's environment, the increase of code coverage after the ith execution is measured as $|b_i \setminus (b_{i-1} \cup ... \cup b_0)|$.

Fig. 5 reports the relative increase of code coverage (using b_0 as baseline) measured during our evaluation, leveraging just four different end-users' environments and 27 different malware samples. The figure clearly shows that in the majority of the cases we have a noticeable relative increase of the code coverage; the average increase is 14.53%, with a minimum of 0.24%, to a maximum of 60.92%. It is worth noting that, although the observed improvements appear minimal, most of the time small percentages correspond to the execution of hundreds of new basic blocks. It is also important to note that certain environments contributed to improve the results with certain malware but did not contribute at all with others. Indeed, the four environments contribute respectively on average 25.35%, 30.86%, 18.14%, and 25.68% of the total increase observed. For example, during the analysis of a variant of SATILOLER, we noticed that the

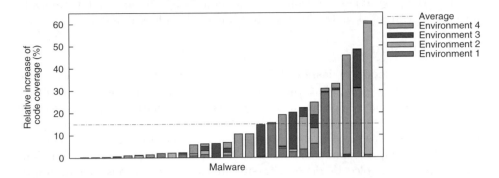

Fig. 5. Relative increase of code coverage obtained by analyzing the tested malware samples in multiple execution environments

monitoring of web activities was triggered only in one of the four environments, when we visited a particular website. Thus, in this environment we observed a 16.54% increase of the relative code coverage, corresponding to the execution of about 140 new unique basic blocks; the observed increase in the other environments did not exceed 3%.

In conclusion, we believe the relative improvements observed during the evaluation testify the effectiveness of the proposed approach at enhancing the completeness of dynamic analysis.

Conceptual comparison with input oblivious analyzers. Input oblivious analyzers are tools capable of analyzing exhaustively a malicious program by systematically forcing the execution of all program paths [7,8]. When an input-dependent control flow decisions is encountered, both program branches are explored. Such systematic exploration is achieved by manipulating the inputs and updating the state of the program accordingly, leveraging constraint solvers, to force the execution of one path and then of the other.

The framework we propose in this paper addresses the same problem through a completely different approach. Although our methodology might appear less systematic, it has the advantage that, by leveraging real execution environments, it can deal with complex trigger conditions that could exhaust the resources of input oblivious analyzers. For example, trigger conditions dominated by a complex program structure might easily generate an unmanageable number of paths to explore and unsolvable constraints. Indeed, several situations are already known to thwart these systems [19,20]. Examples of other situations that can easily render input oblivious analyzers ineffective are malicious programs with payload delivered on-demand (e.g., the Conficker malware [21]) and programs with hidden malicious functionality, like rouge anti-viruses, where the trigger conditions consist in multiple complex asynchronous events. As we assume that sooner or later the malicious program will start to reap victims, we can just sit and watch what a program does in each victim's system, without being affected by the complexity of trigger conditions. At the first sign of malicious activity, we consider the program as malicious; then we can notify all victims, but we could also continue to analyze the program in some of the affected systems.

5 Discussion

Privacy and security issues. The framework we propose can clearly raise privacy issues: by controlling the system calls executed on the systems of an end-user, the security lab can access sensitive user's data (e.g., files, registry keys, GUI events). We are convinced that, considering the current trend, the privacy issues introduced by our approach are comparable to already existing issues. For example, commercial behavior-based detectors incorporate functionality, typically enabled by default, to submit to labs suspicious executables or memory dumps of suspicious processes (which can contain sensitive user data). Thus privacy of users is already compromised. Moreover, the security lab is just a special provider of cloud services: users have to trust it like they trust other providers (e.g., email providers and web storage services).

Detection and evasion. Our framework is sensitive to various forms of detection and evasion. To prevent evasion attacks based on the identification of emulated or analysis environments, it would be sufficient to build our framework on top of undetectable systems for malware analysis [22]. The limitations of our current implementation (e.g., lack of support for inter-process communication) can also offer opportunities for detection and evasion. We believe the majority of the attacks will not be possible with a complete implementation.

6 Related Work

Malware analysis in the cloud. CloudAV is the first implementation of an in the cloud malware detector through which end-users delegate to a central authority the task of detecting if an unknown program is malicious or not [23]. A similar approach, called "collective intelligence", has also been introduced in a commercial malware detector [24]. Such centralized detection gives two major benefits. First, the analysis no longer impacts on end-users' systems, and being centralized, it can be made more fine-grained. For example CloudAV analyzes programs simultaneously, with multiple off-the-shelf detectors. Second, the results of the analysis can be cached to serve future requests of other users at no cost. This paper further enhances these existing solutions by proposing a framework that leverages the systems of potential victims for making the behavioral analysis much more complete.

Behavior-based malware analysis. Our proposed solution is not a malware detector, but is rather a framework that enhances the capabilities of existing dynamic behavior-based detectors. Examples of malware detectors that could integrate our approach are TTAnalyze [1], Panorama [3], CWSandbox [25], and [2]. The problem of the incompleteness of dynamic approaches for malware analysis has been addressed by Moser et al. and Brumley et al. [7,8]. Both systems allow the automatic exploration of multiple execution paths. A thorough comparison between these systems and ours is presented in Section 4.

Sandboxed programs execution. Sun et al. introduced a one-way isolation technique to safely execute untrusted programs [18]. Their approach consists in isolating the effects of an untrusted program from the rest of the system by intercepting system calls that modify the file-system and redirecting them to a cache, invisible to other processes. When the untrusted program terminates, the user can choose to discard these modifications, or to commit them to the real system. The approach we adopt to proxy the access to remote system resources is similar to the one proposed by Sun et al.

Remote system call execution. Remote system call execution has been successfully used to implement a high-throughput computation environment based on Condor [26], where files stored on remote nodes of the environment are made accessible locally and transparently by proxying the appropriate system calls. Similarly, the $\mathcal{V}^2$ project [27] includes support for remote system call execution. Our framework adopts the same strategy, but leverages system call proxying to achieve a completely different goal.

7 Conclusion

In this paper, we presented a framework that enables sophisticated behavior-based analysis of suspicious programs in multiple realistic and heterogeneous environments. We achieve this goal by distributing the execution of the program between the security lab (with unlimited computational resources) and the environments of potential victims of the program (which are heterogeneous by definition and might affect differently the behavior of the analyzed program), by forwarding to the latter certain system calls. We have implemented an experimental prototype to validate our idea and integrated it into an existing behavior-based malware detector. Our evaluation demonstrated the feasibility of the proposed approach, that the overhead introduced is very small, and that the analysis of multiple execution traces of the same malware sample in multiple end-users' environments can improve the results of the analysis.

References

1. Bayer, U., Kruegel, C., Kirda, E.: TTAnalyze: A Tool for Analyzing Malware. In: Proceedings of the Annual Conference of the European Institute for Computer Antivirus Research (2006)
2. Martignoni, L., Stinson, E., Fredrikson, M., Jha, S., Mitchell, J.C.: A Layered Architecture for Detecting Malicious Behaviors. In: Proceedings of the International Symposium on Recent Advances in Intrusion Detection (2008)
3. Yin, H., Song, D., Egele, M., Kirda, E., Kruegel, C.: Panorama: Capturing System-wide Information Flow for Malware Detection and Analysis. In: Proceedings of the Conference on Computer and Communications Security (2007)
4. NovaShield: http://www.novashield.com/
5. Panda Security: True Prevent,
   http://research.pandasecurity.com/archive/
   How-TruPrevent-Works-_2800_I_2900_.aspx
6. Sana Security: http://www.sanasecurity.com/

7. Moser, A., Kruegel, C., Kirda, E.: Exploring Multiple Execution Paths for Malware Analysis. In: Proceeding of the IEEE Symposium on Security and Privacy (2007)
8. Brumley, D., Hartwig, C., Liang, Z., Newsome, J., Song, D., Yin, H.: Towards Automatically Identifying Trigger-based Behavior in Malware using Symbolic Execution and Binary Analysis. Technical Report CMU-CS-07-105, Carnegie Mellon University (2007)
9. Chabbi, M.: Efficient Taint Analysis Using Multicore Machines. Master's thesis, University of Arizona (2007)
10. Nightingale, E.B., Peek, D., Chen, P.M., Flinn, J.: Parallelizing security checks on commodity hardware. In: Proceedings of the international Conference on Architectural Support for Programming Languages and Operating Systems (2008)
11. Ho, A., Fetterman, M., Clark, C., Warfield, A., Hand, S.: Practical Taint-based Protection Using Demand Emulation. In: Proceedings of the EuroSys Conference (2006)
12. F-Secure: Trojan Information Pages: Bancos.VE,
    http://www.f-secure.com/v-descs/bancos_ve.shtml
13. NoAH Consortium: Containment environment design. Technical report, European Network of Affined Honeypots (2006)
14. Goldberg, I., Wagner, D., Thomas, R., Brewer, E.A.: A Secure Environment for Untrusted Helper Applications. In: Proceedings of the USENIX Security Symposium (1996)
15. Hoglund, G., Butler, J.: Rootkits: Subverting the Windows Kernel. Addison-Wesley, Reading (2006)
16. Russinovich, M., Solomon, D.: Microsoft Windows Internals, 4th edn. Microsoft Press, Redmond (2004)
17. Cendio: SeamlessRDP – Seamless Windows Support for rdesktop,
    http://www.cendio.com/seamlessrdp/
18. Sun, W., Liang, Z., Sekar, R., Venkatakrishnan, V.N.: One-way Isolation: An Effective Approach for Realizing Safe Execution Environments. In: Proceedings of the Symposium on Network and Distributed Systems Security (2005)
19. Cavallaro, L., Saxena, P., Sekar, R.: On the Limits of Information Flow Techniques for Malware Analysis and Containment. In: Proceedings of the Conference on Detection of Intrusions and Malware & Vulnerability Assessment (2008)
20. Sharif, M., Lanzi, A., Giffin, J., Lee, W.: Impeding Malware Analysis Using Conditional Code Obfuscation. In: Proceedings of the Annual Network and Distributed System Security Symposium (2008)
21. Porras, P., Saidi, H., Yegneswaran, V.: An Analysis of Conficker's Logic and Rendezvous Points. Technical report, SRI International (2009)
22. Dinaburg, A., Royal, P., Sharif, M., Lee, W.: Ether: Malware Analysis via Hardware Virtualization Extensions. In: Proceedings of the Conference on Computer and communications security (2008)
23. Oberheide, J., Cooke, E., Jahanian, F.: CloudAV: N-Version Antivirus in the Network Cloud. In: Proceedings of the USENIX Security Symposium (2008)
24. Panda Security: From Traditional Antivirus to Collective Intelligence (2007)
25. Willems, C., Holz, T., Freiling, F.: Toward automated dynamic malware analysis using CWSandbox. IEEE Security and Privacy (2007)
26. Livny, M., Basney, J., Raman, R., Tannenbaum, T.: Mechanisms for High Throughput Computing. SPEEDUP Journal (1997)
27. VirtualSquare: Remote System Call,
    http://wiki.virtualsquare.org/index.php/Remote_System_Call

BARTER: Behavior Profile Exchange for Behavior-Based Admission and Access Control in MANETs

Vanessa Frias-Martinez[1,*], Salvatore J. Stolfo[2], and Angelos D. Keromytis[2]

[1] Telefónica Research, Madrid, Spain
[2] Computer Science Department, Columbia University, New York, USA
vanessa@tid.es, {sal,angelos}@cs.columbia.edu

Abstract. Mobile Ad-hoc Networks (MANETs) are very dynamic networks with devices continuously entering and leaving the group. The highly dynamic nature of MANETs renders the manual creation and update of policies associated with the initial incorporation of devices to the MANET (*admission control*) as well as with anomaly detection during communications among members (*access control*) a very difficult task. In this paper, we present *BARTER*, a mechanism that automatically creates and updates admission and access control policies for MANETs based on behavior profiles. BARTER is an adaptation for fully distributed environments of our previously introduced *BB-NAC* mechanism for NAC technologies. Rather than relying on a centralized NAC enforcer, MANET members initially exchange their behavior profiles and compute individual local definitions of normal network behavior. During admission or access control, each member issues an individual decision based on its definition of normalcy. Individual decisions are then aggregated via a threshold cryptographic infrastructure that requires an agreement among a fixed amount of MANET members to change the status of the network. We present experimental results using content and volumetric behavior profiles computed from the ENRON dataset. In particular, we show that the mechanism achieves true rejection rates of 95% with false rejection rates of 9%.

1 Introduction

Mobile Ad-Hoc Networks (MANETs) are composed of devices that enter and leave the network dynamically, quickly changing the network topology and administrative domain membership. MANETs differ from wired/wireless networks in that there is no central control, no base station, and no wireless switches. As a result, any task in the network must be distributed and executed by all its members. These tasks include manually creating and updating policies for the admission as well as the access control of devices over time. Admission control refers to the decision process prior to the incorporation of devices to the

---

* Work performed while a PhD student at Columbia University.

A. Prakash and I. Sen Gupta (Eds.): ICISS 2009, LNCS 5905, pp. 193–207, 2009.

MANET. On the other hand, access control involves the membership update of devices that are already part of the MANET. In general, admission and access control policies are difficult to create manually unless one has a profound understanding of the resource that needs to be controlled. Additionally, the update of policies is even more difficult given the highly dynamic nature of MANETs.

In our previous work, we introduced *BB-NAC*, a behavior-based network admission and access control mechanism for NAC technologies that centralized the decision process on a unique NAC enforcer located at the edge of the network [3] [4] [5]. Behavior was intended to represent the typical communications of network devices *i.e.*, the traffic payload observed or specific volumetric measurements of the traffic such as average number of packets. In this paper, we present BARTER, a behavior-based admission and access control mechanism for MANETs. BARTER is an adaptation of BB-NAC for fully distributed networks. As in the BB-NAC mechanism [5], a newcomer would present its behavior profile to the MANET members during admission control. If an agreement is reached among the members, the newcomer is admitted into the MANET. Analogously, during access control, the traffic exchanged would be checked against the behavior profiles of similar MANET members to perform anomaly detection.

Unlike BB-NAC, the admission and access control decisions in BARTER are distributed among the MANET members rather than being centrally performed by a NAC enforcer. The decision of each individual MANET member is based on the accumulation of knowledge gathered from the behavior profiles of other members. Ultimately, the final admission or access control decision is achieved by building BARTER on top of a threshold cryptographic infrastructure that guarantees not only distributed decision making but also secure communications among MANET members. Due to the limited computational resources of many MANET platforms (such as cellphones or PDAs), the calculation of *clusters of behavior profiles* similar to the one implemented in the BB-NAC mechanism would not be feasible. Instead, BARTER takes advantage of the restrictions imposed by the threshold cryptographic infrastructure as a way to approximate groups of similar behavior within the network.

Apart from the full description of the mechanism, we present an experimental evaluation of BARTER based on content and volumetric behavior profiles computed from the ENRON dataset [2]. Throughout the paper, we assume that there exists a tamper resistance scheme [6] [11] running in the MANET that prevents devices from having multiple identifications (each device has a unique, identifiable ID_i) and that detects manipulations in the packets exchanged between MANET members.

The main contributions of the BARTER mechanism are the following:

– A mechanism that provides automatic and fully distributed creation of admission and access policies for MANETs. Individual decisions are made by each MANET member based on the knowledge accumulated from previous profile exchanges among members. The final admission or access control decision is determined from the aggregation of individual decisions using a threshold cryptographic layer that runs under the BARTER mechanism.

- A mechanism that is robust against attacks from MANET members. The mechanism adjusts over time in order to maintain its robustness even in the presence of malicious devices within the MANET.
- An extensive evaluation of the mechanism using hundreds of content and volumetric behavior profiles computed from the ENRON dataset.

The paper is organized as follows: in Section 2 we describe the foundations of the BARTER mechanism. Section 3 discusses possible attacks to the mechanism and analyzes the costs incurred by the threshold cryptographic infrastructure. Section 4 and Section 5 describe the experimental evaluation for content and volumetric profiles respectively. Section 6 summarizes related work. Finally, Section 7 presents conclusions and future work.

2   The BARTER Mechanism

We start with the assumption that each device in the MANET is running an Anomaly Detection (AD) sensor that allows the device to compute a behavior profile that models its typical behavior. BARTER consists of an initial setup and two main phases: *admission control* and *access control*. Initially, MANET members exchange their behavior profiles in order to build their own individual definition of normal behavior which will later be used during admission and access control. During admission or access control, each MANET member emits an individual decision based on its definition of normal behavior. Individual decisions are aggregated using a threshold cryptographic scheme *(t,n)* that requires at least t out of the total n MANET members to change the status of the network. Next, we describe each of the phases in detail as well as the interaction with the cryptographic infrastructure that runs underneath the mechanism.

2.1   Initial Setup

The principal goal of the setup is for each MANET member to build their own individual definition of normal behavior, which will be ultimately used during admission control. MANET members are not clients or servers but rather peers *i.e.*, all members are considered equal and can execute client or server activities simultaneously. As a result, MANET members can have both input and output behavior profiles for the same service (port). Throughout, we assume that the behavior profiles are computed from previous interactions of the device or alternatively are provided as built-in profiles from the vendor. We further assume that the profiles of the initial MANET members are clean and provide an accurate representation of the typical behavior in the MANET.

During setup, all the initial members broadcast their output behavior profiles to all the other MANET members. Each member proceeds to calculate the distance between its own input behavior profile and the output behavior profiles received from the other devices. Given the distributed nature of the mechanism, MANET members are only required to provide their output behavior profiles.

This step prevents any member from crafting attacks based on the knowledge of the input profiles of the others. The distance between a member i and each of the other MANET members $j = 1, .., n$ is given by $d_{i,j} = d(P_{i,in}, P_{j,out})$, where $P_{i,in}$ is the input behavior profile for i and $P_{j,out}$ is the output behavior profile received from node j. Each pair $(P_{j,out}, d_{i,j})$ computed by member i is then stored as an entry $Q_i[j]$ in its local table Q_i. The entries are sorted by member i according to their distance values such that the closest profiles to $P_{i,in}$ are placed at the top of the table. In general, distances can be interpreted as a measure of confidence between a local device and the rest of the MANET members. Specifically, profiles at shorter distances would be trusted more than their more distant counterparts.

Armed with its sorted table, each MANET member proceeds to calculate its local threshold τ_i that will determine acceptance or rejection of new devices during admission control. The threshold τ_i is defined as the maximum distance between its input profile $P_{i,in}$ and its top t-1 most similar/trusted profiles. In this context, t corresponds to the value from the (t,n) threshold cryptographic scheme. Thus, $\tau_i = Q_i[t-1]$, where $Q_i[t-1]$ represents the $t-1$th entry at the local table of member i.

Simultaneously, the members of the MANET are also responsible for setting up the threshold cryptographic scheme (t,n). This scheme guarantees that all communications among the n MANET members are encrypted using group keys, which can only be reconstructed by any t members of the MANET. The threshold cryptographic scheme also ensures that all decisions within the MANET must meet the approval of at least t members.

The initial setup of the threshold cryptographic scheme is executed in a distributed fashion without a central authority (CA) following the approach proposed by Narasimha et al. [9] using the cryptosystem theory without initial trusted parties from Perdersen [12]. In the approach by Naramsimha et al., the group of all MANET members (M_i, i=1..n) uses Shamir's secret sharing [13] to divide a group secret S into n shares. Specifically, the secret is represented as a polynomial $f(z) = f_1(z) + ... + f_n(z)$, where each $f_i(z)$ is generated by each individual MANET member M_i. Each MANET member M_i computes its share as follows. First, each M_i chooses a random polynomial $f_i(z) \in Z_q$ (where q is a prime number) of degree t-1 such that $f_i(0) = S_i$. Next, each M_i computes M_j's share as $s_i^j = f_i(j)$ (for j=1..n) and securely transmits these values to each j through a secure channel. Finally, M_j computes its share s_j of the secret S (partial signature) by summing all the shares received as $s_j = \sum_{i=1}^{n}(s_i^j)$ and computes its Group Membership Certificate (GMC_i).

Under this scheme, any group of t members among the total n will be able to jointly recover the secret S via Lagrange interpolation. Subsequently, this threshold cryptographic scheme will play a principal role during the admission and access control discussed in the following sections. It is important to note that the merger between BARTER and the threshold cryptographic layer creates a robust mechanism that guarantees distributed admission and access control decisions as well as secure communications among the MANET members.

Cross-Validation. The initial cross-validation seeks to find the ratio t/n that yields the best results for the admission and access control mechanism. In particular, the performance of BARTER for each ratio t/n is measured in terms of false rejection (FR) *i.e.*, number of normal profiles wrongly rejected from entering the MANET, true rejection (TR) *i.e.*, number of anomalous profiles detected as such, cryptographic costs (CC) and possibility of Distributed Denial of Service (DDoS) attacks. The values of the ratios t/n are ranked according to their performance $r = (1 - FR) + TR + (1 - CC) + DDoS$ and the highest ranked value is selected. Here, the cryptographic costs (CC) quantify the total time involved during key (re)generation by the MANET members. For practical purposes, the value of CC is normalized between 0 and 1. On the other hand, $DDoS$ evaluates the robustness against MANET members lying about their decisions in order to manipulate the admission and access control. At the end of the setup and cross-validation, each device will have a sorted local table Q_i, a local threshold τ_i as well as the best t/n ratio for the MANET. The actual computation of the parameters used for the ranking is discussed in more detail in Section 3. Experimental results are presented in Section 4 and Section 5.

2.2   Admission Control

Whenever a new device attempts to enter the MANET, it needs to broadcast its own local output behavior profile to the current members. Initially, the members will check whether the new device is blacklisted. If it passes this check, the members proceed to compute the distance between their own input profile and the output profile of the newcomer. If the distance is within its own local threshold of normalcy, the member emits a favorable vote $v_i = 1$. The final MANET vote v can be expressed as:

$$v = \frac{1}{n} \sum_{i=0..n} v_i$$
$$v_i = 0 \ \ if \ d(P_{i,in}, P_{new,out}) > \tau_i$$
$$v_i = 1 \ \ if \ d(P_{i,in}, P_{new,out}) \leq \tau_i$$

where n is the number of members in the MANET, τ_i is the threshold of member i, $P_{i,in}$ is the input behavior profile of member i and $P_{new,out}$ is the output behavior profile of the newcomer. If t or more members of the MANET emit a favorable vote $v_i = 1$, the newcomer is admitted. Otherwise, the newcomer is rejected and added to a grey list that keeps track of the number of admission attempts by the device. If a device exceeds a fixed number of attempts, it will be added to a blacklist. In order to keep the latest updates, grey and blacklists are exchanged among MANET members.

Upon acceptance of the newcomer, all the members of the MANET submit their output behavior profiles to the new member. The new member stores the profiles together with the distance measures between its own input profile and the output profiles of the remaining members of the MANET in its local table. Then, it proceeds to sort the values in its local table according to their distance. The

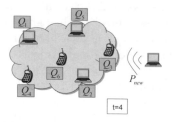

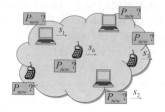

(a) Step 1: New device presents its profile to MANET members.

(b) Step 2: Voting process among MANET members and partial signature distribution.

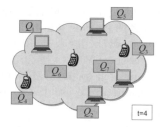

(c) Step 3: New device is accepted and the status of all MANET members is updated.

Fig. 1. Admission Control of a Newcomer *new* to the MANET

maximum distance value among its top $t-1$ profiles determines its local threshold $\tau_{P_{new}}$. The original members of the MANET store the output behavior profile of the newcomer in their local tables and update their distance computations as well as thresholds accordingly.

Whenever a new device enters or leaves the MANET (n increases or decreases), the ratio of t/n will also change. As a result, the mechanism must make the proper adjustment to restore the ratio to its original value that yielded the best performance for the admission control. In order to avoid recalculating t every time that the value of n changes, we set an update window w such that the value of t is changed only when the ratio exceeds the range $t/n \pm w$. If we consider t_0 to be the initial value of t and n_0 the initial number of MANET members, t would be updated as $t = \lceil (t_0/n_0) * n \rceil$, where n is the final size of the MANET. Throughout, we assume the members can *easily* calculate or approximate the total size of the MANET (n).

Every time a newcomer attempts to be admitted into the MANET, BARTER combines with the threshold cryptographic admission control by Narasimha *et al.* [9] as follows:

1. The newcomer M_{new} broadcasts its public key certificate PKC_{new} and its behavior profile $P_{new,out}$ to the MANET members.

2. Members that deem the behavior profile of the newcomer normal $(d(P_{i,in}, P_{new,out}) \leq \tau_i)$ reply with their Group Membership Certificates (GMC_i).

3. M_{new} forms a list of signers SL_{new} and sends it back to each of the members M_j that replied initially.

4. Each M_j computes its partial signature s_j and submits it to M_{new}.

5. M_{new} computes the complete signature s by summing t partial signatures s_j and obtains its own GMC_{new} as well as its partial share s_{new}. In addition, it updates its local table with the behavior profiles of the MANET members.

At the end of the process, if t or more members in the MANET agree on the normal nature of the profile, the newcomer can compute its own GMC and start communications with the MANET. Otherwise, the newcomer will not be able to participate or even eavesdrop because the communications are encrypted. Figure 1 depicts an example of the admission control in a MANET with six initial members and a value of $t=4$.

2.3   Access Control

During access control, communications among the MANET members are continuously screened to ensure that users do not deviate from their declared behavior profiles. In practical terms, each MANET member continuously checks the incoming traffic from any device against its local input behavior profile as well as against the output behavior profile of the sender that was originally saved during the admission of the latter into the MANET. If a device considers some traffic to be anomalous, it requires at least t members of the MANET in order to act against the sender. Thus, the receiver of the anomalous traffic submits the anomaly to its *top t-1 most similar* members drawn from its local table. If the other *t-1* members agree on the anomalous nature of the traffic, the sender is expelled immediately from the MANET. This process relies on the assumption that there exists an scheme that prevents data tampering within the MANET and prevents users from falsifying alerts or replay attacks.

From a threshold cryptographic point of view, if a MANET member detects an anomaly, it adds the anomalous member to its local Certificate Revocation List (CRL) and proceeds to broadcast its own CRL to all the MANET members. In order to ensure that the anomalous member no longer has a vote in the distributed admission and access control, each member will generate new partial signatures that will be submitted to each of the MANET members outside the CRL via point-to-point communications (individual cryptographic channels). This proactive key sharing [7] combines the approaches introduced by Ostrovsky and Yung [10] and by Luo and Lu [8] as follows:

1. Each member M_i defines a polynomial $f_i(z) = f_1 z^1 + f_2 z^2 + ... + f_{t-1} z^{(t-1)}$ with $f_i(0) = S_i$, where $f_1..f_{t-1} \in Z_q$ are randomly selected and q is a prime number.

2. M_i secretly sends $s_i^j = f_i(j) (mod\ q)$ to the MANET members M_j outside the CRL. The members are assumed to have established point-to-point encrypted channels.

3. M_j would reply if and only if it has received t revocation lists (CRL) from different MANET members.
4. M_i decrypts the s_j^i received from the other MANET members and computes its new share s_i.

3   Attacks and Cryptographic Costs

Due to the fully distributed nature of the BARTER mechanism, the main source of attacks derives from MANET members lying about their admission control decisions either to admit members with malicious profiles or else to prevent members with normal profiles from joining the MANET. Small values of the t/n ratio would permit attackers to get a hold of the admission control by compromising only a few MANET members. In contrast, larger t/n ratios could be attacked by compromising a few nodes that would prevent the other members of the MANET from reaching a decision. We quantify the robustness against DDoS attacks via a numerical factor $DDoS$ in the ranking index formula such that $r = (1 - FR) + TR + (1 - CC) + DDoS$. Our assumption is that a $t/n = 0.5$ represents the optimal value to minimize the risk of potential DDoS attacks. As a result, we set $DDoS = 0.5$ for $t/n = 0.5$. We set $DDoS = t/n$ for smaller ratios ($t/n < 0.5$) and assume $DDoS = 1 - (t/n)$ for larger ratios ($t/n > 0.5$). While some t/n ratios may yield better FR or TR rates, the value of $DDoS$ serves as a counterweight to estimate the robustness against DDoS attacks for a certain configuration.

The cryptographic costs (CC) involved in this process are quantified in terms of the total time spent during key regeneration and enter in the evaluation of the ranking index such that $r = (1 - FR) + TR + (1 - CC) + DDoS$. As written, the ranking index penalizes high values of CC and favors more economic key regenerations. During the initial cryptographic setup, each MANET member exchanges shares with all the other members in order to compute its own GMC as well as its partial signature. If we assume that all MANET members exchange their shares in parallel, we can approximate the initial setup cost as $CC = K \times (n_0 - 1)$, where K represents the cost of a single exchange and n_0 is the number of initial members in the MANET. Every time a device enters or leaves the MANET, the mechanism checks that the ratio t/n is within the window w. If the value of t needs to be adjusted, the cost incurred in the key regeneration can be approximated by,

$$CC = K \times \sum_{n_0}^{n_{final}} (update \times n) - 1$$

$$update = \begin{cases} 1 & \text{if } t/n < (t_0/n_0 - w) \quad \text{or if } t/n > (t_0/n_0 + w) \\ 0 & \text{otherwise.} \end{cases} \tag{1}$$

where n_{final} is the final number of MANET members, n is the current number of MANET members, and $update$ is a boolean variable that determines whether an update in the value of t is required. Equation 1 describes the boolean variable that is only *true* whenever the ratio t/n falls below the lower bound of the range $(t/n - w)$ or exceeds the upper bound $(t/n + w)$.

4   Evaluation of BARTER with Content Profiles

In this section, we begin with a description of the AD sensor responsible for the computation of the content behavior profiles and provide experimental results of the BARTER mechanism using this type of profile.

4.1   Semi-supervised Content AD Sensor

We have implemented a content-based AD sensor that represents an adaptation of Shanner's ideas [14]. Shanner proposes an algorithm that incorporates only the most heavily weighted grams to the behavior profile. These grams are the ones that best discriminate between two or more classes of data. Although Shanner is more expensive than other AD sensors, we chose it because it rapidly captures the significant information of the traffic being exchanged.

In our sensor, we consider two classes of data (content): good samples (*goodS*) and bad samples (*badS*). The content of the traffic exchanged is captured as 3-grams. This choice is less computationally expensive than higher n-grams and appropriately captures the specifics of email traffic (as it will be shown in Section 4.3). The weight (frequency) of each 3-gram observed during training is calculated using Shanner's Formula (see Equation 2), where the frequency W of each 3-gram i ($W(i)=F(i)\times U(i)\times A(i)$) is expressed as,

$$W(i) = log(\frac{x_i}{N_g}) \times (\frac{1}{log N_g}) \sum_{j=1}^{N_g} (p_{ij}(log(\frac{1}{p_{ij}}))) \times (1 - (\frac{1}{log L}) \sum_{j}^{goodS,badS} (p_{ij}(log(\frac{1}{p_{ij}}))))$$

(2)

where $F(i)$ measures the frequency of occurrence of each distinct 3-gram i over all the good samples N_g; $U(i)$ measures how uniformly distributed each unique 3-gram i is spread among the set of good samples N_g (p_{ij} represents the probability of seeing 3-gram i in good sample j); and $A(i)$ measures how uniformly distributed each unique 3-gram i is spread across all good and bad samples types ($L=2$). Once all the weights have been calculated, a top percentage of the 3-grams are selected to represent the content profile of the device. We assert that this is a semi-supervised learning technique since the devices store an initial collection of bad 3-grams drawn from known malware samples.

4.2   Behavior Profile Privacy

Due to the fact that the output behavior profiles are exchanged among devices, it may be the case that certain users do not feel comfortable sharing the content they exchange. In order to deal with this possibility, the BARTER mechanism hashes the content behavior profile into Bloom Filters (BF) [1]. Input behavior profiles, although not exchanged, are also converted into BFs so that the comparison with output profiles is fast and straight forward. The way the traffic is mapped to a BF depends on the AD sensor used. The only requirement is that all devices use the same sensor with the same type of mapping. Behavior profiles in BARTER are then easily comparable, since boolean operators allow us to discern similarities or differences between profiles (BFs). For this type of content profiles, the distance $d(P_{i,in}, P_{j,out})$ between two profiles is computed using an exclusive OR (XOR) operator that quantifies the amount of entries that differ between the two profiles: $d(P_{i,in}, P_{j,out}) = |P_{i,in} \oplus P_{j,out}|$, where $\oplus$ represents the XOR operator and $||$ denotes the total number of entries with different values.

4.3   Evaluation Experiments

Having extensively described the foundations of the BARTER mechanism, we proceeded to test the admission control of the mechanism with real content behavior profiles. We focus on the admission control because our main aim is to prove the functionality of the mechanism together with the threshold cryptographic layer. For that purpose, we used the publicly available ENRON dataset [2] that contains 125,218 emails from 140 ENRON employees. The reason for choosing email as a testing dataset is justified based on its use as a primary application on handhelds. Moreover, email constitutes a good approximation of other popular text messaging applications that could be used in MANETs. For each of the 140 users, we computed input and output behavior profiles using Shanner's algorithm [14]. In particular, we first calculated the frequency for each 3-gram in the body of each user's emails and selected the top 5000 most heavily weighted grams. Our choice of 5000 worked well for our experiments, however, other values might be more appropriate for different datasets. The bad samples used to execute Shanner's algorithm were drawn from the signature content of the Snort rules (a total of 58) [15] and from 600 virus samples of vxheavens [17]. Finally, the top 5000 3-grams were hashed into Bloom filters in order to provide privacy to the profiles.

For experimental purposes, we refer to the set of behavior profiles modeled with the content of emails from the ENRON dataset as *pool of normal users* (140 users). The pool of normal users was considered to be clean, composed of normal behavior profiles and *ground truth*. On the other hand, we refer to *pool of bad users* as a set of 60 profiles that represent anomalous behavior (content) that should be rejected from entering the MANET. In order to compute the bad profiles, we used content (3-grams) from 12000 executable files and code files (C or Java). These type of files were chosen because their content is dramatically different from email. Each bad profile was computed with 200 executable/code files with an average of 39 3-grams per file. Once again, behavior profiles were computed using Shanner's algorithm by selecting the top 5000 3-grams and hashing them into Bloom filters.

We defined a group of 80 behavior profiles randomly selected from the pool of normal users as our training set (initial MANET members). The remaining 60

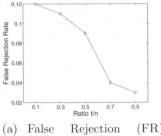
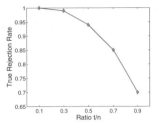

(a) False   Rejection   (FR)
Rates for different ratios t/n.

(b) True   Rejection   (TR)
Rates for different ratios t/n.

Fig. 2. FR and TR for different ratio values t/n

profiles were divided into a cross-validation set (30 profiles) and a testing set (30 profiles). The cross-validation set was used to calculate the best ratio t/n for our dataset determined as the highest ranking index $r = (1 - FR) + TR + (1 - CC) + DDoS$. One by one, each randomly selected profile in the cross-validation set was presented to the MANET members as a newcomer attempting to be admitted into the MANET. From these attempts, we measured the false rejection rate (FR) as the percentage of normal profiles wrongly rejected as anomalous. Next, 30 randomly selected profiles from the pool of bad users were also presented as new devices attempting to gain access into the MANET. The latter experiment allowed us to measure the true rejection rate (TR) by determining the percentage of profiles correctly rejected as anomalous by the MANET members. Finally, we proceeded to determine the cryptographic costs (CC) incurred during the generation of new signatures for the MANET members as well as the robustness against DDoS attacks $(DDoS)$.

The experiments were repeated 60 times for each value of t/n to cover all different evolutions resulting from the random selection of the initial profiles. The results presented here constitute an average over all runs. Five different values of t/n were considered, namely 0.1, 0.3, 0.5, 0.7, and 0.9. These values represent MANETs whereby 10%, 30%, 50%, 70% or 90% of the total members respectively are needed in order to emit an admission control decision. For each ratio, the initial value of t was calculated as $t/n \times 80$ with a window $w = 0.02$. Here, 80 represents the number of total profiles in the training set (initial MANET members). Alternative values of w would produce different numerical results but would follow the same trends observed in our experiments.

Figures 2(a) and 2(b) show the FR and TR rates for different ratio values. As can be seen, smaller ratio values produced larger FR and TR rates. This is most likely related to the fact that smaller ratios reflect a larger number of small sets of profiles. Consequently, the thresholds for the admission control become very restrictive, which results in a larger rejection of normal profiles as well as a larger detection of anomalous profiles. In contrast, larger ratios result in smaller FR and TR rates possibly associated with fewer sets of profiles that define less restrictive thresholds.

We also computed the ranking indices $r = (1-FR)+TR+(1-CC)+DDoS$ for different ratio values t/n for the ENRON dataset, and we found that the highest ranked index corresponded to a ratio $t/n = 0.1$. Such result probably captures the wide variety of content contained in the email exchanges among users. In other words, small sets of normalcy provide a better characterization of the behaviors shared by the users. Armed with the highest ranked index $t/n = 0.1$ obtained from cross-validation, we proceeded to simulate the admission control with randomly selected profiles from the testing set acting as newcomers to the MANET. In order to compute TR and FR, we used the remaining 30 normal and bad profiles drawn from the pool of normal and bad users respectively. For the performance of BARTER, we obtained a false rejection FR=13%, a true rejection TR=100% and cryptographic costs CC=179 × K.

5   Evaluation of BARTER with Volumetric Profiles

Rather than content, volumetric profiles capture the typical characteristics of the communications such as number of emails exchanged, number of different people contacted (clique), and frequency of usage. In this Section, we describe the volumetric AD sensor used to compute the profiles. This is followed by an actual evaluation of the BARTER mechanism using volumetric behavior profiles computed from the ENRON dataset.

5.1   Histogram-Based Volumetric AD Sensor

In order to compute volumetric input and output behavior profiles, we used the EMT tool (Email Mining Toolkit) [16]. The behavior profile of each user is represented as a daily histogram that reflects the behavior of a user exchanging emails. In order to be able to compute the initial behavior profiles of the MANET members, we presume that members have an archive of stored emails from previous interactions in other environments. Alternatively, one can always provide the members with an initial set of training samples chosen according to the type of user.

EMT computes two types of daily histograms: *hourly histograms* and *grouped histograms*. Hourly histograms divide the day in 24 bins where each bin represents the average number of emails (sent or received) per hour. Grouped histograms, on the other hand, divide the day in 4 bins of 6 hours each, where each bin is the average number of emails sent or received during a 6-hour period. Hereafter, we will refer to the number of bins in which the day is divided as bin granularity (bg). In particular, we shall use $bg = 24$ for hourly modeling and $bg = 4$ for grouped modeling. Each profile $P_{i,d}$ is a vector with bg entries, where d represents the direction of the traffic i.e., either input ($P_{i,in}$) or output emails ($P_{i,out}$). Each histogram entry represents a bin b_j that contains the average value a and standard deviation σ for the number of emails sent or received by user i during a time frame j. The average and standard deviation values for each time frame j are averaged throughout the duration of the training period. Hence,

$P_{i,d} = \{b_1, ..., b_{bg}\}$ and $b_j = \{(a, \sigma)\}$ where $j \in [1..24]$ for hourly histograms or $j \in [1..4]$ for grouped histograms.

The *grouped histograms* are intended to save bandwidth usage by exchanging smaller behavior profiles among MANET members. Nonetheless, it is only through cross-validation tests that an appropriate bin granularity that both minimizes the behavior profile size while maximizing BARTER performance can be properly selected.

5.2   Evaluation Experiments

Our evaluation of the BARTER mechanism for volumetric profiles is similar to the one presented for content profiles. Again, we used the publicly available ENRON dataset to compute the volumetric behavior profiles of 140 users. For each user, we computed its input and output volumetric profiles in two formats: hourly and grouped histograms. Behavior profiles were computed by calculating the average number of emails sent or received by a user throughout the duration of the training period. For experimental purposes, the set of 140 volumetric profiles modeled with emails from the ENRON dataset is referred to as *pool of normal users* and is considered *ground truth*. In order to compute a *pool of bad users*, we produced volumetric behavior profiles one, two, and three standard deviations away from the top *t-1* entries in the local table of each MANET member. Our assumption is that the *t-1* top entries represent the most similar counterpart to a particular profile. As a result, behavior profiles separated by one or more standard deviations from this set constitute potential anomalous profiles. We repeated this process for all the members of the MANET and obtained a final pool of bad users for each ratio t/n.

As in the experiments with content profiles, we simulated an environment where a number of profiles attempt to gain admission into an already formed MANET. The pool of normal users (140 profiles) was divided into three sets: the training set (80 randomly selected profiles), the cross-validation set (30 randomly selected profiles), and the testing set (the remaining 30 profiles). Armed with these sets, we measured the FR rate of the BARTER mechanism with volumetric profiles. Next, we created additional cross-validation and testing sets with 30 profiles each randomly selected from the pool of bad users. The latter sets were used to compute the TR rate of the mechanism.

The purpose of the cross-validation experiments is to determine the combination of t/n ratio and type of histogram that yields the highest ranking index r. We experimented with five different values for the ratio t/n: 0.1, 0.3, 0.5, 0.7, 0.9 and two types of histograms: hourly and grouped. Simulations were repeated 60 times to account for the random draw of the initial profiles, and the results were averaged among the 60 simulations. For each combination of parameters, we computed the ranking index r and selected the highest ranked.

Figures 3(a) and 3(b) depict our TR and FR results for a wide variety of ratio values as well as two types of histograms (hourly and grouped). As can be seen, grouped histograms outperform hourly histograms in terms of FR an TR rates. Our interpretation is that hourly histograms likely produce a too fine grained

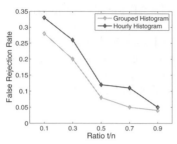

(a) False Rejection (FR) Rates for different ratios t/n.

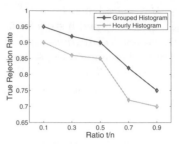

(b) True Rejection (TR) Rates for different ratios t/n.

Fig. 3. FR and TR for different ratio values t/n

modeling for our dataset. In contrast, grouped histograms can identify behaviors more effectively thus improving the performance of BARTER. In general, higher t/n ratios translate into smaller FR and TR rates.

We note that the highest ranked index occurs for grouped histograms and a ratio $t/n = 0.5$. Such ratio indicates that the best admission results take place when 50% of the MANET members are needed to make a decision. We can also interpret this result as an indication of few distinct behaviors within the ENRON dataset. Taking the highest ranked index parameters ($t/n = 0.5$ and grouped histograms), each randomly selected profile from the testing set was presented to the MANET members as a newcomer attempting to be admitted into the MANET. From these admission control experiments, we measured FR=8%, TR=90% and cryptographic costs CC=1571 × K. These results demonstrate the feasibility of BARTER using volumetric as well as content behavior profiles.

6   Related Work

There is a body of work about the use of threshold cryptography for admission control in ad-hoc networks. Narasimha et al. [9] and Ostrovsky et al. [10] studied possible adaptations of existing threshold cryptographic schemes to MANETs. However, none of the previous works have discussed the implementation of the decision process during admission control. BARTER enhances threshold cryptographic approaches by automatizing the individual admission decision at each device. AD sensors have been widely used to implement access control in MANETs. The main idea is that profiles computed from audit data can be used as a representation of the normal behavior. As a result, any behavior that deviates from the profile is considered anomalous [18]. However, the current literature does not offer a satisfactory explanation on the interaction of ADs with secure cryptographic platforms. BARTER provides an access control that uses AD sensors at an application level rather than at the routing level. Additionally, our work describes the interaction between the AD sensors and the cryptographic layer.

7   Conclusions and Future Work

We have presented BARTER, a mechanism that automatically creates admission and access control policies for MANETs. Individual decisions regarding admission and access control are issued based on a local definition of normal behavior computed from the knowledge of the behavior profiles from other members. A threshold cryptographic layer *(t,n)* that runs underneath the mechanism aggregates the individual decisions by requiring at least t devices to participate in the decision. We have discussed experimental results using both content and volumetric behavior profiles computed from the ENRON dataset. Our results show that the mechanism can successfully perform under both types of behavior profiles with FR rates ranging from 9% to 12% and TR rates between 95% and 100%. Future work will evaluate how to best determine the most defining behavioral characteristics of a host using techniques such as bagging or boosting.

References

1. Bloom, B.H.: Space/Time tradeoffs in hash coding with allowable errors. Communications of the ACM 13(7) (1970)
2. ENRON Dataset (2004), www.cs.cmu.edu/~enron
3. Frias-Martinez, V., Stolfo, S.J., Keromytis, A.D.: Behavior-Based Network Access Control: A Proof-of-Concept. In: Wu, T.-C., Lei, C.-L., Rijmen, V., Lee, D.-T. (eds.) ISC 2008. LNCS, vol. 5222, pp. 175–190. Springer, Heidelberg (2008)
4. Frias-Martinez, V., Stolfo, S.J., Keromytis, A.D.: Behavior-Profile Clustering for False Alert Reduction in Anomaly Detection Sensors. In: ACSAC (2008)
5. Frias-Martinez, V., et al.: A Network Access Control Mechanism Based on Behavior Profiles. In: ACSAC (2009)
6. Hastad, J., et al.: Funkspiel Schemes: An Alternative to Conventional Tamper Resistance. In: Proc. of the 7th ACM Conf. on Computer Commun. Security (2000)
7. Herzberg, A., et al.: Proactive Secret Sharing Or: How to Cope with the Perpetual Leakage. In: Coppersmith, D. (ed.) CRYPTO 1995. LNCS, vol. 963, pp. 339–352. Springer, Heidelberg (1995)
8. Luo, H., Lu, S.: Ubiquitous and Robust Authentication Services for Ad Hoc Wireless Networks, Technical Report, UCLA (2000)
9. Narasimha, M., et al.: On the utility of Distributed Cryptography in P2P and MANETs: the case of Membership Control. In: Proc. of the 11th ICNP (2003)
10. Ostrovsky, R., Yung, M.: How To Withstand Mobile Virus Attacks. In: Proc. of the 10th ACM Symp. on the Principles of Distributed Computing (1991)
11. Papadimitratos, P., Haas, Z.J.: Secure Data Transmission in Mobile Ad Hoc Networks. In: Proceedings of the ACM Workshop on Wireless Security, WiSe (2003)
12. Pedersen, T.P.: A Threshold Cryptosystem without a Trusted Party. In: Davies, D.W. (ed.) EUROCRYPT 1991. LNCS, vol. 547. Springer, Heidelberg (1991)
13. Shamir, A.: How to share a secret. Communications ACM 22(11) (1979)
14. Shaner, R.A.: US Patent No. 5,991,714 (November 1999)
15. Snort Rulesets, http://www.snort.org/pub-in/downloads.cgi
16. Stolfo, S.J., et al.: Behavior-based Modeling and its Application to Email Analysis. ACM Transactions on Internet Technology (TOIT) 6(2) (2006)
17. VXHeavens, vx.netlux.org
18. Zhang, Y., Lee, W., Huang, Y.: Intrusion Detection Techniques for Mobile Wireless Networks. Mobile Networks and Applications 9(5) (2003)

Automatic Identification of Critical Data Items in a Database to Mitigate the Effects of Malicious Insiders

Jonathan White and Brajendra Panda

Department of Computer Science and Computer Engineering, University of Arkansas,
Fayetteville, Arkansas, 72703, USA
{jlw09,bpanda}@uark.edu

Abstract. A major concern for computer system security is the threat from malicious insiders who target and abuse critical data items in the system. In this paper, we propose a solution to enable automatic identification of critical data items in a database by way of data dependency relationships. This identification of critical data items is necessary because insider threats often target mission critical data in order to accomplish malicious tasks. Unfortunately, currently available systems fail to address this problem in a comprehensive manner. It is more difficult for non-experts to identify these critical data items because of their lack of familiarity and due to the fact that data systems are constantly changing. By identifying the critical data items automatically, security engineers will be better prepared to protect what is critical to the mission of the organization and also have the ability to focus their security efforts on these critical data items. We have developed an algorithm that scans the database logs and forms a directed graph showing which items influence a large number of other items and at what frequency this influence occurs. This graph is traversed to reveal the data items which have a large influence throughout the database system by using a novel metric based formula. These items are critical to the system because if they are maliciously altered or stolen, the malicious alterations will spread throughout the system, delaying recovery and causing a much more malignant effect. As these items have significant influence, they are deemed to be critical and worthy of extra security measures. Our proposal is not intended to replace existing intrusion detection systems, but rather is intended to complement current and future technologies. Our proposal has never been performed before, and our experimental results have shown that it is very effective in revealing critical data items automatically.

1 Introduction

Intrusion detection systems are important tools in the fight against malicious attackers on computing systems. These tools monitor different system activities and report on activities that can be construed as malicious. The system administrator or security engineers look at this information, and based on experience to some extent, determine which of these actions are indeed malicious. In this work, we propose a more quantitative approach to help these system administrators make sound judgments about where to focus their security efforts and to better identify data items that are critical to the system. When these critical data items are automatically identified, the security engineers can provide better and more thorough protection to these items.

A. Prakash and I. Sen Gupta (Eds.): ICISS 2009, LNCS 5905, pp. 208–221, 2009.
© Springer-Verlag Berlin Heidelberg 2009

Existing intrusion detection systems suffer shortcomings in this regard. First, not many of them do a good job in handling threats from malicious insiders [1]. These attacks, which are often considered to cause the majority of major security breaches, are a significant threat to all computing systems. The insider threat is of paramount importance when designing security systems, and more work needs to be done on classical intrusion detection systems to counteract the malicious insider [7].

A second concern with existing intrusion detection systems is that they do not typically allow system administrators the ability to focus on mission critical data [8]. It is very hard, if not impossible, to protect all data on a system against all forms of misuse. Without guidance on what is and is not critical to the system, it is difficult to focus preventative and detection measures on those assets that are deemed critical, and without such focus the efforts at data collection and analysis are likely to be overwhelmed by the "noise" produced in classical intrusion detection systems. These sources of noise produced by classical intrusion detection systems include lesser offenses that will not cause extensive damage, mistakes made unintentionally by non-malicious users, and the like.

As a corollary to this, modern information systems contain a constantly shifting collection of gigabytes, if not terabytes, of data and information. It is unlikely that static lists of critical files and processes will remain relevant over time as the system changes. The identification of critical data in a system must be dynamic, and the information about what is critical in the system must be able to be altered as the system changes [5].

Also, classical intrusion detection systems tend to rely on the fact that security engineers are generally familiar with the data systems that they are charged to protect. However, this assumption is a dangerous one as data systems continue to expand, sometimes exponentially. A malicious insider may have intimate knowledge about what files or databases are important to their part of the business, but this expert knowledge does not necessarily transfer to other layers of the organization, even to the group tasked with computer security. Security engineers, though insiders themselves, may not be familiar with what data items are critical as they might be outside of their normal scope of knowledge.

These several factors lead us to propose a new method that can be used to automatically identify data items that are critical. In our research, we have identified two approaches to this process. One involves identifying critical data items by content alone, and the second method involves examining the usage of the data system and detecting which data items influence a large number of other data items and at what frequency this influence occurs. As the identification of critical data items by content typically requires expert knowledge, we have chosen not to focus on that at this time. However, it is an area of future work, and we will be examining this method later.

The second proposal uses statistical data relationship oriented models. This method attempts to locate critical data without necessarily being concerned about the content of the data. Attributes that identify critical data items would include ownership, file size, view count, time of last access, file location, and what data items were written to after reading this data item (influence). These methods may identify data items that are not necessarily the most popular in the computing system but nonetheless influence a large portion of the database. We are going to use this statistical approach in our work as it does not require expert knowledge about the content of the data and is applicable to all database systems. We will use the metrics of view count, time of access, and influence.

Our approach is different from classical intrusion detection systems in that we will enable the system administrator to automatically identify which data items are critical. As listed in [6], establishing critical assets is one of the key strategies in order to minimize the impacts of insider threats. In a database, a critical data item is one on which many other data items in the system depend on. That is, if such a data item gets maliciously updated or deleted, many other items will consequently be affected, resulting in incorrect queries that will require repair procedures. Therefore, it is necessary to enforce tighter access control and also monitor access to these items more thoroughly. Next, we briefly define our technique for identifying these critical sets.

We detect these critical data items by considering data dependency relationships. The database log is scanned, and one or more disjoint and directed graphs are formed that show the can-influence relationships and the amount of times that the data items were accessed over this period. The can-influence graph shows the sets of relationships that occurred where two nodes connected by a directed edge indicates that the data item pointed by the arrow was influenced by the other data item. That is, if the latter is modified, there is a possibility that the former will be affected. Furthermore, by analyzing the graph for sinks (nodes to which many arrows point), sets of critical data items are identified by way of an algorithm that we have designed, tested, and evaluated.

The advantage of our approach is that it is a flexible and resource efficient technique. It solves the problem of identifying critical data items, and it also avoids the pitfalls of using static lists of critical data items. Also, as data systems change constantly, the proposed algorithm can be invoked to process this dynamically changing environment. By identifying the critical data items, system administrators can deploy tighter and more focused access policies, more detailed monitoring systems, and other focused insider detection tools, such as honeypots and honeynets.

The rest of the paper is organized as follows. In section 2 we briefly discuss why insiders are a threat to critical data items and what work has been done previously in detecting data items that can influence other data items, which is the starting point of our work. Section 3 details our proposed approach, defines the necessary definitions of our work, and shows an example of how our approach operates. Section 4 concludes the paper with an evaluation of the results and future areas of improvements.

2   Background and Related Work

In the following section, we will identify why we are trying to mitigate the effects of insider threats by identifying the data in the system that is critical. We define what a malicious insider is, what their motives are, the opportunities that are unique to insiders to cause damage using critical data, and the methods that insiders use that make them hard to defend against. We also summarize past work on using graphs to track certain data items in a database.

2.1   Insider Threats in Relation to Critical Data

CERT defines a malicious insider as a current or former employee, contractor, or business partner who has or had authorized access to an organization's network, system, or data and intentionally exceeded or misused that access in a manner that negatively affected the confidentiality, integrity, or availability of the organization's information or information systems [4]. This definition of a malicious insider has a wide reaching scope and is a good starting point for defining why insider threats are so hard to mitigate against. Insider threats are an ever increasing problem, with the recent E-Crime Watch Survey conducted by the US Secret Service, CERT, Microsoft, and others reporting that in cases where respondents could identify the perpetrator of an electronic crime, in 31% of those cases the crimes were committed by insiders. Also, 49% of the respondents reported experiencing at least one malicious, deliberate attack by an insider within the last calendar year. The impact of insider crime can truly be devastating; in one recent case an employee stole blueprints on a new and classified process worth an estimated $100 million and sold them to a Taiwanese competitor with the hope of obtaining future employment with that organization [4].

The motive for a malicious attack can be grouped into three main areas: IT sabotage, theft/modification for financial gain, and theft/modification for a business advantage [4]. An example of IT sabotage occurs when a disgruntled employee who has recently been fired causes intentional damage to a database they are charged to maintain, knowing that this will cause a lack of availability for the organization in the time following their leaving the company. IT saboteurs target systems that are critical to the business; otherwise their malicious actions would be easily repairable or ignored and the sense of revenge over the precipitating event would not be fulfilled. Insiders who steal data for financial gain would include individuals who secretly sell proprietary data to an outsider with the hope of a monetary reward. Again, malicious insiders whose motive is financial gain will not target non crucial data as it would not be as valuable to an outsider. The final motive for insiders involves individuals who steal/modify data in order to bring it with them to a new job or to start up their own business. An example would be a salesman who copies the customer list from the database and brings it with them to a new job. Again, typically only important data will be taken [9]. So, the motivation for an insider to commit a crime involving critical data items is quite high [12], [13], [14].

Insiders have significant unique opportunities over others (including the system administrators and security engineers) when it comes to committing an electronic crime [10]. Insiders, by design, can bypass physical and technical security measures designed to prevent unauthorized access; the data must be made available to them in order for their business function to work properly. In terms of methods, insiders can often use the same methods that they use everyday to access the data. As mentioned before, most systems are tuned to detect threats from outside the system, not necessarily internal threats. Insiders are also aware of the policies, procedures, technologies, and the associated vulnerabilities that are linked with them. They are able to exploit flaws in the system because of their expert knowledge; they work with these critical data items everyday. This unique opportunity that is afforded to malicious insiders of familiarity and their knowledge of the methods required in order to access the important data is what makes identifying what is and is not critical in the data system such an important task in order to mitigate this risk [16].

2.2 Previous Work

The idea of using graphs in insider threat detection has been used before, though not in relation to automatic identification of critical data items. In [1] and [11], attack tree graphs were used to identify malicious attacks from users who were performing seemingly innocuous actions in the system. In [3], a graph was developed that showed what data items could potentially influence other data items were an attack to occur. Then, in the recovery process, only the items that were influenced by the malicious action would need to go through the recovery process; those that were not in the scope of influence could be ignored, saving time and resources. In [2], a scalable graph based network vulnerability analysis was performed, identifying potential network targets. Graphs and attack trees have been proven to be a good tool at identifying and stopping potential insider threats. We have chosen to use some of these basic ideas in identifying critical data items, and some of the theorems that were proven in the previous work will be applied to our graph based system.

Previous insider threat works have called for more effort on the identification of critical data items [15]. In [5], it was pointed out that clear definitions are needed regarding what constitutes critical assets on a system in order to protect it from insider misuse. Without such guidance, most protection measures are doomed to failure. In [6] it was stated that it is important to focus R&D and operational measures on those items within an information system that are critical. It posed the question about whether procedures could be developed by which critical information within a system could be automatically identified by using expert systems and/or rule-based approaches in order to expedite this process.

3 Automatic Identification System

Our automatic identification of critical data item system works briefly as follows. We begin by developing a directed graph architectural model by scanning the database log. The log is scanned for items which are typically read before some other data item is written to or used for some business process. These data items are considered to have "influenced" the latter item because information flow occurred; based on the value of the previous item, the latter item was changed accordingly. The frequency that this influence occurs is maintained, as well as the total number of instances that the particular data item is used. Also, the average time between influences is calculated during this process. This results in several potentially disjoint graphs that will then be traversed, starting at the leaf nodes, until no more internal nodes remain for each tree. A function will be called for each item in order to determine this level of criticality, taking into account the number of items that are influenced, the number of times this item was used, and the rate at which this influence occurs. Ultimately, each item in the database will be associated with a criticality value, and those items with a relatively large critical value will be afforded greater protection. As we are focusing on those items that are critical from a usage point of view as opposed to a content based viewpoint, our algorithm may not find the items that are the most important based on the confidentiality level of the data. Rather, our approach is content independent, and will find those data items, which if damaged or altered, would cause the most damage due to their highly influential status in the system.

In the following sections we describe each component of our system in details. We begin by describing how our process scans the database logs in order to form the criticality graph.

3.1 Requisite Terminologies

Several intrusion detection systems scan the historical database logs in order to establish the normal operation of the data system. Most anomaly detection systems work by comparing known good behavior to present behavior, and when deviations occur, further security procedures are activated. We scan the database log, taking note of the following, in order to identify potential critical data items: 1. Items in the read set of the transactional sequence; 2. Items in the write set of the transactional sequence; 3. Time stamp of the transaction.

For instance, suppose the following transaction is found in the database logs: *r(x) w(a,b) timestamp: 11:32 AM, July 14, 2009.* We would then conclude that a and b were influenced by x at that particular time. This scanning of the logs is performed for each transaction that occurred over a representative time period. Also, if a transaction views a data item and does not write to another item, this is also maintained as a field. For example, this type of operation would occur when a student executes a query to view the classes that are offered for the next semester but does not register because a class is currently closed. The following definitions help in understanding these concepts.

Definition 1. A transactional sequence is an ordered list of read and/or write operations with an associated timestamp value. We denote a transactional sequence s by $< O_1(d_a), O_2(d_b), \dots O_n(d_n) \mid T_s >$ where $O_i \in \{r, w\}$, d_x is a unique data item with $1 \leq x \leq n$, and T_s being the time s was committed to the database.

Definition 2. The read set of a transactional sequence s for a data item x is the ordered list with the format $< r(d_a), r(d_b), \dots r(d_n), w(x) \mid T_s >$ which represents that the transaction s reads all data items $d_a, d_b, \dots d_n$ *before* the transaction updates data item x. It must be noted that each data item may have several read sequences each having different length. All these sequences together are called the transactional read set of this data item.

The notation $r_s(x)$ is used to represent the transactional read set for transaction s on data item x. For example, consider the following update statement in a transaction: *Update table1 set x = a+b+c where d > 100 .*

In this statement, the values of a, b, c, and d must be read before the potential updating of x. So, $< r(a), r(b), r(c), r(d) \ w(x) \mid T_s > \in r_s(x)$ and a, b, c, and d all potentially influenced x. It should be noted that the database log only contains before and after images of x instead of the exact mathematical operation used for calculating x. The above example is only used for illustrating the concept of a read sequence. The database log entry containing the above transaction may in fact look like:

$$< r(m), r(n), w(y), r(u), r(v), r(a), r(b), r(c), r(d), w(x), r(d), w(c), w(v) \mid T_s >$$

Table 1. Hypothetical Data obtained by log scanning

Item	Infl.	Freq.	$\Delta t_{avg.}$
A	B	12	30
A	C	13	45
A	-	9	180
B	D	12	480
B	-	20	10
C	G	19	10
C	J	11	15
D	E	50	16
D	F	37	7
D	J	25	10
E	G	3	60
E	-	2	120
F	H	17	15
F	E	25	23
G	-	14	10
H	I	10	15
H	G	7	14
H	-	3	5
I	-	12	47
J	-	17	5
W	Y	5	15
W	-	3	19
X	Y	3	2
X	Z	2	34
Y	-	11	57
Z	-	0	-
Z	Z	67	18

Definition 3. The write set of a transactional sequence s is the list with the format $<$ $r(d_1), r(d_1),\ldots r(d_n), w(d_a), w(d_b), \ldots w(d_k) \mid T_s >$ which represents that the transaction s reads all data items $d_1, d_2,\ldots d_n$ *before* the transaction updates data items $d_a, d_b, \ldots d_k$. Therefore, data items $d_a, d_b, \ldots d_k$ were each influenced by data items $d_1, d_2,\ldots d_n$.

Definition 4. The maximum time between any two transactional sequences is called T_{max}. T_{max} is calculated as $T_{end} - T_{start}$, where T_{end} and $T_{start} \in < T_x, T_y, \ldots T_z >$ and $\min(< T_x, T_y, \ldots T_z >) = T_{end}$ and $\max(< T_x, T_y, \ldots T_z >) = T_{start}$.

The T_{max} value will be used to define the maximum time period upon which the transactions were recorded. If a transactional read/write sequence only occurs once in the database logs, then it will have a length between influences of T_{max}.

   The table on the previous page shows a hypothetical scanning of the logs, detecting the data items that influenced other data items, the rate at which this transactional influence occurred, and also the number of times the data item was used without influencing another item. All of this information is necessary for the algorithms that will be presented in the sections that follow. The $\Delta t_{avg.}$ column in Table 1 shows the average time between each event that occurred in the corresponding row. This is recalculated for each new access that occurs. For simplicity, in the following descriptions, the time values used are measured in minutes, though this unit of time measure is not required algorithmically.

3.2 Criticality Graphs

Then, from this tabular information, one or more directed graphs are formed to represent this information. From the above example, two disjoint graphs will be formed, one with data item A as the root, and another disjoint graph with no roots. These graphs are presented on the following page and will be used as examples to show several important definitions and properties about this graphing process.

3.3 Formal Definition of Criticality Graph

The following definitions and properties formally define what the criticality graph is and how it will be used to locate and identify critical data items in the database. The first definition has been taken from [2] with slight modification.

Definition 5. Data item a "influences" data item b if data item a is read in order to update or write to data item b in a single, atomic transaction s that is recorded in the logs of the database with a discrete time stamp, T_s. This relationship is denoted as a $\rightarrow$ b in the graph structure. The following properties hold: 1. Reflexive: $a \rightarrow a$; 2. Non-commutative: $a \rightarrow b \,!\Rightarrow b \rightarrow a$; 3. Transitive: $a \rightarrow b \cap b \rightarrow c \Rightarrow a \rightarrow c$.

Definition 6: A criticality graph is a rooted or rootless graph structure defined as CT = (A, E, C), where

1. A is the set of nodes in the graph corresponding to the different data items that are related by some sphere of influence. The set A can be partitioned into two subsets, leaf_nodes and internal_nodes such that
    a) leaf_nodes $\cup$ internal_nodes = A,
    b) leaf_nodes $\cap$ internal_nodes = ϕ.
2. E $\subseteq$ A x A constitutes the set of edges in the criticality graph. An edge (v_i, v_j) $\in$ E represents the "influences" relationship transition from a parent node v_i $\in$ A to a child node v_j $\in$ A in the graph. The edge (v_i, v_j) is said to be "emergent from" v_i and "incident to" v_j. Further if edges (v_i, v_j) and (v_i, v_k) exists in the set of edges, then v_j and v_k represent the same transition.
3. C is a set of criticality labels. A label $l \in$ C is associated with either a node or a transitional edge as previously defined. If $S \in$ A is a node then the criticality label l_s is given by the tuple <f, t> where f $\in$ integers and ≥ 0, and t $\in$ reals and $\phi \leq t \leq T_{max}$. The item f is termed the frequency of influence and item t is termed the average time between influences.

For example, the criticality tree in Figure 1 consists of the nodes A,B,C,D,E,F,G,H,I, and J. In node A, the internal criticality label is <9, 180> signifying that it was read 9 times without being used to influence other items with an avg. time between these events being 180 min. The label <12, 30> from node A to node B represents the 12 times A was used to update B with an average time between these influences being 30 minutes.

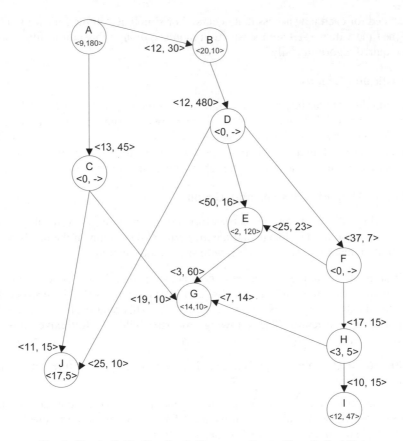

Fig. 1. Simple Criticality Graph Corresponding to Hypothetical Data

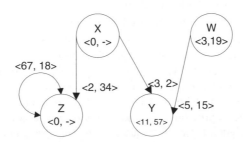

Fig. 2. Second, Disjoint Criticality Graph Corresponding to Hypothetical Data

Definition 7. Given a node $v_i \in$ A in a criticality tree, then $v_i \in$ internal_nodes iff. $\exists$ some $(v_i, v_j) \in$ E emergent from v_i that is not incident to v_i.

Definition 8. Given a node $v_k \in$ A in a criticality tree, then $v_k \in$ leaf_nodes iff. $!\exists$ some $(v_k, v_l) \in$ E emergent from v_k that is not incident to v_k and $\exists$ some $(v_k, v_m) \in$ E incident to v_k.

In Figure 2, node Z is actually a leaf node. It does have an edge that leaves the node, but the edge returns to the same node. This models when a transaction reads a data item and then writes back to the same item. This would occur, for example, when a query reads the current salary, increases it by 5%, and then writes back to the salary location.

3.4 Calculating Criticality

We now use the criticality graph to determine the criticality of each data item element in the graph. The algorithm below shows all the steps in the process, but the process is briefly explained in the following. The graph is traversed, starting at the leaf nodes, and criticality is calculated for each node. As the leaf nodes influence no other items, the criticality calculation is relatively straightforward. For the parent nodes, the criticality algorithm takes into account the frequency/average time of use of that item when it was not being used to influence other items to arrive at an internal criticality value. Then, this value is summed with each data item that is influenced, taking into account the child's criticality, and also the frequency and average time that this influence occurred. During the traversal, the leaf nodes are removed, and ultimately criticality values are calculated for each item. As we wish to find the items that influence several other items at a high rate of time and frequency, frequency of use and influencing several other influential items is considered to add to the criticality value. If the average time between each event is relatively high, this means that the influence takes a long time to spread, so this is a negative contributor to the criticality.

Starting with the leaf nodes of the graph, the criticality value for a generic leaf K, called C_K, is calculated as the number of uses (f_K) times a scaling constant minus a penalty value if the average time between uses (t_K) is over a certain acceptable threshold:

$$C_K = K_1 * f_K - P_K \tag{1}$$

where K_1 is a constant used to weight the criticality value towards or away from the number of uses and P_K is:

$$P_K = \begin{cases} 0 \mid t_K < t_{min} \\ \dfrac{K_1 * f_k}{t_{max} - t_{min}} * (t_k - t_{min}) \mid t_{min} \le t_K \le t_{max} \\ K_1 * f_K \mid t_K > t_{max} \end{cases} \tag{2}$$

where t_{min} is the bound on the time between use that is considered to happen so often that no penalty is needed to be assessed to the criticality value because the event occurs so often that its influence will spread quickly and t_{max} is the upper bound on the time between usage that is considered to be so infrequent that it results in the data item not being critical because security procedures are adequate enough to repair any damage that might be caused by malicious uses of that item. When t_k is between t_{min} and $t_{max,}$ the penalty is a linear progression from 0 to the maximum penalty of K_1*f_k. For the following examples, we will use a K_1 value of 1. Also, it is important to note that:

$$0 \le C_{LK} \le K_1 * f_K \qquad (3)$$

so the criticality can not be negative. As a future work, we may consider how having negative criticality values would better enable us to rank low criticality value data items. Therefore, the criticality of the leaf nodes will consist of the sum of the instances when the item was read without influencing other data items and the instances when the data item was used to influence itself, as this is the definition of what a leaf node is.

Then, once the criticality is calculated for each leaf node, the leaf nodes are removed, and the critical values are stored. This results in a new set of leaf nodes that were once parents. The links that they once had to the children are still maintained in order to calculate the next set of criticality values. The criticality for a node N with edges $v_i...v_k$ each associated with a frequency $f_i...f_k$, average time duration of $t_i...t_k$ and criticality of $C_i...C_k$, then the criticality for node N is:

$$C_N = \sum_{i=0}^{i=j} (C_i (K_2 * f_{N \to i} - P_{N \to i})) + K_1 * f_N - P_N \qquad (4)$$

where K_2 is a constant to weigh the criticality value of a parent towards or away from the criticality value of the link to the child. For the examples that follow, we assume K_2 to be 1. In the above equation, the $f_{N \to I}$ and $P_{N \to I}$ values are the frequency and average time between events for a particular edge I which is summed for each link. The summation is also multiplied times the criticality of the child that the link points to. Finally, the reflexive criticality for the node is added once to give the final critical value for the node.

These operations are performed for each node until no more remain in the graph. While one may assume that the criticality would increase as the graph is traversed upwards, this is not always the case due to the penalty assessed by the average time between influence events. The ultimate output of this process is a list of every data item with an associated criticality value. This process is automatic and requires little input from the system administrator.

3.5 Criticality Example

We will now show, by way of example, how our proposed algorithm operates. We will use the criticality graph that was shown in Figure 1 along with all the frequency and time averages associated with it. We will also assume that the t_{min} and t_{max} are 10 minutes and 60 minutes respectively. Again the constants K_1, and K_2 in the above criticality equations are defined to be one.

First, the criticality for nodes G, I and J are calculated as they are leaf nodes:

$$C_G: 14 - 0 = 14 \qquad C_I: 12 - \frac{12}{60 - 10}(47 - 10) = 3.12 \qquad C_J: 17 - 0 = 17$$

For the following nodes, the self-criticality is calculated first. Then the contributions from the child nodes are calculated in the order given. The criticality for the parents (C, H, and E) of nodes G, I, and J is calculated as follows:

C is the parent of J and G; C_C: $0+17\left(11-\dfrac{11}{60-10}(15-10)\right)+14(19-0)=434.3$

H is the parent of I and G;

C_H: $(3\text{--}0)+3.12\left(10-\dfrac{10}{60-10}(15-10)\right)+14\left(7-\dfrac{7}{60-10}(14-10)\right)=121.24$

E is the parent of G; C_E: $(2-2)+14(3-3)=0$
Then C, H, and E are removed and the criticality for the next set of node(s) is:
F is the parent of E and H;

C_F: $0+0\left(25-\dfrac{25}{60-10}(23-10)\right)+121.24\left(17-\dfrac{17}{60-10}(15-10)\right)=1854.97$

Then the criticality for node D is calculated:
D is the parent of J, E, and F;

C_D: $0+17(25-0)+0\left(11-\dfrac{50}{60-10}(16-10)\right)+1854.97(37-0)=69,058.9$

Then node B:
B is the parent of D; C_B: $(20-0)+69,058.9(12-12)=20$
Finally, the criticality of node A is calculated:
A is the parent of B and C;

C_A: $20\left(12-\dfrac{12}{60-10}(30-10)\right)+434.3\left(13-\dfrac{13}{60-10}(45-10)\right)=1837.77$

So, node D is the most critical data item in the database based on its frequency of usage, time betweens uses, and the criticality and rate of the data items that it influences. This is not something that is immediately obvious by looking at the logs, and our algorithm was very capable of revealing the most critical data items automatically. The most critical data items, in order of importance, are D, F, A, C, H, B, J, G, I, and then E, in that order.

3.6 Bidirectional Criticality

There are cases where information flow or influence can go two ways. For example in Figure 3 below data item A influenced data item B 89 times and data item B influenced A 44 times. In the cases where the influence is bidirectional, the above criticality calculation requires some minor adjustments. The original criticality graph is broken down into two sub graphs, and the bidirectional links are separated, one for each direction. Then, the criticality of the affected data items are calculated separately, resulting in the total criticality of the affected nodes.

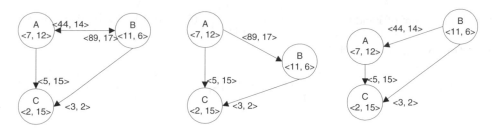

Fig. 3. A criticality graph with a bidirectional edge is shown at left. It is decomposed into two sub criticality graphs, which are shown in the center and right.

4 Conclusions and Future Work

In this paper, we propose a new and novel method to detect critical data items in a database automatically. Our system is intended to complement existing intrusion detection systems to help fight the threat of malicious insiders abusing critical data items. We develop a quantitative framework that applies very well to determining which data items are critical in that they influence a significant amount of other data items that are significant themselves. Also, our algorithm takes into account the number of uses and the average time between uses in order to better model a realistic system. The advantage of our approach is that it is a flexible and resource efficient technique that can be applied to any system that maintains a log of the transactions that are operated on the database. While our approach is aimed to be used by system administrators in a defensive mode of operation, it is also applicable to individuals who wish to use it in an offensive mode in order to efficient target the areas of the data system where malicious actions will cause the most damage and disruption to the enemy.

We plan to further our work by extending the algorithm to the level of the user. A criticality graph will be developed for each user, and if the monitoring system can be tuned to be specific to particular users, better security can be achieved. As the criticality of certain documents is very different to different users, extending our work to that level will be a good and worthwhile improvement.

Acknowledgement

This work has been supported in part by US AFOSR under grant FA9550-08-1-0255. We are thankful to Dr. Robert Herklotz for his support, which made this work possible.

References

1. Ray, I., Poolsappasit, N.: Using Attack Trees to Identify Malicious Attacks from Authorized Insiders. In: di Vimercati, S.d.C., Syverson, P.F., Gollmann, D. (eds.) ESORICS 2005. LNCS, vol. 3679, pp. 231–246. Springer, Heidelberg (2005)
2. Hu, Y., Panda, B.: Identification of Malicious Transactions in Database Systems. In: 7th Intl. Database Engineering and App. Symposium (IDEAS 2003), p. 329 (2003)
3. Zuo, Y., Panda, B.: A Service Oriented System Based Information Flow Model for Damage Assessment. In: 6th IFIP WG 11.5 Working Conference on Integrity and Internal Control in Information Systems, Lausanne, Switzerland, November 13-14 (2003)

 4. Cappelli, D., Moore, A., Shimeall, T., Trzeciak, R.: Common Sense Guide to Prevention and Detection of Insider Threats, Carnegie Mellon University (2008)
 5. Insider Threat Integrated Process Team, Department of Defense (DoD-IPT), 2000. DoD Insider Threat Mitigation, U.S. Department of Defense (2000)
 6. Anderson, R., Bozek, T., Logstaff, T., Meitzler, W., Skroch, M., Wyk, K.V.: Research on mitigating the insider threat to information sys., RAND Corporation Report CF-163 (2000)
 7. Whitman, M.: Enemy at the Gate: Threats to Information Security. Communications of the ACM 46(8) (2003)
 8. Abbadi, I., Alawneh, M.: Preventing Insider Information Leakage for Enterprises. In: Proceedings of the 2008 Second International Conference on Emerging Security Information, Systems and Technologies, pp. 99–106 (2008)
 9. Anderson, R., Brackney, R.: Understanding the Insider Threat. In: Proceedings of a March 2004 Workshop, RAND National Defense Research Institute (2004)
10. Ha, D., Upadhyaya, S., Ngo, H., Pramanik, S., Chinchani, R., Mathew, S.: Insider Threat Analysis Using Information Centric Modeling. In: Craiger, P., Shenoi, S. (eds.) Advances in Digital Forensics III. Springer, Boston (2007)
11. Sheyner, O., Haines, J., Jha, S., Lippmann, R., Wing, J.: Automated Generation and Analysis of Attack Graphs. In: Proc. IEEE Symposium on Sec. and Priv., Oakland (2002)
12. Cathey, R., Ma, L., Goharian, N., Grossman, D.: Misuse detection for information retrieval systems. In: CIKM 2003: Proceedings of the twelfth international conference on Information and knowledge management, New York, NY, USA, pp. 183–190 (2003)
13. White, J., Panda, B.: Implementing PII Honeytokens to Mitigate Against the Threat of Malicious Insiders. In: Proc. of the IEEE International Conference on Intelligence and Security Informatics (ISI 2009), Dallas, Texas, p. 233 (2009)
14. White, J., Panda, B., Yaseen, Q., Nguyen, K., Li, W.: Detecting Malicious Insider Threats using a Null Affinity Temporal Three Dimensional Matrix Relation. In: Proc. of the 7th Inl. Workshop on Security in Info. Sys (WOSIS 2009), Milan, pp. 93–102 (2009)
15. Meza, B., Burns, P., Eavenson, M., Palaniswami, D., Sheth, A.: An ontological approach to the document access problem of insider threat. In: Kantor, P., Muresan, G., Roberts, F., Zeng, D.D., Wang, F.-Y., Chen, H., Merkle, R.C. (eds.) ISI 2005. LNCS, vol. 3495, pp. 486–491. Springer, Heidelberg (2005)
16. Bradford, P., Brown, M., Perdue, J., Self, B.: Towards proactive computer-system forensics. In: Proceedings of ITCC, pp. 648–652 (2004)

Database Relation Watermarking Resilient against Secondary Watermarking Attacks

Gaurav Gupta[1,2] and Josef Pieprzyk[1]

[1] Centre for Advanced Computing - Algorithms and Cryptography,
Department of Computing, Macquarie University, Australia
[2] Centre for Policing, Intelligence and Counter Terrorism,
Macquarie University, Australia
{ggupta,josef}@science.mq.edu.au
www.comp.mq.edu.au/~ggupta

Abstract. There has been tremendous interest in watermarking multimedia content during the past two decades, mainly for proving ownership and detecting tamper. Digital fingerprinting, that deals with identifying malicious user(s), has also received significant attention. While extensive work has been carried out in watermarking of images, other multimedia objects still have enormous research potential. Watermarking database relations is one of the several areas which demand research focus owing to the commercial implications of database theft. Recently, there has been little progress in database watermarking, with most of the watermarking schemes modeled after the *irreversible* database watermarking scheme proposed by Agrawal and Kiernan. Reversibility is the ability to re-generate the original (unmarked) relation from the watermarked relation using a secret key. As explained in our paper, reversible watermarking schemes provide greater security against secondary watermarking attacks, where an attacker watermarks an already marked relation in an attempt to erase the original watermark. This paper proposes an improvement over the reversible and blind watermarking scheme presented in [5], identifying and eliminating a critical problem with the previous model. Experiments showing that the average watermark detection rate is around 91% even with attacker distorting half of the attributes. The current scheme provides security against secondary watermarking attacks.

1 Introduction

The world is rapidly becoming a smaller place with the advancements in high-speed network and availability even in remote regions. Free file hosting services such as RapidShare and peer-to-peer networks make data sharing very convenient. However, this also poses a threat to the entertainment industry and also to organizations dealing with sensitive information such as currency exchange rates and stock prices. Digital watermarking is one of the solutions to the problem, involving embedding of a digital watermark in a multimedia object such that it satisfies the following properties:

A. Prakash and I. Sen Gupta (Eds.): ICISS 2009, LNCS 5905, pp. 222–236, 2009.

- *Detectable/ Extractable*: The watermark should be recovered or detected from the watermarked copy.
- *Robust*: The watermark should satisfy detectability property even after distortions introduced by the attacker.
- *Limited distortion*: The watermark should cause minimal distortion (measured by statistical metrics, such as average) to the original data.
- *Low false positives*: The probability of detecting watermark in a document, or its parts, that do not contain a watermark, should be negligible.
- *Blindness*: Watermark detection process should require only the supposedly watermarked object and a secret key.
- *Randomness*: The watermark should be distributed across the object so that localized attacks are ineffective.
- *Capacity*: The watermark-carrying capacity should be sufficient to embed the desired watermark.

In this paper, we provide an improvement over the scheme presented in [5]. By identifying and eliminating a critical error in the concerned scheme, we provide a more secure watermarking model.

1.1   Scenario

The problem is described in the following scenario. Alice publishes a database relation R (for example, forecasts of currency rates) and shares the watermarked version R_w with Bob and Mallory. The watermark proves Alice's ownership over R_w and also introduces "small" changes in the data such that Bob and Mallory can get a fair estimate of the document's usefulness but still cannot afford to risk using it directly (because it is an approximation of the accurate data). The degree of changes can be adjusted by the owners to suit their requirements.

If Mallory inserts his own watermark in R_w and sells the re-watermarked version R_{w_2} (this process is called secondary watermarking attack), then Alice should be identified as the rightful owner of R_{w_2}. Bob and Mallory can purchase a key and recover R from R_w.

If Mallory purchases the key and obtains the original relation from Alice, he legally agrees to the fact that Alice is the owner of the relation. Hence, even if Mallory later claims ownership over a watermarked copy of the relation, Alice can produce the transaction details as the proof of ownership.

1.2   Organization of Paper and Notations Used

In Section 2, we provide an overview of existing watermarking schemes and discuss watermarking scheme from [1]. Our algorithms are presented in Section 3, with analysis in Section 4, and experimental results in Section 5. The paper is concluded in Section 6 with a note on future research directions.

We use the following notations throughout the paper; R is a Relation, r represents a Tuple, $r.P$ its Primary Key and $r.A_i^j$, the jth bit of its ith attribute. $bin(x)$ is used for the binary value of x, $len(x)$ for its length (in bits). $insert(x, pos, b)$

function inserts bit b at the pos^{th} LSB of x while $replace(x, pos, b)$ function replaces bit at the pos^{th} LSB of x by bit b. $bit(x, pos)$ gives the bit at pos^{th} LSB in x (Specifically, $bit(x, 0)$ gives the least significant bit of x). $int(x)$ is the integer part of a real number x and $frac(x)$is the fraction part of real number x. Finally, cap gives the number of bits allocated to store fraction part (we assume that $cap = 16$).

2   Related Work

There have been several numerical database watermarking schemes proposed in the past decade in [2,1,4,8,7]. Here, we discuss the fundamental watermarking algorithm proposed in [1] and difference expansion [9] applied for reversible watermarking.

2.1   Agrawal-Kiernan Watermarking Scheme

One of the early works in database relation watermarking was carried out by Agrawal and Kiernan and presented in [1]. Several schemes followed with modifications to the original watermarking model and were described in [7,8].

The function $\mathcal{F}(r.P) = \mathcal{H}(\mathcal{K}\|\mathcal{H}(\mathcal{K}\|(r.P))$, where $\mathcal{H}$ is a one-way hash function, $\mathcal{K}$ is a secret key and $\|$ stands for the concatenation operation. The value of this function depends on the primary key $r.P$ of the tuple r and the secret key $\mathcal{K}$. The tuple, attribute, and bit carrying a watermark bit are calculated using $\mathcal{F}(r.P)$. The bit embedded is calculated as $\mathcal{H}(\mathcal{K}\|r.P)$ (mod 2). Assuming the primary key and the secret key are available during the detection process, the exact watermark bit can easily be identified and compared with $\mathcal{H}(\mathcal{K}\|r.P)$ (mod 2) to determine if they match, in which case the watermark bit is successfully recovered. There is a minimum threshold on the fraction of bits to be correctly recovered in order to ascertain presence of a watermark. The threshold is determined by parameter α in Algorithm 2. This controls the probability of false positives. The watermark insertion and detection algorithms from [1] are provided in Algorithm 1 and Algorithm 2, respectively.

Input   : Relation R, secret key $\mathcal{K}$, fraction $\frac{1}{\gamma}$, LSB usage ξ, Markable
              attributes $\{A_1, A_2, \ldots, A_v\}$
Output: Watermarked relation R_w
forall *tuples* $r \in R$ **do**
  if $\mathcal{F}(r.P)$ (mod γ) $= 0$ **then**
      Mark attribute $i = \mathcal{F}(r.P)$ (mod v);
      Mark bit $j = \mathcal{F}(r.P)$ (mod ξ);
      $r.A_i^j = \mathcal{H}(\mathcal{K}\|r.P)$ (mod 2);
  end
end

Algorithm 1. Watermark insertion [2]

While the scheme is secure against distortion attacks due to the pseudo-random distribution of watermark based on keyed-hash function, and also against sorting attacks due to independent watermarking of each tuple, the scheme does not provide security against secondary watermark attacks. In the scenario described in Section 1.1, Mallory will be identified as the owner for relation R_{w_2} instead of the rightful owner Alice.

Input   : Relation R, secret key $\mathcal{K}$, fraction $\frac{1}{\gamma}$, LSB usage ξ, threshold α
Output: Watermark Status $\in \{true, false\}$
$matchcount = totalcount = 0$;
forall *tuples* $r \in R$ **do**
    if $\mathcal{F}(r.P) \pmod \gamma = 0$ **then**
        Marked attribute $i = \mathcal{F}(r.P) \pmod v$;
        Marked bit $j = \mathcal{F}(r.P) \pmod \xi$;
        if $\mathcal{H}(\mathcal{K}\|r.P) \pmod 2 = r.A_i^j$ **then**
          | $matchcount = matchcount + 1$;
        end
        $totalcount = totalcount + 1$;
    end
end
$\tau = \min(\theta) : \text{B}(\theta, totalcount, 1/2) < \alpha$;
if $matchcount \geq \tau$ **then**
    | return true;
else
    | return false;
end

Algorithm 2. Watermark detection [2]

2.2   Reversible Watermarking Scheme

Difference expansion refers to a series of arithmetic operators on two integer values and a bit that result into a pair of modified integers from which original pair of integers and the bit can be re-generated [9,6]. Difference expansion has previously been applied in image watermarking [3]. But application in database watermarking introduces an additional constraint of limiting distortion.

An integer pair x, y $(x \geq y)$ can be encoded as a pair of it's integral average and difference between the integers using Equation 1. The values x, y can be recovered from the derived from Equation 2. Proof 2.1 shows that the recovered values are in fact the original values.

$$avg = \lfloor \frac{(x+y)}{2} \rfloor, dif = x - y \tag{1}$$

$$x_{recover} = avg + \lfloor \frac{(dif + 1))}{2} \rfloor, y_{recover} = avg - \lfloor \frac{dif}{2} \rfloor \tag{2}$$

Proof (2.1). $x_{recover} = x, y_{recover} = y$

if($x \pmod 2$)==$y \pmod 2$) (both even or both odd)
{

$$x_{recover} = avg + \lfloor \frac{(dif+1)}{2} \rfloor = \lfloor \frac{x+y}{2} \rfloor + \lfloor \frac{x-y+1}{2} \rfloor = (\frac{x+y}{2}) + (\frac{x-y}{2}) = x$$
$$y_{recover} = avg - \lfloor \frac{(dif)}{2} \rfloor = \lfloor \frac{x+y}{2} \rfloor - \lfloor \frac{x-y}{2} \rfloor = (\frac{x+y}{2}) - (\frac{x-y}{2}) = y$$

}
else
{

$$x_{recover} = avg + \lfloor \frac{(dif+1)}{2} \rfloor = \lfloor \frac{x+y}{2} \rfloor + \lfloor \frac{x-y+1}{2} \rfloor = (\frac{x+y-1}{2}) + (\frac{x-y+1}{2}) = x$$
$$y_{recover} = avg - \lfloor \frac{(dif)}{2} \rfloor = \lfloor \frac{x+y}{2} \rfloor - \lfloor \frac{x-y}{2} \rfloor = (\frac{x+y-1}{2}) - (\frac{x-y-1}{2}) = y$$

} □

Let x, y be the two attributes selected to carry a watermark bit b. The scheme works as follows: The average avg and difference dif is computed using Equation 1. The integer dif is then expanded considering the bit to be inserted using Equation 3. The expanded difference is odd for 1-bit and even for 0-bit. The new watermarked values x', y' are computed from Equation 4.

$$dif' = 2 \times dif + b \tag{3}$$

$$x' = avg + \lfloor \frac{(dif'+1)}{2} \rfloor, y' = avg - \lfloor \frac{dif'}{2} \rfloor \tag{4}$$

The average of the new pair remains the same as the average of the old pair. This has been demonstrated in Proof 2.2.

During detection, the average avg' and difference dif' are calculated. Equation 5 shows that the bit inserted is 0 if the difference is even, otherwise odd. Then the difference is compressed to the original value using Equation 6. Average need not be changed, as shown in Proof 2.2. The original values and the watermark values can be recovered at detection using Equation 7. The recovered values are the original values, as proved in Proof 2.1.

Proof (2.2). $avg' = avg$

$$avg' = \lfloor \frac{x'+y'}{2} \rfloor$$
$$= \lfloor \frac{avg + \lfloor \frac{dif'+1}{2} \rfloor + avg - \lfloor \frac{dif'}{2} \rfloor}{2} \rfloor \text{ (From Equation 4)}$$
$$= \lfloor \frac{2 \times avg + \lfloor \frac{dif'+1}{2} \rfloor - \lfloor \frac{dif'}{2} \rfloor}{2} \rfloor$$

$$= \begin{cases} \lfloor \frac{2 \times avg+1}{2} \rfloor & \text{if } dif' \text{ is odd} \\ \lfloor \frac{2 \times avg}{2} \rfloor & \text{if } dif' \text{ is even} \end{cases}$$

$$= avg \qquad \qquad \square$$

$$b = dif' \pmod 2 \tag{5}$$

$$dif_{old} = \lfloor \frac{dif'}{2} \rfloor \tag{6}$$

$$x_{old} = avg + \lfloor \frac{(dif + 1))}{2} \rfloor, y_{old} = avg - \lfloor \frac{dif}{2} \rfloor \tag{7}$$

It can also be proved that the values of x and y thus recovered are in fact the original values. We have already proved that the average of the modified pair x', y' is same as the average of the original pair x, y. The difference recovered is also the same as the original difference, proved in Proof 2.3. Obtaining the original average and difference directly implies recovery of correct original values.

Proof (2.3). $dif_{old} = dif$

$$dif_{old} = \lfloor \frac{dif'}{2} \rfloor$$
$$= \lfloor \frac{2*dif+b}{2} \rfloor \text{ (From Equation 3)}$$
$$= dif \qquad \qquad \Box$$

The major drawback of this scheme is that it requires two attributes to embed a single watermark bit and the amount of distortion introduced in the attributes directly proportional to the numerical difference of the two attributes. A single attribute carrying a watermark bit would be a far better option, and this is precisely our objective in this research project.

We proposed a reversible watermarking scheme in [5]. In that scheme, the empirical results were slightly lower than theoretical results in terms of security. This was initially attributed to the quality of automated data generation but we realized that when small distortions are made to items in the neighborhood of powers of 2, they jump over from $2^x - y$ to $2^x + z$ and thereby the MSB of these items change, which means that during detection, they are classified as *non-marked* with a probability of $\frac{\gamma-1}{\gamma}$. While this is a small concern in terms of security (only few items lie in this region), it has massive implications in reversibility because even if a single bit is not recovered successfully, the whole watermark is said to not have been recovered successfully. We have placed proper checks on such boundary values and thus ensure that these *jumps* from one side of powers of 2 to the other do not occur, thereby preserving MSBs during detection.

3   Proposed Scheme

This section describes the operations we use to build our watermarking scheme and the following three algorithms used in the scheme:

1. *Insert(R, K)* → R_w: Relation R is watermarked using secret key K to get relation R_w.
2. *Detect(R_w, K)* → $(R, status)$: Detecting a watermark in relation R_w with a secret key. Value *status* provides indication of whether watermark was detected or not and also returns the original relation, R (if the watermark is detected).
3. *Owner($\mathcal{R}$, U)*: Identifies the rightful owner from a set of candidates U with $u_i \in U$ claiming ownership of $R_i \in \mathcal{R}$ such that $R_i \approx R_j$, $i \neq j$.

3.1   Mathematical Model

In this section, we provide the watermarking model representing inputs and outputs of watermark insertion and detection and also constraints under which watermarking should be performed. Given a value $x \in \mathbb{R}$, bit b, and secret key K, the objective of the watermarking scheme is to find $x' \in \mathbb{R}$, such that:

1. $(x, b, K) \rightarrow x'$: We can obtain x' from the knowledge of (x, b, K)
2. $(x', K) \rightarrow (x, b)$: We can obtain (x, b) from the knowledge of (x', K)
3. $(1 - \sigma) \le \frac{x'}{x} \le (1 + \sigma)$ $(\sigma \approx 0.03)$: Distortion to individual attributes is limited to approximately $(100 \times \sigma)\%$.

3.2   Attacks

The following four attacks should be considered in a secondary watermarking scheme:

- **Subtractive attack:** Attacker deletes some tuples from the database.
- **Distortive attack:** Attacker introduces a random distortion in the relation.
- **Sorting attack:** Attacker rearranges the tuples based on one or more attributes.
- **Additive attack/Secondry watermarking:** Attacker inserts watermark in the relation already watermarked in an attempt to erase the old watermark.

3.3   Proposed Algorithms

Algorithm 3 describes the process of embedding one bit in an attribute. The operation involves extracting bit $oldBit$ from the integer portion of the attribute before replacing it by the watermark bit and inserting it in the fraction portion of the attribute. Thus, the watermark bit can be recovered during detection and the attribute can be restored to it's unmarked value by replacing the watermark bit with the original bit extracted from the fraction part. The process of detecting a single bit in an attribute and regenerating the original value is illustrated in Algorithm 4.

As a working example, let $A = 612.875$ and $b = 0$. The value $len(int(A)) = 10$ contains the length of binary representation of 612 (=10 0110 0100) and $len(frac(A)) = 3$ contains the length of binary representation of 0.875 (=.111). Both integral and fraction bits have positions starting from 0, where position 0 is for the bit next to the decimal point. For example, in 6.5 (110.1), integer bit at position 0 is 0, at position 1 is 1, and at position 2 is 1 while fraction bit at position 0 is 1. Let $pos_1 = 2, pos_2 = 3$, The watermarking condition from Algorithm 3 is satisfied. The bit at position 2 (=1) (the first LSB is at position 0) is replaced by the bit $b = 0$ to be embedded. Upon this change, the integer portion becomes 608 (10 0110 0000). The bit removed from the integer part is 1 and is inserted in the fraction part at position 3, thereby changing it to 0.9375

```
Input  : Bit b, Attribute A, F(r.P)
Output: Watermarked attribute A_w
pos_1 = F(r.P)   (mod len(int(A)));
pos_2 = F(r.P)   (mod len(frac(A)));
if len(int(A)) > (pos_1 + ε) and len(frac(A)) < cap then
    oldBit = bit(int(A), pos_1);
    replace(int(A), pos_1, b);
    insert(frac(A), pos_2, oldBit);
end
```

$$\textbf{Algorithm 3. } embed(b, A)$$

(.1111). The final watermarked value is 608.9375 from which the original value can be extracted using Algorithm 4. During detection, given that the primary key and the secret key remain the same, the same attribute is symmetrically identified and the watermark bit is checked in it. The value of the watermarked value is 608.9375, integer part being 608 (10 0110 0000) and fraction part being .9375 (.1111). Again $pos_1 = 2, pos_2 = 3$ are calculated using the secret key and primary key. We check the bit at position $pos_1 = 2$ in the integer part (0) and compare with $\mathcal{H}(\mathcal{K}\|r.P)$ (mod 2). We then remove the bit at $pos_2 = 3$ from the fraction part (1) and put it at position pos_1 of the integer part, thereby regenerating the original attribute 612.875.

```
Input  : Bit b, Attribute A, F(r.P)
Output: Watermark detection status
pos_1 = F(r.P)   (mod len(int(A)));
pos_2 = F(r.P)   (mod len(frac(A)));
if len(int(A)) > (pos_1 + ε) then
    if bit(int(A), pos_1) == b and len(frac(A)) < cap then
        match = true;
        oldBit = bit(frac(A), pos_2);
        replace(int(A), pos_2, oldBit);
    else
        match = false;
    end
end
return match;
```

$$\textbf{Algorithm 4. } check(b, A)$$

The rationale behind placing the condition $len(int(A)) > (pos_1 + ε)$ to embed a watermark bit is to ensure that the attribute value is at least $2^ε$ times larger than the modification, and therefore the distortion fraction to δ calculated using Equation 8. We can decrease δ by by increasing the value of ϵ. This ensures that the watermarked values are not in the *neighbourhood* of powers of two which might cause MSB distortion with a high probability.

$$\delta = \frac{2^{(\lfloor log_2(A) \rfloor - \epsilon)}}{A} \tag{8}$$

The second condition that should be satisfied to insert a watermark bit is that $len(frac(A)) < cap$. That is, the length of the bit representation of the attribute's fraction part should be at least one less than the total number of bits available to contain the fraction part. If this is not true, the new bit inserted in the fraction part will knock out the LSB of the fraction, thereby introducing irreversible data loss.

$$\mathcal{F}(r.P) = \mathcal{H}(\mathcal{K} \| \mathcal{H}(\mathcal{K} \| (r.P))) \tag{9}$$

Input   : relation R, secret key K, fraction $\frac{1}{\gamma}$, LSB usage ξ, Markable attributes
            $\{A_1, A_2, \ldots, A_v\}$, primary key P
Output: Watermarked relation R_w
forall *tuples* $r \in R$ **do**
  if $\mathcal{F}(r.P) \pmod{\gamma} = 0$ **then**
    Mark attribute $i = \mathcal{F}(r.P) \pmod{v}$;
    Mark bit $j = \mathcal{F}(r.P) \pmod{\xi}$;
    $b = \mathcal{H}(\mathcal{K} \| r.P) \pmod{2}$;
    $embed(r.A_i^j)$;
  end
end

Algorithm 5. Watermark insertion

We use this simple insertion and detection process in conjunction with the keyed tuple and attribute selection performed in [1] to accomplish a comprehensive watermarking scheme. The insertion and detection algorithms are given in Algorithm 5 and Algorithm 6, respectively. We use a confidence level θ (typically between 0.60 and 0.75 since keeping θ too low will result in huge false positives and keeping it too high would compromise security) to determine the presence of the watermark. If less than $(\theta \times 100)\%$ bits are correctly identified, the presence of the watermark cannot be ascertained.

To combat secondary watermarking attacks, we propose another algorithm that identifies whether watermark of a party p_1 is detected in a relation R whose ownership is claimed by a party p_2. Since false positive probability is negligible (see Equation 12), R must have been watermarked by p_1 before p_2, thus identifying the rightful owner. Party p_2 can distort a relation before inserting it's own watermark but the distortions need to be limited to preserve relation usability for the party p_2. In our experiments, we test secondary watermarking survival with 30% attributes distorted. (an attack that distorts $x\%$ attributes is referred to as $x\%$ distortive attack).

Input : relation R, private key K, primary key P, fraction $\frac{1}{\gamma}$, LSB usage ξ,
     confidence level θ
Output: Watermark Status $\in \{true, false\}$
$matchcount = totalcount = 0$;
$oldRelation = R$;
forall *tuples* $r \in R$ **do**
 if $\mathcal{F}(r.P) \pmod{\gamma} = 0$ **then**
  Marked attribute $i = \mathcal{F}(r.P) \pmod{v}$;
  Marked bit $j = \mathcal{F}(r.P) \pmod{\xi}$;
  $b = \mathcal{H}(\mathcal{K}\|pk) \pmod{2}$;
  if $check(b, r.A_i^j) == true$ **then**
   | $matchcount = matchcount + 1$;
  end
  $totalcount = totalcount + 1$;
 end
end
$fractionDetected = \frac{matchcount}{totalcount}$;
if $fractiondetected \geq \theta$ **then**
 | return *true*;
else
 | $R = oldRelation$;
 | return *false*;
end

Algorithm 6. Watermark detection

4   Security Analysis

In this section, we describe the security of our schemes against reshuffling, subtractive, distortive and additive (or secondary watermarking) attacks. We present the experimental results obtained which confirm our claims about the security of the scheme in Section 5.

Confidence level: In our scheme, we set confidence level θ such that the detection algorithm must correctly identify at least θ fraction of watermark bits in order to determine presence of the watermark beyond reasonable doubts. In our experiments, we have kept the value θ between 0.60 and 0.75.

Subtractive attack: Subtractive attacks refer to the attacker deleting a certain proportion of tuples in an attempt to destroy the watermark. Assuming that the relation R is watermarked with γ fraction of tuples watermarked and the attacker deletes k randomly chosen tuples out of the n tuples, the relation R' with the remaining $n - k$ tuples is checked for watermark presence. Since each tuple is independently watermarked, the number of watermarked tuples left are $(n-k)/\gamma$. Each of these tuples successfully return presence of a watermark bit, and the watermark presence is determined. Assuming that the attacker deletes the tuples randomly, the probability of deleting all $\omega = n/\gamma$ watermarked tuples depends on the number of tuples k chosen for deletion. The first condition evidently is

```
Input: Potential owners U = {u₁, u₂, ..., uₙ}. Secret parameter list of each uᵢ,
       ℐᵤᵢ = {𝒦ᵢ, γᵢ, υᵢ, ξᵢ}, confidence level θ, Potential owners' versions of the
       watermarked relation {R₁, R₂, ..., Rₙ}
Output: Owner O
forall uᵢ ∈ U do
   if detect(Rᵢ, ℐᵤᵢ) == {false, R'ᵢ} then
   |   U = U \ uᵢ;
   end
   if detect(Rᵢ, ℐᵤᵢ) == {true, Rᵢʳᵉᵛ} then
   |   if {uⱼ : detect(Rᵢʳᵉᵛ, uᵢ) == {true, Rₜₑₘₚ}, ∀j ≠ i} ≠ null then
   |   |   U = U \ uᵢ;
   |   end
   end
   return U;
end
```

Algorithm 7. Rightful owner identification in presence of secondary watermarking

$k \geq \omega$. The probability of deleting ω tuples is given in Equation 10. If R contains 200 tuples, out of which 50 tuples are marked, and the attacker removes half of the tuples, the probability of erasing the watermark is approximately 2^{-50}, which is negligible. Deleting more than half tuples in the relation marginally increases the probability of erasing the watermark but at the same time, makes the data less useful for the attacker.

$$P(d) = \frac{\frac{k!}{(k-\omega)!} \times (n-\omega)!}{n!} = \sum_{i=0}^{\omega-1} \left(\frac{k-i}{n-i} \right) \tag{10}$$

Sorting/ Shuffling attacks: Since each tuple is watermarked independently, sorting and shuffling attacks are ineffective against the watermarking scheme.

Distortive attacks: We assume that attacker knows the value of ξ. The fraction of attributes distorted by the attacker is λ, hence the total tuples modified are $\zeta = n/\lambda$. The attacker randomly chooses ζ tuples and distorts all ξ bits in these. The objective of the attacker is to change at least $\tau = (1 - \theta) \times \omega$ watermark bits in order to render the watermark undetectable. Equation 11 [1] gives the probability of success for such attacks. Experimental results show that for $\lambda = 2$, the watermark scheme survival rate is close to 91%.

$$\mathcal{P}(\mathcal{A}) = \sum_{i=\tau}^{\omega} \frac{\binom{\omega}{i}\binom{n-\omega}{\zeta-i}}{\binom{n}{\zeta}} \tag{11}$$

False Positives: The watermarking scheme has a false positive probability provided in Equation 12. We attempted to detect our watermark in 20,000 randomly generated unmarked relations and we had zero detections, confirming that the probability of false positives is negligible. The average percentage of watermark bits detected in the 20,000 relations were 50.049% which is understandable given that each randomly chosen bit can have values 0 or 1 with equal probabilities.

$$P(\frac{mc}{tc} \geq \theta) = \sum_{i=1}^{tc \times (1-\theta)} 2^{-tc} \tag{12}$$

Additive attacks/Secondary watermarking: If parties $\{p_1, \ldots, p_n\}$ watermark different instances of the same relation and claim ownership of the watermarked relation (R_i is the watermarked copy of p_i), the aim is to identify the rightful owner from these n candidates.

If the watermark of p_i is detected in R_j ($i \neq j$), it implies that p_i owns a relations from which R_j is eventually derived, thereby eliminating p_j from the contention. Thus, if **only** p_x's watermark is detected for relation R_x, then p_x is the rightful owner. Algorithm 7 identifies the correct owner from multiple potential candidates. We used the watermarking scenario described in Figure 1 for testing our claims. We watermarked the relations with different keys for different users after introducing 30% distortions in an attempt to destroy the previous watermark. The results of the experiments are given in Table 1. We assume that the candidates are $\{C, u_2, u_4, u_7, u_{10}, u_{12}\}$ and the other users are not located.

The experiments show that watermark of only the watermark of C was detected in relation R_1 implying that C is the rightful owner. Watermark of at least one other party was detected in relations claimed by parties other than C. Watermark of C was not detected only in R_{12} since the concerned relation had been distorted sequentially by four parties, thereby making effective distortion to be $1 - 0.7^4 = 76\%$.

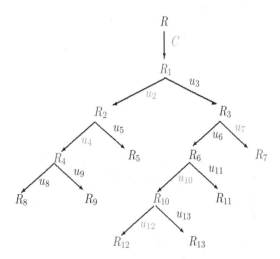

Fig. 1. Secondary watermarking scenario - identified users highlighted in red and their relations in blue

Table 1. Rightful owner identification results ($\checkmark$: detected, $\rtimes$: not detected)

	C	u_2	u_4	u_7	u_{10}	u_{12}
R_1	$\checkmark$	$\rtimes$	$\rtimes$	$\rtimes$	$\rtimes$	$\rtimes$
R_2	$\checkmark$	$\checkmark$	$\rtimes$	$\rtimes$	$\rtimes$	$\rtimes$
R_4	$\checkmark$	$\checkmark$	$\checkmark$	$\rtimes$	$\rtimes$	$\rtimes$
R_7	$\checkmark$	$\rtimes$	$\rtimes$	$\checkmark$	$\rtimes$	$\rtimes$
R_{10}	$\checkmark$	$\rtimes$	$\rtimes$	$\rtimes$	$\checkmark$	$\rtimes$
R_{12}	$\rtimes$	$\rtimes$	$\rtimes$	$\rtimes$	$\checkmark$	$\checkmark$

If Alice publishes a relation R and the watermarked version R_w is given to Mallory. Mallory likes the data and purchases the key to get the original relation, in which case Alice and Mallory sign an agreement stating that the key to recover R was purchased by Mallory from Alice. It is possible that Mallory now embeds his own watermark and distributes the watermarked relation to make a profit. In such a situation, Alice can always use the agreement between her and Mallory as a proof that the relations being distributed belong to her.

5   Experimental Results

We generated 270 sets of random documents each containing 10 attributes and 200 to 2000 tuples to test our scheme for security against distortive attacks. We carried out experiments with θ between 0.6 to 0.75 and distortive attacks ranging from 10% to 50%. These experiments were carried out under mix and match environment of distortive plus subtractive attacks. The overall average detection rate for 20%-50% distortions and 60%-75% confidence levels was 94.125%. This is significantly higher than the detection rate after attack of [1]. Figure 2 illustrates the detection success rates with varying θ, λ for $\gamma = 10$.

Experiments were carried out to test the effect of varying the fraction of tuples watermarked, γ. We set $\theta = 0.40$ and the results indicate that having a smaller fraction and thereby a higher number of watermark-carrying tuples is beneficial

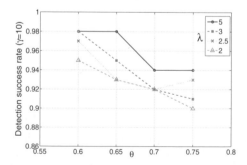

Fig. 2. Changes in survival rate with varying confidence level θ and attack level λ (watermarking fraction γ fixed at 10)

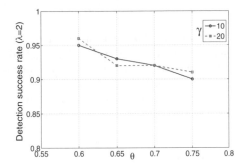

Fig. 3. Changes in survival rate with varying watermarking fraction γ and confidence level θ (attack level λ fixed at 2)

for detection of watermark. The most critical set of experiments were carried out with $\theta = 0.50$ and the results of the experiments are illustrated in Figure 3. We can see that the detection success rate is around 91% for the values of γ between 50 and 100.

6   Conclusion

In this paper, we have proposed an improvement over the reversible and blind watermark scheme proposed in [5] that offers high security against subtractive, distortive, shuffling, and additive (secondary watermarking) attacks. The scheme does not suffer from the *neighbourhood* of powers of two problem described in the paper. Our scheme has the following features which mark significant improvement over other models for watermarking database relations:

1. The scheme introduces less distortion in the data items, with an adjustable upper bound, in order to maintain usability.
2. Experiments show that the scheme has an average successful detection rate of 91% even if half the values in the relation distorted by the attacker, which is a significant improvement over previous schemes proposed in [2,1].
3. The scheme has extremely low false positives confirmed with experimental results showing no accidental watermark detections in 20,000 randomly generated unmarked relations.
4. Even if the attacker re-watermarks an already marked database relation, the rightful owner can be identified by the virtue of reversibility.

The current assumption in database watermarking is that the attacker cannot change the primary key. This enables us to symmetrically identify the tuples and attributes carrying the watermark. Our future work is directed towards eliminating this requirement and constructing a watermarking scheme that detects watermarks under the presence of attacks, including primary key modifications.

References

1. Agrawal, R., Kiernan, J.: Watermarking relational databases. In: Proceedings of the 28th International Conference on Very Large Databases VLDB (2002)
2. Agrawal, R., Kiernan, J.: Watermarking relational data: framework, algorithms and analysis. The VLDB Journal 12(2), 157–169 (2003)
3. Alattar, A.: Reversible watermark using the difference expansion of a generalized integer transform. IEEE Transactions on Image Processing 13(8), 1147–1156 (2004)
4. Gross-Amblard, D.: Query-preserving watermarking of relational databases and xml documents. In: Proceedings of the 20th ACM Symposium on Principles of Database Systems, pp. 191–201 (June 2003)
5. Gupta, G., Pieprzyk, J.: Reversible and blind database watermarking using difference expansion. In: eForensics 2008: Proceedings of 1st International Conference on Forensic applications and techniques in telecommunications, information, and multimedia workshop, ICST, Brussels, Belgium, pp. 1–6 (2008); ICST (Institute for Computer Sciences, Social-Informatics and Telecommunications Engineering)
6. Tsai, C.-S., Chu, Y.-P., Feng, J.-B., Lin, I.-C.: Reversible watermarking: Current status and key issues. International Journal of Network Security 2(3), 161–171 (2006)
7. Li, Y., Deng, R.H.: Publicly verifiable ownership protection for relational databases. In: Proceedings of the 2006 ACM Symposium on Information, computer and communications security, ASIACCS 2006, pp. 78–89. ACM, New York (2006)
8. Sion, R., Atallah, M., Prabhakar, S.: On watermarking numeric sets. In: Petitcolas, F.A.P., Kim, H.-J. (eds.) IWDW 2002. LNCS, vol. 2613, pp. 130–146. Springer, Heidelberg (2003)
9. Tian, J.: Reversible data embedding using a difference expansion. IEEE Transactions on Circuits and Systems for Video Technology 13(8), 890–896 (2003)

A Robust Damage Assessment Model for Corrupted Database Systems

Ge Fu[1,2], Hong Zhu[1], and Yingjiu Li[2]

[1]Huazhong University of Science and Technology, 430074, Wuhan, P.R. China
[2]Singapore Management University, 80 Stamford Road, 178902, Singapore
fuge@smail.hust.edu.cn, yjli@smu.edu.sg, whzhuhong@gmail.com

Abstract. An intrusion tolerant database uses damage assessment techniques to detect damage propagation scales in a corrupted database system. Traditional damage assessment approaches in a intrusion tolerant database system can only locate damages which are caused by reading corrupted data. In fact, there are many other damage spreading patterns that have not been considered in traditional damage assessment model. In this paper, we systematically analyze inter-transaction dependency relationships that have been neglected in the previous research and propose four different dependency relationships between transactions which may cause damage propagation. We extend existing damage assessment model based on the four novel dependency relationships. The essential properties of our model is also discussed.

Keywords: Data integrity, database recovery, damage assessment.

1   Introduction

A database system being able to detect intrusions and recover compromised data back to a consistent state is claimed to be an intrusion tolerant database system (or attack resistant, or self healing system) [1][2][3][4][5]. As it is shown in Fig. 1, most intrusion tolerant database systems consist of the following modules: System Log, Intrusion Detector, Damage Assessor, and Data Repairer. The clients commit various transactions to execute the application logic, and these transactions affect the integrity and consistency of a database system. The Intrusion Detector tracks clients' behaviors, and detects intrusion activities of malicious clients based on the system log. For the data that is corrupted by malicious transactions, the Damage Assessor detects the scale of damage propagation and the Data Repairer generates compensation transactions to repair the compromised data. An intrusion tolerant database is built based on a traditional relational model. It can be considered as an extension to the relational database system since the modules can be either built into the kernel of DBMS [3][4][5][6] or developed on top of DBMS (serves as a middleware between DBMS and the clients)[1][2].

The technologies of intrusion detection, transaction processing, and database auditing can be used to develop an intrusion tolerant database system. Damage Assessment is the most critical phase during the whole damage recovery

A. Prakash and I. Sen Gupta (Eds.): ICISS 2009, LNCS 5905, pp. 237–251, 2009.
© Springer-Verlag Berlin Heidelberg 2009

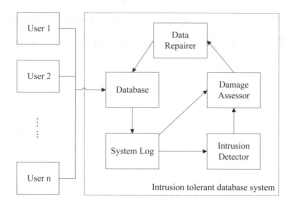

Fig. 1. Architecture of a fault tolerant database system

process[7]. The Damage assessor concerns the issues on how the damage appears and in what way the damage can be detected and exposed. Nowadays, most damage assessment algorithms rely on a model on how innocent data are affected in a compromised database system (denoted damage spreading patterns). The model evaluates damage spreading patterns by analyzing the dependencies between transactions. A *Read-Write Dependency* is the most common damage spreading pattern: in a transaction history H: T_1, ..., T_2.... Supposing transaction T_2 reads the results modified by transaction T_1 (we claim that transaction T_2 is read-write dependent upon T_1), and then writes data x to the database system, then we say transaction T_2 is affected by T_1 and data x is corrupted. Existing damage assessment models deal with this kind of damage spreading pattern, and various algorithms and prototypes were developed based on it. However, except for the Read-Write Dependency, do there exist any other dependency relationships between transactions that cause damage spreading? To answer this question, some deeper issues towards the inter-transaction dependencies should be referred to. In essence, the dependency between transactions derives from the issue of data sharing. The read or write operations in different transactions towards the same data may generate a dependency relationship between the transactions. For a data item x and transaction T_1 and T_2 (T_2 is scheduled after T_1), there are totally four data sharing modes that may connect T_1 and T_2 together: 1)∃ a read operation r_1 in T_1 and a read operation r_2 in T_2, r_1 and r_2 read x; 2)∃ a read operation r_1 in T_1 and a write operation w_2 in T_2, r_1 read x and w_2 write x; 3)∃ a write operation w_1 in T_1 and a read operation r_2 in T_2, w_1 write x and r_2 read x; 4) ∃ a write operation w_1 in T_1 and a write operation w_2 in T_2, both w_1 and w_2 write x. We denote above four situations Read-Read mode, Write-Read mode, Read-Write mode, and Write-Write mode separately. The Read-Read and Write-Read modes do not lead to a dependency relationship from T_2 to T_1 because the read operation in transaction T_2 can not cause a state transition for database system (we claim that only write operations can change the DB state). So we focus on the Read-Write and Write-Write modes, and extract dependency relationships between transactions due to the two categories of data sharing modes.

In this paper, we systematically analyze the dependency relationships between transactions corresponding to the Read-Write and Write-Write data sharing modes. We proposed four novel inter-transaction dependency relationships which may lead to damage propagation, and illustrate how these dependencies help the damages to spread to a larger scale. Based on that, we propose our damage assessment model to detect affected transactions that are corrupted by the malicious transactions due to the new proposed inter-transaction dependencies. The model is an essential extension to existing read-write dependency model, and makes the results of damage recovery more accurate.

The rest of the paper is organized as follows: section 2 is devoted to the review of existing damage assessment methods and damage repair systems. In section 3 we analyze the dependency relationships between transactions according to the Read-Write and Write-Write data sharing modes, and give the formal descriptions of four inter-transaction dependencies which may cause damage propagation. In section 4, we propose an extended damage assessment model by taking the new dependency relationships into account. Section 5 discusses the essential features of our model.

2 Related Work

There are mainly two categories of damage assessment models. The first is *Application Level Damage Tracking* [6][8]. In this model, an application-program-analyzer module is constructed to capture the damage propagation in the application layer. Supposing a variable x in a program is corrupted by a malicious user, damage can be spread to the data whose producer references to the variable x. Furthermore, in case that an IF-ELSE code fragment references to the variable x, the control logic for the program can be changed and the damage may be propagated due to the corrupted logic control caused by variable x. Application level damage tracking is devoted to capture above damage spreading patterns and record the related information so as to facilitate the recovery activities (e.g. the before image of corrupted data). The second damage assessment model is *Inter-Transaction Dependency Tracking*. This model assesses the damage scale in the layer of database system. Transactions which have a dependency relationship with the malicious transactions are identified as affected and those data whose producer is affected are labeled corrupted. A Read-Write Dependency is the most common damage spreading pattern investigated so far. Yu *et al.* proposed another damage spreading pattern: Control Dependency [9]. Transaction T_2 being control dependent on T_1 indicates that the execution of transaction T_2 is determined by transaction T_1. In database layer, the control dependency is mainly caused by triggers. A control dependency on a malicious transaction causes damage spreading to an incorrect execution path. Since triggers can be considered as a fragment of code, so to some extent, the control dependency is much similar to application level tracking.

Comparing the two models, the application level damage tracking is more accurate and effective. In the application layer, the inherent program structure can describe the read-write dependency relationship between data evidently, while on the contrary, the SQL is not capable to express the complicated semantics (the sequence, branch and cycle structure (IF-ELSE, WHILE etc.)) if stored procedure is not used. However, in database level, a log of transaction history can be easily obtained from the inherent mechanisms in DBMS such as auditing and trigger, so that the damage tracking becomes not so complicated based on the transaction log. Due to the simplicity and efficiency of database level tracking, the inter-transaction dependency tracking model draws much attention in recent decades. Up to now, most self-healing systems still adopt the inter-transaction dependency tracking model for the damage assessment [3][10][11][12].

Existing inter-transaction dependency tracking model is incomplete, and certain dependencies between transactions have not been concerned. Consequently, the damage assessment algorithms causes a violation to Completeness Criteria for damage recovery [9]. To address this problem, we systematically discuss the inter-transaction dependencies that may cause damage spreading in this paper.

3   Inter-transaction Dependency Relationships Analysis

As it is described above, the damage propagation is mainly caused by the Read-Write mode and Write-Write mode of data sharing. Extracting the Read-Write Dependency relationship between transactions is the basic resolution in current damage assessment model. This method mainly contributes to discover the damage propagation caused by the Read-Write mode. In this section, we focus on the Write-Write data sharing mode and analyze which kind of inter-transaction dependency relationships related to this data sharing mode may cause damage spreading. We discover four categories of inter-transaction dependency relationships which may produce compromised data.

There is a special dependency relationship between transactions: In a transaction history $H : T_1...T_2...$ where transaction T_2 is not read-write dependent on transaction T_1. If we construct a new transaction history $H' : ...T_2...$ which indicates that if transaction T_1 doesn't execute, then in transaction history H', transaction T_2 should have read some data which were modified by transaction T_1 in history H. Furthermore, if T_1 is malicious, T_2 should be regarded as an affected transaction and captured by the damage assessment. It seems that T_1 and T_2 are connected with some phantoms data which T_2 should have read in semantics (see an example in Fig.2). We refer to this kind of inter-transaction dependency as *Phantoms Dependency* (note that the concept has been mentioned in [6][13][14]). The Phantoms Dependency is an important damage propagation pattern which has significant destructive power on database systems. Unfortunately, the former inter-transaction dependency tracking model does not consider the Phantoms Dependency, thus the damage assessment algorithms are not completely effective.

Application Logic:
An increase of commodity prices: we need the price of commodity whose price is more than *$500* increased by *10%*.
Intrusion Activity:
Assume that before the price increase activity occurs, there is a malicious transaction B_1 modifies the product rice's price
from *$400* to *$600*. The correspondent transaction history is described as follows:
Correlated Database Layer SQL statements:
G_0: UPDATE *product* SET *price* = 600 WHERE *product_name* = "*rice*";
B_1: UPDATE *product* SET *price* = 400 WHERE *product_name* = "*rice*";
G_1: UPDATE *product* SET *price* = $1.1 * price$ WHERE *price* > 500;

- In the application above, we can see that transaction G_1 did not read from B_1, and thus there was no read-write dependency from G_1 to B_1. So in traditional inter-transaction damage tracking model, G_1 would not been treated as an affected transaction, and only malicious transaction B_1 would be undone.
- Suppose we only undid malicious transaction B1, then the price of product rice was written back to *$400*. But is that the correct recovery result? Obviously no, because all products' prices increased by *10%*, except for the product rice! Therefore, we conclude that the execution of transaction B_1 did affect transaction G_1, and G_1 was no longer innocent.
- In a deeper sight, if B_1 did not exist, G_1 should have read the record "rice" and made modifications on its price. But in fact, the transaction B_1 did exist, and the undo transaction for B_1 made the recovery result incomplete for the product rice's price did not increase. Some modifications requested by transaction G_1 were lost. In the common sense, It seemed that G_1 was affected by B_1 for G_1 read a phantom data "rice". We denote the dependency from G_1 to B_1 as *Phantoms Dependency*. A novel damage assessment approach should be proposed to track this dependency and identify G_1 as an affected transaction.

Fig. 2. Phantoms Dependency between transactions

In a transaction history, some transactions' execution is dependent on other transactions so as to satisfy the inherent integrity constraints in DBMSs, such as Entity Integrity, Domain Integrity, and Reference Integrity). On the point of security, the integrity constrains may also help to propagate damage in the context of data sharing: Suppose that an innocent transaction's execution is dependent upon a malicious transaction so that the integrity constraints are bypassed for the innocent transaction, it can be indicated that the innocent transaction is not benign any more and it is probable to cause damage propagation. We summarize three categories of inter-transaction dependencies related to the inherent integrity constraints as follows:

Pseudo-Identity Dependency. In some cases, the execution of an innocent transaction is dependent upon a malicious transaction so that it bypasses the Entity Integrity Constraint. For the instance described in Fig.3, malicious transaction B deletes a record (*product_id*="*P002*") in table product (subfigure (b)), and then innocent transaction G inserts a new tuple with the same primary key *product_id P002* (see subfigure (c)). In this transaction history, it is obvious

product_id (PK)	name	price
P000	rice	$400
P001	banana	$230
P002	orange	$120
P003	apple	$100
P004	flour	$460

(a) Initial state of table *product*

product_id (PK)	name	price
P000	rice	$400
P001	banana	$230
P003	apple	$100
P004	flour	$460

(b) Malicious transaction B deletes the record with *product_id="P002"*

product_id (PK)	name	price
P000	rice	$400
P001	banana	$230
P003	apple	$100
P004	flour	$460
P002	grape	$320

(c) innocent transaction G inserts a new record with *product_id="P002"*

Fig. 3. Pseudo-Identity Dependency between transactions

that the execution of transaction G is dependent on B (if the product *P002* was not deleted by transaction B, transaction G could not have been executed successfully). In our intuitive feeling, transaction G creates a new entity with a pseudo identity to substitute the historical object so as to satisfy the entity integrity constraint. We denote this kind of dependency from G to B as *Pseudo-Identity Dependency*. The transactions that have a pseudo-identity dependency relationship with a malicious transaction should be considered as affected. Unfortunately, the Pseudo-Identity Dependency can not be captured by current damage assessment algorithms.

Domain-Integrity Dependency. The execution of an innocent transaction is dependent upon a malicious transaction so that it can satisfy the Domain Integrity Constraint. There are mainly two categories of domain integrity constraints (namely *CHECK* constrains) in DBMSs: field integrity constraint (e.g. *CHECK*($column1 < 50$)) and row integrity constraint (e.g. *CHECK*($column1 < colmn2$)). The inherent row integrity constraints in DBMSs protect the security of database systems; however, they are not capable to prevent all damage spreading patterns. For the example in Fig.4, suppose that the application logic requires the purchase price be lower than retail price and imposes a row integrity constraint *CHECK*($p\_price < r\_price$). The initial state for table *product* is given in Subfigure (a). Now consider the following scenario: malicious transaction B modifies product *P000*'s *p_price* to *$350* (Subfigure (b)), and then, innocent transaction G renews product *P000*'s *r_price* to *$360* (Subfigure (c)). In this transaction history, there seems no *CHECK* constrains violation, but

product_id (PK)	p_price	r_price
P000	$400	$500
P001	$230	$246
P002	$460	$486

(a) Initial state of table *product*, where a domain integrity constraint $CHECK(p\_price < r\_price)$ is imposed on table *product*

product_id (PK)	p_price	r_price
P000	$350	$500
P001	$230	$246
P002	$460	$486

(b) Malicious transaction B updates the record with *product_id="P000"* and decreases *purchase_price* to *$350*

product_id(PK)	p_price	r_price
P000	$350	$360
P001	$230	$246
P002	$460	$486

(c) Innocent transaction G *UPDATE* the record with *product_id="P000"* and decreases *retail_price* to *$360*

Fig. 4. Domain-Integrity Dependency between transactions

the damage spreading does occur: transaction G's UPDATE operation is dependent on B; in other words, if B did not exist, G would not have been executed successfully due to the *CHECK* constraint imposed on table *product* (if B did not exist, G renewed *r_price* to *$360*, then the function $CHECK(\$400<\$360)$ would return a value *false*). Therefore, the *CHECK* can not deal with this pattern of damage propagation, and even worse, one can not recover the product *P000*'s *p_price* to the correct value (because when the recovery activity to undo the product's *p_price* to *$400* was launched, the function $CHECK(\$400<\$360)$ would return a value *false*). In our work, we denote the dependency relationship from transaction G to B as *Domain-Integrity Dependency*, and incorporate it in our damage assessment model.

Reference-Integrity Dependency. As we all know, the inherent Reference Integrity Constraints in DBMSs provides the SET-NULL and CASCADE policy to protect data consistency in data sharing [15]. However, these two policies also help to propagate new damage if they are utilized by an intruder: A malicious DELETE operation on the main table will impose a negative impact on the slave table if a SET-NULL or CASCADE policy exists in the main and slave tables. Fortunately, the trigger mechanism in DBMSs facilitates traditional damage assessment models to recover the cascade deleted data in slave tables (the cascade delete operations in the slave tables can be captured by triggers). However, there is still a possibility that some innocent transactions depend upon a malicious transaction and thus bypass the reference integrity Constraint and cause damage propagation. For the instance in Fig.5, the main table *product* and the slave table *order* with a foreign key constraint *order (p_id)* referencing *product(product_id)* (see Subfigure (a) and (b)). Now assume that a malicious transaction B creates a product *P002* (see Subfigure (c)) and that an innocent transaction G

product_id (PK)	p_price	r_price
P000	$400	$500
P001	$230	$246

(a) Main table *product*

order_id(PK)	p_id(FK)	quantity
O001	P000	500
O002	P001	300

(b) Initial state of slave table *order*, where a foreign key constraint in which *order(p_id)* references to *product(product_id)* without any CASCADE policy

product_id (PK)	p_price	r_price
P000	$400	$500
P001	$230	$246
P002	$460	$486

(c) Malicious transaction *B* inserts a product with *product_id="P002"* into main table *product*

order_id(PK)	p_id(FK)	quantity
O001	P000	500
O002	P001	300
O003	P002	260

(d) Innocent transaction *G* inserts a new order that references to product *P002*

Fig. 5. Reference-Integrity Dependency between transactions

generates a new order *O003* referencing product *P002*. It is obvious that the execution of transaction *G* is dependent on *B*. This dependency relationship should be captured by damage assessment algorithms. We refer to this kind of dependency from *G* to *B* as *Reference-Integrity Dependency*. Traditional damage assessment models cannot discover the damage spreading patterns caused by Reference-Integrity Dependency. Even worse, the corrupted data caused by *B* could not be recovered in traditional models: the rollback transaction for *B* would delete product *P002* in the main table *product*. If a DO-NULL policy is used for the reference integrity constraint, the DELETE operation will return an error; otherwise, if a SET-NULL policy is imposed on the tables, the recovery for transaction *B* is incomplete because the order *O003* still existed with the foreign key *p_id* being set to *null*. Only the CASCADE policy will bring a complete recovery.

4   Damage Assessment Model

In this section, we give the formal definitions for the Phantoms Dependency, Pseudo-Identity Dependency, Domain-Integrity Dependency and Reference-Integrity Dependency between transactions. Meanwhile, a detail on how these inter-transaction dependencies cause damage spreading is explained. Finally, we propose our extended damage assessment model which is devoted to discover the new damage propagation patterns relative to the new defined inter-transaction dependencies.

4.1   Preliminaries

Before we propose the damage assessment model, we first introduce some basic concepts. A transaction history to be repaired is a serializable history generated under the *two phase locking principle*. We denote the committed malicious transactions in a history by a set $B=\{B_1, B_2, ..., B_m\}$, and the committed benign transactions in a history by a collection $G=\{G_1, G_2, ..., G_n\}$. For a transaction history H over $B \cup G$, we define $<_H$ as the usual partial order on $B \cup G$ for history H, where $T_i <_H T_j$ indicates that the operations of T_i are scheduled before the conflicting operations of T_j. Two operations conflict if they are on the same data item and at least one is write operation. Two transactions conflict if they have conflicting operations[1]. Even if transactions T_i and T_j are not conflict transactions, we still use the notation $T_i <_H T_j$ to denote that T_i is scheduled before T_j by DBMS.

As our best knowledge, in DBMS, a write-involved SQL statement t is executed in the following process: 1) DBMS loads the data blocks requested by t to the main memory; and 2) DBMS writes back the modified data from main memory to DB files after t is executed. So on this point, we assume that when a write-involved SQL statement executes a write operation requesting data set x, implicitly, it has a read operation towards x firstly. For example, a write-involved SQL statement could be UPDATE *product* SET *price* $= 1.1 * price$ WHERE *price* > 500. In semantics, it is equivalent to the sequence: SELECT *price* FROM *product* WHERE *price* > 500, and UPDATE *product* SET *price* $= 1.1*price$ WHERE *price* > 500. Therefore a write-involved SQL statement can be divided into a read operation and a succeeding write operation (this method was used in the damage assessment algorithms in [3][6]). In our work, when we mention the read operation, it not only refers to the SELECT operation, but also the read operations in the write-involved statements. Formally, a read operation on a data item x for transaction T is denoted by *[SELECT, x, img, T]*[1].

The UPDATE statement has the semantics that it modifies certain data to new values. In a transaction history, it can be assumed that an UNDATE statement is equivalent to a sequence of a DELETE operation and a succeeding INSERT operation (for example, for a UPDATE involved statement UPDATE *product* SET *price* $= \$100$ WHERE *product_id* $=$ ”*P001*”, the statement first deletes the product *P001*'s price and then inserts a new value *$100* in the same position). For simplicity, we use DELETE operations to denote the DELETE statements and the DELETE semantics for UPDATE involved statements; similarly, we refer to the INSERT statements and the INSERT semantics for UPDATE involved statements as INSERT operations. Therefore, an UPDATE statement can be substituted by the sequence of an DELETE operation and a succeeding INSERT operation. Meanwhile, we claim that the write operation consists of INSERT and DELETE operations (the objective is to omit UPDATE

---

[1] In the label *[SELECT, x, img, T]*, *img* represents the value of data item x. We denote data item x with a three-tuple $x(table,v\_pk,column)$ where v_pk refers to the value of the primary key of *table*, and it identifies the row number of data x.

operations for simplicity). Formally, a write operation is denoted as *[OPTYPE, item, b_img, a_img, tran_id]*[2].

The existing models to detect the damage propagation are mainly based on the Read-Write Dependency relationship between transactions. Previous works [1][16] give the definition of Read-Write Dependency relationship, and we introduce it to our work.

Definition 1 (*Read-Write Dependency*). Transaction T_j is Read-Write Dependent upon transaction T_i in a transaction history if there exists a data item x such that:

1) T_j reads x after T_i wrote x;
2) T_i does not abort before T_j reads x;
3) every transaction that writes x between the time when T_i writes x and the time when T_j reads x is aborted.

In our work, we use the notation $\to_W$ to denote the Read-Write Dependency. Transaction T_j is Read-Write Dependent upon transaction T_i is denoted by $T_i \to_W T_j$.

4.2   Phantoms Dependency

Section 3 describes the problem for phantoms dependency. Intuitively, transaction T_2 is dependent on T_1 because T_2 reads a phantoms data from T_1. In other words, if we change the transaction history and add an undo transaction UT_1 behind T_1, then in the new transaction history, T_2 may read from T_1. On this point of view, we propose the formal definition for the phantoms dependency as follows:

Definition 2 (*Phantoms Dependency*). Consider a transaction history $H{:}..., T_1, ..., T_2,...$ that satisfies:

1) there exists a write operation op_1 in T_1 and an read operation op_2 in T_2;
2) $T_1 <_H T_2$;
3) $T_1 \to_W T_2$ does not hold.

Let s_1 be the set of data written by op_1. Assume that transactions are executed according to another transaction history $H'{:}..., T_2, ...$ (where transaction T_1 is removed from transaction history H). Let s_2 be the set of data read by op_2 in transaction history H'. If $s_1 \cap s_2 \neq \varnothing$, we say T_2 is Phantoms Dependent upon T_1, and operations op_1 and op_2 are Phantoms Conflict operations.

We use the notation $\to_P$ to denote the Phantoms Dependency. Transaction T_j being phantoms dependent upon transaction T_i is denoted by $T_i \to_P T_j$.

---

[2] Here *[OPTYPE, item, b_img, a_img, tran_id]* means that the transaction *tran_id* writes the data *item* and modifies its value from *b_img* to *a_img*. OPTYPE∈{INSERT, DELETE}. For *OPTYPE*=DELETE, *a_img* is *null* while for *OPTYPE*=INSERT, *b_img*=*null*.

4.3 Pseudo-identity Dependency

As described in section 2, some transactions' execution is dependent on some other transactions so that the Entity Integrity Constraint may be bypassed. This inter-transaction dependency may cause damage propagation if a malicious transaction is dependent. This dependency should be considered in the damage assessment model.

Definition 3 (*Pseudo-Identity Dependency*). Given a transaction history $H{:}...$, $T_1,..., T_2,...$ and two conflict transactions T_1 and T_2 that satisfy:

1) $T_1 <_H T_1$;
2) there exist a DELETE operation op_1 *[DELETE, x, b_img, -, T_1]* in T_1 and an INSERT operation op_2 *[INSERT, x, -, a_img, T_2]* in T_2, where $x.column$ is the PRIMARY KEY or UNIQUE KEY of $x.table$.

Then we say transaction T_2 is Pseudo-Identity Dependent upon T_1, and operations op_1 and op_2 are Pseudo-Identity conflict operations.

We use the notation $\rightarrow_I$ to denote the Pseudo-Identity Dependency. Transaction T_j being pseudo-identity dependent upon transaction T_i is denoted by $T_i \rightarrow_I T_j$.

4.4 Domain-Integrity Dependency

The domain integrity dependency is derived from the row level domain integrity constraint. It means that if two transactions each has a INSERT operation towards the same row and if the data items that the INSERT operations write are restricted by the *CHECK* constraint, then there is a domain integrity dependency relationship between the two transactions.

Definition 4 (*Domain-Integrity Dependency*). Given a transaction history $H{:}...$, $T_1, ..., T_2,...$ and two transactions T_1 and T_2 ($T_1 <_H T_2$) in H that satisfy:

1) there exist INSERT operations op_1 *[INSERT, x, -, v_1, T_1]* and op_2 *[INSERT, y, -, v_2, T_2]* satisfying that $x.v\_pk = y.v\_pk$, and $x.table = y.table$;
2) there exists a row-level domain integrity constraint $CHECK[col_1, col_2, ..., col_n]^3$ ($n \geq 2$) on $x.table$ and $x.column, y.column \in \{col_1, col_2, ..., col_n\}$.

we say transaction T_2 is Domain-Integrity Dependent upon T_1, and operations op_1 and op_2 are Domain-Integrity conflict operations.

We use the notation $\rightarrow_D$ to denote the Domain-Integrity Dependency. Transaction T_j being domain-integrity dependent upon transaction T_i is denoted by $T_i \rightarrow_D T_j$.

4.5 Reference-Integrity Dependency

The reference integrity constraints also lead to dependency relationships between transactions: when a transaction with an INSERT operation which references to

---

[3] Here col_1, col_2, ..., col_n denote the constrained columns for the *CHECK* constraint.

another table, this dependency is formulated. We define this kind of dependency as follows:

Definition 5 (*Reference-Integrity Dependency*). Consider a transaction history $H:..., T_1, ..., T_2,...$ and two transactions T_1 and T_2 ($T_1 <_H T_2$) in H that satisfy:

1) there exist INSERT operations op_1 *[INSERT, x, -, v_1, T_1]* and op_2 *[INSERT, y, -, v_2, T_2]* and

2) there exists a reference integrity constraint from *y.table (y.column)* to *x.table (x.column)* so that the insertion of v_2 is referenced to the value of v_1.

We say transaction T_2 is Reference-Integrity Dependent upon T_1, and operations op_1 and op_2 are Reference-Integrity conflict operations.

We use the notation $\rightarrow_R$ to denote the Reference-Integrity Dependency. Transaction T_j being reference-integrity dependent upon transaction T_i is denoted by $T_i \rightarrow_R T_j$.

4.6   Damage Assessment Model

With a set of malicious transactions as input, the damage assessment algorithm outputs the affected transactions as well as the corrupted data in a transaction history so as to recovery the database to a consistent state. The assessment process is based on a transaction dependency relation which is maintained in the execution period of transactions. The transaction dependency relation keeps track of phantoms dependency, pseudo-identity dependency, domain-integrity dependency and reference-integrity dependency between transactions. The formal definition of transaction dependency relation is given below:

Definition 6 (*Transaction Dependency Relation for a Transaction History*). Given a transaction history H, and a binary relations $D = \{< T_i, T_j > | T_i \rightarrow_W T_j$, or $T_i \rightarrow_P T_j$, or $T_i \rightarrow_I T_j$, or $T_i \rightarrow_D T_j$, or $T_i \rightarrow_R T_j\}$ in H, the transaction dependency relation D_H in history H is defined to satisfy $D_H = t(D)$ (here $t(D)$ represents the transitive closure of relation D).

Notation "$\rightarrow$" is introduced to denote the transaction dependency between two transactions. Let $T_i \rightarrow T_j$ denote $< T_i, T_j > \in D_H$.

In a transaction history $H: B \cup G$, where B is the set of malicious transactions and $G = \neg B$. The damage assessment discovers the set of affected transactions A according to following recursive definition:

1) if $< B_k, T_i > \in D_H$, where D_H is the transaction dependency relation in H, then $T_i \in A$;

2) if $T_i \in A$ and $< T_i, T_j > \in D_H$, then $T_j \in A$.

5   Discussion

To explain the damage assessment model, we construct a transaction history H based on tables *product* and *order* in Fig.6 as follows:

p_id (PK)	name	p_price	r_price
P000	apple	$400	$500
P001	orange	$600	$700
P003	rice	$100	$110

(a) Initial state of table *product*

o_id(PK)	p_id(FK)	quantity
O001	P000	500
O002	P001	300

(b) Initial state of table *order*.

– A foreign key constraint in which *order(p_id)* references to *product(product_id)*, and a domain integrity constraint $CHECK(p\_price < r\_price)$ are imposed on table *product*.

Fig. 6. A sample database to explain our damage assessment model

– T_0: INSERT INTO *product* VALUES (”*P004*”,”*flour*”, 30, 50);
– T_1: INSERT INTO *product* VALUES (”*P002*”,”*grape*”, 460, 486);
– T_2: UPDATE *product* SET *r_price* = ”650” WHERE *p_id* = ”*P001*”;
– T_3: SELECT *p_id* FROM *product* WHERE *name* = ”*grape*”;
  UPDATE *shopping_cart* SET *quatity* = 1 WHERE *p_id* = ”*P002*”;
– T_4: UPDATE *product* SET *r_price* = 1.1∗*r_price* WHERE *r_price* > 680;
– T_5: UPDATE *product* SET *p_id* = ”*P008*” WHERE *name* = ”*apple*”;
– T_6: INSERT INTO *product* VALUES (”*P000*”,*banana*, 100, 120);
– T_7: UPDATE *product* SET *p_price* = 80 WHERE *p_id* = ”*P003*”;
– T_8: UPDATE *product* SET *r_price* = 90 WHERE *p_id* = ”*P003*”;
– T_9: INSERT INTO *order* VALUES (”*O003*”,”*P002*”, 700);
– T_{10}: UPDATE *product* SET *r_price* = 150 WHERE *p_id* = ”*P004*”;

According to our transaction dependency definitions, we can derive: $T_1 \rightarrow_W T_3$, $T_2 \rightarrow_P T_4$, $T_5 \rightarrow_I T_6$, $T_7 \rightarrow_D T_8$, $T_1 \rightarrow_R T_9$, $T_0 \rightarrow_W T_{10}$. In transaction history H, the transaction dependency relation is $D_H = \{< T_1, T_3 >, < T_2, T_4 >, < T_5, T_6 >, < T_7, T_8 >, < T_1, T_9 >, < T_0, T_{10} >\}$. If the malicious set of transactions is $B = \{T_1, T_2, T_5, T_7\}$, then according to our damage assessment model, the affected transactions set is $A = \{T_3, T_4, T_6, T_8, T_9\}$. Traditional damage assessment model only regards transaction T_3 as affected transactions. In fact, T_4, T_6, T_8, and T_9 are also affected by malicious transactions. Therefore, our model captures a larger scale of damage propagation.

Finally, we discuss some essential features of the four novel transaction dependencies. In essence, the four dependencies can be regarded as an extension to the read-write dependency. For Phantoms Dependency, in above transaction history H, we have $T_2 \rightarrow_P T_4$, since transaction T_4 should have read the record whose *p_id* = ”*P001*” (the UPDATE operation can be seen as a combination operation of SELECT and UPDATE in semantics). The execution process of T_4, can be divided into two steps: 1) looking up all records and picking up the records whose *r_price* > 680; 2) updating the fields ”*r_price*” for related records. From step 1), it's reasonable for us to consider that T_4 has read all records in table *product* including the record whose *p_id* = ”*P001*”. Namely, transaction T_4 implicitly reads from transaction T_2. Therefore, on this point, we can say Phantoms Dependency is an extension of read-write dependency. For Pseudo-Identity dependency in transaction history H, we have $T_5 \rightarrow_I T_6$. The execution process of T_6 can be divided into the following steps: 1) Integrity constrain check: checking whether there is a record in table *product* has the primary key $p\_id = "P000"$; 2) Inserting a new record. In step 1), the integrity constrain check can be considered that transaction T_6 implicitly reads the primary keys of all records, including the records which have been deleted. Consequently, Pseudo-Identity dependency can also be considered as an extension to the read-write dependency. For Domain Integrity and Reference Integrity dependencies, we can consider that the affected transaction implicitly read from another transaction in the period of constraint checking. Therefore, in essence, the four dependencies can be seen as an extension to the read-write dependency. Furthermore, from a technical point of view, it is a complicated process to capture the four dependencies. For Phantoms and Pseudo Identity dependencies, an additional table should be maintained to record the before image of each update involved operations. This is because maintaining the modification history is essential for damage assessment. For Domain Integrity and Reference Integrity dependencies, the constraints check should be transformed to a appropriate "implicit read" action. These properties require a more complicated technical resolution than handling read-write dependency. This also proves the useability of our work.

6   Conclusion and Future Work

In this paper, we systematically analyze the inter-transaction dependencies which may cause damage propagation. We propose to consider four new dependencies in damage assessment. An extended damage assessment model is built according to the dependencies. We also discuss some essential features of these dependencies. Though these dependencies can be regarded as an extension to the read-write dependency, they must be independently evaluated in damage assessment and recovery. We are currently building a damage assessment and recovery prototype based on our model by revamping the kernel of Dameng [17] database system. The evaluation results will be reported in an extension work of this paper.

Acknowledgments

The work presented in this paper is partly supported by 863 hitech research and development program of China (granted number: 2006A A01Z430).

References

1. Ammann, P., Jajodia, S., Liu, P.: Recovery from malicious transactions. IEEE Trans. Knowl. Data Eng. 14(5), 1167–1185 (2002)
2. Luenam, P., Liu, P.: Odar: An on-the-fly damage assessment and repair system for commercial database applications. In: Olivier, M.S., Spooner, D.L. (eds.) DBSec. IFIP Conference Proceedings, vol. 215, pp. 239–252. Kluwer, Dordrecht (2001)

3. Chiueh, T.-c., Pilania, D.: Design, implementation, and evaluation of a repairable database management system. In: ICDE, pp. 1024–1035. IEEE Computer Society, Los Alamitos (2005)
4. Bai, K., Yu, M., Liu, P.: Trace: Zero-down-time database damage tracking, quarantine, and cleansing with negligible run-time overhead. In: Jajodia, S., Lopez, J. (eds.) ESORICS 2008. LNCS, vol. 5283, pp. 161–176. Springer, Heidelberg (2008)
5. Lomet, D., Vagena, Z., Barga, R.: Recovery from "bad" user transactions. In: SIGMOD 2006: Proceedings of the 2006 ACM SIGMOD international conference on Management of data, pp. 337–346. ACM, New York (2006)
6. cker Chiueh, T., Bajpai, S.: Accurate and efficient inter-transaction dependency tracking. In: ICDE, pp. 1209–1218. IEEE, Los Alamitos (2008)
7. Gollmann, D., Meier, J., Sabelfeld, A. (eds.): ESORICS 2006. LNCS, vol. 4189. Springer, Heidelberg (2006)
8. Panda, B., Haque, K.A.: Extended data dependency approach: a robust way of rebuilding database. In: SAC, pp. 446–452. ACM, New York (2002)
9. Yu, M., Liu, P., Zang, W., Jajodia, S.: Trusted recovery. Secure Data Management in Decentralized Systems 33, 59–94 (2007)
10. Luenam, P., Liu, P.: Odam: An on-the-fly damage assessment and repair system for commercial database applications, pp. 446–452 (2003)
11. Yu, M., Zang, W., Liu, P.: Database isolation and filtering against data corruption attacks. In: ACSAC, pp. 97–106. IEEE Computer Society, Los Alamitos (2007)
12. Yu, M., Liu, P., Zang, W.: The implementation and evaluation of a recovery system for workflows. J. Network and Computer Applications 32(1), 158–183 (2009)
13. Zhu, H., Fu, G., Zhu, Y., Jin, R., Lü, K., Shi, J.: Dynamic data recovery for database systems based on fine grained transaction log. In: IDEAS 2008: Proceedings of the 2008 international symposium on Database engineering & applications, pp. 249–253. ACM, New York (2008)
14. Xie, M., Zhu, H., Feng, Y., Hu, G.: Tracking and repairing damaged databases using before image table. In: FCST 2008: Proceedings of the 2008 Japan-China Joint Workshop on Frontier of Computer Science and Technology, Washington, DC, USA, pp. 36–41. IEEE Computer Society, Los Alamitos (2008)
15. Garcia-Molina, H., Ullman, J.D., Widom, J.D.: Database Systems: the Complete Book, 5th edn. Prentice Hall, Englewood Cliffs (2001)
16. Fayad, A., Jajodia, S., McCollum, C.D.: Application-level isolation using data inconsistency detection. In: ACSAC, pp. 119–126. IEEE Computer Society, Los Alamitos (1999)
17. Dameng: http://www.dameng.com/

A Generic Distortion Free Watermarking Technique for Relational Databases

Sukriti Bhattacharya and Agostino Cortesi

Dipartimento di Informatica
Universita Ca' Foscari Venezia
Via Torino 155, 30170 Venezia, Italy
sukriti@dsi.unive.it, cortesi@unive.it
http://www.unive.it

Abstract. In this paper we introduce a distortion free watermarking technique for relational databases based on the Abstract Interpretation framework. The watermarking technique is partition based. The partitioning can be seen as a virtual grouping, which does not change neither the value of the table's elements nor their physical positions. Instead of inserting the watermark directly to the database partition, we treat it as an abstract representation of that concrete partition, such that any change in the concrete domain reflects in its abstract counterpart. The main idea is to generate a binary image of the partition as a watermark of that partition, that serves as ownership proof as well as tamper detection.

Keywords: Database Watermarking, HMAC, Galois Connection, Abstract Interpretation.

1 Introduction

Watermarking is a widely used technique to embed additional but not visible information into the underlying data with the aim of supporting tamper detection, localization, ownership proof, and/or traitor tracing purposes [1]. Watermarking techniques apply to various types of host content. Here, we concentrate on relational databases. Rights protection for such data is crucial in scenarios where data are sensitive, valuable and nevertheless they need to be outsourced. Unlike encryption and hash description, typical watermarking techniques modify the ordinal data and inevitably cause permanent distortion to the original ones and this is an issue when integrity requirement of data are required. Database watermarking consists of two basic processes: watermark insertion and watermark detection [1], as illustrated in Figure 1. For watermark insertion, a key is used to embed watermark information into an original database so as to produce the watermarked database for publication or distribution. Given appropriate key and watermark information, a watermark detection process can be applied to any suspicious database so as to determine whether or not a legitimate watermark can be detected. A suspicious database can be any watermarked database or innocent database, or a mixture of them under various database attacks.

A. Prakash and I. Sen Gupta (Eds.): ICISS 2009, LNCS 5905, pp. 252–264, 2009.

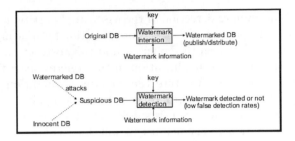

Fig. 1. Basic watermarking process

Watermarking has been extensively studied in the context of multimedia data for the purpose of ownership protection and authentication [11] [8]. The increasing use of relational database systems in many real life applications created an ever increasing need for watermarking database systems. As a result, watermarking relational database systems is now merging as a research area that deals with the legal issue of copyright protection of database systems.

The first well-known database watermarking scheme for relational databases was proposed by Agrawal and Kiernan [1] for watermarking numerical values. The fundamental assumption is that the watermarked database can tolerate a small amount of errors. Since any bit change to a categorical value may render the value meaningless, Agrawal and Kiernan's scheme cannot be directly applied to watermarking categorical data. To solve this problem, Sion [14] proposed to watermark a categorical attribute by changing some of its values to other values of the attribute (e.g., 'red' is changed to 'green') if such change is tolerable in certain applications. There have been other schemes proposed for watermarking relational data. In Sion et al.'s [15] scheme, an arbitrary bit is embedded into a selected subset of numeric values by changing the distribution of the values. The selection of the values is based on a secret sorting. In another work, Gross-Amblard [9]designs a query preserving scheme which guarantees that special queries (called local queries) can be answered up to an acceptable distortion.

All of the work cited so far ([1][9][2][14][15]) assume that minor distortions caused to some attribute data can be tolerated to some specified precision grade. However some applications in which relational data are involved cannot tolerate any permanent distortions and data's integrity needs to be authenticated. In order to meet this requirement, we further strengthen this approach: we propose a distortion free watermarking algorithm for relational databases, and we discuss it in the abstract interpretation framework proposed by Patrick and Radhia Cousot [5] [6] [7]. In [3], we presented a first proposal in this direction, focusing on partitions based on categorical values present in the table and generating a watermark as a permutations of the ordering of the tuples. Here we go one step further, by removing the constraints on the presence of categorical values in the table: we consider now any partitioning, and we generate out of it a binary image which contains the same number of rows but one less number of columns of the actual partition. The contribution of this paper is thus much more sophisticated and completely orthogonal to [8]. The binary image serves the purpose of the ownership proof and tamper detection of the associated partition. We prove that this is an abstract representation of the actual partition by showing the existence of a Galois connection between the concrete and the abstract partition (i.e. the binary image). Therefore, any modification in the concrete partition will reflect in the abstract counterpart. We state the soundness condition regarding this alteration. The robustness of the proposed watermarking obviously depends on the size of the individual groups, so it is specifically designed for large databases. The resulting watermark is robust against various forms of malicious attacks and updates to the data in the table.

The paper is organized as follows. In Section 2, we formalize the definition of tables in relational database, and a formal definition of watermarking process of a table in relational database is given. Section 3 illustrates how distortions and watermarking are related. In Section 4, we show the data partitioning algorithm. In Section 5, we present the watermark generation algorithm for a data partition, and we explain why this watermark is considered as an abstract representation of the concrete partition. In Section 6, we propose the watermark detection algorithm. The robustness of the technique is discussed in Section 7. Finally, we draw our conclusions in Section 8.

2   Preliminaries

This section contains an overview of Galois connection and some formal definitions of tables in relational database and database watermarking [4] [10].

Definition 2.1 (Partial Orders)
A partial order on a set D is a relation $\sqsubseteq \in \wp(D \times D)$ with the following properties:

- $\forall d \in D : d \sqsubseteq d$ (reflexivity)
- $\forall d, d' \in D : (d \sqsubseteq d') \wedge (d' \sqsubseteq d) \Longrightarrow (d = d')$ (antisymmetry)
- $\forall d, d', d'' \in D : (d \sqsubseteq d') \wedge (d' \sqsubseteq d'') \Longrightarrow (d \sqsubseteq d'')$ (transitivity)

A set with a partial order defined on it is called partially ordered set, poset. Following are definitions of some commonly used terms with respect to Partial order $(L, \sqsubseteq)$.

Definition 2.1.1 (Lower Bound)
X $\subseteq$ L has $l \in$ L as lower bound if $\forall$ l' $\in$ X : $l \sqsubseteq$ l'.

Definition 2.1.2 (Greatest Lower Bound)
X $\subseteq$ L has $l \in$ L as greatest lower bound l if $l_0 \sqsubseteq l$ whenever l_0 is another lower bound of X. It is represented by the operator $\sqcap$. glb(X)= $\sqcap$ X.

Definition 2.1.3 (Upper Bound)
X $\subseteq$ L has $l \in$ L as upper bound if $\forall$ l' $\in$ X : l' $\sqsubseteq$ l.

Definition 2.1.4 (Least Upper Bound)
X $\subseteq$ L has $l \in$ L as least upper bound if $l \sqsubseteq l_0$ whenever l_0 is another upper bound of X. It is represented by the operator $\sqcup$. lub(X)= $\sqcup$ X.

Definition 2.2 (Complete Lattice)
A complete lattice $(L, \sqsubseteq, \sqcup, \sqcap, \top, \bot)$ is a partial ordered set $(L, \sqsubseteq)$ such that every subset of L has a least upper bound as well as a greatest lower bound.

- The greatest element $\top = \sqcup L$
- The least element $\bot = \sqcap L$

For instance $(L, \sqsubseteq, \sqcup, \sqcap, \top, \bot)$ where $L = \{1, 2, 3, 4, 6, 9, 36\}$, the partial order $\sqsubseteq$ is defined by $n \sqsubseteq m \Leftrightarrow (m \bmod n = 0)$, $\bot = 1$ and $\top = 36$ is a complete lattice. It can be represented using Hasse diagram as shown below

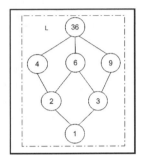

Fig. 2. Complete Lattice

Definition 2.3 (Galois Connection)
Let C (concrete) and A (abstract) be two domains (or lattices). Let $\alpha : C \rightarrow A$ and $\gamma : A \rightarrow C$ be an abstraction function and a concretization function, respectively. The pair of functions (α, γ) form a Galois Connection if:

- both α and γ are monotone (order preserving).
- $\forall\, a \in A : \alpha(\gamma(a)) \sqsubseteq a$
- $\forall\, c \in C : c \sqsubseteq \gamma(\alpha(c))$

α and γ uniquely determine each other.

Definition 2.4 (Function)
Let Π_i be the projection function which selects the i-th coordinate of a pair. F is a function over the set A into set B $\Leftrightarrow F \in \wp(A \times B) \bigwedge (\forall p_1, p_2 \in F : p_1 \neq p_2 \Rightarrow \Pi_1(p_1) \neq \Pi_1(p_2)) \bigwedge \{\Pi_1(p) | p \in F\} = A$.

Definition 2.5 (Set Function)
A set function is a function in which every range element is a set. Formally, let F is a set function $\Leftrightarrow$ F is a function and $(\forall c \in dom(F) : F(c)$ is a set).
For instance, we can express information about companies and their locations by means of a set function over the domain {Company, Location}. Namely, (Company;{'Natural Join', 'Central Boekhuis', 'Oracle', 'Remmen & De Brock'}) (Location, {'New York', 'Venice', 'Paris'}).

Definition 2.6 (Table)

Given two sets H and K, a table over H and K is a set of functions T over the same set H and into the same set K. i.e. $\forall\, t \in T$: t is a function from H to K. For instance consider a table containing data on employees:

Table 1. Employee

emp_no	emp_name	emp_rank
100	John	Manager
101	David	programmer
103	Albert	HR

The table is represented by the set of functions t_1, t_2, t_3 where $dom(t_i) =$ emp_no, emp_name, emp_rank and for instance t_1(emp_name) = John.

There is a correspondence between tuples and functions. For instance, t_1 corresponds to the following tuple: (emp_no, 100), (emp_name, John), (emp_rank, manager). The first coordinates of the ordered pairs in a tuple are referred to as the attributes of that tuple.

Definition 2.7 (Watermarking)

A watermark W for a table T over H into K, is a predicate such that W(T) is true and the probability of $W(T')$ being true with $T' \in \wp(H \times K)\backslash T$ is negligible.

3   Distortions by Watermarking

It is often hard to define the available *bandwidth* for inserting the watermark directly. Instead, allowable distortion bounds [14][15]for the input data can be defined in terms of consumer metrics. If the watermarked data satisfies the metrics, then the alterations induced by the insertion of the watermark are considered to be acceptable. One such simple yet relevant example for numeric data, is the case of maximum allowable mean squared error (MSE), in which the usability metrics are defined in terms of mean squared error tolerances as

$$(S_i - V_i)^2 < t_i, \forall i = 1...n \quad and \tag{1}$$

$$\sum_i^n (S_i - V_i)^2 < t_{max} \tag{2}$$

where
$\mathbb{S} = s_1, ..., s_n \subset \mathbb{R}$, is the data to be watermarked,
$\mathbb{V} = v_1, ..., v_n$ is the result,
$\mathbb{T} = t_1, ..., t_n \subset \mathbb{R}$ and
$t_{max} \in R$ define the guaranteed error bounds at data distribution time.

In other words $\mathbb{T}$ defines the allowable distortions for individual elements in terms of MSE and t_{max} its overall permissible value.

However, specifying only allowable change limits on individual values, and possibly an overall limit, fails to capture important *semantic features* associated with the data, especially if the data is structured. Consider for example, the *age* data in an Indian context. While a small change to the age values may be acceptable, it may be critical that individuals that are younger than 21 remain so even after watermarking if the data will be used to determine behavior patterns for under-age drinking. Similarly, if the same data were to be used for identifying legal voters, the cut-off would be 18 years. In another scenario, if a relation contains the start and end times of a web interaction, it is important that each tuple satisfies the condition that the end time be later than the start time. For some other application it may be important that the relative ages, in terms of which one is younger, not change. Other examples of constraints include: *uniqueness*, each value must be unique; *scale*, the ratio between any two number before and after the change must remain the same; and *classification*, the objects must remain in the same class (defined by a range of values) before and after the watermarking. As is clear from the above examples, simple bounds on the change of numerical values are often not sufficient to prevent side effects of a watermarking operation.

4   Data Partitioning

In this section we present a data partitioning algorithm that partitions the data set based on a secret key $\Re$. The data set D is a database relation with scheme $D(P, C_0, ..., C_{v-1})$, where P is the primary key attribute, $C_0, ..., C_{v-1}$ are it's v attributes, and η is the number of tuples in D. The data set D is to be partitioned into m non overlapping partitions, $[S_0], ..., [S_{m-1}]$, such that each partition $[S_i]$ contains on average $\left(\frac{\eta}{m}\right)$ tuples from the data set D. Partitions do not overlap, i.e., for any two partitions $[S_i]$ and $[S_j]$ such that $i \neq j$ we have $[S_i] \cap [S_j] = \emptyset$. In order to generate the partitions, for each tuple $r \in D$, the data partitioning algorithm computes a message authenticated code (MAC) using HMAC [12].

Using the property that secure hash functions generate uniformly distributed message digests this partitioning technique places $\left(\frac{\eta}{m}\right)$ tuples, on average, in each partition. Furthermore, an attacker cannot predict the tuples-to-partition assignment without the knowledge of the secret key $\Re$ and the number of partitions m which are kept secret. Keeping it secret makes it harder for the attacker to regenerate the partitions. The partitioning algorithm is described below:

Algorithm 1. get_partitions(D, $\Re$, m)

1: **for** each tuple $r \in D$ **do**
2:     partition ← HMAC($\Re$ | r.P) mod m
3:     insert r into $S_{partition}$
4: **end for**
5: **return** $(S_0, ..., S_{m-1})$

Consider the lattice $A = \langle \mathbb{N}, \bigcup\{\bot, \top\}, \sqsubseteq \rangle$, where $\bot \sqsubseteq i \sqsubseteq \top$ and $\forall$ i, j $\in \mathbb{N}$, $i \neq j$, i and j are uncomparable with $\sqsubseteq$. The lattice is shown in Figure 3.

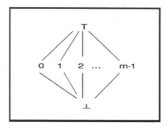

Fig. 3. Lattice of the abstract domain

Given a data set $D \in (P \times C_0 \times C_1 \times ... \times C_{v-1})$ and m partitions $\{[S_i], 0 \leq i \leq (m-1)\}$, for each set $T \subseteq D$, and given a set of natural number i $\in \mathbb{N}$, we can define a concretization map γ as follows:
$\gamma(\top) = D$
$\gamma(\bot) = \emptyset$

$$\gamma(i) = \begin{cases} T \subseteq D & \text{if } \forall t \in T : i = HMAC(\Re | t.P) \mod m \\ \emptyset & \text{Otherwise} \end{cases} \tag{3}$$

The best representation of a set of tuples is captured by the corresponding abstraction function α :

$$\alpha(T) = \begin{cases} \bot \text{ if } S = \emptyset \\ i \text{ if } \forall t \in T : HMAC(\Re | t.P) \mod m = i \\ \top \text{ } Otherwise \end{cases} \tag{4}$$

The two functions α and γ described above yield a Galois connection [6] between D, i.e. the actual data set and the lattice depicted in figure 2.

5   Watermark Generation

We are interested in a watermark generation process starting from a partition $[S_k]$ $0 \leq k \leq m]$, in a relational database table. The partitioning can be seen as a virtual grouping which does not change the physical position of the tuples. Let the owner of the relation D possess a watermark key $\Re$, which will be used in both watermark generation and detection. In addition, the key should be long enough to thwart brute force guessing attacks to the key. A cryptographic pseudo random sequence generator [13] G is seeded with the concatenation of watermark key $\Re$ and the primary key r.P for each tuple $r \in S_k$, generating a sequence of numbers. The MSBs (most significant bits) of the selected values are used for generating the watermark. Formally, the watermark W_k corresponding to the kth partition $[S_k]$ is generated as follows,

Algorithm 2. genW($\mathbf{S_k}, \Re$)

1: **for** each tuple r $\in S_k$ **do**
2:     construct a row t in W_k
3:     **for** (i=0; i< v; i=i+1) **do**
4:         j= $G_i(\Re, r.P)$ mod v
5:         $t.W_k^i$ = MSB of the jth attribute in r
6:         delete the jth attribute from r
7:     **end for**
8: **end for**
9: **return**(W_k)

Let us illustrate the above algorithm for a single tuple in any hypothetical partition of a table Employee = ($emp\_id, emp\_name, salary, location, position$), where emp_id is the primary key which is concatenated along with the private key $\Re$ as in line 2 in the above algorithm to select random attributes. Here (1011) is the generated watermark for the tuple (Bob, 10000, London, Manager), where MSBs 1, 1, 1 and 0 are associated to Bob, 10000, London and Manager respectively.

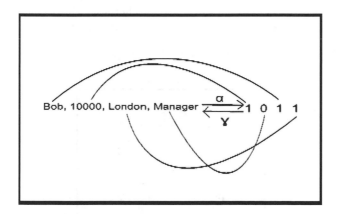

Fig. 4. Watermark generation for a single tuple

So if there are n number of tuples in the partition [S_k], $genW$ generates a binary image $W_k^{n,v}$ as a watermark for [S_k] partition. The whole process does not introduce any distortion to the original data. The use of MSBs is for thwarting potential attacks that modify the data. Namely, subset alteration attack where the attacker alters the tuples of the database through operations such as linear transformation. The attacker hopes by doing so to erase the watermark from the database.

5.1   Functional Abstraction

Theorem 1 (Galois Connection)

Given a table $D \subseteq C_0 \times C_1 \times C_2 \times ... C_{v-1}$, let $\mathbb{B}^v$ is the set of all binary sequences of length v. We can define abstraction and concretization function between $\wp (C_0 \times C_1 \times C_2 \times ... C_{v-1})$ and $\wp(\mathbb{B}^v)$ as follows

$\alpha(S) = \{genW(\mathrm{S}, \Re)(\mathrm{r}) \mid \mathrm{r} \in \mathrm{S} \}$

$\gamma(W) = \{\mathrm{t} \in \mathrm{S} \subseteq \mathrm{D} \mid genW(\mathrm{S}, \Re)(\mathrm{t}) \in \mathrm{W}\}$. Then α and γ form a Galois connection [6].

Proof:

$\alpha(S) \subseteq W$

$\Leftrightarrow \{genW(\mathrm{S}, \Re)(\mathrm{r}) \mid \mathrm{r} \in \mathrm{S} \} \subseteq \mathrm{W}$

$\Leftrightarrow \forall\, \mathrm{r} \in \mathrm{S} : genW(\mathrm{S}, \Re)(\mathrm{r}) \in \mathrm{W}$

$\Leftrightarrow \mathrm{S} \subseteq \{\, \mathrm{r} \mid genW(\mathrm{S}, \Re)(\mathrm{r}) \in \mathrm{W}\}$

$\Leftrightarrow \mathrm{S} \subseteq \gamma(\mathrm{W}).$

The data set (table) $D \subseteq \wp(C_0 \times C_1 \times ... C_{v-1})$ and the watermark $W \subseteq \wp(\mathbb{B}^v)$. By Theorem 1 (D, W, α, γ) form a Galois Connection. The function $genW : D \to W$ is the watermark generation function described above. $\forall t \in D,\ f_{alt} : D \to D$ and $\forall t^{\#} \in W,\ f_{alt}^{\#} : W \to W$ are the alteration functions that alter the tuples in both concrete and abstract domain, respectively. Therefore the soundness condition with respect to the alteration function can be stated as follows:

$$\forall t \in D : \alpha(f_{alt}(t)) \sqsubseteq f_{alt}^{\#}(\alpha(t))$$

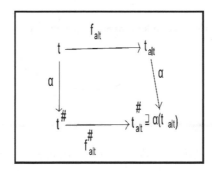

Fig. 5. Soundness

This means that, the proposed watermark process is sound whenever the diagram above commutes.

6   Watermark Detection

A very important problem in a watermarking scheme is synchronization, that is, we must ensure, that the watermark extracted is in the same order as that generated. If synchronization is lost, even if no modifications have been made, the embedded watermark cannot be correctly verified. In watermark detection, the watermark key $\Re$ and watermark W_k are needed to check a suspicious partition S'_k of the suspicious database relation D'. It is assumed that the primary key attribute has not been changed or else can be recovered.

Algorithm 3. $\det W(S'_k, \Re, W_k)$

1: matchC=0
2: **for** each tuple r $\in$ S_k **do**
3:     get the rth row, t of W_k
4:     **for** (i=0; i < v; i = i+1) **do**
5:       j= $G_i(\Re, r.P)$ mod v
6:       **if** $t.W_k^i$ = MSB of the jth attribute in r **then**
7:           matchC = matchC + 1
8:       **end if**
9:       delete the jth attribute from r
10:     **end for**
11: **end for**
12: **if** matchC=ω **then**
13:     // ω = number of rows $\times$ number of columns in W_k
14:     **return** true
15: **else**
16:     **return** false
17: **end if**

The variable matchC counts the total number of correct matches. We consider the watermark $W_k^{t,i}$, t= 1 to q_k(number of tuples in S_k) and i= 1 to v (number of attributes in relation). At the statement number 6 the authentication is checked by comparing the generated watermark bitwise. And after each match matchC is increased by 1. Finally at statement number 12, the total match is compared to the number of bits in the watermark image W_k associated with partition S_k to check the final authentication.

7 Robustness

We analyze the robustness of our scheme by Bernoulli trials and binomial probability as in [6]. Repeated independent trials in which there can be only two outcomes are called Bernoulli trials in honor of James Bernoulli (1654-1705).The probability that the outcome of an experiment that consists of n Bernoulli trials has k successes and n - k failures is given by the binomial distribution

$$b(n, k, p) = \binom{n}{k} p^k (1 - p)^{n-k}$$

$$\binom{n}{k} = \frac{n!}{k!(n-k)!} \qquad 0 \le k \le n$$

where the probability of success on an individual trial is given by p.

The probability of having at least k successes in n trials, the cumulative binomial probability, can be written as

$$B(n, k, p) = \sum_{i}^{k} b(n, i, p)$$

We will discuss our robustness condition based on two parameters *false hit* and *false miss*.

7.1   False Hit

False hit is the probability of a valid watermark being detected from non-watermarked data. The lower the false hit, the better the robustness. When the watermark detection is applied to non-watermarked data, each MSB in data has the same probability $\frac{1}{2}$ to match or not to match the corresponding bit in the watermark. Assume that the non-watermarked data partition S_q has the same number q of tuples and has the same primary keys as the original data. Let $\omega = vq$ is the size of the watermark. where v is the no of attributes being watermarked and r is the number of tuples in partition S_r. The false hit is the probability that at least $\frac{1}{\mathfrak{T}}$ portion of ω can be detected from the non-watermarked data by sheer chance. When $\mathfrak{T}$ is the watermark detection parameter. It is used as a tradeoff between false hit and false miss. Increasing $\mathfrak{T}$ will make the robustness better in terms of false hit. Therefore, the false hit F_h can be written as

$$F_h = B(\omega, \lfloor \frac{\omega}{\mathfrak{T}} \rfloor, \frac{1}{2}).$$

7.2   False Miss

False miss is the probability of not detecting a valid watermark from watermarked data that has been modified in typical attacks. The less the false miss, the better the robustness. For tuple deletion and attribute deletion, the MSBs in the deleted tuples or attributes will not be detected in watermark detection; however, the MSBs in other tuples or attributes will not be affected. Therefore, all detected MSBs will match their counterparts in the public watermark, and the false miss is zero. Suppose an attacker inserts ς new tuples to replace ς watermarked tuples with their primary key values unchanged. For watermark detection to return a false answer, at least $\frac{1}{\mathfrak{T}}$ MSBS of those newly added tuples (which consists of $v\varsigma$ MSBs) must not match their counterparts in the watermark (which consists of $\omega = vq$ bits, if the partition contains q tuples). also in this case $\mathfrak{T}$ is the watermark detection parameter, used as a tradeoff between false hit and false miss. Increasing $\mathfrak{T}$ will make the robustness worse in terms of false miss. Therefore, the false miss F_m for inserting ς tuples can be written as

$$F_m = B(v_\varsigma, \lfloor \frac{v_\varsigma}{\mathfrak{T}} \rfloor, \frac{1}{2})$$

The formulae F_h and F_m together, give us a measure of the robustness of the watermark.

8   Conclusions

As a conclusion, let us stress the main features of the watermark technique presented in this paper,

- it does not depend on any particular type of attributes (categorical, numerical);
- it is partition based, we are able to detect and locate modifications as we can trace the group which is possibly affected when a tuple t_m is tampered;
- neither watermark generation nor detection depends on any correlation or costly sorting among data items. Each tuple in a table is independently processed; therefore, the scheme is particularly efficient for tuple oriented database operations;
- it does not modify any database item; therefore it is distortion free.

Acknowledgements

Work partially supported by Italian MIUR COFIN '07 project "SOFT".

References

1. Agrawal, R., Kiernan, J.: Watermarking relational databases. In: In 28th Int Conference on Very Large Databases, Hong Kong, pp. 155–166 (2002)
2. Al-Haj, A., Odeh, A.: Robust and blind watermarking of relational database systems. Journal of Computer Science 4(12), 1024–1029 (2008)
3. Bhattacharya, S., Cortesi, A.: A distortion free watermarking framework for relational databases. In: Proc. 4th International Conference on Software and Data technology, ICSOFT 2009, Sofia, Bulgaria, pp. 229–234 (2009)
4. Collberg, C., Thomborson, C.: Watermarking, tamper-proofing, and obfuscation - tools for software protection. IEEE Trans. Software Eng. 28, 735–746 (2000)
5. Cousot, P.: Abstract interpretation based formal methods and future challenges. In: Wilhelm, R. (ed.) Informatics: 10 Years Back, 10 Years Ahead. LNCS, vol. 2000, pp. 138–156. Springer, Heidelberg (2001)
6. Cousot, P., Cousot, R.: Abstract interpretation: a unified lattice model for static analysis of programs by construction or approximation of fixpoints. In: POPL 1977: Proceedings of the 4th ACM SIGACT-SIGPLAN symposium on Principles of programming languages, pp. 238–252. ACM Press, New York (1977)
7. Cousot, P., Cousot, R.: Abstract interpretation frameworks. Journal of Logic and Computation 2, 511–547 (1992)
8. Cox, I.: Digital Watermarking: Principles and Practice. Morgan Kaufman Publ. Inc., San Francisco (2001)

9. Gross-Amblard, D.: Query-preserving watermarking of relational databases and xml documents. In: Proc. of the Twenty-Second ACM SIGACT-SIGMOD-SIGART Symposium on Principles of Database Systems, San Diego, CA, USA, June 9-12, pp. 191–201 (2003)
10. de Haan, L., Koppelaars, T.: Applied Mathematics for Database Professionals. Apress, Berkely (2007)
11. Sushil, Z.J., Duric, J.N.F.: Information hiding: steganography and watermarking. In: Attacks and countermeasures. Kluwer Academic Publishers, Dordrecht (2000)
12. Mineta, N.Y., Shavers, C.L., Kammer, R.G., Mehuron, W.: The keyed-hash message authentication code (HMAC). Federal Information Process Standards Publication (2002)
13. Schneier, B.: Applied Cryptography. John Wiley & Sons, Chichester (1996)
14. Sion, R.: Proving ownership over categorical data, vol. 0, p. 584. IEEE Computer Society, Los Alamitos (2004)
15. Sion, R., Atallah, M., Prabhakar, S.: Rights protection for relational data, vol. 16, pp. 1509–1525. IEEE Computer Society, Los Alamitos (2004)

On Some Weaknesses in the Disk Encryption Schemes EME and EME2

Cuauhtemoc Mancillas-López, Debrup Chakraborty,
and Francisco Rodríguez-Henríquez

Department of Computer Science, CINVESTAV-IPN, Av. IPN 2508, Col: San Pedro
Zacatenco, Mexico City 07360, Mexico
mancilla@computacion.cs.cinvestav.mx, debrup@cs.cinvestav.mx,
francisco@cs.cinvestav.mx

Abstract. Tweakable enciphering schemes are a certain type of block-cipher mode of operation which provide security in the sense of a strong pseudo-random permutation. It has been proposed that these types of modes are suitable for in-place disk encryption. Currently there are many proposals available for these schemes. EME is one of the efficient candidate of this category. EME2 is a derivative of EME which is currently one of the candidates of a draft standard for wide block modes by the IEEE working group on storage security. We show some weakness of these two modes assuming that some side channel information is available.

Keywords: Tweakable Enciphering Schemes, Disc Encryption, Modes of operation, EME.

1 Introduction

A mode of operation is a specific way to use a block-cipher to encrypt arbitrary long messages. Several classes of modes have been proposed in the last few years to provide different security services for various kind of scenarios. In particular, a Tweakable Enciphering Scheme (TES), is a length preserving enciphering scheme that provides security in the sense of a strong pseudo-random permutation. This means that an efficient adversary given access to the outputs of the TES encryption and decryption algorithms, will not be able to distinguish them from a random permutation and its inverse with non-negligible probability. For length preserving encryption this is the highest form of security that can be guaranteed. Some of the most important TES proposals published to date can be found in [9,10,7,19,6,15,5,8,18]. In [9], it was suggested that TES is the natural choice for the application of in place disk encryption.

TES can be used in low-level disk encryption by placing a hardware/software realization of this scheme in the disk controller, where it will be in charge of performing both, run-time encryption of the sectors to be written and run-time decryption of the sectors to be read. Thus, the data contained in the disk sectors remains at all times in encrypted form. Note that under this model, a TES has

A. Prakash and I. Sen Gupta (Eds.): ICISS 2009, LNCS 5905, pp. 265–279, 2009.

no knowledge of the high level partitions of the disk, such as files and directories. Moreover, due to the nature of the application, a secure length preserving encryption scheme (such as a TES) is required.

Since nowadays encrypting data recorded in bulk storage devices like hard-disks and flash memory portable devices has become a strategic problem, the design of secure TES has attracted considerable attention. Currently, there is also an on-going standardization effort carried out by the IEEE security in storage working group, that has produced a draft standard for wide-block encryption making it available for public scrutiny at [1].

Among the different TES found in the literature EME [10] is one of the efficient candidates, whereas EME2 [1], a derivative of EME, is currently a candidate of the draft standard proposed by [1]. Both, EME and EME2 work on n bit binary strings which are viewed as elements of the finite field $GF(2^n)$. Hence, the n-bit strings can be treated as polynomials of degree less than n with coefficients in $GF(2)$. The addition of the elements of such a field is defined as the regular polynomial addition and the multiplication is done as multiplication of two polynomials modulo a fixed irreducible polynomial $\tau(x)$ of degree n. Let $L \in \{0, 1\}^n$. One operation of particular interest is the product xL, which means multiplication of the polynomial L by the monomial x modulo the irreducible polynomial representing the field. We shall further call this operation as *xtimes*. If the irreducible polynomial $\tau(x)$ representing the field is primitive then the monomial x would be a generator of the cyclic group formed by the non-zero elements of $GF(2^n)$. This means that $x, x^2, x^3, \ldots, x^{2^n-1}$ will all be distinct. This property has found many cryptographic applications. In particular in the modes EME and EME2 a sequence of the form $x^i L$, $1 \le i < 2^{n-1}$, for some unknown L is used to mask certain data streams. These masks can be efficiently generated by repeatedly applying *xtimes* on L. The operation xL can be performed quite efficiently, but as we shall discuss in the rest of this paper, if not carefully crafted, that operation may leak information regarding L.

Our Contribution. We analyze the mode of operations EME and EME2 and point out certain weaknesses in the modes if side channel information is available. We use a previously reported observation that *xtimes* leaks much information in terms of timings and power utilization. Assuming the insecurity of the *xtimes* operation we systematically develop attacks on EME and EME2. Specifically we show that for both EME and EME2, given side channel information and access to the encryption algorithm, an adversary can efficiently mount distinguishing attacks. For EME we show a stronger attack, where an adversary can decrypt any ciphertext C without querying the decryption algorithm at C with very high probability. Also for EME, given access to the encryption algorithm the adversary can produce ciphertext of any given plaintext P, without querying the encryption algorithm at P.

The possible side channel weakness of EME and two of its derivatives EME$^+$ and EME* were pointed out in an appendix of [16], but the true vulnerabilities were not analyzed in details. We claim that our analysis is substantially different from that in [16]. In [11], Antoine Joux presented a cryptanalysis of EME mode.

Joux's cryptanalysis operates on a flawed version of EME (this version can be found in [17], which is significantly different from the final mode as reported in [10]). Right after Joux attack, the EME mode was repaired and the attacks by Joux are not applicable to the corrected version of EME which has been reported in [10]. We note that, the attacks in [11] does not require any access to side channel information and that our attacks are un-related to those reported in [11].

2   Adversaries with Access to Side Channel Information

Modern security guarantees provided by security proofs, are based on complexity theoretic arguments and assumptions on abstract notions of computations. For security definitions, one models the adversary as a probabilistic polynomial time algorithm with access to input/outputs of a protocol. The adversary knows the algorithm which produces the outputs for his chosen inputs, but has no knowledge of a secret quantity which is called the key. Moreover, as the computation model is assumed to be an abstract one, hence the state of the algorithm is also assumed to be invisible to an adversary, who cannot know the branches taken, subroutines called, etc. by the algorithm during its execution.

However, this is not a realistic scenario, since computations must be done on a physical device, and that device can leak various kinds of information. This can motivate attacks from the adversary who by applying measurements on the leaked information may be able to gain access to sensitive data related to the computation being performed. In the past few years there have been numerous studies which point out insecurity of many established cryptographic algorithms if certain side channel information is available to the adversary.

Researchers have considered the possibilities of using different types of side channel information for breaking crypto-systems. Some of the categories of side channel attacks are timing attacks [13], power analysis attacks, differential power analysis attacks [14], electromagnetic radiation attacks[2], fault attacks [3] etc. These attacks utilize the leakages that are associated with any type of computation that takes place in a physical device.

3   Notations

In what follows we shall mean by $\mathsf{msb}(L)$ the most significant bit of a binary string L. For two strings L and M, $L\|M$ will denote the concatenation of L and M. By $L << k$ we shall mean left-shift of L by k bits. $\mathsf{take}_k(L)$ will mean the k most significant bits of L. If b is a bit, then $\bar{b}$ will mean the complement of b. We shall treat n bit strings as polynomials with coefficients in $GF(2)$. Thus, an n bit string can be treated as an element in $GF(2^n)$. For two n bit strings X and Y, $X \oplus Y$ will denote the addition in the field, which can be realized by a bitwise xor of the strings X and Y. Multiplication of two n bit strings would be represented as XY which will mean the multiplication of the two corresponding $(n - 1)$ degree polynomials modulo an n degree irreducible polynomial $\tau(x)$. Particularly, for $X \in \{0,1\}^n$, xX would mean the multiplication of the polynomials x and X modulo $\tau(x)$. By an n-bit block cipher we shall mean a function $E : \mathcal{K} \times \{0,1\}^n \rightarrow \{0,1\}^n$, where $\mathcal{K} \neq \emptyset$ is the key space and for any $K \in \mathcal{K}$, $E(K,.)$ is a permutation. We shall often write $E_K(.)$ instead of $E(K,.)$.

4   Side Channel Weakness in the *xtimes* Operation

The implementation of the *xtimes* operation is very efficient. Let $\tau(x)$ denote the n degree irreducible polynomial representing the field $GF(2^n)$, let Q be the n bit representation of the polynomial $\tau(x) \oplus x^n$. Then xL can be realized by the algorithm in Fig. 1.

Algorithm *xtimes*(L)
1. $b \leftarrow \mathsf{msb}(L)$
2. $L \leftarrow L << 1$
3. **if** $b = 1$,
4. $L \leftarrow L \oplus Q$
5. **return** L

Fig. 1. The algorithm *xtimes*

This is the most efficient (and the usual) way of implementing *xtimes* where the basic operations involved are a left shift and a conditional xor. As it is obvious from the algorithm that line 4 gets executed only when the most significant bit (MSB) of L is a one. The power utilization in this algorithm would be different in the cases where $\mathsf{msb}(L) = 0$ and $\mathsf{msb}(L) = 1$. This difference of power consumption if measured can give information regarding the MSB of L.

Above described weakness of the *xtimes* operation is widely known. The *xtimes* operation on an n bit string can also be implemented by linear feedback shift registers (LFSR). The vulnerability of LFSRs to side channel attacks has been extensively studied and also there are experimental evidences that such systems leak a lot of information [12][4]. Thus with the support of the evidence as found in the literature and without going into technical/experimental details of side channel attacks in the rest of this paper we shall make the following assumption:

Assumption 1. *If the operation xL is implemented according to the algorithm xtimes as shown in Fig. 1 then the MSB of L can be obtained as a side channel information.*

Repeated application of *xtimes* on L can reveal much more information about L. In particular, based on Assumption 1 we can state the following proposition.

Proposition 1. *If xtimes is applied k ($k \leq n$) times successively on L then the k most significant bits of L can be recovered.*

> **Algorithm** $Recover(Q, k)$
> 1. $D \leftarrow\, < d_{n-1}, d_{n-2}, \ldots, d_0 > \leftarrow 0^n;$
> 2. $B \leftarrow$ Empty String;
> 3. **for** $i = 1$ to k,
> 4. $b \leftarrow \mathsf{SC}(L_1 \leftarrow xL)$; $(\mathsf{SC}(L_1 \leftarrow xL)$ gives the MSB of $L)$
> 5.   **if** $d_{n-1} = 0$,
> 6. $B \leftarrow B||b;$
> 7.   **else,**
> 8. $B \leftarrow B||\bar{b}$
> 9.   **end if**
> 10. $D \leftarrow D << 1;$
> 11.   **if** $b = 1$,
> 12. $D \leftarrow D \oplus Q$
> 13.   **end if**
> 14. $L \leftarrow L_1$
> 15. **end for**
> 16. **return** B

Fig. 2. The algorithm to recover k bits of L

In lieu of proof of the above proposition we present the procedure to recover the k bits of L in the algorithm in Figure 2.

The algorithm *Recover* as shown in Fig. 2 takes in as input the number of bits to be recovered k along with another n bit string Q which encodes the polynomial $x^n \oplus \tau(x)$. The algorithm also have access to some side-channel information, which gives it the information of the MSB of L, this is shown as $\mathsf{SC}(L_1 \leftarrow xL)$ in line 4. The algorithm, initializes an n bit string D with all zeros (d_i represents the i-th bit of D in the algorithm) and initializes B by an empty string. The output of the algorithm is a k bit string B whose bits would be the same as the k most significant bits of L. It is not difficult to see the correctness of the algorithm. Note that we simulate in D the same changes that takes place in L. After executing the i-th iteration of the for loop we obtain in line 4 the most significant bit of $x^{i-1}L$. This bit would be equal to the i-th bit of L if the MSB of D is zero, otherwise the i-th bit of L would be the complement of the most significant bit of $x^{i-1}L$.

5   Security of Tweakable Enciphering Schemes

In this section we shall review the security requirements of tweakable enciphering schemes. The material in this section is based on [9,10].

A tweakable enciphering scheme is a function $\mathbf{E} : \mathcal{K} \times \mathcal{T} \times \mathcal{M} \rightarrow \mathcal{M}$, where $\mathcal{K} \neq \emptyset$ and $\mathcal{T} \neq \emptyset$ are the key space and the tweak space respectively. The message and the cipher spaces are $\mathcal{M}$. We shall write $\mathbf{E}_K^T(.)$ instead of $\mathbf{E}(K, T, .)$. The inverse of an enciphering scheme is $\mathbf{D} = \mathbf{E}^{-1}$ where $X = \mathbf{D}_K^T(Y)$ if and only if $\mathbf{E}_K^T(X) = Y$.

Let $\mathrm{Perm}^{\mathcal{T}}(\mathcal{M})$ denote the set of all functions $\boldsymbol{\pi} : \mathcal{T} \times \mathcal{M} \to \mathcal{M}$ where $\boldsymbol{\pi}(\mathcal{T}, .)$ is a length preserving permutation. Such a $\boldsymbol{\pi} \in \mathrm{Perm}^{\mathcal{T}}(\mathcal{M})$ is called a tweak indexed permutation.

An adversary A is a probabilistic algorithm which has access to some oracles and which outputs either 0 or 1. Oracles are written as superscripts. The notation $A^{\mathcal{O}_1, \mathcal{O}_2} \Rightarrow 1$ denotes the event that the adversary A, interacts with the oracles $\mathcal{O}_1, \mathcal{O}_2$, and finally outputs the bit 1. In what follows, the notation $X \xleftarrow{\$} \mathcal{S}$, will denote the event of choosing X uniformly at random from the finite set $\mathcal{S}$.

For a tweakable enciphering scheme $\mathbf{E} : \mathcal{K} \times \mathcal{T} \times \mathcal{M} \to \mathcal{M}$, we define the advantage an adversary A has in distinguishing $\mathbf{E}$ and its inverse from a random tweak indexed permutation and its inverse in the following manner.

$$\mathbf{Adv}_{\mathbf{E}}^{\pm \widetilde{\mathrm{prp}}}(A) = \left| \Pr\left[K \xleftarrow{\$} \mathcal{K} : A^{\mathbf{E}_K(\cdot, \cdot), \mathbf{E}_K^{-1}(\cdot, \cdot)} \Rightarrow 1 \right] \right.$$

$$\left. - \Pr\left[\boldsymbol{\pi} \xleftarrow{\$} \mathrm{Perm}^{\mathcal{T}}(\mathcal{M}) : A^{\boldsymbol{\pi}(\cdot, \cdot), \boldsymbol{\pi}^{-1}(\cdot, \cdot)} \Rightarrow 1 \right] \right|. \qquad (1)$$

Here, $\boldsymbol{\pi} \xleftarrow{\$} \mathrm{Perm}^{\mathcal{T}}(\mathcal{M})$ means that for each ℓ such that $\{0, 1\}^{\ell} \subseteq \mathcal{M}$ and $T \in \mathcal{T}$ we choose a tweakable random permutation π^T from $\mathrm{Perm}(\ell)$ independently.

A TES is considered to be secure if $\mathbf{Adv}_{\mathbf{E}}^{\pm \widetilde{\mathrm{prp}}}(A)$ is small for all efficient adversaries. The definition of advantage of an adversary A above suggests the task of the adversary is to distinguish the output of an algorithm from random outputs. The adversary is given oracle access to both the encryption and decryption algorithms, which means that the adversary is free to see ciphertexts corresponding to the plaintexts of his choice and also decryptions of ciphertexts of his choice. Such an adversary is called a chosen-ciphertext (CCA) adversary Moreover, the adversary is at liberty to choose the tweaks.

The definition of advantage of an adversary A above does not take into account the information leaked by a physical implementation of the algorithm. It is practical to consider CCA adversaries, but in real life an adversary may have more information than only access to ciphertexts (plaintexts) of his/her chosen plaintexts (ciphertexts). As discussed in Section 2 given access to a physical implementation of a cryptographic algorithm, the adversary may perform other kinds of measurements and thus obtain more information. In the attacks that we construct we shall consider efficient adversaries with access to side channel information. In what follows by an oracle access to an algorithm we would mean that the adversary gets outputs of the algorithm along with certain side channel information.

6   The EME Mode of Operation

ECB-Mask-ECB (EME)[10] is an efficient tweakable enciphering scheme. EME consists of two electronic code-book layers with a masking layer in between. The encryption and decryption algorithm are given in Fig. 3.

EME takes in an m block message along with a tweak T. The algorithm is self explanatory, but an important feature to note is that in the masking layer,

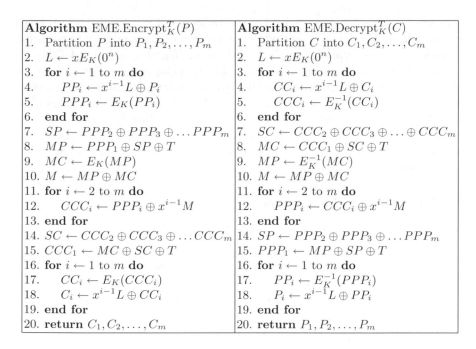

Algorithm EME.Encrypt$_K^T(P)$	**Algorithm** EME.Decrypt$_K^T(C)$
1. Partition P into $P_1, P_2, \ldots, P_m$	1. Partition C into $C_1, C_2, \ldots, C_m$
2. $L \leftarrow xE_K(0^n)$	2. $L \leftarrow xE_K(0^n)$
3. **for** $i \leftarrow 1$ to m **do**	3. **for** $i \leftarrow 1$ to m **do**
4. $PP_i \leftarrow x^{i-1}L \oplus P_i$	4. $CC_i \leftarrow x^{i-1}L \oplus C_i$
5. $PPP_i \leftarrow E_K(PP_i)$	5. $CCC_i \leftarrow E_K^{-1}(CC_i)$
6. **end for**	6. **end for**
7. $SP \leftarrow PPP_2 \oplus PPP_3 \oplus \ldots PPP_m$	7. $SC \leftarrow CCC_2 \oplus CCC_3 \oplus \ldots \oplus CCC_m$
8. $MP \leftarrow PPP_1 \oplus SP \oplus T$	8. $MC \leftarrow CCC_1 \oplus SC \oplus T$
9. $MC \leftarrow E_K(MP)$	9. $MP \leftarrow E_K^{-1}(MC)$
10. $M \leftarrow MP \oplus MC$	10. $M \leftarrow MP \oplus MC$
11. **for** $i \leftarrow 2$ to m **do**	11. **for** $i \leftarrow 2$ to m **do**
12. $CCC_i \leftarrow PPP_i \oplus x^{i-1}M$	12. $PPP_i \leftarrow CCC_i \oplus x^{i-1}M$
13. **end for**	13. **end for**
14. $SC \leftarrow CCC_2 \oplus CCC_3 \oplus \ldots CCC_m$	14. $SP \leftarrow PPP_2 \oplus PPP_3 \oplus \ldots PPP_m$
15. $CCC_1 \leftarrow MC \oplus SC \oplus T$	15. $PPP_1 \leftarrow MP \oplus SP \oplus T$
16. **for** $i \leftarrow 1$ to m **do**	16. **for** $i \leftarrow 1$ to m **do**
17. $CC_i \leftarrow E_K(CCC_i)$	17. $PP_i \leftarrow E_K^{-1}(PPP_i)$
18. $C_i \leftarrow x^{i-1}L \oplus CC_i$	18. $P_i \leftarrow x^{i-1}L \oplus PP_i$
19. **end for**	19. **end for**
20. **return** $C_1, C_2, \ldots, C_m$	20. **return** $P_1, P_2, \ldots, P_m$

Fig. 3. Encryption and Decryption using EME

the mask M is dependent on all the plaintext blocks and the mask is distributed to all the blocks suitably. This makes each block of ciphertext dependent on all blocks of plain texts. This is a necessary criteria for any disk encryption mode.

EME has some message length restrictions. If the block length of the underlying block cipher is n then EME cannot encrypt more than n blocks of messages. Also the message length should always be a multiple of n. EME is proved to be a secure tweakable enciphering scheme.

7   The Attack on EME

Note that EME uses three layers of *xtimes* operation. These operations can leak information about the internal variables L and M. Utilizing this leaked information one can attack the mode. We show two attacks. One attack is a distinguishing attack, which shows that an adversary with oracle access to only the encryption oracle of the mode and the side channel information can distinguish with probability 1 between the real oracle from the one which produces only random strings. We also show a stronger attack, where the adversary can successfully decrypt any given ciphertext C by querying the decryption oracle with ciphertexts other than C. Similarly, without knowledge of the key an adversary can produce a valid cipher text from a given plaintext P and tweak T by querying the encryption oracle (but not at P).

The main observation that makes these attacks possible is Proposition 1. From the algorithm in Fig. 3 it is clear that on encryption or decryption of m plaintext or ciphertext blocks *xtimes* is applied m times on $E_K(0^n)$ and $m - 1$ times on M. This information would be crucial in mounting the attacks. For an m block query the side channel information that we are interested in is the information regarding M and $E_K(0^n)$ further we shall say that the M-side-channel and L-side-channel gives the side channel information regarding M and $E_K(0^n)$. So after an m block encryption or decryption query the M-side-channel and the L-side-channel will give the $(m - 1)$ significant bits of M and m significant bits of $E_K(0^n)$ respectively.

7.1   The Distinguishing Attack

First we note down the basic steps followed by the adversary:

1. Apply an arbitrary encryption query of n blocks with an arbitrary tweak.
   - Obtain the n bits of $E_K(0^n)$ from the L-side-channel .
   - Compute $L = xE_K(0^n)$.
2. Apply an encryption query with plaintext L and tweak $x^{-1}L$. Let C be the response of this query.
3. If C is equal to $(1 \oplus x)x^{-1}L$ output EME otherwise output random.

It is easy to see why this attack works. When applying the query in step 1, the adversary recovers the n bits of $E_K(0^n)$. From line 2 of the algorithm in Fig. 3 we can see that $L = xE_K(0^n)$, thus the adversary can compute L. Following the algorithm in Fig. 3 we see that for the second query (in step 2) the value of PP_1 would be 0^n hence the value of PPP_1 would be $E_K(0^n)$. As the query consists of only one block, so values of both SP and SC would be zero. So, MP would be computed as $PPP_1 \oplus T$. Note that $T = x^{-1}L = E_K(0^n)$. So MP would be 0^n and CCC_1 would also be 0^n. Thus, we would obtain the output as

$$C = E_K(0^n) \oplus L = E_K(0^n) \oplus xE_K(0^n)$$
$$= (1 \oplus x)x^{-1}(xE_K(0^n)) = (1 \oplus x)x^{-1}L$$

7.2   The Stronger Attack

Here we describe a stronger attack, in which assuming that the adversary has access to the M-side-channel and L-side-channel can decrypt any given ciphertext by querying the decryption oracle with ciphertexts other than the ciphertext in question. Before we present the attack we note down an important but obvious characteristics of EME in the proposition below:

Proposition 2. *An oracle access to the blockcipher E_K is enough to encrypt any plaintext $P_1||P_2|| \ldots ||P_m$ with arbitrary tweak T using the EME mode of operation which uses the key K. Similarly, with an oracle access to both E_K^{-1} and E_K one can decrypt any arbitrary ciphertext $C_1, C_2, \ldots, C_m$ with an arbitrary tweak T which has been produced by the EME mode of operation with key K.*

The truth of the above proposition can be easily verified from the algorithm in Fig. 3. Following the algorithm in Fig. 3, if we write the dependence of the ciphertext (resp. plaintext) with the plaintext (resp. ciphertext), then the only unknown terms would be of the form $E_K(X)$, for some X, which can be obtained by querying the oracle E_K at X. Similar argument hold for the decryption oracle.

In the attack that follows we shall show that given access to the encryption algorithm of EME along with the L-side-channel and M-side-channel, an adversary can use it as an oracle for the blockcipher $E_K()$. Similarly given an access to the decryption algorithm of EME along with the M-side-channel and L-side-channel, the adversary can use it as an oracle for E_K^{-1}. So, by Proposition 2 the adversary can compute ciphertext (plaintext) corresponding to any plaintext (ciphertext) for EME. We describe the steps undertaken by the adversary to obtain $E_K(X)$ given an oracle access to the encryption algorithm of EME in Fig. 4. We assume that the procedure $\mathbf{AdvSCA}^{\mathrm{EME}_K(\cdot,\cdot)}(X)$ has an access to to the EME encryption algorithm, we also assume that n (the block length of the block cipher E_K) is even[1].

$\mathbf{AdvSCA}^{\mathrm{EME}_K(\cdot,\cdot)}(X)$

1. Apply an arbitrary encryption query of n blocks with an arbitrary tweak.
   - Obtain the n bits of L using the L-side-channel .
2. Apply an encryption query with tweak X and the following plaintext:

$$\underbrace{Y \oplus L, Y \oplus xL, \ldots, Y \oplus x^{n-1}L}_{n \text{ blocks}}.$$

   where $Y \in \{0,1\}^n$ is chosen arbitrarily.
   - Obtain $(n-1)$ significant bits of M using the M-side-channel , call this as M_1.
3. Output $M_1 \oplus \mathsf{take}_{n-1}(X)$

Fig. 4. The side channel adversary with access to EME encryption algorithm producing $n-1$ bits of $E_K(X)$ for arbitrary $X \in \{0,1\}^n$

Proposition 3. *The procedure* $\mathbf{AdvSCA}^{\mathrm{EME}_K(\cdot,\cdot)}(X)$ *as shown in Fig. 4 outputs* $\mathsf{take}_{n-1}(E_K(X))$.

Proof. In step 1 the information regarding L is obtained. For the query in step 2 according to the algorithm (see Fig. 3), we obtain $PP_i = Y$. Thus,

$$SP = PPP_2 \oplus PPP_3 \oplus \cdots \oplus PPP_n$$
$$= E_K(Y) \oplus \underbrace{(E_K(Y) \oplus \cdots \oplus E_K(Y))}_{n-2} = E_K(Y)$$

---

[1] This assumption is not strong, as we do not know of any blockcipher whose block length is odd.

$$\mathbf{AdvSCB}^{\mathrm{EME}_K(\cdot,\cdot)}(X, \mathsf{take}_{n-1}(E_K(X)))$$

1. Apply an arbitrary encryption query of n blocks with an arbitrary tweak.
   - Obtain the n bits of L using the L-side-channel .
2. $Z \leftarrow \mathsf{take}_{n-1}(E_K(X))$
3. $S \leftarrow \mathbf{AdvSCA}^{\mathrm{EME}_K(\cdot,\cdot)}(Z\|1 \oplus x^{-1}L)$
4. Apply a query with tweak $Z\|1$ and plaintext $X \oplus L$
   - Get the output as C
5. If $\mathsf{take}_{n-1}(C \oplus L) = S$ output $Z\|1$
   else output $Z\|0$

Fig. 5. The side channel adversary with access to EME encryption algorithm producing $E_K(X)$

So we have,

$$MP = PPP_1 \oplus SP \oplus X = E_K(Y) \oplus E_K(Y) \oplus X = X$$

Thus, $MC = E_K(X)$, and $M = MP \oplus MC = X \oplus E_K(X)$. Hence $M \oplus X = E_K(X)$. In step 2, only $n-1$ bits of M would be obtained, hence the procedure $\mathbf{AdvSCA}^{\mathrm{EME}_K(\cdot,\cdot)}(X)$ outputs $n-1$ bits of $E_K(X)$. $\square$

Now we design another adversary which on given access to the EME encryption algorithm and X and $\mathsf{take}_{n-1}(E_K(X))$ can produce $E_K(X)$ with high probability. We call this procedure as $\mathbf{AdvSCB}^{\mathrm{EME}_K(\cdot,\cdot)}(X, \mathsf{take}_{n-1}(E_K(X)))$, which is shown in Fig. 5.

Proposition 4. *Let the procedure* $\mathbf{AdvSCB}^{\mathrm{EME}_K(\cdot,\cdot)}(X, \mathsf{take}_{n-1}(E_K(X)))$ *be as described in Fig. 5, then*

$$\Pr[\mathbf{AdvSCB}^{\mathrm{EME}_K(\cdot,\cdot)}(X, \mathsf{take}_{n-1}(E_K(X)) = E_K(X)] \geq 1 - \frac{1}{2^{n-1}}$$

Proof. Let us first see what is done in the procedure described in Fig. 5. The adversary knows X and the $(n-1)$ significant bits of $E_K(X)$. He wants to predict the missing bit of $E_K(X)$. We call the $(n-1)$ bits of $E_K(X)$ as Z. He guesses that the missing bit is 1 and tries to verify if his guess is correct. First let us concentrate on the query made at step 4. The query is made with a tweak $Z\|1$ and a single block of plaintext $X \oplus L$. If his guess regarding the last bit of $E_K(X)$ is correct, then $Z\|1$ would be $E_K(X)$, and in such a case the response C obtained would be

$$C = L \oplus E_K(E_K(X) \oplus E_K(0^n)) = L \oplus E_K(E_K(X) \oplus x^{-1}L). \tag{2}$$

This can be easily verified from the algorithm in Fig. 3. In the third step of the procedure, S is the output of $\mathbf{AdvSCA}^{\mathrm{EME}_K(\cdot,\cdot)}$ on $Z\|1 \oplus x^{-1}L$. So according to Proposition 3

$$S = \mathsf{take}_{n-1}(E_K(Z\|1 \oplus x^{-1}L)). \tag{3}$$

So if the guess is correct then from eq. (2) and eq. (3) we get that

$$\mathsf{take}_{n-1}(C \oplus L) = S.$$

Thus, if the last bit of $E_K(X)$ is 1, then the procedure will always output the correct value of $E_K(X)$. On the other hand if the guess is wrong, i.e., the last bit of $E_K(X)$ is zero, then the response to the query in step 4 would be as

$$C = L \oplus E_K(E_K(X) \oplus E_K(0^{n-1}1))$$

And in this case the check in step 5 will pass with a probability less than $\frac{1}{2^{n-1}}$. Thus, the probability with which a correct guess can be made is greater than $(1 - \frac{1}{2^{n-1}})$. □

So using the procedures described in Fig 4 and Fig 5 the side channel adversary can compute $E_K(X)$ for a X of his choice with very high probability. Using the same technique the adversary can compute $E_K^{-1}(X)$ for any X given access to the decryption algorithm of EME.

Thus, we can conclude that given access to the encryption and decryption algorithms of EME and the relevant side channel information, an adversary can compute the encryption of a plain-text P of his choice without querying the encryption algorithm at P. Similarly, (s)he can decrypt any ciphertext C without querying the decryption algorithm at C.

8   EME2 Mode of Operation

EME2 adds certain functionalities which are not present in EME, for example, EME2 can handle arbitrary long messages (recall that EME cannot securely encrypt messages larger than n blocks long). Additionally EME2 can handle arbitrarily long tweaks (EME can only handle n bit tweaks, where n is the block length of the block cipher). The description of EME2 is a bit different from that of EME, the primary difference being that it encrypts the tweak. The description of EME2 is given in Fig. 6. The description given in Fig 6 is not the full description, if we assume that both the tweak length and the block length are multiples of the block length of the block cipher and the number of blocks are less less or equal to the block length of the block cipher, then the original description of EME2 translates to the description given in Fig. 6. But the above stated restrictions are not valid for the EME2 mode, the full description of the mode can handle plaintexts which do not satisfy these restrictions. For the full description of the mode see [1]. The main difference of the restricted description of EME2 compared to EME is in the handling of the tweak, as it can handle arbitrarily long tweaks and converts an arbitrary long tweak to a n bit value which is used in the mode. Also, EME2 uses three n bit keys, for processing the tweak it uses the key K_3, and the value of L which is used to mask the plain-texts and the ultimate outputs is first set to the value of K_2 and the bulk encryption is done by the key K_1.

9   A Distinguishing Attack on EME2

As evident from the algorithm in Fig. 6 there are four layers of *xtimes* operations performed in the algorithm. Thus, based on Assumption 1 and Proposition 1 one can get information about K_2, K_3 and M from the algorithm. We will call them as the K2-side-channel, K3-side-channel and M-side-channel respectively. Using these side-channel information one can mount a distinguishing attack on EME2. The adversary performs the following steps:

1. Apply an n block encryption query with no tweak.
   - Obtain K_2 using the K2-side-channel.
2. Apply an arbitrary encryption query with a n block tweak.
   - Obtain K_3 using the K3-side-channel.
3. Apply an encryption query with a one block tweak where $T = 0^n$, and a $n - 1$ block message $P = P_1||P_2||\ldots||P_{n-1}$, where $P_i = x^{i-1}K_2 \oplus xK_3$
   - Obtain $(n - 2)$-bits of M using the M-side-channel . Call this as M_1.

Algorithm EME2.Encrypt$_{K_1,K_2,K_3}^{T}(P)$

1. Partition P into $P_1, P_2, \ldots, P_m$
2. **if** len(T)= 0 **then** $T^* = E_{K_1}(K_3)$
3. **else**
4.   Partition the tweak T to $T_1, T_2, \ldots, T_r$
5.   **for** $i = 1$ to r
6. $K_3 \leftarrow xK_3$
7. $TT_i \leftarrow E_{K_1}(K_3 \oplus T_i) \oplus K_3$
8. $T^* = TT_1 \oplus TT_2 \oplus \cdots \oplus TT_r$
9. **end if**
10. $L \leftarrow K_2$
11. **for** $i = 1$ to m
12. $PPP_i \leftarrow E_{K_1}(L \oplus P_i)$
13. $L \leftarrow xL$
14. **end for**
15. $MP \leftarrow PPP_1 \oplus PPP_2 \oplus \cdots \oplus PPP_m \oplus T^*$
16. $MC \leftarrow E_{K_1}(MP)$
17. $M \leftarrow MP \oplus MC$
18. **for** $i \leftarrow 2$ to m
19. $M \leftarrow xM$
20. $CCC_i \leftarrow PPP_i \oplus M$
21. **end for**
22. $CCC_1 \leftarrow MC \oplus CCC_2 \oplus \cdots \oplus CCC_m \oplus T^*$
23. $L \leftarrow K_2$
24. **for** $i \leftarrow 1$ to m
25. $C_i \leftarrow E_{K_1}(CCC_i) \oplus L$
26. $L \leftarrow xL$
27. **end for**
28. **return** $C_1, C_2, \ldots, C_m$

Fig. 6. Encryption using EME2

4. Apply an encryption query with a one block tweak $T = 0^n$, and one block of message $P = P_1 = xK_3 \oplus K_2$
   – Obtain the corresponding ciphertext and call it C_1.
5. If the first $(n-2)$ bits of $C_1 \oplus xK_3 \oplus K_2$ are equal to M_1 output "EME2" otherwise "random".

To see why this attack works, note that according to the algorithm in Fig. 6, for query 3 we have the following:

Firstly, as there is a single block of tweak and the tweak is zero hence we get

$$T^* = E_{K_1}(xK_3) \oplus xK_3 \tag{4}$$

further, from line 12 of Fig. 6 we have, for all $i = 1, \ldots, n-1$,

$$PPP_i = E_K(x^{i-1}K_2 \oplus P_i) = E_K(x^{i-1}K_2 \oplus x^{i-1}K_2 \oplus xK_3) = E_K(xK_3)$$

Now, according to line 15 of the algorithm in Fig. 6 we have

$$MP = PPP_1 \oplus PPP_2 \oplus \ldots \oplus PPP_{n-1} \oplus T^* \tag{5}$$

$$= E_K(xK_3) \oplus T^* \tag{6}$$

$$= E_K(xK_3) \oplus E_{K_1}(xK_3) \oplus xK_3 \tag{7}$$

$$= xK_3 \tag{8}$$

Equation (6) follows from eq. (5) because the PPP_is are all equal and we assume that n is even. Equation (7) follows from eq. (6) by substituting the value of T^* in eq. (4). Thus, the value of M gets computed as

$$M = MP \oplus E_{K_1}(MP) = xK_3 \oplus E_{K_1}(xK_3) \tag{9}$$

Thus the value M_1 obtained in step 3 consists of the first $(n-1)$ bits of M as in eq. (9).

In the query in step 4, the tweak is again a single block and its value is zero, thus the value of T^* would be same as in eq. (4), and $PPP_1 = E_{K_1}(xK_3)$. Thus we would have $M = xK_3 \oplus E_{K_1}(xK_3)$, which is same as the value of M obtained as side channel information from query 3 (eq. (9)). Continuing, according to the algorithm in Fig. 6 we would have the cipher text C_1 computed as $C_1 = E_{K_1}(xK_3) \oplus K_2$. So, we have

$$C_1 \oplus xK_3 \oplus K_2 = xK_3 \oplus E_{K_1}(xK_3) \tag{10}$$

So comparing eq. (10) and eq. (9), we obtain $C_1 \oplus xK_3 \oplus K_2 = M$. The $(n-2)$ significant bits of M has been obtained from the side channel information in query 3. So if the check in step 5 is successful then with overwhelming probability the adversary can say that he is communicating with EME2.

The strong attack discussed in Section 7.2 for EME cannot be applied in the case of EME2. The strong attack for EME utilizes the fact that by obtaining the value of M one can obtain the block-cipher encryption of the tweak. As in EME the tweak can be freely chosen, hence one can get encryption of any string by suitably choosing the tweak. In EME2, the tweak is encrypted, this prevents one to apply the strong attack applicable to EME.

10 Conclusion

We presented some attacks on EME and EME2 assuming that *xtimes* leaks some information. These attacks does not contradict the claimed security of the modes, as the security definition and the security proofs for these modes does not assume any side-channel information being available to the adversary. Also the consequences of these attacks shown are not immediate. But, it points out that using *xtimes* indiscriminately may give rise to security weakness in true implementations.

Acknowledgements. The second author acknowledges the support from the CONACyT project 90775.

References

1. Draft standard architecture for wide-block encryption for shared storage media, https://siswg.net/index2.php?option=com_docman&task=doc_view &gid=84&Itemid=41
2. Agrawal, D., Archambeault, B., Rao, J.R., Rohatgi, P.: The EM side-channel(s). In: Kaliski Jr., B.S., Koç, Ç.K., Paar, C. (eds.) CHES 2002. LNCS, vol. 2523, pp. 29–45. Springer, Heidelberg (2003)
3. Anderson, R.J., Kuhn, M.G.: Low cost attacks on tamper resistant devices. In: Christianson, B., Crispo, B., Lomas, T.M.A., Roe, M. (eds.) Security Protocols 1997. LNCS, vol. 1361, pp. 125–136. Springer, Heidelberg (1998)
4. Burman, S., Mukhopadhyay, D., Veezhinathan, K.: LFSR based stream ciphers are vulnerable to power attacks. In: Srinathan, K., Rangan, C.P., Yung, M. (eds.) INDOCRYPT 2007. LNCS, vol. 4859, pp. 384–392. Springer, Heidelberg (2007)
5. Chakraborty, D., Sarkar, P.: A new mode of encryption providing a tweakable strong pseudo-random permutation. In: Robshaw, M.J.B. (ed.) FSE 2006. LNCS, vol. 4047, pp. 293–309. Springer, Heidelberg (2006)
6. Chakraborty, D., Sarkar, P.: HCH: A new tweakable enciphering scheme using the hash-counter-hash approach. IEEE Transactions on Information Theory 54(4), 1683–1699 (2008)
7. Halevi, S.: EME*: Extending eme to handle arbitrary-length messages with associated data. In: Canteaut, A., Viswanathan, K. (eds.) INDOCRYPT 2004. LNCS, vol. 3348, pp. 315–327. Springer, Heidelberg (2004)
8. Halevi, S.: Invertible universal hashing and the TET encryption mode. In: Menezes, A. (ed.) CRYPTO 2007. LNCS, vol. 4622, pp. 412–429. Springer, Heidelberg (2007)
9. Halevi, S., Rogaway, P.: A tweakable enciphering mode. In: Boneh, D. (ed.) CRYPTO 2003. LNCS, vol. 2729, pp. 482–499. Springer, Heidelberg (2003)
10. Halevi, S., Rogaway, P.: A parallelizable enciphering mode. In: Okamoto, T. (ed.) CT-RSA 2004. LNCS, vol. 2964, pp. 292–304. Springer, Heidelberg (2004)
11. Joux, A.: Cryptanalysis of the EMD mode of operation. In: Biham, E. (ed.) EUROCRYPT 2003. LNCS, vol. 2656, pp. 1–16. Springer, Heidelberg (2003)
12. Joux, A., Delaunay, P.: Galois LFSR, embedded devices and side channel weaknesses. In: Barua, R., Lange, T. (eds.) INDOCRYPT 2006. LNCS, vol. 4329, pp. 436–451. Springer, Heidelberg (2006)

13. Kocher, P.C.: Timing attacks on implementations of diffie-hellman, RSA, DSS, and other systems. In: Koblitz, N. (ed.) CRYPTO 1996. LNCS, vol. 1109, pp. 104–113. Springer, Heidelberg (1996)
14. Kocher, P.C., Jaffe, J., Jun, B.: Differential power analysis. In: Wiener, M. (ed.) CRYPTO 1999. LNCS, vol. 1666, pp. 388–397. Springer, Heidelberg (1999)
15. McGrew, D.A., Fluhrer, S.R.: The security of the extended codebook (XCB) mode of operation. In: Adams, C., Miri, A., Wiener, M. (eds.) SAC 2007. LNCS, vol. 4876, pp. 311–327. Springer, Heidelberg (2007)
16. Phan, R.C.-W., Goi, B.-M.: On the security bounds of CMC, EME, EME^+ and EME^* modes of operation. In: Qing, S., Mao, W., López, J., Wang, G. (eds.) ICICS 2005. LNCS, vol. 3783, pp. 136–146. Springer, Heidelberg (2005)
17. Rogaway, P.: The EMD mode of operation (a tweaked, wide-blocksize, strong PRP). Cryptology ePrint Archive, Report 2002/148 (2002), http://eprint.iacr.org/
18. Sarkar, P.: Improving upon the TET mode of operation. In: Nam, K.-H., Rhee, G. (eds.) ICISC 2007. LNCS, vol. 4817, pp. 180–192. Springer, Heidelberg (2007)
19. Wang, P., Feng, D., Wu, W.: HCTR: A variable-input-length enciphering mode. In: Feng, D., Lin, D., Yung, M. (eds.) CISC 2005. LNCS, vol. 3822, pp. 175–188. Springer, Heidelberg (2005)

TWIS – A Lightweight Block Cipher

Shri Kant Ojha[1], Naveen Kumar[2], Kritika Jain[2], and Sangeeta[2]

[1] Joint Cipher Bureau, Department of Defence R & D, Metcalfe House,
Delhi-110054, India
[2] Department of Computer Science, University of Delhi, Delhi-110007, India

Abstract. A new 128-bit block cipher, TWIS is proposed. It uses key size
of 128-bits. The design targets to software environment for resource constrained applications. It is inspired from existing block cipher, CLEFIA.
Although the proposed design uses less resources as compared to CLEFIA,
it compares favorably with CLEFIA in terms of security provided.

Keywords: Cipher, CLEFIA, lightweight cryptography, and S-Box.

1   Introduction

Cryptographic techniques are used to protect sensitive and valuable information
against any undesirable third party. In cryptography, we encrypt plaintext i.e.
original message to be sent, using a key, which produces ciphertext i.e encrypted
message. The encrypted message is decrypted by the receiver to get plaintext.
There are in general two types of cryptographic algorithms, secret key (or symmetric key) and public-key (or asymmetric key) algorithms. While symmetric key
algorithms use the same secret key to encrypt and decrypt a message, asymmetric algorithms use different keys for encryption and decryption. The symmetric
key algorithms are further classified as block ciphers and stream ciphers whereas
asymmetric key algorithms work only as block ciphers.

While block ciphers encrypt a block of data at a time, stream ciphers produce
a series of data bits called keystream bits (a sequence of bits used as a key).
In case of stream ciphers, encryption is accomplished by xoring the plaintext
bits with key stream bits. Generation of keystream bits is independent of the
plaintext. Hence, the ciphertext produced by a stream cipher for the same unit of
plaintext may differ depending on where it appears. In contrast, the ciphertext
produced by a block cipher depends on plaintext and secret key only. Hence they
will always produce same output after encryption when provided with particular
pair of plaintext block and secret key. Some of the common examples of stream
cipher include Geffe, Grain, Trivium, Lex, Salsa20. DES, AES, RSA, are some
common examples of block ciphers. Whereas former two are symmetric block
ciphers, the latter is an asymmetric block cipher.

Conventional algorithms such as AES although quite secure, are not suitable
for the extremely resource constrained applications such as RFID tags and sensor networks. The field of lightweight cryptography deals with designing ciphers
for such environments. It deals with refining existing cryptographic algorithms

A. Prakash and I. Sen Gupta (Eds.): ICISS 2009, LNCS 5905, pp. 280–291, 2009.
© Springer-Verlag Berlin Heidelberg 2009

or discovering new algorithms for providing high security in constrained environments [2],[1]. In lightweight cryptography there is trade-off between security, cost, and performance; and it is highly difficult to optimize all the three [2]. One also needs to carry out the trade off between - hardware level and software level optimization. For example, bit permutations can be implemented in hardware without any cost but can slow down performance in software, and large substitution tables are good to implement in software but they are relatively difficult to implement in hardware [2].

A number of symmetric lightweight block ciphers have been proposed in the literature - for example DESL [5], PRESENT [1], HIGHT [3], CLEFIA [10], LCASE [9], Cobra-H64 [6] and Cobra-H128 [6]. DESL [2],[5] is the modification of well known cipher DES. It modifies DES by replacing 8-S boxes of DES by one cryptographically stronger S-box [5]. This lightweight variant uses approximately 20% smaller chip than DES and 1,850 gate equivalents(GEs) against 2,310 GEs used in DES. PRESENT [1] is a new lightweight block cipher based on SPN with 32 rounds, a block size of 64 bits, and a key size of 80 or 128 bits. Design of PRESENT is very simple and it provides good performance in both hardware and software. Its structure favors repetition and hence it can be compactly implemented in hardware. As it requires only 1570 GEs its hardware requirements are competitive with today's leading stream ciphers. HIGHT [3] uses 64-bit block lenght and 128-bit key length.It is a hardware oriented cipher, based on 32-round iterative strucutre which is modification of Generalized Fiestel structure. HIGHT uses vary simple operations such as XOR, addition mod 2^8, and left bitwise rotation, and can be implmented with 3048 GE's on $0.25 \mu m$ technology. Hence it is suitable for low-cost, low-power, and ultra-light implementation. CLEFIA [11] is another lightweight block cipher using variable block length and variable key size of 128, 192 and 246 bits. It is based on 4-branch compact but Generalized Feistel structure. Diffusion matrices and two S-box system is used to provide high security. LCASE [9] exploits inherent parallelism of the cellular automata for designing a high speed cipher. It improves over ICEBERG and AES significantly in terms of hardware complexity. Cobra-H64 [6] and Cobra-H128 [6] are two new high speed ciphers that make use of cryptographic primitives based on data-dependent permutations. They support variable plaintext lengths of size 64-bit and 128-bit. The ciphers exploit switchable operations to prevent weak keys. The authors have shown through hardware implementation of the ciphers that they are suitable for high-speed networks [6].

In this paper, we propose a new lightweight block cipher, TWIS. The proposed cipher is inspired from CLEFIA [10,11]. TWIS is a 128-bit block cipher which uses key of size 128 bit. It consists of two parts: Key scheduling part and Data processing part. It employs a 2-branch Generalized Fiestel structure which employs key whitening parts at the beginning and at the end of the cipher. The number of rounds taken by TWIS before producing a ciphertext is 10. TWIS also uses an S-Box and a diffusion matrix that enables good diffusion properties [4] while generating keystream.

TWIS is designed to employ good balance between three fundamental features: security, speed and cost of implementation. The salient features of TWIS are as under:

1. G-function used is same for both encryption and decryption.
2. We have used only 11 round keys. Each round key is of 4 bytes, totaling only 44 bytes.
3. Each of the 10 rounds during encryption or decryption process uses two round keys. G-function as defined in section 2.3 is called twice in one iteration, each call to G-function uses a single round key.

The paper is organized as follows: section 2 gives the design criteria and discusses the algorithm of the cipher. Section 3 describes the cryptanalysis of the cipher and the complexity of the cipher is discussed in section 4. Finally we conclude the paper in section 5.

2   Design Criteria

The design of the cipher is inspired from CLEFIA with an aim to make it lighter without compromising the security. The security requirements correspond to a computational complexity of 2^{128}, equivalent to exhaustive key search. For making the cipher lighter than CLEFIA, we have to take into account both time and space taken by the cipher in software.

The proposed cipher has 10 rounds for encryption/decryption. The repeated use of 64-bit G-function is to have a strong encryption algorithm, a single round of encryption might constitute a weak algorithm [7]. Each round of encryption/decryption uses two rounds of Fiestel network to scramble all bits of text block. The S-Box is used in the cipher to have good diffusion properties [4] while generating a ciphertext. It uses diffusion matrix [11] while generating round keys. The cipher also makes use of key whitening steps to increase the difficulty of key search attacks against the remainder of the cipher.

An overview of the different blocks of cipher for encryption/ decryption is shown in Fig.2 and Fig.3. The cipher uses a 2-branch Generalized Fiestel structure with additional key whitening of the input and output. It is divided into two parts namely, key scheduling and data processing.

2.1   Key Scheduling

The key scheduling part of the cipher deals with generation of round keys used in data processing part. Let K be the 128-bit initial key, which will produce 11 round keys, denoted by RK_i $(0 \le i \le 10)$, of 32-bit each. The key, K is divided into 16 bytes, denoted by $K[i]$ for $(1 \le i \le 16)$.

The complete algorithm for Key scheduling is as under:

1. for *round_counter* $\leftarrow$ 1 to *number_rounds* + 1 do the following:
   (a) $K = K <<< 3$ ▷ left rotate the key by 3 bits

(b) $K[round\_counter] \leftarrow S(K[round\_counter].0x3f)$

(c) $K[15] \leftarrow S(K[15].0x3f)$

(d) $K[16] \leftarrow K[16] \oplus round\_counter$

(e) $(y_0, y_1, y_2, y_3) \leftarrow (K[13], K[14], K[15], K[16])$

(f) $RK^t_{round\_counter-1} \leftarrow M(y_0, y_1, y_2, y_3)^t$

S is nonlinear 8-bit S-box, and M is 4×4 matrix defined later in subsequent sections.

2.2   Data Processing

The data processing part of TWIS consists of an encryption part, ENC_r and a decryption part, DEC_r for decryption. ENC_r and DEC_r are based on the 2-branch Generalized Feistal structure. Let $P, C \in \{0, 1\}^{128}$ be a plaintext and corresponding ciphertext respectively, and let $P_i, C_i \in \{0, 1\}^{32}$ $(0 \le i < 4)$ be divided plaintext and ciphertext where $P = P_0|P_1|P_2|P_3$ and $C = C_0|C_1|C_2|C_3$, and $RK_i \in \{0, 1\}^{32}$ $(0 \le i \le 10)$ be round keys provided by the key scheduling part. Then 10-round encryption function ENC_r is defined as follows and is as shown in figure 2:

ENC_r :

1. $T_0|T_1|T_2|T_3 \leftarrow (P_0 \oplus RK_0)|P_1|P_2|(P_3 \oplus RK_1)$
2. for $round\_counter \leftarrow 1$ to 10, repeat steps (a) to (g)
    (a) $X_0|X_1 \leftarrow G - Function(RK_{round\_counter-1}, T_0, T_1)$
    (b) $T_2 \leftarrow X_0 \oplus T_2$
       $T_3 \leftarrow X_1 \oplus T_3$
    (c) $T_1 \leftarrow T_1 <<< 8$
       $T_3 \leftarrow T_3 >>> 1$
    (d) $T_0|T_1|T_2|T_3 \leftarrow T_2|T_3|T_0|T_1$
    (e) $X_0|X_1 \leftarrow G - Function(RK_{round\_counter}, T_0, T_3)$
    (f) $T_1 \leftarrow X_0 \oplus T_1$
       $T_2 \leftarrow X_1 \oplus T_2$
    (g) $T_2 \leftarrow T_2 >>> 1$
       $T_3 \leftarrow T_3 <<< 8$
3. $C_0|C_1|C_2|C_3 \leftarrow (T_0 \oplus RK_2)|T_1|T_2|(T_3 \oplus RK_3)$

The 10-round decryption function is just reverse of encryption process and is defined as follows and is shown in figure 3:

DEC_r :

1. $T_0|T_1|T_2|T_3 \leftarrow (C_0 \oplus RK_2)|C_1|C_2|(C_3 \oplus RK_3)$
2. for $round\_counter \leftarrow 10$ down to 1, repeat steps (a) to (g)
    (a) $T_2 \leftarrow T_2 <<< 1$
       $T_3 \leftarrow T_3 >>> 8$

(b) $X_0|X_1 \leftarrow G - Function(RK_{round\_counter}, T_0, T_3)$

(c) $T_1 \leftarrow X_0 \oplus T_1$

  $T_2 \leftarrow X_1 \oplus T_2$

(d) $T_0|T_1|T_2|T_3 \leftarrow T_2|T_3|T_0|T_1$

(e) $T_1 \leftarrow T_1 >>> 8$

  $T_3 \leftarrow T_3 <<< 1$

(f) $X_0|X_1 \leftarrow G - Function(RK_{round\_counter-1}, T_0, T_1)$

(g) $T_2 \leftarrow X_0 \oplus T_2$

  $T_3 \leftarrow X_1 \oplus T_3$

3. $P_0|P_1|P_2|P_3 \leftarrow (T_0 \oplus RK_0)|T_1|T_2|(T_3 \oplus RK_1)$

2.3 TWIS Building Blocks

In this subsection we will describe the building blocks i.e. G-function, F-function, S-box, and diffusion matrix 'M' used in the cipher.

G-Function

It takes two inputs, 32 bit round key and 64 bit data. It calls F-function, that takes input of 32-bit round key and 32-bit intermediate ciphertext or plaintext. Mathematically, G-function can be written as in equation 1:

$$G - function = \begin{cases} \{0,1\}^{32} \times \{0,1\}^{64} \rightarrow \{0,1\}^{64} \\ (RK_{(32)}, X_{(64)}) \mapsto Y_{(64)} \end{cases} \tag{1}$$

The algorithm employed by G-function is as under:

1. $T_0|T_1 \leftarrow X$
2. $T_0 \leftarrow T_1 \oplus F(RK, T_0)$
3. $Y_0|Y_1 \leftarrow T_1|T_0$

F-Function

It takes two 32-bit inputs and produces 32-bit output. The input/output functions are defined by equation 2 [10].

$$F = \begin{cases} \{0,1\}^{32} \times \{0,1\}^{32} \rightarrow \{0,1\}^{32} \\ (RK_{(32)}, x_{(32)}) \mapsto y_{(32)} \end{cases} \tag{2}$$

The F-function used takes 32-bit round key RK and 32-bit intermediate plaintext or ciphertext, depending on encryption or decryption, denoted by X. The 32-bit output is returned in Y. The algorithm used by F-function is as under:

1. $T_0|T_1|T_2|T_3 \leftarrow RK \oplus X$
2. $T_0 \leftarrow S(T_0.0x3f)$

  $T_1 \leftarrow S(T_1.0x3f)$

  $T_2 \leftarrow S(T_2.0x3f)$

  $T_3 \leftarrow S(T_3.0x3f)$

3. $Y_0|Y_1|Y_2|Y_3 \leftarrow T_2|T_3|T_0|T_1$

Table 1. S-box - S used

	.0	.1	.2	.3	.4	.5	.6	.7	.8	.9	.a	.b	.c	.d	.e	.f
0.	90	49	d1	c6	2f	33	74	fb	95	6d	82	ea	0e	b0	a8	1c
1.	28	d0	4b	92	5c	ee	85	b1	c4	0a	76	3d	63	f9	17	af
2.	bf	bf	19	65	f7	7a	32	20	16	ce	e4	83	9d	5b	4c	d8
3.	ee	99	2e	f8	d4	9b	0f	13	29	89	67	cd	71	dd	b6	f4

S-box

The cipher employs an S-box with 6-bit input which yields 8-bit output. The S-Box used by TWIS is shown in Table 1.

Diffusion Matrix

The diffusion matrix is employed at the round key generation step to ensure diffusion at the key level making it difficult for the cryptanalyst to know exact key. The diffusion matrix M [10] is defined as follows:

$$
M = \begin{pmatrix}
0x01 & 0x02 & 0x04 & 0x06 \\
0x02 & 0x01 & 0x06 & 0x04 \\
0x04 & 0x06 & 0x01 & 0x02 \\
0x06 & 0x04 & 0x02 & 0x01
\end{pmatrix}
$$

3 Cryptanalysis

In this section, we consider some general attacks that are possible on block ciphers and investigate to what extent TWIS is resistant to them. In ideal situation there should be no attack faster than exhaustive key search having computational complexity 2^{128}.

3.1 Statistical Testing

NIST Statistical Test Suite, SP800-22 [12] is widely used testing software for pseudo random sequence generator. It is provided with 16 tests which test the random nature of bits generated by any cipher algorithm[1]. The results of statistical test on TWIS are shown in Table 2.

We used 100 files each containing 10^7 bits sequence, using default parameters. Table 2 indicates that when we convert the block cipher to stream cipher, the bits produced are random in nature.

3.2 Avalanche Effect

Avalanche effect states that if there is single bit change in key or plaintext, then there must be at least 50% change in number of ciphertext/ round key bits.

---

[1] The details of the tests can be referred in [12] and test suite can be downloaded from http://csrc.nist.gov/groups/ST/toolkit/rng/index.html

Table 2. Statistical Results of TWIS

Statistical Tests	P-value (TWIS)
Frequency	0.727003
Block Frequency (m = 128)	0.880692
Cumulative Sum - Forward	0.577018
Cumulative Sum - Backward	0.318680
Runs	0.711364
Long Runs of Ones (M = 10000)	0.753960
Rank	0.331621
Spectral DFT	0.654639
Non-overlapping Templates (m = 9 , B = 000000001)	0.970310
Overlapping Template	0.299256
Universal (L = 7, Q = 1280)	0.517380
Approximate Entropy (m = 10)	0.677380
Random Excursions (x = +1)	0.078587
Random Excursions Variant (x = -1)	0.732206
Linear Complexity (M = 500)	0.489456
Serial (m = 5, $\nabla \psi_m^2$)	0.130827

Effect on Round Keys on Changing Single Bit of Key

When a single bit of key is changed, there should be change in at least half of the
bits of the round keys generated from the initial key. When this test is applied
to TWIS, we found that there is at least 50% change of bits in round key on
single bit change of key.

The cipher produces 11 round keys, each of 32 bits. Thus, having 352 bits in
total. As we can see from the graph in figure 1, for 100 executions of the cipher
for different single bit change in key, there is approximately 50% change in bits
of round key. Thus, the avalanche effect requirement is satisfied by TWIS.

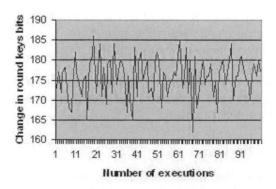

Fig. 1. Effect on round key

Effect on Ciphertext on Changing 1 bit of key keeping Plaintext Constant

A set of 1000 keys were generated randomly. For each of 1000 128-bit random key, 128-bit ciphertext is obtained keeping the plaintext fixed. We changed a single bit of key, and again obtained corresponding ciphertext. We found the number of bits changed in two ciphertexts by xoring them. We organized the the number of bits changed in five classes; 0-58, 59-62, 63-65, 66-69, and 70-128 [8]. The observations are shown in Table 3.

Table 3. Key/Ciphertext Avalanche Effect keeping plaintext fixed

Class	Frequency for Number of bits uncorrelated
0-58	156
59-62	231
63-65	211
66-69	235
70-128	167

From Table 3, it is concluded that in TWIS 61.3% times atleast half of the bits of key/keystream are uncorrelated, satisfying avalanche effect.

Effect on Ciphertext on Changing 1 bit of Plaintext keeping Key Constant

A set of 1000 random plaintexts are generated. For each of 1000 128-bit random plaintexts, 128-bit ciphertext is obtained keeping key fixed. We changed a single bit of plaintext, and again computed corresponding ciphertext. We find the number of bits changed in two ciphertexts by xoring them. After finding change in bits, we classified them into into 5 classes; 0-58, 59-62, 63-65, 66-69, and 70-128 [8]. The observations are shown in Table 4.

Table 4. Plaintext/Ciphertext Avalanche Effect keeping key fixed

Class	Frequency for Number of bits uncorrelated
0-58	156
59-62	217
63-65	234
66-69	230
70-128	163

From Table 4, it is concluded that 62.7% of times atleast half of the bits of key/keystream are uncorrelated, satisfying avalanche effect.

4   Complexity

The major goal behind the design of the cipher is to make it lighter so that it can be used in extremely resource-constrained environment like RFID tag and sensor

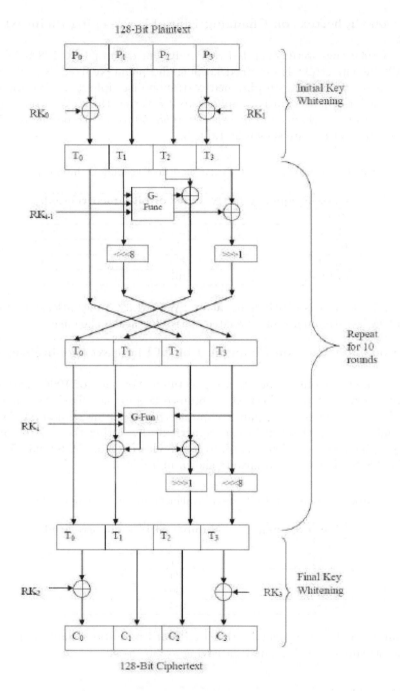

Fig. 2. The Encryption Process

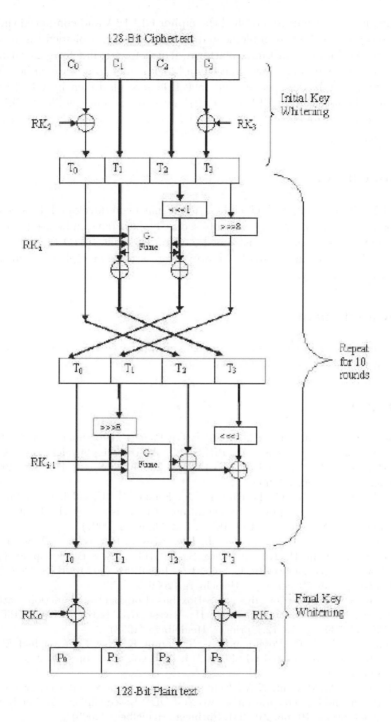

Fig. 3. The Decryption Process

networks. For this, we have modified the cipher CLEFIA and compared the time and memory it takes when implemented in software. By implementing both the ciphers on gcc compiler in Linux platform, it was found that for generating 10^7 bits using counter mode, which converts a block cipher to stream cipher, TWIS takes approximately 0.98 seconds against 1.98 seconds taken by CLEFIA. On examining the space, CLEFIA takes 121 bytes of memory while TWIS takes only 114 bytes of memory. However, both the ciphers take key length of 128 bits, having computational complexity of 2^{128}.

5   Conclusion

A new 128-bit lightweight block cipher, TWIS has been developed. It is designed with the motivation of building a highly secure cipher that can be used in devices used in extremely resource-constrained environment like RFID tags and sensor networks. As part of future work, we propose to study the cipher for linear and differential cryptanalysis.

Acknowledgment

The authors would like to acknowledge the support from research grant of University of Delhi: Dean(R)/R&D/2008/230.

References

1. Bogdanov, A., Knudsen, L.R., Leander, G., Paar, C., Poschmann, A., Robshaw, M.J.B., Seurin, Y., Vikkelsoe, C.: PRESENT: An Ultra-Lightweight Block Cipher. In: Paillier, P., Verbauwhede, I. (eds.) CHES 2007. LNCS, vol. 4727, pp. 450–466. Springer, Heidelberg (2007)
2. Eisenbarth, T., Paar, C., Poschmann, A., Kumar, S., Uhsadel, L.: A Survey of Lightweight Cryptography Implementations, Copublished by the IEEE CS and the IEEE CASS, 0740-7475/07/. IEEE, Los Alamitos (2007)
3. Hong, D., Sung, J., Hong, S., Lim, J., Lee, S., Koo, B., Lee, C., Chang, D., Lee, J., Jeong, K., Kim, H., Kim, J., Chee, S.: HIGHT: A New Block Cipher Suitable for Low-Resource Device. In: Goubin, L., Matsui, M. (eds.) CHES 2006. LNCS, vol. 4249, pp. 46–59. Springer, Heidelberg (2006)
4. Kim, K.: Construction of DES-like S-Box based on Boolean Functions satisfying the SAC. In: Matsumoto, T., Imai, H., Rivest, R.L. (eds.) ASIACRYPT 1991. LNCS, vol. 739, pp. 59–72. Springer, Heidelberg (1993)
5. Leander, G., Paar, C., Poschmann, A., Schramm, K.: New Lightweight DES Variants. In: Biryukov, A. (ed.) FSE 2007. LNCS, vol. 4593, pp. 196–210. Springer, Heidelberg (2007)
6. Sklavos, N., Moldovyan, N.A., Koufopavlou, O.: High Speed Networking Security:Design and Implementation of Two New DDP-Based Ciphers. Mobile Networks and Applications 10, pp. 219–231. Springer, Heidelberg (2005)
7. Scheiner, B., Kelsey, J., Whiting, D., Wagner, D., Hall, C., Ferguson, N.: Twofish: A 128-bit Block Cipher. In: Counterpane System, Berkeley, California (1998)

8. Soumez, M., Doganaksoy, T.A., Calik, C.: Detailed Statistical Analysis of Synchronous Stream Ciphers. In: SASC 2006: Stream Cipher Revisited (2006)
9. Tripathy, S., Nandi, S.: LCASE: Lightweight Cellular Automata-based Symmetric-key Encryption. International Journal of Network Security 8(2), 243–252 (2009)
10. The 128-bit Block Cipher CLEFIA: Algorithm Specification. On-line document, 2007. Sony Corporation (2007)
11. The 128-bit Block Cipher CLEFIA: Design Rationale. Revision 1.0, 2007. Sony Corporation (2007)
12. NIST Special Publication 800-22. A Statistical Test for Random and Pseudo-random Number Generators for Cryptographic Application [EB/OL].[2001-05-15] (2001)

Quantitative Analysis of a Probabilistic Non-repudiation Protocol through Model Checking

(Short Paper)

Indranil Saha[1] and Debapriyay Mukhopadhyay[2]

[1] Computer Science Department
University of California, Los Angeles, CA 90095, USA
indranil@cs.ucla.edu
[2] Rebaca Technologies Pvt. Ltd.
Block EP & GP, Sector V, Kolkata-91, India
debapriyaym@gmail.com

Abstract. In the probabilistic non-repudiation protocol without a trusted third party as presented in [5], the recipient of a service can cheat the originator of the service with some probability. This probability indicates the degree of fairness of the protocol and is referred as ϵ-fairness. In this paper, we analyze the protocol quantitatively through probabilistic model checking. The ϵ-fairness is quantitatively measured by modeling the protocol in PRISM model checker and verifying appropriate property specified in PCTL. Moreover, our analysis gives proper insight to choose proper values for different parameters associated with the protocol in such a way that certain degree of fairness can be achieved and therefore answers the reverse question, given the degree of fairness ϵ, how should one choose the protocol parameters to ensure fairness.

1 Introduction

In an electronic world, requests for a service from a client and eventually its getting the service from the service provider and then sending an acknowledgment, considered as a proof of getting the service, to the service provider are all implemented as network protocols. The service provider is called the *originator* of the service and the client is called the *recipient* of the service. Repudiation is defined as "denial by one of the entities involved in a communication of having participated in all or part of the communication". Solutions to these problems offer non-repudiation services and the protocols implementing these solutions are thus called non-repudiation protocols.

In this paper we consider the probabilistic non-repudiation protocol [5] that offers non-repudiation service guaranteed with a certain probability. The protocol does not require to involve any trusted third party. *Fairness* property of a non-repudiation protocol here is replaced by ϵ-*fairness* which ensures that at each step of the protocol run, either both parties receive their expected items,

A. Prakash and I. Sen Gupta (Eds.): ICISS 2009, LNCS 5905, pp. 292–300, 2009.

or the probability that the cheating party gains any valuable information, while the other party gains nothing, is $\leq \epsilon$ (with $\epsilon \in [0, 1]$). ϵ is called the *degree of fairness*. It is to note that lower the value of ϵ, the better the non-repudiation protocol is in terms of fairness.

In this work we view the probabilistic non-repudiation protocol proposed in [5] as a 2-player game [4] between the originator (O) of a service and the recipient(R) of the service, wherein the originator cannot cheat the recipient, but the recipient can cheat the originator. We use probabilistic model checking to quantitatively analyze the game. This protocol has been previously modeled and analyzed to estimate the fairness using process algebraic techniques by reducing it to an equivalence problem between two appropriately defined systems [1,2]. In [6], the protocol has been modeled as Probabilistic Timed System, which has then been translated into PRISM specifications for relating degree of fairness of the protocol with the other parameters of the protocol. Our work deviates significantly from these prior works in the approach and the kind of results we present.In [6], the originator and the recipient have been modeled such that infinite rounds of the protocol is possible. We deviate from this thought as this assumption of infinite number of rounds is not realistic. We introduce two new parameters in our model - 1) the maximum number of rounds r_{max} originator may take to finish the protocol; 2) for a particular run of a protocol originator chooses the number of rounds it will take to send the message according to a geometric distribution with success probability p_{geo}. In all the earlier works recipient has always sent the acknowledgement with a fixed probability, but what is more natural from a malicious recipient's point of view is that it decreases the acknowledgement probability as the protocol proceeds. This aspect has also been captured in our analysis. We have carried out analysis considering all the parameters of the protocol and have tried to figure out the impact of a particular parameter on the degree of fairness. Actually, along with measuring the degree of fairness quantitatively, we answer the reverse question: given the degree of fairness ϵ, how the originator can choose the protocol parameters at its end to ensure fairness. This is missing in all the earlier works including [6], wherein probability of breaking fairness has been related only with the recipient's probability for sending an acknowledgement. Our main motivation is to help deployer of the protocol to provide with a tool with which he can properly set the protocol parameters to ensure the desired degree of fairness.

2   Probabilistic Non-repudiation Protocol

In this section, we briefly describe the probabilistic non-repudiation protocol without a trusted third party [5]. Such a protocol should ensure fair exchange of messages between the originator O who offers a service, and the recipient R who is expected to confirm having received the service. During the protocol, in addition to the message, a non-repudiation of origin (NRO) token and a non-repudiation of receipt(NRR) token have to be transmitted as evidences usable to resolve possible future disputes.

The protocol starts when the recipient R sends a request for a message to the originator O of the message. Having received the request, O chooses a number r, the number of rounds it will take to send the message, according to a geometric distribution. Though using geometric distribution to choose the number of rounds may lead to infinite steps, for practical purpose we assume that the originator will fix a maximum number of rounds r_{max}. If the process of finding out the number of rounds does not stop before the maximum number of rounds, the originator would consider the value of maximum number of rounds to be the number of rounds to send the message. The value of r is neither disclosed to R nor it is possible for R to compute it. The originator O also computes r functions $f_1, \ldots, f_r$ which are parts of a function composition. If the requested message is M, then the functions f_i's are such that

$$f_r(M) \circ f_{r-1}(M) \circ \ldots \circ f_1(M) = M$$

$f_i(M)$'s are called *message components*.

In step i, O sends $f_{r-i+1}(M)$ to R. R sends an acknowledgement for receiving every message component. As the messages are sent in reverse order, R has to receive all these component messages to get the requested message. Moreover, the composition function is chosen in such a way that it is not commutative. So R cannot compute the part of the message before getting all the message components. To cheat O, R needs to guess the last round and not to send acknowledgement in that very round.

3   Modeling and Analysis of Probabilistic Non-repudiation Protocol

We carry out our analysis of the non-repudiation protocol by probabilistic model checker PRISM [3]. Non-repudiation protocol exhibits both non-deterministic and probabilistic behavior and hence can be best modeled as a Markov Decision Process (MDP). The originator chooses the number of rounds it will take to send the message according to a geometric distribution with success probability p_{geo} and the maximum number of rounds r_{max} it may take to finish the protocol. The success of the originator depends on choosing these two parameters. On the other hand, recipient's success to cheat the originator depends on the probability of sending the acknowledgement after getting each message component. We call this probability the *acknowledgement probability*. The recipient may always send the acknowledgement with a fixed probability, or it may decrease the probability by a fixed amount d at each step. The *acknowledgement probability* and d forms the *trust profile* of a recipient. The trust profile of a recipient is formally represented as a tuple $\{p_{ack}, d\}$.

For a recipient with a particular trust profile, our objective is to enable an originator to come up with specific strategy so that the fairness of the non-repudiation protocol can be achieved. We show that probabilistic model checking is a promising approach to achieve this goal. We use probabilistic model checker PRISM to formally model the probabilistic behavior of the originator and the recipient and quantitatively measure the *cheating probability* in different setting by specifying a suitable PCTL property. Finally we show how the originator can precisely obtain the values of r_{max} and p_{geo} to defeat a recipient with a particular trust profile.

3.1 MDP Models for Recipient and Originator

The MDP models for the recipient and the originator are shown in Figure 1(a) and Figure 1(b) respectively . At the beginning, the recipient stays in state R0. The recipient starts the protocol by sending a request message to the originator, and moves to state R1. In the model, a boolean variable *req* initially set to 0 is changed to 1 during this transition. Another boolean variable *ready_recipient*, initially set to 0, is used to denote that the recipient is ready to receive message from the originator. During the transition from state R0 to state R1, this boolean variable is set to 1. In state R1, the recipient receives the message component sent by the originator. Now, the recipient can send acknowledgement to the originator for the message component with probability p_{ack} and move to state R2, or it may not send the acknowledgement with probability $1 - p_{ack}$ and move to state R3. During both the transitions, *ready_recipient* is set to 0. If the recipient moves to state R2 it sets a boolean flag *ack* to 1 to indicate that it has sent the acknowledgement. Moreover, the recipient decreases the probability p_{ack} by a specific value d which is a component of its trust profile. From state R2, the recipient goes back to the state R1, and during this transition, it sets the flag *ack* to 0, and the flag *ready_recipient* to 1. If the protocol stops after fair transactions, then the recipient stays in state R1 at the end of the protocol. If the recipient reaches state R3, it may or may not be able to cheat the originator based on whether it has moved to state R3 in the last round of the transaction.

The originator starts the protocol being in state O0. The originator model uses three boolean flags: *msg* is used to indicate that the current message component

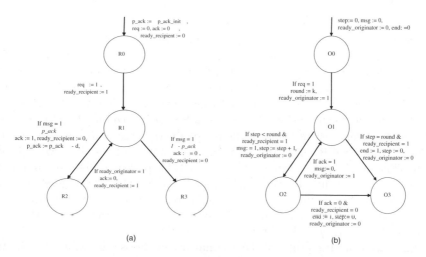

(a)   (b)

Fig. 1. Probabilistic Model for (a) Recipient (b) Originator

has been sent, *ready_originator* is used to denote that the originator is ready to send the current message component, and *end* is used to denote the end of the current transaction. Initially, all these flags are set to 0. Moreover, the originator uses a variable *round* to indicate the number of steps it will take to send the complete message, and another variable *step* to indicate in which step of the transaction it is currently in. In state O0 the originator waits for a request for a message from the recipient. When the flag *req* is 1, the originator starts its preparation phase to send the message. In this phase the originator chooses the value of *round* according to geometric distribution with success probability p_{geo} and maximum value for *round* r_{max} (In Figure 1, the chosen value for round has been shown as k). Choosing the success probability p_{geo}, and the maximum value for *round* is the part of originator's strategy to have a fair transaction done. After choosing the value for *round*, the originator sets *ready_originator* to 1 and moves to state O1. In state O1, the originator checks if *step* is less than *round*. If that is the case, it sends the current message component to the recipient and moves to state O2. During this transition, boolean variable *msg* is set to 1, *step* is incremented by 1 and the flag *ready_originator* is set to 0. If *step* is equal to *round* in step O1, then the required message components have been sent. In that case, the originator sets the flag *end* to 1, variable *step* and flag *ready_originator* to 0, and moves to state O3. In state O2, the originator waits for the acknowledgement from the recipient. While staying in state O2, if the originator finds *ack* to be 1, it sets *msg* to 0, sets the flag *ready_originator* to 1, and moves to state O1. But if *ack* does not become 1, but the flag *ready_recipient* becomes 0 (which, in fact, indicates that the recipient has moved to state R3), the originator decides that the recipient has cheated. In that case it stops the protocol by setting the flag *end* to 1, and moves to state O3. During this transition, the variable *step* and the flag *ready_originator* is set to 0.

3.2   Experimental Results

In this section we discuss the experiment we have carried out with the model checker PRISM to analyze non-repudiation protocol quantitatively. We are mainly interested to know with what probability the recipient would be able to cheat the originator in different settings, and try to find out what should be the originator's strategy to make this probability as low as possible. We refer this probability as *cheating probability*. To measure the cheating probability we use the following PCTL property: $P_{min} = ?[trueU((step = round) \wedge (r\_state = 3))]$ where r_state denotes the state of the recipient. $(r\_state = 3)$ denotes that the recipient is in state R3, i.e., the recipient does not send the acknowledgement for the current message component. So, the PCTL property finds the minimum probability that eventually the originator sends the last message component, but the recipient ends up not sending the corresponding acknowledgement. We consider calculating the minimum probability as we are interested in the lower bound of the *cheating probability*.

While executing the protocol the originator can choose the values for the two parameters: the maximum value for *round* r_{max} and the success probability p_{geo}

for the geometric distribution with which the originator decides the number of rounds for the current protocol run. Now for a message recipient with a particular trust profile, the originator would like to ensure that the cheating probability is below a threshold by properly choosing the values of r_{max} and p_{geo}. First we consider that the recipient sends acknowledgement with a fixed probability p_{ack} in each round, thus $d = 0$. Later, we shall introduce $d > 0$ in our experimental results.

Figure 2(a) shows how cheating probability varies with success probability of geometric distribution for maximum number of rounds equals to 6 and three different values of acknowledgement probability. The figure shows that cheating probability increases with the increase in the success probability for a fixed value of the maximum number of rounds and for any p_{ack}. Also, with the increase in the value of p_{ack}, the rate at which cheating probability increases decreases. That means, though intuitive, higher is the value for p_{ack} lower will be the cheating probability for a fixed value of p_{geo} and maximum number of rounds. Figure 2(b) shows how cheating probability varies with maximum number of rounds for success probability of geometric distribution equals to 0.5. The figure shows that cheating probability slightly decreases with increase in the maximum number of rounds, and asymptotically approaches to a constant value. This suggests that for a fixed value of p_{ack} and p_{geo}, it is not possible for the originator to bring the cheating probability below a certain limit only by increasing the maximum number of rounds.

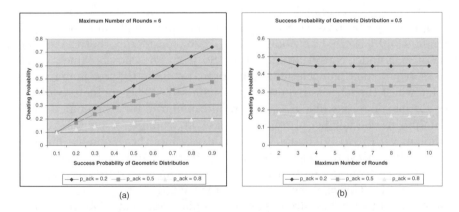

Fig. 2. Variation of cheating probability with (a) p_{geo}, (b) r_{max} for different p_{ack}

From our experiment, it is clear that to achieve a low value of degree of fairness, the originator should choose lower success probability for geometric distribution with which it chooses the number of rounds, and also it should choose higher value for maximum number of rounds. Lower success probability and higher value for maximum number of rounds cause lengthy transaction, thus increasing the communication cost. So there is a clear trade-off between security and cost of communication. If the message is costly, the originator should pay more price in terms of communication cost.

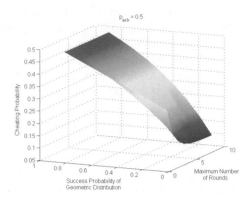

Fig. 3. Variation of cheating probability with maximum number of rounds and success probability of geometric distribution for acknowledgement probability equals to 0.5

Now given a degree of fairness ϵ, we shall show how the originator can perform the protocol to ensure the fairness. Figure 3 shows how cheating probability varies with maximum number of rounds and success probability of geometric distribution for acknowledgement probability to be equal to 0.5. For a recipient with $p_{ack} = p'_{ack}$ the originator first generates such a figure for acknowledgement probability to be equal to p'_{ack}. Then the originator chooses a value for maximum number of round, and tries to find out the maximum possible value for p_{geo}, for which the fairness condition is satisfied. It is to note that a fairness requirement may not always be possible to be ensured for any small value of r_{max}. For example, $\epsilon = 0.1$ is achievable only for $r_{max} \geq 6$ (considering that the minimum value of p_{geo} under consideration is 0.1). So if for the chosen value r_{max}, the fairness requirement is achievable, the originator finds the maximum value of p_{geo} for which the fairness requirement is achievable. The originator would like to go for maximum possible p_{geo}, as it would minimize the communication cost by minimizing the number of rounds. To give an example, if ϵ equals to 0.3 for a recipient with $p_{ack} = 0.5$ and the originator wants the maximum number of rounds to be 6, then to achieve the fairness, the originator should select p_{geo} to be equal to 0.4 (considering that the originator is interested to select p_{geo} to be multiple of 0.1). This is also evident from Figure 2(a).

Now we shall show how decreasing the acknowledgement probability at each round (i.e., $d > 0$ in the trust profile of the recipient) effects the cheating probability. Figure 4(a) shows how cheating probability varies with success probability of geometric distribution for three different values of d ($d = 0.001$, $d = 0.01$ and $d = 0.1$) when maximum number of rounds equals to 6 and the initial value of acknowledgement probability equals to 0.8. Figure 4(b) shows how cheating probability varies with maximum number of rounds for three different values of d when success probability of geometric distribution equals to 0.5 and the initial value of acknowledgement probability equals to 0.8. As expected, the value of cheating probability increases with increase in the value of d, though the increase in the value of cheating probability is not very prominent when d

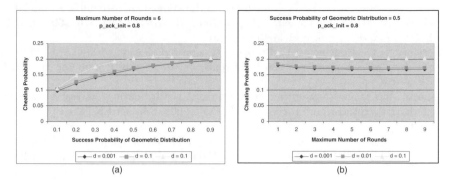

Fig. 4. Variation of cheating probability with (a) p_{geo}, (b) r_{max} for different d's

increases from 0.001 to 0.01. Now to ensure that a recipient with trust profile $\{p_{ack\_init} = 0.8, d = 0.1\}$ will not be able to cheat with probability more than 0.2, the originator needs to choose p_{geo} to be greater than 0.5 if maximum number of rounds is taken as 6 (From Figure 4(a)). Similarly, to take $p_{geo} = 0.5$ the originator needs to choose maximum number of rounds to be at least 6 for the same purpose(From Figure 4(b)). Now for such a trust profile, the originator can summarize the effect of success probability of geometric distribution and maximum number of rounds on cheating probability in a 3D plot like Figure 3, which can be used to choose the value of p_{geo} and r_{max} for any fairness requirement.

4   Conclusion

In this paper we quantitatively analyze a probabilistic non-repudiation protocol without a trusted third party as presented in [5] by PRISM model checker. We have shown through model checking how originator's strategy of choosing protocol parameters influences its chance to ensure the fairness of the transaction. The approach described in this paper would be helpful for an originator of a service in the Internet domain to estimate the required parameters precisely to achieve a successful(fair) transaction.

References

1. Aldini, A., Gorrieri, R.: Security analysis of a probabilistic non-repudiation protocol. In: Hermanns, H., Segala, R. (eds.) PROBMIV 2002, PAPM-PROBMIV 2002, and PAPM 2002. LNCS, vol. 2399, pp. 17–36. Springer, Heidelberg (2002)
2. Aldini, A., Di Pierro, A.: On Quantitative Analysis of Probabilistic Protocols. In: Proc. 2nd Workshop on Quantitative Aspects of Programming Languages (QAPL 2004). ENTCS, vol. 112, pp. 131–148 (2004)
3. Hinton, A., Kwiatkowska, M., Norman, G., Parker, D.: PRISM: A tool for automatic verification of probabilistic systems. In: Hermanns, H., Palsberg, J. (eds.) TACAS 2006. LNCS, vol. 3920, pp. 441–444. Springer, Heidelberg (2006)

4. Kremer, S., Raskin, J.-F.: A game-based verification of non-repudiation and fair exchange protocols. In: Larsen, K.G., Nielsen, M. (eds.) CONCUR 2001. LNCS, vol. 2154, p. 551. Springer, Heidelberg (2001)
5. Markowitch, O., Roggeman, Y.: Probabilistic non-repudiation without trusted third party. In: Proceedings of the 2nd Conference on Security in Communication Networks (1999)
6. Lanotte, R., Maggiolo-schettini, A., Troina, A.: Automatic Analysis of a Non-Repudiation Protocol. In: Proceedings of QAPL 2004. Elsevier ENTCS, pp. 113–129 (2004)
7. Zhou, J., Gollman, D.: Observations on non-repudiation. In: Kim, K.-c., Matsumoto, T. (eds.) ASIACRYPT 1996. LNCS, vol. 1163, pp. 133–144. Springer, Heidelberg (1996)

Method-Specific Java Access Control via RMI Proxy Objects Using Annotations

(Short Paper)

Jeff Zarnett, Patrick Lam, and Mahesh Tripunitara

University of Waterloo
Waterloo, Ontario, Canada

Abstract. We propose a novel approach for granting to remote clients partial access on arbitrary objects at the granularity of methods. The applications that we target use Remote Method Invocation (RMI). We automatically build proxy objects, and give them to untrusted clients instead of the originals. Proxy objects expose a subset of methods to prevent potentially dangerous calls from clients. We present the system's semantics, implementation, and its evaluation. Creating a proxy takes an order of magnitude less time than the corresponding RMI lookup.

1 Introduction

Access control is a key security feature that protects sensitive information. Type-safe languages such as Java help prevent arbitrary accesses to memory and contribute to the development of secure systems. Java's built-in security features are fairly coarse-grained. Existing approaches, such as stack inspection [1,2], provide the ability to grant fine-grained partial access to an object's methods. However, they must consider all remote accesses to be untrusted, as the client's call stack is unavailable to the server.

We present a method for providing security through proxy objects. In our technique, developers specify which methods to allow and deny; we use this information to automatically construct proxy objects. As they expose only a permitted subset of methods, proxies are safe by construction and may be passed to untrusted clients. Our system works with Remote Method Invocation (RMI).

We have implemented our system and analyzed its performance. Our system imposes minimal overhead (see Section 5); creation of a proxy object takes an order of magnitude less time than the corresponding RMI lookup. Our contributions include an approach to automatically generate RMI proxy objects for security, an algorithm for deriving proxy interfaces, and an experimental evaluation of the feasibility and performance of our system.

2 Motivating Example

Our technique handles cases where a heterogeneous software system needs to share objects with subsystems that are not fully trusted. We are able to

A. Prakash and I. Sen Gupta (Eds.): ICISS 2009, LNCS 5905, pp. 301–309, 2009.

expose only parts of an object's functionality to a client. This is useful when it is undesirable or dangerous to grant the client unrestricted access.

Consider a software-as-a-service case with three parties: a software developer (the service provider), a store owner (service client), and store customers (who buy from the online store). The developer creates a customizable application, ShipItems, for online commerce. The clients (store owners) purchase an account and customize their instance of ShipItems according to their needs. They use the application to organize and track product shipments to their customers. Customers place orders.

As the software developer cannot foresee all the business rules of store owners (service clients), he can either guess at the rules the store owner wants and provide rule templates for those cases, or give out full access to the Java objects. If the store owner cannot implement her business logic using the given rules or templates, then a human must verify every order before it goes out. This is costly and error-prone. Alternately, the owner can access the Java objects directly.

Suppose ShipItems validates that the Postal/ZIP Code field is not empty. The store owner will ship only within Canada. She tries to add a rule that the postal code must conform to the Canadian format (e.g., A1B 2C3). If the developer did not grant the owner the ability to define the formatting for this box, then the owner must verify her rule manually. Alternatively, if given the address object, the store owner might change the name of the object that represents Canada. A modification to the Canada object affects every user. Likewise, by navigating the object graph, the store owner could access other stores' confidential data.

We could write a restrictive interface and provide this to the client, with the data objects implementing the interface. Deriving this interface manually is time-consuming and error-prone, and it must be kept up to date when the original object changes. Our system supports the automatic generation of such interfaces, based on light-weight annotations.

The developer writes the general system (ShipItems) and sells it to the store owner, who applies her specific business rules to the system. We propose a way to allow the store owner to programmatically apply her business rules, while limiting her access to the Java objects.

3   Proxy Objects

Our solution enables servers to give out Java objects such that recipients cannot adversely change the state of the system. We build custom proxy objects from the original Java objects, and give those to clients in place of the originals. Proxy objects are stand-ins generated from the originals that expose a subset of the original's methods. We require a pre-processing step between the Java Compiler and the RMI Compiler (see Section 4).

Developers may specify policies at three levels: global, class and method. Our system applies the policy closest to the method. If a method is annotated with a policy, our system uses the declared method-level policy. Otherwise, if the method's defining class is annotated with a policy, then our system uses the class-level policy for the method. If both the method and class lack annotations, our system uses the global policy for the method. The developer must specify a global policy, which can be seen as the default for the system.

We support two kinds of policies: permit and deny. A developer specifies that a permit policy using a "safe" annotation, and a deny policy with an "unsafe" annotation. If we infer that a method has an effective unsafe annotation, then this method is invisible to and uncallable by untrusted clients.

An object can have one or more proxies. Each proxy represents an original object residing at the server. Proxies forward method execution to originals.

A developer annotates a method or class by adding @Safe or @UnSafe above it. These annotations impose no requirements upon the methods or classes they accompany; they do not affect the method's behaviour. Below is the @Safe annotation; @UnSafe is identical except "Safe" is replaced with "UnSafe".

```
@Retention(RetentionPolicy.RUNTIME)
public @interface Safe { }
```

If a method is annotated safe, then untrusted clients can invoke that method with their choice of arguments. Clients can invoke methods that are annotated unsafe as well, but only via other methods. Clients then do not have direct control over the arguments with which these unsafe methods are invoked. We assume that it is safe to invoke these methods from other methods that are safe.

Consider the following example. A system has a global default permit policy (configured at compile-time); all methods are visible unless marked as unsafe. A class O carries a default-deny annotation, while its a() method is marked as safe to invoke. Since precedence goes from most- to least-specific, all methods in the program are visible, except for those in the class O, because O has a policy of default deny. Also, the method-level annotation at a() overrides the class-level policy, so that untrusted clients see only a().

```
// Global Policy: Default Permit

@UnSafe // Class O Policy: Default Deny
public class O {
    @Safe // Method a() is safe
    public int a() { ... } // Permitted method
    // Unannotated method b() receives the annotation of its class
    public void b(String s) { ... } // Denied method
}
```

This system has trusted clients (T) and untrusted clients (U). Figure 1 shows the placement of the proxy object P in the system.

As a is safe, U can invoke a on the proxy, and the proxy invokes the corresponding method on the original object O. Method b is unsafe, so b cannot be invoked on the proxy object because it does not exist on the proxy. Conversely, because trusted client T can access O directly, it is free to invoke b. However, even if b is unsafe in general, it may be safe when invoked with specific parameters. In this scenario, it is meaningful and appropriate for a safe method to invoke an unsafe one, under controlled circumstances.

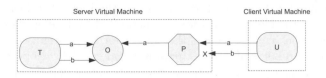

Fig. 1. Proxy Object P Guards O from Untrusted Client U

We can create a proxy for any object. Any class C induces a derived interface, defined by its declared and inherited methods. To enable callers to use proxy objects in place of the corresponding real objects, a proxy object P implements the derived interface of the original class C. Our interface builder (see Section 4) creates an interface I based on C's derived interface. Furthermore, a method appears in I only if it is allowed by the policy.

Our solution is impervious to Java reflection attacks. Consider a proxy object that is accessed remotely using RMI. Although the proxy object keeps a reference to the original, the original remains inaccessible, because reflection cannot be used on a remote object [3]. RMI hides all fields of the implementation class from remote clients; fields do not appear on the client-side stub. We require that arbitrary access to memory on the server side is not permitted. We do not make assumptions about the client side virtual machine, as it is untrusted.

3.1   Semantics of Annotation

We use First Order Logic [4] to express the semantics of our approach precisely.

To express that a method m has annotation a in its definition in class c, we adopt the predicate annotatedMethod (m, c, a). The counterpart corresponding to annotatedMethod for a class is annotatedClass (c, a). To express the global annotation, we adopt the constant **globalAnnotation**. To model the inheritance and method-definition aspects of Java, we adopt the predicates inherits (c_2, c_1) to express that class c_2 directly inherits c_1, and definedIn (c, m) to express that method m is defined in the class c. Figure 2 presents our inference rules.

$$\text{annotatedClass}\,(c, a) \longleftarrow (\textbf{globalAnnotation} = a) \land (a \neq a') \land \neg \text{annotatedClass}\,(c, a') \quad (1)$$

$$\text{annotatedMethod}\,(m, c, a) \longleftarrow$$
$$\text{definedIn}\,(c, m) \land \text{annotatedClass}\,(c, a) \land (a \neq a') \land \neg \text{annotatedMethod}\,(m, c, a') \quad (2)$$

$$\text{annotatedMethod}\,(m, c_2, a) \longleftarrow$$
$$\neg \text{definedIn}\,(c_2, m) \land \text{annotatedMethod}\,(m, c_1, a) \land \text{inherits}\,(c_2, c_1) \quad (3)$$

Fig. 2. Inference Rules for Determining Safe and Unsafe Annotations for Methods

For a semantics, we specify a model $\mathcal{M}$ and an environment l [4]. The set of concrete values, A, that we associate with $\mathcal{M}$ is $A = A_c \cup A_m \cup A_a$, where A_c is the set of classes, A_m is the set of methods and $A_a = \{\text{safe}, \text{unsafe}\}$. We associate one of the values from A_a with the constant **globalAnnotation**. We consider only environments in which our variables have the following mappings for our five predicates annotatedMethod (m, c, a), annotatedClass (c, a), definedIn (c, m), inherits (c_2, c_1), and $a \neq a'$. The variables c, c_1 and c_2 map to elements of A_c, m to an element of A_m, and a and a' to elements of A_a.

To compute $\mathcal{M}$, we begin with a model $\mathcal{M}_0$, with A as its universe of concrete values. In $\mathcal{M}_0$, we populate the relations that make our predicates concrete with those values that we glean from the Java code. For example, inherits$^{\mathcal{M}_0}$ contains every pair $\langle c_2, c_1 \rangle$ for which class c_2 extends c_1. Similarly, we instantiate annotatedMethod$^{\mathcal{M}_0}$ to those $\langle m, c, a \rangle$ tuples such that the method m has the annotation a in its definition in class c. We point out that an annotation can exist for a method in a class in the code only if the method is defined in that class. Also, there is at most one annotation in the code for each method in a class. There is also at most one annotation for a class. We define $\mathcal{M}$ to be the least fixed point from applying the rules from Figure 2. There exists an algorithm for computing $\mathcal{M}$ whose worst-case time is $O\left(|A_c|^2\right)$.

To construct a proxy object for a particular class c, we can instead use a "bottom-up" algorithm that is linear in $|A_c| + |A_m|$. We first identify all methods that are defined in c by a breadth- or depth-first search of the inheritance graph in reverse, starting at c. We can then identify the annotation of each method in c in constant time.

$\mathcal{M}$ is sound and complete. Soundness means that a method has at most one annotation in $\mathcal{M}$. Completeness means that a method that is defined in a class has at least one annotation in $\mathcal{M}$.

3.2 Semantics of Invocation

To express that a method m in class c may be safely invoked, we adopt the predicate canSafelyInvoke (m, c). We use the predicate invokes (m_1, m_2) to indicate that method m_1 invokes method m_2. We introduce a constant, **safe**, to indicate the safe annotation. Figure 3 presents our inference rules. Our semantics are specified as in the previous section. In our model $\mathcal{M}$, **safe**$^{\mathcal{M}}$ = safe.

$$\text{invokes}\,(m_1, m_3) \longleftarrow \text{invokes}\,(m_1, m_2) \wedge \text{invokes}\,(m_2, m_3) \tag{4}$$
$$\text{canSafelyInvoke}\,(m, c) \longleftarrow \text{annotatedMethod}\,(m, c, \textbf{safe}) \tag{5}$$
$$\text{canSafelyInvoke}\,(m_2, c) \longleftarrow \text{canSafelyInvoke}\,(m_1, c) \wedge \text{invokes}\,(m_1, m_2) \tag{6}$$

Fig. 3. Inference Rules associated with Invocation

4 Implementation

Bytecode generation and modification lie at the heart of our implementation. We modify RMI-enabled classes and generate interface class files. We employ an interface builder, which examines classes, and creates a modified derived interface I. As the interface builder does not need to produce arbitrary executable code, but rather only the limited subset of bytecode needed to define interfaces, we can create our interfaces without a full-featured code generation library. Our interface building routine is based on the code by McManus [5].

Although I contains only safe methods, we alter some method signatures. We leave unmodified all methods that return a primitive type (e.g., `int`) or a `String`. For all other methods, we replace the return type with a proxy type.

At run-time, we also employ a `ProxyObject` class, which we provide. This class is registered as the invocation handler for all proxy objects. If the method exists in the modified derived interface I, then the proxy passes the invocation on to O; O executes the method as requested. If some parameters are proxy objects, the invocation handler replaces those proxies with their corresponding originals before forwarding the execution. The `ProxyObject` class also intercepts returns of a non-proxy object and performs the appropriate substitution. If a method is not permitted, it did not appear in I and hence is not available for invocation on the proxy P. This ensures that only safe methods may be invoked.

The interface builder runs during a compile-time preparation step that takes place between compiling the source files and running the RMI Compiler (`rmic`). No modifications to the Java compiler or `rmic` are necessary. Figure 4 depicts this process on a typical class `Example`.

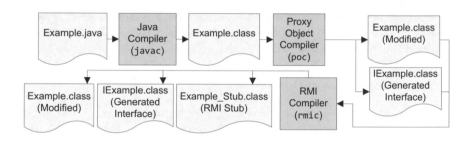

Fig. 4. Proxy Object Compiler Processing `Example.java`

A developer has written the `Example.java` file, and compiled it into a class file using `javac`. We identify `Example` as being a remote-accessible object (it extends `UnicastRemoteObject`), and give it to the proxy object compiler (`poc`). The `poc` examines `Example` and derives interface `IExample`, which contains only safe methods. The `poc` modifies `Example.class` so it implements `IExample`. Once our modifications are complete, we invoke `rmic` on the resultant class files, and the RMI compiler produces `Example_Stub.class`. All compile-time steps are complete and the application may be started normally.

5   Performance Analysis

To examine our system's performance, we use micro-benchmarks. Creating a proxy of an object with no defined methods, save those inherited from `Object`, takes 0.56 ms, on average. Thereafter, each method of the object adds a small penalty. The time to create a proxy object is linear with the number of methods.

The first time a proxy object of a particular class is created, there is an additional, one-time, server-side cost to derive the interface. After the interface is created and loaded, it is cached, so thereafter the cost of creating the interface is negligible. Furthermore, testing reveals that when the interface is created multiple times, the virtual machine optimizes or caches the derivation of the interface after the first time it is created. Hence, to get consistent results, we conducted our analysis by restarting the Java virtual machine each time. Deriving the object's interface is linear in the number of methods in the object. Although the initial interface creation may be costly, we reiterate that it is a one-time cost; once derived, the interface is cached and is never re-created.

Table 1 summarizes the mean times (in ms) for both types of tests. Figure 5 presents a graph of the data, including standard deviations (which are small).

Table 1. Mean Object Creation & Interface Build Times (in ms)

Methods	0	25	50	75	100
Object Creation	0.563	1.856	3.207	4.487	5.834
Interface Build	21.51	30.43	34.67	38.85	42.15

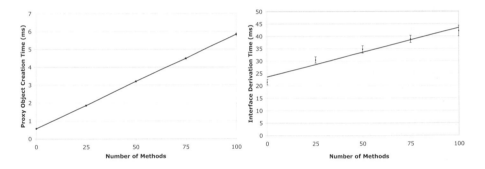

Fig. 5. Proxy Creation (L) and Interface Derivation (R): Linear Performance with the Number of Methods in the Object

Finally, our tests reveal that locally invoking a proxy in place of the original has negligible overhead. Over 1 000 000 tests, invoking the proxy took, on average, 0.002 ms longer than invoking the original. This is below the noise threshold for our test. Therefore, the overhead of invoking a proxy is negligible.

To provide perspective, we conducted a comparison to how long it takes to do a Java RMI lookup of a simple example object (not a proxy). The server, RMI registry, and client ran on the same machine and used the same network interface. These tests reveal that over 1 000 tests, a lookup takes 89.2 ms on average (with a standard deviation of 8.52 ms). Creation of a proxy object, even one with 100 methods, takes an order of magnitude less than the RMI lookup. Even deriving the interface is on the same order as the RMI lookup. Thus, our system's overhead is small in practice.

6   Related Work

While type safety obviates many security concerns, access control remains a key issue. Pandey and Hashii [6] investigate bytecode editing to enforce access controls, but do not discuss RMI. Wallach et al [1] enforce access controls using Abadi, Burrows, Lampson, and Plotkin (ABLP) Logic, where authorization is granted or denied on the basis of a statement from a principal allowing or denying access. However, their approach does not work with RMI, and, as acknowledged by the authors, does not handle a dynamic system with classloading well.

Stack inspection can provide effective access control, but the client call stack is unavailable to the server, and even if it were available, it would be untrustworthy. A stack inspection scheme would therefore have to consider all remote accesses untrusted, while proxies can differentiate between trusted and untrusted RMI calls. Furthermore, the time to perform a stack inspection increases linearly with the depth of the stack [1], while the proxy object overhead is constant. Stack inspection suffers from difficulties with results returned by untrusted code, inheritance, and side effects [2]. Proxy objects are more resistant to these difficulties, because they do not trust any results from untrusted code, are designed with inheritance in mind, and are intended as a tool to avoid harmful side effects. Proxy objects and stack inspection have different principles of trust. In proxies, a caller is trusted if it receives a reference to the original object. In stack inspection, the callee verifies its caller and all transitive callers.

Interface derivation is already in use in practice. For instance, Bryce and Razafimahefa [7] generate dynamic proxies to go between objects, and restrict access to methods. These bridges do not restrict access to fields; our solution allows only safe method invocations.

7   Conclusions

We presented a technique for method-level access control within the RMI applications using the Java programming language. Our technique computes whether a method is safe or unsafe based on program annotations. To capture the semantics of our system, we described them using First Order Logic.

Proxy objects have very little overhead in practice. We showed that creation of a proxy object takes an order of magnitude less time than the RMI lookup. Deriving the interface—a one-time cost—is on the same order as the RMI lookup.

References

1. Wallach, D., Appel, A., Felten, E.: SAFKASI: A Security Mechanism for Language-based Systems. ACM Transactions on Software Engineering and Methodology (TOSEM) 9, 341–378 (2000)
2. Fournet, C., Gordon, A.: Stack Inspection: Theory and Variants. ACM Transactions on Programming Languages and Systems (TOPLAS) 25, 360–399 (2003)
3. Richmond, M., Noble, J.: Reflections on Remote Reflection. In: Proceedings of the 24th Australasian Conference on Computer Science, vol. 11, pp. 163–170 (2001)

4. Hugh, M., Ryan, M.: Logic in Computer Science, 2nd edn. Cambridge University Press, Cambridge (2004)
5. McManus, E.: Build your own interface—dynamic code generation (2006), http://weblogs.java.net/blog/emcmanus/archive/2006/10/ build_your_own.html (accessed, 2009-05-22)
6. Pandey, R., Hashii, B.: Providing Fine-Grained Access Control for Java Programs. In: Guerraoui, R. (ed.) ECOOP 1999. LNCS, vol. 1628, pp. 449–473. Springer, Heidelberg (1999)
7. Bryce, C., Razafimahefa, C.: An Approach to Safe Object Sharing. In: Proceedings of the 15th ACM SIGPLAN Conference on Object-Oriented Programming, Systems, Languages, and Applications, pp. 367–381 (2000)

Let Only the Right One IN: Privacy Management Scheme for Social Network
(Short Paper)

Nagaraja Kaushik Gampa, Rohit Ashok Khot, and Kannan Srinathan

Center for Security,Theory and Algorithmic Research (CSTAR),
International Institute of Information Technology, Hyderabad
{kaushik,rohit_a}@research.iiit.ac.in, srinathan@iiit.ac.in

Abstract. Current social networking sites protect user data by making it available only to a restricted set of people, often friends. However, the concept of 'friend' is illusory in social networks. Adding a person to the friends list without verifying his/her identity can lead to many serious consequences like identity theft, privacy loss, etc. We propose a novel verification paradigm to ensure that a person (Bob) who sends a friend request (to Alice) is actually her friend, and not someone who is faking his identity. Our solution is based on what Bob might know and verify about Alice. We work on the premise that a friend knows a person's preferences better than a stranger. To verify our premise, we conducted a two stage user study. Results of the user study are encouraging. We believe our solution makes a significant contribution, namely, the way it leverages the benefits of preference based authentication and challenge response schemes.

Keywords: Privacy over social networks, preference based authentication, friend verification, and challenge response schemes.

1 Introduction

Security experts often say that users are the weakest link in a security system. Users misunderstand how to use security mechanisms and do not realize the need for such a protection. They are happy to circumvent the security measures, if security measures try to impede their primary tasks. Attackers exploit user's lack of understanding and their tendencies of not complying with security protocols and policies by developing simple yet effective social engineering attacks. This problem is inherent in social networks. Social networking sites are highly popular among teenagers, which are having more than 150 million users each and a growth rate of 3% per week [2]. This growth bounds to attract many malicious people. Social networking sites are a rich source of sensitive private data about millions of users. If such a data gets into the hands of malicious people, then there could be serious side effects.

Current social networking sites protect user data by making it semi-public [2] which is only restricted to a set of people often friends. However, the definition

A. Prakash and I. Sen Gupta (Eds.): ICISS 2009, LNCS 5905, pp. 310–317, 2009.

of friend is rather illusory in a social networking environment. Each person can have different kinds of friends. Most notable categories of friends are: Direct or close friends, acquaintances and Internet friends. The third category of Internet friends, is the most troublesome category. This category includes friends whom they never met personally. Therefore, the only form of communication with these friends is via Internet. There is no easier way to verify their true identity, so they are no different than a stranger. Users never realize that many among them could be potential attackers trying to steal their important data and impede their social privacy. Therefore adding strangers as friends, without verifying is not advisable. However, teens do not share the same risk perception. Most of them think friendship as a loyal and harmless relation. Moreover, it is often difficult to say 'no' to a friend request. Moreover, a common belief among teens is more the number of friends they have, more the popular and cool they become [3]. Thus, they blindly accepts most of the friend requests and grant a power to the added person to view all the contents of their profile, without being aware of when and what they view [5].

We propose a simple yet effective verification paradigm to ensure that the person who sends you a friend request is actually your friend and not someone who is faking his/her identity. Our solution is based on what a person might know and can verify about the other person. We work on a premise that a friend can tell about his/her friend's preferences better than a stranger. To verify our premise, we did a two stage user study. Results of the user study are encouraging.

2   Background and Related Work

Primary reason behind the success of social networking sites has been the range of socially compelling services that they offer. Three most important of those services [4] are: Identity, Relationships and Communities.

- **Identity:** Social networking sites allow user to create a public or semi-public profile inside a bounded system. Biggest advantage of profile pages is that it let users to say who they are and in a manner they want.
- **Relationships:** Social networking sites let user to make new friends, rediscover old friends and keep in touch with the current ones. A user is able to traverse accepted friend's connections and can meet new friends. In this way, network of friends grows and is often measured in millions.
- **Communities:** Third compelling factor about social networking site is the communities in social networks. Like minded people come together and start communities on common subject of interest.

According to Maslow hierarchy of human needs [10], the urge to sociality is highly motivating force. Above social compelling services often make users to neglect the associated risks. By sharing the personal data to a stranger, is an open invitation to attackers whose consequences can be: loss of privacy, identity theft, Sexual and mental harassments, etc[11]. Therefore, users are often advised not to reveal any sensitive and personal information on social network. However, doing so defeats the purpose of social networks, which is an healthy exchange of ideas across the connections.

2.1   Related Work

In recent times multiple techniques have been implemented to protect the data over the Social Networking Sites. First solution is based on identifying the honest nodes [14]. Honest nodes are the ones with good connectivity with the rest of the social networks. Results show that users blindly accept the request from forged identity that is already confirmed by their friends[11]. Lucas et.al [9] has proposed an encryption scheme that presents the user data in an encrypted form. However, their solution needs secure distribution of encryption keys which is an overhead. A related solution to the privacy problem is using the shared knowledge between the persons [12]. However, this solution requires active involvement from both the parties. A CAPTCHA based technique is proposed in [13]. They ask users to identity content (e.g. person's name) of a shared image. However, user's appearances do change over time, therefore, it might be difficult even for a legitimate user to identify the person in the image. As a result, most of the proposed solutions are yet far from the perfection.

3   Motivation

Let us first look at how friends are formed in a social networks. We follow Facebook model, where it involves three basic steps. For clarity, we name the persons involved in interaction as *Alice* and *Bob*. The role of malicious user faking Bob's identity is done by *Mallory*. Bob first sends a friend request containing his profile summary to Alice. Alice therefore, can see and verify Bob's profile. Alice can also communicate with Bob by sending messages to which Bob can reply. Alice generally accepts the request if Bob and Alice share some mutual friends [1]. However, Bob's data can be easily available and forged from public records. Thus, Alice can easily be tricked into accepting a request from a fake profile. To mitigate such attacks, a possible way of sender verification is with challenge response schemes.

Challenge response schemes are popular means of fallback authentication scheme [8]. In the challenge response schemes, system verifies whether the user remembers the answers to the questions mostly about their personal life e.g. mother's maiden name, date of birth, etc. It has been conceived that answers to these questions are not available in public records and only the legitimate person knows the correct answers. However, this assumption has recently been proved faulty [11]. these schemes are found particularly vulnerable against insider attacks, i.e. family members, friends, etc., who know answers of many such questions. Therefore, why can't we use these questions to authenticate them instead of the user? We can thus verify the person sending the friend request by Challenge Response schemes in following two ways:

1. Ask the sender, the questions related to his/her own life.
2. Ask the sender, the questions related to the life of the person (receiver) to whom the friend request has been sent.

Below we describe the approaches and argue why the second approach is better.

3.1 Naive Approach: Verify about the Sender

Alice can ask Bob to prove his identity by asking him questions related to his life. Answers of which only Alice and Bob know. If Alice is satisfied with the answers, she will accept Bob's request else decline. However, this solution will work only if the following two conditions are satisfied.

1. Question formed should be automated and require minimal effort from Alice.
2. Answers to these questions should not be publically available.

First, finding appropriate challenge questions automatically for every other user is difficult. Alice must constantly be involved in the process of question forming and verification. A perfect solution should expect most of the work from malicious Bob (actually Mallory who is impersonating Bob) than Alice. Secondly, since the identity of Bob is already forged, chances that Mallory might able to correctly answer some of the questions from the mined data.

4   Our Approach: Verify about the Receiver

Instead we let Alice to ask Bob questions about her life. If Alice is satisfied with the answers, she will accept Bob's request else decline. Steps followed are summarized in Fig.1.

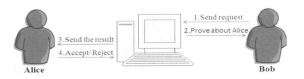

Fig. 1. Better approach of verifying the receiver

There are two distinct advantages with this approach. It requires minimal efforts from Alice's side. Alice can prepare a set of challenge questions concerning her and ask a subset of them for any friend request that comes. Thus there is no need to separately prepare the questions for new friend request and verify them. Secondly forming questions can be automated to a certain degree. However, we desire answers to these questions should not be mined easily from public records. User preferences are generally not publically available online, we utilize this fact and design our scheme around user preferences.[6]

4.1 User Verification Using Preferences

Each person has unique set of likes and dislikes for range of items. We strongly believe that a friend can tell about a friend's preferences better than a stranger. Our proposed scheme works in three simple steps:

1. **Building preferences:** Alice builds a list of preferences for different categories. We ask Alice about her preferences (likes and dislikes) for number of different items belonging to each category and save these preferences in a secure database.
2. **Verification Test:** When Bob sends a friend request to Alice, we pick a random subset of items from the preferences database of Alice and ask Bob to identify Alice preferences. Bob then tries to answer maximum of those questions.
3. **Result:** The results of Bob performance test is shown to Alice along with his Profile history. Thereafter it is up to Alice, to Accept or reject Bob's request.

We list below, the distinct advantages of the proposed design.

- User preferences are generally not available online [6]. Thereby the proposed scheme probably safe against data mining of public records.
- The scheme gives minimal overhead to a person receiving the friend request.
- The scheme can be easily automated once the preference database is formed.
- The scheme is simple and easy to understand for users.

5 User Study

To test the viability of our approach we conducted a two phase user study. In the first phase, a pilot study was conducted on a group of 75 student volunteers of which 49 were male while 26 were female with their age in the range of 19 to 28. The questionnaire was prepared with eight categories namely: Sports, Video Games, Music, Hobbies and interests, Food, Movies, TV shows and Academic subjects of interest. Participants were asked to respond with their likes and dislikes for each of the categories. The aim of the pilot study was to know two things: 1. Commonly liked and disliked items and 2. Correlations among the liked and disliked Items. The most liked items are cricket,books,rap music, etc., and the most disliked items are Swimming, Fashion designing, Heavy metal, etc., which are easily predicted by most of the users. We therefore, eliminated them from the second stage questionnaire.

We next describe correlations among the items within each category. We wanted to combine these items for the second phase study. Fig.2 shows the results of the correlation study. The graph is split into two parts where left part shows liking for each item in the sport category and right part shows the liking for the items in the interest category. We can observe that, items like volley ball and basket ball are liked equally by the participants. Similarly items like sleeping and travelling got equal votes.

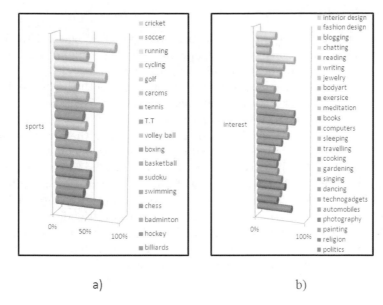

a)   b)

Fig. 2. Liking for the items belonging to (a) Sports category (b) Interest category

At the first stage, we wanted to eliminate items that can be easily guessed. As a result, 42 items were removed from the first stage questionnaire, leaving behind 92 items. We then combined the items that have equal liking or disliking responses. Our motivation behind doing it is to improve the usability as well as the security. To clarify it better, let us take an example of items: chess and carom. We found that 50.94% of participants liked chess while 48.16% participants loved caroms. Now if we combine these two in a single question and ask user that which one or both among them you liked the most, then user wont feel the burden of answering two questions and security is also improved in a sense attackers can not easily identify whether the legitimate user likes one or both or neither of these two items (security is improved from 2 bit to 4 bit).

5.1   Second Phase User Study

At the end of first stage user study, we were left with 92 items that after combining created 48 questions. We then introduced a new category 'Personality', loosely based on the Big Five personality factors [7] of a person into second phase. This phase was conducted on a different set of volunteers which consisted of 32 volunteers, comprising of 20 male and 12 female volunteers. These set of 32 volunteers has been chosen in such a way that for each and every participant there would be a friend of the participant and a complete stranger to the participant. We asked each user to fill three questionnaires one for themselves, one for his/her friend and one for a stranger whom he/she does not know personally. Participants were free to choose either or both items as likes. Items that are not selected are considered as dislikes.

5.2   Our Results

We collected the forms from all the participants and cross checked the entries written for the friend as well as the strangers with their original answers. The analysis has been carried out in the following manner:

If the participant has guessed correctly either one or both the items are liked or disliked by a stranger and a friend then we rewarded a point. But if the participant is able to guess only one correct answer, i.e. if the friend or stranger has liked both the items of single row or guessed both or them wrong then no point was rewarded. Our results show that a participant is able to correctly guess about her friend for 45.86% time whereas she can only able to guess for 30.69% of a stranger. There exists a distinct gap of 15.17% that distinguishes between a stranger and a friend. We can see the results in Table 1. After getting the results of how much a person can distinguish between a friend and a stranger, the next aim is to find out in which one of the categories there was much of the differences in guesses for friend and stranger. The graph shows the percentage difference between friends and strangers for each category.

As we can see from the graph, the personality and the interest categories shows the maximum difference of 21.43% and 17.43% respectively between a friend and a stranger. It is obvious that the personality and interests of a person can be better known to their friends than to a stranger. In a similar manner, the two categories where the guesses about friends and strangers closely match are music and the movies categories. We thus can say these two categories are not good estimates of differentiation among friends and strangers.

At the end, we can conclude that our theory of distinguishing friends from the stranger using like and dislike preferences will work given that there exist a distinct gap of 15% or more in the guesses for the friends and the strangers.

Table 1. Guesses of participants about their friends and strangers

Total no. of participants	Guess about Friends	Guess about Strangers
32(20 male + 12 female)	45.86%	30.69%

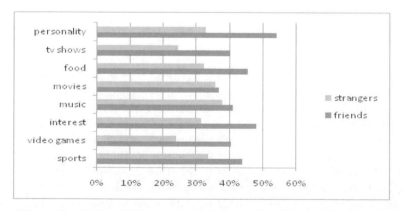

Fig. 3. Prediction difference by participants for friend and a stranger

6   Conclusion and Future Work

In this paper we investigated a novel idea of verifying friends from strangers using a challenge response schemes. In addition, we have used the big five personality traits to make a stranger more difficult to identify the user. We showed the consequences of adding a stranger without verifying and possible applicable countermeasures. Results of the user study show that our proposed approach provides a viable option to privacy management in social networks. In future, we wish to extend the work for differentiating friends.

References

1. Bilge, L., Strufe, T., Balzarotti, D., Kirda, E.: All your contacts are belong to us: automated identity theft attacks on social networks. In: WWW 2009: Proceedings of the 18th international conference on World wide web, pp. 551–560. ACM, New York (2009)
2. Boyd, D., Ellison, N.: Social network sites: Definition, history, and scholarship. Journal of Computer-Mediated Communication 13(1), 210–230 (2008)
3. Boyd, D.: Why Youth (Heart) Social Network Sites: The Role of Networked Publics in Teenage Social Life, pp. 119–142. MIT Press, Cambridge (2007)
4. Grimmelmann, J.: Facebook and the social dynamics of privacy (August 2008)
5. Gross, R., Acquisti, A.: Information revelation and privacy in online social networks (the Facebook case). In: Proceedings of the 2005 ACM workshop on Privacy in the electronic society, pp. 71–80 (2005)
6. Jakobsson, M., Stolterman, E., Wetzel, S., Yang, L.: Love and authentication. In: CHI 2008: Proceeding of the twenty-sixth annual SIGCHI conference on Human factors in computing systems, pp. 197–200. ACM, New York (2008)
7. John, O.P., Srivastava, S.: The big five trait taxonomy: History, measurement, and theoretical perspectives, pp. 102–138. Guilford Press, New York (1999)
8. Just, M.: Designing and evaluating challenge-question systems. IEEE Security and Privacy 2(5), 32–39 (2004)
9. Lucas, M.M., Borisov, N.: Flybynight: mitigating the privacy risks of social networking. In: WPES 2008: Proceedings of the 7th ACM workshop on Privacy in the electronic society, pp. 1–8. ACM, New York (2008)
10. Maslow, A.H.: A theory of human motivation. Psychological Review 50, 370–396 (1943)
11. Rabkin, A.: Personal knowledge questions for fallback authentication: security questions in the era of facebook. In: SOUPS 2008: Proceedings of the 4th symposium on Usable privacy and security, pp. 13–23. ACM, New York (2008)
12. Toomim, M., Zhang, X., Fogarty, J., Landay, J.A.: Access control by testing for shared knowledge. In: CHI 2008: Proceeding of the twenty-sixth annual SIGCHI conference on Human factors in computing systems, pp. 193–196. ACM, New York (2008)
13. Yardi, S., Feamster, N., Bruckman, A.: Photo-based authentication using social networks. In: WOSP 2008: Proceedings of the first workshop on Online social networks, pp. 55–60. ACM, New York (2008)
14. Yu, H., Gibbons, P.B., Kaminsky, M., Xiao, F.: Sybillimit: A near-optimal social network defense against sybil attacks. In: SP 2008: Proceedings of the 2008 IEEE Symposium on Security and Privacy, Washington, DC, USA, pp. 3–17. IEEE Computer Society, Los Alamitos (2008)

Detecting and Resolving Misconfigurations in Role-Based Access Control

(Short Paper)

Ravi Mukkamala, Vishnu Kamisetty, and Pawankumar Yedugani

Old Dominion University, Department of Computer Science,
Norfolk, Virginia 23529-0162, USA
mukka@cs.odu.edu, {vishnuteja,pawan.y}@gmail.com

Abstract. In Role Based Access Control (RBAC) systems, formulating a correct set of roles, assigning appropriate privileges to roles, and assigning roles to users are the fundamental design tasks. Whether these tasks are performed by a human (e.g., system administrator) or by a machine (e.g., expert system), misconfigurations are likely to occur. The misconfigurations could manifest as under-privileges (fewer privileges assigned) or over-privileges (more privileges than necessary). In this paper, we describe an approach based on role mining to detect and correct such misconfigurations. Here, the overlap among the users and privileges of different roles is used to identify possible misconfigurations.

Keywords: Access control, failed accesses, misconfigurations, role-based access control, role mining.

1 Introduction

Due to its simplicity and flexibility, role-based access control (RBAC) has been popular among medium to large organizations in assigning and enforcing privileges [1]. Whenever organizations attempt to switch to RBAC, they face the challenge of determining roles, role-privilege assignment, and user-role assignment [2], [3]. Two approaches are in vogue to solve this problem---top-down approach and bottom-up approach. In a top-down approach, based on the organizational structure and functionalities (e.g., job descriptions), administrators arrive at role definitions and assign privileges to roles, and users to roles. This approach is rather expensive and time-consuming. In a bottom-up approach, on the other hand, the existing user-privileges are examined to identify appropriate roles, based on observed commonalities. This is referred to as role-mining problem in [4], [5], and [6].

In a typical solution to the role mining problem, attempt is made to minimize the number of derived roles, yet maintaining the resulting user-privilege assignments as an exact replica of the input [4],[6]. Their effort to retain the exact user-privilege assignment throughout this process is similar to being "over-fit" in data mining terminology [7].

The existence of misconfigurations and the importance of identifying them in the context of access control has been underscored in the past [8]. In our approach, we

A. Prakash and I. Sen Gupta (Eds.): ICISS 2009, LNCS 5905, pp. 318–325, 2009.

extend the role mining solutions to identify such potential misconfigurations (over- and under-privileges), correct them if so identified, and arrive at a new set of roles. While typically resulting in a reduced set of roles, correcting misconfigurations could sometimes result in increased roles.

In this paper, we describe the details of the proposed technique and summarize the results. The paper is organized as follows. In section 2, related work is summarized. Section 3 describes our role-mining based approach to identifying misconfigurations. Section 4 summarizes the results of experiments with our approach. In section 5, we summarize our contributions and describe plans for the future.

2 Related Work

Role-based access control (RBAC) has been adopted by several commercial organizations primarily due to its simplicity and its close match with the security needs of the organizations [1]. However, for organizations that are transitioning from non-RBAC to RBAC, one of the challenges is to determine the roles. A trivial role assignment such as creating a new role for each user with the existing privileges is not in line with the spirit of RBAC. Instead, one needs to arrive at a minimal set of roles that satisfy the organizational needs. One approach towards this direction is a top-down approach that analyzes each job description in the organization and arrives at a set of roles. This is often a tedious approach. Another approach is the bottom-up approach that takes the existing user-privilege assignment and arrives at asset of roles, role-privilege assignment, and role-user assignment. This is the approach taken by several researchers [2-6].

In [2], Vaidya et al discuss a method of migrating to RBAC with minimal perturbation. The idea here is to discover an optimal set of roles form existing user permissions that are similar to the currently deployed roles. They propose a heuristic solution based on FastMiner algorithm [10]. This algorithm generates candidate roles by intersecting all unique user pairs. The new heuristic defined some similarity measures for roles. In [4], the same authors employ a tiling approach to discover the roles. This is the work that we expanded on to identify misconfigurations.

In [5], the authors introduce a comprehensive framework to compare different role mining algorithms. For the purpose of evaluation, they introduce two algorithms for generating user-permissions with role hierarchies: tree-based data generator and enterprise RBAC data generators. They compare nine role mining algorithms including the ones by Vaidya et al [2-4] that we have adopted for our work. They recommend under-assignment of privileges rather than over-assignment to be in line with the principle of least privilege [9]. However, in our work we deviate from this philosophy since failed accesses are as unproductive as excess privileges.

In [6], the authors describe a bottom up approach for the RBAC problem. Once again, the idea is to arrive at a solution with minimal set of roles. They propose a fast graph-reduction technique to solve the problem that is very close to the optimal solution.

Bauer et al [8] propose a method to detecting misconfigurations in access control by applying association rule mining to the history of accesses. Their idea is to predict required changes to access control based on users' intentions. Like our own system, this system requires the feedback from the administrator for the final changes. Once again, primary idea is to reduce failed accesses. This is in line with our own objective of identifying misconfigurations ahead of time.

3 Employing Role Mining for Identifying Misconfigurations

The basis of our work is the solution to role mining problem (RMP) suggested by Vaidya et al [4]. Here, we start from the given user-privilege assignment (UPA) with rows representing users and columns representing privileges. A "1" in UPA[i,j] means that user "i" is assigned privilege "j"; "0" means that privilege "j" is not assigned to user "i". Rectangular areas in the matrix that contain contiguous 1s are referred to as tiles. Each tile corresponds to a role, the rows of the tile represent the users to whom the role has been assigned, and the columns of the tile represent the privileges assigned to that role. Identifying the minimum number of tiles that cover all 1s in the UPA is the objective. This is achieved using two algorithms. Algorithm 1, called RMP, finds the minimum tiling for the given user-privilege assignment (UPA). These tiles are then converted to roles (ROLES), assignment of privileges to roles (PA), and assign users to roles (UA). To identify the tiles, it uses LUTM function. Algorithm 2 implements the LUTM function.

Our work starts from these tiles produced by the above algorithms for a given UPA. Once the initial tiles are identified by Algorithms 1 and 2, we find common sets of users and common sets of privileges between each pair of tiles. The basis behind this is as follows. Let US_i and US_j be the sets of users in tiles T_i and T_j. Similarly, let PS_i and PS_j be the sets of privileges in the two tiles. Let $CU_{ij} = US_i \cap US_j$ and $CP_{ij} = PS_i \cap PS_j$, representing common users and privileges, respectively. Four cases arise here.

Case i. $CU_{ij} = \phi$ and $CP_{ij} = \phi$. This refers to disjoint sets of users with disjoint sets of privileges. We can ignore this case since it neither indicates under privileges nor over privileges.

Case ii. $CU_{ij} \neq \phi$ and $CP_{ij} = \phi$. This is a case where common users have some additional privileges which other peer(s) do not have. This refers to either under privileges or over privileges. This is handled as follows: (i) Form a new matrix that contains users $US_i \cup US_j$ and privileges $PS_i \cup PS_j$. (ii) For each user in US_i-US_j, test if the privileges in PS_j be allocated (under-privilege misconfiguration) by determining the percentage of users to whom each privilege in PS_j has been allocated. If the percentage exceeds a threshold, then consider the 0s for this privilege as a misconfiguration. (iii) For each user u in $US_i \cap US_j$, test if the privileges in PS_j be removed (over-privilege misconfiguration)——find the number of total privileges that user u shares with each of the other users in PS_j, from the original UPA. If this is lower than the minimum threshold, then consider that the privileges in PS_j are over- privileges to u and hence be recommended to be removed.

Case iii. $CU_{ij} = \phi$ and $CP_{ij} \neq \phi$. This is a case where some common privileges are shared among a disjoint set of users. This too refers to either under privileges or over privileges. This is handled as follows: (i) Form a new matrix M_{ij} that contains $US_i \cup US_j$ as users and $PS_i \cup PS_j$ as privileges. (ii) For each user u in US_i, test if privileges in $(PS_j - PS_i)$ be allocated (under-privilege misconfiguration) by determining the percentage of users to whom each privilege in PS_j has been allocated. If the percentage exceeds a threshold, then consider the 0s for this privilege as a misconfiguration. (iii) For each user u in US_j, repeat test (ii) for privileges in $(PS_i - PS_j)$.

Case iv. $CU_{ij} \neq \phi$ and $CP_{ij} \neq \phi$. Since the tiles produced by Algorithms 1 and 2 are non-overlapping, this case does not occur and may be ignored.

Let us look at cases (ii) and (iii) in more detail. How do we know whether we are dealing with a case of under privileges or over privileges? While in reality the answer depends on the decision of the administrator, as a general rule we can say that misconfigurations should be in the minority and the correct classification is the majority case. To be more specific, consider case ii. Suppose $US_i=\{U_1,U_2,U_3,U_4\}$, $PS_i=\{P_1,P_2\}$, $US_j=\{U_1,U_5,U_6,U_7\}$, and $PS_j=\{P_3\}$. So $CU_{ij}=\{U_1\}$ and $CP_{ij}=\phi$. So U_1 has privilege P_3 which not all other users in US_i have. Two possibilities exist: (a) No other user in US_i has these privileges. So either U_1 has an additional role which others don't have or U_1 should not be allotted this privilege (case of over privilege). (b) All users except U_2,

Users	Privileges					
	P1	P2	P3	P4	P5	P6
U1	0	1	1	1	1	1
U2	1	1	1	1	1	1
U3	1	0	1	1	1	1
U4	1	1	0	1	1	0
U5	1	1	1	1	1	1

(a)

Tile 1: <{U2, U3, U4, U5}, {P1, P4, P5}>
Tile 2: <{U1, U2, U5}, {P2,P3}>
Tile 3: <{U4}, {{P2}>
Tile 4: <{U1}, {P4}>
Tile 5: <{U3}, {P3}>

(b)

Users	Privileges					
	P1	P2	P3	P4	P5	P6
U1	**1**	1	1	1	1	1
U2	1	1	1	1	1	1
U3	1	**1**	1	1	1	1
U4	1	1	**1**	1	1	**1**
U5	1	1	1	1	1	1

(c)

Fig. 1. (a) Original UPA. (b). Resulting tiles. (c). Modified UPA.

for example, have this privilege. So it could be a case of under privilege and hence U_2 should be granted this privilege. In general, there could be some ambiguous cases and some clear cut cases. The decision of which is right may be resolved by the administrator or an expert system.

We now illustrate our approach using UPA in Figure 1a. Using algorithms 1 and 2, five tiles are identified as shown in Figure 1b. The five tiles correspond to five roles. Our objective is to identify and correct any misconfigurations.

Table 1. %increase in 1s in UPA and %reduction in roles with 20 users

#of users	%increase in 1s in UPA	%reduction in #of roles
2	38.1	33.3
3	20.0	20.0
4	17.5	16.7
5	14.6	12.5
6	13.6	11.1
7	7.2	10.0
8	3.8	16.7
9	4.3	9.1
10	3.0	6.7
11	4.5	6.7
12	5.2	12.5
13	4.0	5.9
14	5.1	10.5
15	2.0	10.5

Table 2. Results of reverse engineering: Detected changes vs. injected changes

#of injected changes	#of detected changes by the algorithm					
	4 users	6 users	8 users	10 users	12 users	15 users
1	1	1	0	1	1	1
2	2	2	2	2	1	2
3	3	3	2	3	3	3
4	4	3	4	4	4	2
5	4	4	4	4	4	4
6	4	5	5	5	5	6
7	5	7	6	6	5	5
8	7	8	6	6	6	6
9	5	9	6	8	6	5
10	5	6	8	8	8	9

Tiles 1 and 2 have no overlap, so is represents case (i) and we ignore it.

Tiles 1 and 3 have U1 common. It represents case (ii). We form a new privilege matrix with users {U2,U3,U4,U5} and privileges {P1, P2,P4,P5}. From UPA, we get $DM_{13}=1/20*100=5\%$. Definitely, this is a case for corrections. Carrying forward the remaining analysis, we can recommend that the under-privilege of P2 to U3 be corrected.

Now consider tiles 1 and 4. This represents case (iii). Here, we need to test if user U1 be allocated the privileges {P4, P5} or remove the privilege P4 from U1. Here, N0 =1 and N1=14. So, $DM=1/15*100=6.7\%$. In other words, there is a strong indication that we should consider the possibility of misconfigurations. There are three privileges to consider {P1, P4, P5}. P4 and P5 are assigned to all 5 users {U1-U5}. Hence, there are no misconfigurations to consider. For P1, there is one 0 and four 1s. Thus, $n0/(n0+n1)*100=20\%$. This does suggest that missing (U1,P1) is a possible misconfiguration. The recommendation is that U1 should be assigned P1.

Tiles 1 and 5 correspond to case (ii). We form a new privilege matrix with users {U2,U3,U4,U5} and privileges {P1,P3,P4,P5}. From UPA, we get $DM_{13}=1/16*100=6.25\%$. Definitely, this is a case for corrections. Carrying forward the remaining analysis, we can recommend that the under-privilege of P3 to U4 be corrected.

Tiles 2 and 3 correspond to case (iii). Here, we need to test if user U4 be allocated the privilege P3 or remove the privilege P2 from U4. Here, N0 =1 and N1=7. So, $DM=1/8*100=12.5\%$. In other words, there is an indication that we should consider the possibility of misconfigurations. There are two privileges to consider {P2, P3}. P2 is assigned to all 4 users. For P3, there is one 0 and three 1s. Hence, $n0/(n0+n1)*100=25\%$. This does suggest that missing (U4,P3) is a possible misconfiguration. The recommendation is that U4 be assigned P3.

Tiles 2 and 4 have no overlap, so they correspond to case (i). Thus, we ignore it.

Tiles 2 and 5, correspond to case (ii). Further analysis shows that the missing (U3,P2) is a possible misconfiguration.

Tiles 3 and 4, tiles 3 and 5, and tiles 4 and 5 also have no overlap, so they correspond to case (i), and hence are ignored.

In summary, the suggestion is that the 4 missing privileges need to be assigned (under privilege). There are no over privileges. The modified UPA after repeating steps 2-4 is shown in Figure 1c. This is just one tile representing one role. Thus, by detecting and correcting four misconfigurations we have reduced 5 roles to 1 role. Of course, this is an exception, and in reality the results are not so drastic.

4   Results

In order to validate the algorithm, we have carried out two types of experiments: forward engineering and reverse engineering.

Under forward engineering, we randomly generated UPA matrices for a given number of users and a number of privileges. Each UPA was then first subjected to Algorithms 1 and 2 resulting in an initial set of tiles, corresponding to roles, privilege-role assignment and user-role assignment. We have then applied our misconfigurations algorithm and noted the modified role set and assignments. We varied the number of users from 2 to 25 and the number of privileges also from 2 to 25. In the following results, we have focused our attention only on under privileges. Thus, the measurements include: Number of changes made (i.e., number of under-privileges detected), number of roles after resolving the under-privileges, percentage Reduction in number of roles, percentage reduction in total number of 1's in the binary matrix, and maximum percentage increase in privileges for the affected users.

The results from forward engineering are summarized in Table 1. The percentage reduction in the number of roles is significant over the entire spectrum of number of users of 2-15. In fact, when we consider specific UPAs instead of randomly generated ones, we found the reduction in the roles to be much more. This observation is consistent with other work that concluded that random test data results in conservative estimate of the outcome [11].

In the above analysis, we have generated random UPAs, so we don't know exactly whether all potential changes were detected or not. In order to verify the correctness and effectiveness of our algorithm, we have carried out what we refer to as *reverse engineering*. Here, we start with a UPA representing certain roles and corresponding assignments, and intentionally introduce certain misconfigurations. In this paper, for brevity, we only present our results with introducing under privileges; i.e., some of the 1s in the UPA are changed to 0s. We now check how many of these misconfigurations were detected by our algorithm. The following metric was recorded: the number of privileges introduced versus the number of privileges detected. The results are summarized in Table 2.

It may be noticed that the proposed method is very effective in detecting the injected changes. This is yet another illustration to show that the methods such as this are more effective in specific systems rather than random data. Clearly, the proposed method is able to identify almost all the injected changes. Other runs (results not shown here) showed similar behavior.

In summary, we find the role-mining based method is quite effective in identifying the misconfigurations. While the results we have shown primarily focused on under-privileges, the same thing is true of over privileges also.

5   Conclusion and Future Work

In this paper, we addressed the aspects of identification and correcting the misconfigurations that exist in role-based access control systems. While the basic methodology itself is also applicable to other access control systems, the fact that the roles are much smaller than the number of users makes the system efficient and a practical tool (in terms of computability).

First, we have discussed a means to identify misconfigurations by adopting role mining techniques. In particular, we have used the tiling technique of Vaidya et al [4]. Here, roles are identified as a set of non-overlapping tiles that are minimal in number. We have developed a methodology that analyzes the tiles and identifies possible misconfigurations, both over-privileges and under-privileges, with the result that the number of roles is typically smaller than the original set.

We are currently working on conducting more experiments to understand the behavior of the above method and understand when and where this will be most effective.

Acknowledgements. We wish to thank Professor Vijay Atluri, Professor Jaideep Vaidya, and Q. Guo of Rutgers University for their helpful discussions and for letting us use the implementation code of Algorithms 1 and 2 presented in this paper.

References

1. Sandhu, R., Coyne, E., Feinstein, H., Youman, C.: Role-based Access Control Models. IEEE Computer 29(2), 38–47 (1996)
2. Vaidya, J., Atluri, V., Guo, Q., Adam, N.: Migrating to Optimal RBAC with Minimal Perturbation. In: 13th ACM Symposium on Access Control Models and Technologies, pp. 11–20. ACM Press, New York (2008)
3. Vaidya, J., Atluri, V., Warner, J., Guo, Q.: Role Engineering via Prioritized Subset Enumeration. In: IEEE Transactions on Dependable and Secure Computing, October 2008, vol. 28. IEEE Computer Society Digital Library, IEEE Computer Society, Los Alamitos (2008), http://doi.ieeecomputersociety.org/10.1109/TDSC.2008.61
4. Vaidya, J., Atluri, V., Guo, Q.: The Role-Mining Problem: Finding a Minimal Descriptive Set of Roles. In: 12th ACM Symposium on Access Control Models and Technologies, pp. 175–184. ACM Press, New York (2007)
5. Molloy, I., Li, N., Li, T., Lobo, J.: Evaluating Role Mining Algorithms. In: 14th ACM Symposium on Access Control Models and Technologies, pp. 21–30. ACM Press, New York (2009)
6. Ene, A., Horne, W., Milosavljevic, N., Rao, P., Schreiber, R., Tarjan, R.E.: Fast Exact and Heuristic Methods for Role Minimization Problems. In: 13th ACM Symposium on Access Control Models and Technologies, pp. 21–30. ACM Press, New York (2008)
7. Witten, I.H., Frank, E.: Data Mining: Practical Machine Learning and Techniques, 2nd edn. Morgan Kaufmann Publishers, San Francisco (2005)
8. Bauer, L., Garriss, S., Reiter, M.K.: Detecting and Resolving Policy Misconfigurations in Access-Control Systems. In: 13th ACM Symposium on Access Control Models and Technologies, pp. 185–194. ACM Press, New York (2008)
9. Bishop, M.: Computer Security: Art and Science. Addison-Wesley Professional, Reading (2002)
10. Vaidya, J., Atluri, V., Warner, J.: Roleminer: mining Roles Using Subset Enumeration. In: 13th ACM Conference on Computer and Communications Security, pp. 144–153. ACM Press, New York (2006)
11. Mukkamala, R., Jajodia, S.: Effects of Distributed Database Modeling on Evaluation of Transaction Rollbacks. In: 22nd Winter Simulation Conference, pp. 839–845. IEEE Press, Los Alamitos (1990)

Author Index

Printing: Mercedes-Druck, Berlin
Binding: Stein+Lehmann, Berlin